THANK YOU, COMRADE STALIN!

THANK YOU, COMRADE STALIN!

SOVIET PUBLIC CULTURE FROM
REVOLUTION TO COLD WAR

Jeffrey Brooks

PRINCETON UNIVERSITY PRESS   PRINCETON, NEW JERSEY

Copyright © 2000 by Princeton University Press
Published by Princeton University Press, 41 William Street,
Princeton, New Jersey 08540
In the United Kingdom: Princeton University Press,
3 Market Place, Woodstock, Oxfordshire OX20 1SY
All Rights Reserved

Third printing, and first paperback printing, 2001
Paperback ISBN 0-691-08867-5

*The Library of Congress has cataloged the cloth edition of this
book as follows*

Brooks, Jeffrey, 1942–
Thank you, comrade Stalin! : Soviet public culture from revolution
to Cold War / Jeffrey Brooks.
    p.   cm.
Includes bibliographical references and index.
ISBN 0-691-00411-0 (cloth : alk. paper)
1. Popular culture—Soviet Union.   2. Soviet Union—Civilization.
3. Journalism—Soviet Union.   I. Title.
DK266.4.B76   1999
947—dc21   99-25331

This book has been composed in Times Roman

Printed on acid-free paper. ∞

www.pup.princeton.edu

Printed in the United States of America

10   9   8   7   6   5   4   3

Contents

Illustrations _____

Acknowledgments

I DEDICATE this book to my wife, Karen Brooks.

I thank my daughters, Elizabeth and Emily. They grew up with the book and encouraged me. We had some good times while I was writing it. I hope in some small way that what I have written will allow their generation better to understand the world before and behind them.

I am also pleased to thank many institutions and individuals who provided support and encouragement over the years of preparation of this book. The Simon Guggenheim Foundation, the National Council for Soviet and East European Research (contract numbers 728-7 and 802-11), and the International Researches and Exchanges Board provided financial support that is gratefully acknowledged. The Johns Hopkins University granted me a sabbatical leave in 1996–97.

Many friends, colleagues, and students were willing to help me. I am grateful to the following who read the entire manuscript: Elena Artemova, Karen McConnell Brooks, John Baldwin, Stephens Broening, Georgiy Cherniavskiy, Aaron Cohen, Jeff Horstein, David Joravsky, Ruth Judson, Peter Kenez, Anna Krylova, Tom Leonard, Vernon Lidtke, Lary May, Dmitry Shlapentokh, Vladimir Shlapentokh, Grant Ujifusa, and Sergei Zhuk. I also thank those who commented on various parts or chapters, including Sara Berry, John Covington, Joyce Feltzer, Robert Forster, Morris Gelfand, Louis Galambos, Kirstie McClure, Sidney Mintz, John Pocock, Dorothy Ross, Gabrielle Spiegel, Dan Todes, Mack Walker, and Judith Walkowitz. The book is much improved by their suggestions, many of which are reflected in the text. Lastly, I would like to acknowledge the help and suggestions I received from Brigitta von Rheinberg, history editor at Princeton University Press, and the assistance of Rita Bernhard, who copyedited my manuscript.

I presented early versions of many chapters at the Seminar of the History Department at the Johns Hopkins University at which I received many useful comments and suggestions from colleagues and students. I also delivered versions of chapters as papers at professional meetings and at other universities and received additional suggestions and often very helpful criticism.

I enjoyed the stimulation of the three universities where I taught while researching and writing, the University of Chicago, the University of Minnesota, and the Johns Hopkins University. At each, colleagues were generous with advice. Librarians were helpful as well, particularly June Ferris at Chicago, Miranda Beaven at Minnesota, and Thomas Izbiki and Agnes Flannery-Denner at Johns Hopkins. I am also grateful to those who helped me at the Lenin Library in Moscow and the Public Library in St. Petersburg.

Some short passages from the book have appeared in articles published over the years in the *Slavic Review, The Russian Review, The Journal of Popular Culture,* and *The American Historical Review,* as well as in several book chapters. None of these earlier essays is reproduced as a chapter. I borrowed most, however, from my essays, "Socialist Realism in *Pravda,*" which was originally published in the *Slavic Review,* and "The Origins of the Soviet Success Story," which originally appeared in the *Journal of Popular Culture.* I thank both journals for permission to reprint parts of these essays.

Prologue

THE BOLSHEVIKS seized the public lectern in October 1917, at a time when the balance between state and society in Imperial Russia had tilted toward civil society and individual initiative. By the early twentieth century, the country was acquiring a secular and pluralistic public culture reflecting increased urbanization, industrialization, and the importance of market transactions in Russian life. Schooling had become readily available, and children and their parents valued its advantages. In the Russian Empire in 1913 the probability that a child aged seven to fourteen would attend school for more than one year in their lifetimes was 70 percent for boys and 40 percent for girls.[1] Literate peasants exposed to a wider world adopted new values. Some bought urban clothes, new farm implements, tin roofs and brick stoves for their homes, soap, and kerosene lanterns.[2] The legal restraints that divided Russian society into nearly hereditary castes were eroding, and the social structure accommodated professions such as those of writer and journalist in which fame and fortune were independent of the state.

Russia shared in the market-based European and American cultural movements of aesthetic modernism and commercial popular culture, creating national versions of each.[3] Stravinsky, Chagall, Kandinsky, Malevich, and others testify to the power of Russian modernism. The popular culture is less known, but a vast self-help literature appeared, including information for small farmers and stories akin to Horatio Alger's American fantasies of social mobility. In addition, Russian publishers issued tens of millions of copies of cheap fiction in other classic Western genres before World War I, including adventure, romance, and detection. More than twenty million detective stories were published in the decade before 1914 alone, and nearly two thousand Russian films appeared largely in the same genres from 1908 through 1917.[4]

The victorious revolutionaries reversed this process and brought authoritarian and statist values to the fore. They created a monopoly of the press and other media and used it to halt the drift toward pluralism, commercialism, and international linkages. They obliterated the commercial popular culture by nationalizing local firms, destroying existing stocks of goods, halting foreign imports, and curtailing translations of printed materials. They also suppressed aesthetic modernism and murdered some of its greatest luminaries. In their rendering of the Soviet experience from 1917 to 1953, the early Bolsheviks and their successors sacralized the state and its leader, diminished the stature of citizens as free agents, and nurtured an international identity that eventually resided in a vision of Soviet exceptionalism and beneficence.

The official public culture included art, music, literature, film, drama, public lectures, radio, and much more, but its most commanding voices were the Party newspaper, *Pravda,* compared by Communists of the 1920s to the medieval Bible in influence and authority, the government paper *Izvestiia,* the army paper *Red Star,* and central national dailies for workers, peasants, and young people. Some observers might argue that the official press was ignored or peripheral to Soviet culture. I disagree. The press was not coterminous with all public expression, but it contextualized the Soviet experience and imposed a structure on thinking even among nonbelievers, much as censorship imposed a structure on belles lettres. It was the deepest reservoir of the "dark and magical night" to which Andrei Sinyavsky paid sad tribute in his essay *On Socialist Realism.*[5] It set the standard for purposive lying about one's convictions and for historical amnesia, which Czeslaw Milosz has described.[6] The press largely retained its monopoly of information after Stalin's death as the font of falsehood with which Aleksandr Solzhenitsyn and Andrei Sakharov long contended. The press and the official public culture retained much of their distinctive character until Mikhail Gorbachev introduced glasnost—"openness" or "transparency"—after 1985.

In its heyday under Stalin, the Soviet system of public information precluded reflection and discussion. Although public consideration of a limited range of issues was permitted after Stalin's death, the informational system retained much of its restrictive quality, and, in passing, left a void where public analysis of issues and common experiences did not take place. Decades of constrained formulaic commentaries about politics, nationality, ethnicity, human rights, and the economy shaped the consciousness and memory of people in postcommunist societies and now limit current efforts to understand these and other vital issues. Open dialogue under the old Soviet regime took place in private sitting rooms and at kitchen tables, and ideas and opinions that might have served society well were confined there. Other ideas and misconceptions that might have been weakened by the give and take of a more fluid public discussion were contrarily protected from wider scrutiny. The consequences of this claustrophobic informational world are apparent in the ongoing expression of chauvinism, xenophobia, anti-Semitism, and ignorance among people who are, on average, unusually well educated by world standards.

Lenin initiated this monopoly on information, and Stalin oversaw its fullest realization. On seizing power in 1917, Bolshevik leaders suppressed rival publications and sealed their personal control over public expression with an invasive censorship. Faced with a diverse and often hostile populace during the civil war of 1918–20, they instilled a vision of the world that precluded other ways of seeing, even as they disagreed among themselves. During the decade and a half before the Nazi invasion of June 22, 1941, Stalin and his supporters made the press the hegemon of information, and it remained so to the end of Communism. The shift came in the traumatic years of the First Five-Year Plan (1928–32) and collectivization, "the great break" when Stalin and his colleagues, fresh from triumphs over Trotsky and others, promised ordinary people a better life. Although they built factories and power stations, living standards collapsed and millions died. Yet the government's accountability to the population was nil, and the official press presented the plan and collectivization as gratifying and splendid, as indeed they seemed to many supporters. On front pages, images of enthusiasm and determination gave way to those of gratitude and triumph.

On December 30, 1936, the official trade union newspaper, *Labor,* carried a front-page picture of Stalin as Grandfather Frost, the Russian Santa Claus. Bright-faced smiling children circled a "New Year's tree" decorated with schools, buses, planes, and other such "gifts." The tree, first permitted in 1935, marked New Year's Day as a surrogate Christmas; the picture signified Stalin's accession as the country's benefactor. Eight years later, in 1943, when the Red Army liberated Kharkov, *Pravda* carried a tribute to Stalin from grateful inhabitants: "Thank you, dear Marshal, for our freedom, for our children's happiness, for life."[7]

These citations are not mere oddities of Stalin's cult. They express an official core Soviet value: the idea that citizens are immeasurably beholden to the leader, the Party, and the state. Lenin and Stalin advanced this formulation of economic and social relations in which citizens received ordinary goods and services as gifts from a generous and solicitous leadership. In Lenin's time, the press informed citizens that they owed their well-being to "the revolution," "Soviet power," "the Party," or occasionally "the working people." Later, Stalin became the center of public obligation and loyalty. The effect in each case was to diminish the role of individual citizens as historical actors and shift "agency"—that is, the motive and moving force in daily life—from society to the state and leader.[8]

This was more than entitlement in the British or American sense of society's consensual obligation to members who qualify for particular services and thereby attain rights to them. It was an extension of a contorted "moral economy" in which the state was presumed to dispense necessary goods and services, and the tremendously beholden citizens were obligated to provide their labor in return.[9] I use the term *moral economy* to describe the official effort to represent economic relationships as moral relationships, following upon the early Marx of *Capital,* who defined the allocation to factors other than labor by the pejorative term *exploitation.*

Soviet authorities shaped economic life with appeals to moral incentives from the earliest days. Beginning on May 10, 1919, citizens cleaned streets and performed similar tasks without pay on special days (*subbotniki*), often Saturdays, which Lenin later praised as "the factual beginning of communism."[10] Similar were the "socialist competitions" between groups of workers to overfulfill production targets that were institutionalized in the late 1920s and continued until the fall of Communism. The same logic shaped the slogan "Let us

give!"—as in "Let us give more coal!"—employed sporadically from the First
Five-Year Plan (1928–32) to the Brezhnev era.[11] The government made explicit the moral economy that underlay such rhetoric on Stalin's seventieth
birthday in December 1949, by orchestrating the mass "giving" of trainloads of
gifts from Soviet and foreign citizens, who were presumably indebted to him
for peace and prosperity.

The economy of the gift signified an abrupt departure from economic and social values expressed in the prerevolutionary Russian print media. It was, moreover, in clear contrast to the economic relationships in a market economy. In
the latter, gifts exchanged and obligations incurred in the workplace supplement the functioning of the labor market, which remains primary. In the Soviet
case, the moral economy of the gift supplanted the labor market, enmeshing
people in a web of relationships as separate from those of a capitalist market as
its feudal antecedents.

Stalin and others employed rituals of theater to draw citizens into public displays of support. Political activity has always been akin to drama, and this was
more than ever the case in the Nazi, fascist, and communist states.[12] Journalists created a context in which Stalin could display himself and the new order
he claimed to have created, an omnipresent magic theater in which all active
participants in Soviet public life acquired ancillary roles. The core of this performative culture was the cult of Stalin, whose promoters manipulated a quasi-religious iconography to lend his persona a near-sacred character. In accord
with the official culture's theatricality, party leaders stopped explaining publicly what they were doing and made the reason why something was done less
important than the orders to do it. Ceasing to appeal to the reason and common
sense of imagined readers, they thereby distanced themselves in their articulation of public policy from the rationality of the European socialist tradition.
They demanded belief and respect for authority in the person of the leader,
much as the Nazis did. An audience of officials, enthusiasts, and others who satisfied this requirement entered into the Stalinist political theater. Speaking as
exemplary representatives of society, Stalin and his supporters magnified the
performance in the manner of a classical Greek chorus, but whereas the Greek
chorus often queried public values, the Soviet chorus certified them.

For those who identified with the project of "building socialism," the militant wishfulness that flooded Russian newspapers of the 1930s signified faith
in achievement as well as a denial of any evidence of adversity. For others who
hesitated or were less convinced, participation was a means of securing a place
in a society that was ruthless toward outsiders and misfits. Khrushchev recalled
how, under Stalin, he organized spectacles of "cheap theater."[13] Such performances restricted the flow of information throughout society. Condemned perforce to perform in this theatrical realm, journalists dissociated themselves from
negative features of the surrounding world and ceased to integrate much read-

ily available information into their reportage. The press then acquired the
dreamlike qualities characteristic of the 1930s: paeans to official heroes, denunciations of stigmatized villains, and hosannahs to Stalin. The government
secured conformity with these practices through terror, and no questioning
voices sounded openly. Varlam Shalamov summed up the power of this vision
in his *Kolyma Tales,* when he recorded a cynical camp saying, "If you don't believe it, take it as a fairy tale."[14] But, in fact, Soviet people could not take the
public culture as a fairy tale because it infiltrated every aspect of their lives.

The Nazi invasion threatened this mendacious performance, undermined the
symbolism of the dictator's "gift," and interrupted the government's public conversation with officials and sympathizers. The military threat was real to the entire society, and an effective response could only come from the whole country. While Stalin monopolized the stage, defeats could hardly be explained
without implicating him. Whereas the British made Dunkirk a national epic and
the Nazis used the defeat at Stalingrad to energize their forces, Soviet authorities forced journalists to ignore the loss of Minsk on June 28 and that of
Smolensk and Kishinev on July 16.[15] Soon, however, new public narratives
arose in which soldiers, partisans, civilians, and also journalists played greater
roles. The press told these stories during the crisis years of 1941 and 1942, when
society was mobilized in self-defense.

Following the victories at Stalingrad in late 1942 and at Kursk in July 1943,
Stalin and his supporters restaged the performance on which their rule had formerly depended. In the postwar period, citizens' obligations to the state were
reaffirmed. "Thank you, Comrade Stalin" again became the choral refrain and
the United States and other enemies appeared in an official moral drama rivaling that of the 1930s.

After the war Stalin and his supporters extended the obligation due the state
and leader as the empire expanded and the cold war progressed. The press then
portrayed the Soviet Union as a benefactor of other nations, who were presumed
to be grateful for the defeat of Germany and Japan, and, in the case of the new
peoples' republics, also for the gift of the socialist way of life. After Stalin's
death Khrushchev increased public expectations about the quantity and quality
of the state's gift to society, but his promises to match and surpass Western living standards went unfulfilled. The Soviet Union continued to suffer perpetual
shortages as buying power outpaced the economy's ability to deliver consumer
goods. The public's accommodation to scarcity and to the implicit relationships
behind simple economic transactions was evident in the question asked when-
ever a line formed in the 1970s and 1980s: "What are they giving out?" By the
end of the Soviet era, despite chronic shortages, many people nevertheless expected a paternalistic state to provide housing, health care, and even sausage at
subsidized prices.

Along with the emphasis on consumerism, Khrushchev opened society to a degree by limiting repression and easing censorship. Intellectuals took advantage of Khrushchev's "thaw" to champion "sincerity," the antithesis of the performative ethos, but nonetheless left much of the performative culture intact. In the end, neither Khrushchev nor his successors were willing to discard the ritualistic certainties from which they derived legitimacy. The performative culture lingered on in a semi-moribund state until Brezhnev inadvertently turned it into self-parody.

The holding power of the official public culture owed much to its eclectic and evolutionary character. The world as the press formulated it during the 1920s differed markedly from that of the 1930s, and representations of the wartime years and the postwar period were also distinct. Soviet leaders and their supporters drew upon utopian strains of Marxism and a contemporary faith in science and technology, as well as a rich mix of Russian secular and religious traditions stretching back to the middle ages. The layered quality of the performative culture made it possible for the press to represent the leader simultaneously as the coryphaeus of science and a sacred potentate in the Byzantine or Oriental tradition. The performance promoted the Soviet way of life as unique and exceptional, and at the same time as the object of the natural striving of honorable people throughout the world. The press presented a normative standard for society as a whole and a practical guide to public behavior for all citizens. It was a hierarchical system in which *Pravda*'s editorials constituted the last word.

How a diverse and accomplished people verbalized its historical experience in this constricting idiom and the price they paid for sustaining it is the story told in the eight chapters that follow. The first is about the institutional foundation for the monopolization of the media. The second presents conflicting images of the state and citizens in the first decade of Soviet rule. The third and fourth concern the public culture under Stalin from 1928 until the Nazi invasion and representations of citizens' indebtedness to the leader and the state. The fifth and sixth pertain to the incorporation of literature and the arts into social performance, and the division of society into those who fulfilled obligations and enemies who did not. In the seventh and eighth chapters I describe the wartime disruption of the prewar culture and its reformulation from 1945 until Stalin's death. The persistence of elements of this culture until Gorbachev's era of glasnost and its long-term effects are explored in the epilogue.

The book is based on a close reading of the press from the early days of the October Revolution to Stalin's death in March 1953. I describe how editors and journalists covered the events of their time, but I also sample newspapers to trace the changing content of reportage. The result is an investigation of the public culture over nearly four decades and a quantitative analysis of its varying themes and characteristics. For example, to reveal the evolving image of America in the 1920s and 1930s I read commentaries on events and measured the space and frequency of different types of stories about America in *Pravda, Labor,* and *The Peasant Newspaper.*

I do not make a statistical analysis that tests hypotheses about Soviet culture, but I do attempt a rigorous presentation of descriptive statistics of prominent themes and issues and their interpretative context. One sample consisted of every tenth editorial in *Pravda* from 1917 to Stalin's death; another comprised articles published on important holidays; and a third included all reports on domestic affairs in a random sample of several issues of *Pravda* per year from 1917 to the end of World War II, more than twenty-five hundred articles in all. I stress *Pravda* because it was the center of the informational system, and it was more influential and more closely scrutinized by the authorities and concerned citizens than any other publication. As Stalin wrote to his chief facilitator, Viacheslav Molotov, in the autumn of 1930, "every issue of *Pravda* is "an address," "an appeal."[16] I include other newspapers in additional samples to answer questions about images of other countries and foreigners; changing representations of science, literature, and the arts; and the construction of individual identities in obituaries and human-interest stories. The results of this elementary quantification are subsumed in conclusions and presented in the footnotes, so as not to burden the reader with tables requiring lengthy explanations.

The questions I asked blended those that could be quantified straightforwardly with issues requiring subjective judgments. Among the easily quantifiable topics was the comparative amount of space allotted to various countries and regions over time; for example, did *Pravda* give more space in a given year to Europe or the United States, to the colonial world or Russia's traditional sphere of interest, the Balkans? More subtle issues required the exercise of greater judgment, for example, to assess the recurrence of metaphors used to frame a picture of society, such as "the path to Communism," "class war," or "the gift" of social benefits. Most subjective of all was my evaluation of the correlation between competing stories and social values in such issues as the shifting balance between cosmopolitanism and xenophobia, changing images of "enemies of the people," and the evolution and extension of Stalin's cult.

In each case the statistics greatly assisted my efforts to impose order on a vast sea of words. I always shaped and guided the quantification, however, according to my judgment and choice of relevant issues and categories. Often the data led me to reject one line of interpretation and seek another, but the study is that of a cultural historian rather than a statistician, a personal reflection on a historical phenomenon rather than a fully replicable examination of data. I believe the outcome is a new understanding of how leaders and participants in the Soviet project shaped the perception and ultimately the history of their society.

One final note. I began this book during the late Soviet era. Now, after the collapse of Communism, the quantity of primary material about the Soviet experience has multiplied manyfold. I have used new published materials, including autobiographies, private letters and journals, official documents, and monographs. I have not availed myself of the opportunity to work in Russian archives on the press. The quantity of material in the press itself was more than sufficient for this project. Nevertheless archival material will undoubtedly offer new perspectives as a new generation of scholars attempts to understand the cultural and intellectual dimensions of Russia's experience under communist rule.

THANK YOU, COMRADE STALIN!

One

The Monopoly of the Printed Word:
From Persuasion to Compulsion

THE BOLSHEVIKS' first step upon seizing power was to nationalize the publishing industry. On November 9, 1917, the new authorities issued the "Decree on the Press" over the signature of Vladimir Ilich Lenin, closing down newspapers that preached "open opposition or insubordination to the worker-peasant government."[1] They had ruled for a day. A week later, at the All-Russian Central Executive Committee of the Soviets, Lenin and Trotsky justified the decree by stressing current exigencies, but the measure was never rescinded. John Reed, the American radical who attended and described the meeting in *Ten Days That Shook the World,* foresaw a time when "capitalist owners of printing presses and of paper cannot be the all-powerful and exclusive manufacturers of public opinion."[2] This was the sentiment of Article 14 on freedom of the press in the July 10, 1918, Constitution of the Russian Socialist Federative Republic:

> To guarantee working people real freedom to express their opinions, the Russian Socialist Federation of the Soviet Republic terminates the press's dependence on capital and puts all technical and material means for publishing newspapers, brochures, books, and other printed material in the hands of the working class and poor peasantry and ensures their free distribution throughout the whole country.[3]

Many socialists shared Lenin's belief that Party leaders should direct political struggle and, if necessary, manipulate audiences. Closing "bourgeois" presses was less accepted but also unremarkable. Lenin believed that the bourgeoisie had monopolized publishing to solidify its dominance, and he thought revolutionaries should do the same.[4] Somewhat contradictorily, he also saw the press after 1917 as a means of popular self-expression, but pragmatism overshadowed theory. He sketched a proposal on November 17, 1917, for the nationalization of paper factories and publishing houses, but, in accord with his most populist essay, *The State and Revolution,* he promised any group of ten thousand citizens or more the right to print its views.[5] The promise was not kept, and nationalization moved forward.[6] "The printing press is our strongest weapon," he wrote in 1918.[7]

The Bolsheviks did not seek pluralism, and the civil war, which lasted from the spring of 1918 until November 1920 and was followed by the Polish-Soviet War from April 1920 until March 1921, did not encourage legal niceties. As one revolutionary explained, the bourgeois parties had "printing houses and auto-mobiles, telephones and telegraphs."[8] The "Decree on the Press" of November 9, 1917, justified expropriations.[9] In fact, the Bolsheviks could hardly have accepted a free press. "We announced earlier we would close bourgeois newspapers if we took power. To tolerate these newspapers would mean not to be a socialist," Lenin chided a leftist critic.[10] The revolutionaries nationalized the Petrograd Telegraph Agency on November 18, 1917, and banned private advertisements two days later.[11] In 1918 they closed the remaining socialist newspapers.[12] They nationalized the material side of publishing in 1918 under the Supreme Council of the National Economy, including production of paper and cardboard.[13] The centralized allocation of raw materials enhanced control. Finally, in September 1918 the Party took over the production of news by establishing the All-Russian Telegraph Agency (ROSTA), which was partially replaced in 1925 by TASS.[14]

Censorship was the scourge of nineteenth-century Russian intellectuals, and it took bravado for the Bolsheviks to reestablish it. Soon after taking power they appointed a commissar for press affairs under the Petrograd Soviet, and a Revolutionary Tribunal of the Press began work as a censor in January 1918.[15] Lenin signed a decree making the tribunal a court to judge editors and journalists for "crimes" against "the people."[16] In practice, the wrong news as well as news the leaders considered inaccurate was cause for punishment.[17] The tribunal's three judges, chosen by the Soviet, could impose fines, close publications, confiscate presses and buildings, imprison, exile, and take away the political rights of those found guilty. The guards, militia, the Red Army, and other "executive organs" implemented their orders. The All-Russian Extraordinary Commission for Combating Counterrevolution, Speculation, and Delinquency in Office (Cheka) also silenced dissident editors and publishers. Suppression, control, and intimidation of the press were widely accepted by the early Bolshevik elite.[18] Others on the Left were outraged. "Russia's tragedy follows its path," noted the writer V. G. Korolenko on witnessing the destruction of the non-Bolshevik press in Poltava.[19]

In June 1922 the government replaced the tribunal with the Chief Administration of Literary and Publishing Affairs (Glavlit), which lasted to the end of Soviet Communism.[20] Formally housed under the Commissariat of Education, it soon came under the authority of the Cheka and the Central Committee's division on agitation and propaganda. According to one account, Glavlit's employees later wore uniforms of the Joint State Political Administration (OGPU), the Cheka's successor, and their salaries were paid by that institution through the Commissariat of Education from the late 1920s.[21] Glavlit entered every avenue of Soviet life. In December 1922, after six months of existence, it ordered the removal from printed articles of facts and figures "which compromise Soviet power and the Communist Party."[22] By 1925 it censored radio and musical publications, posters, advertising, postal envelopes, and even matchbox covers.[23] Yet it remained small. By one account there were only eighty-six censors in 1926, fifty-two of whom were Communists.[24]

As it grew, Glavlit cloaked politics in secrecy, silenced opponents, and obscured policies likely to spark opposition. It suppressed information on members of the government and Central Committee, including their personal lives and travel plans. It circulated lists of forbidden topics to publishers and editors. One from 1925 banned reports on armed clashes with peasants over tax and fiscal measures, sanitary conditions at places of imprisonment, numbers of crimes and Party affiliations of the accused, numbers of death sentences, and suicides or cases of insanity resulting from unemployment or hunger.[25] In 1924 Glavlit forbade mention of government policy in setting relative prices of manufactured goods and agricultural products, which discriminated against peasants.[26] In the second half of the 1920s, the organization banned the names of Stalin's opponents from the press. It restricted reports of accidents and disasters and forbade mention of itself. Glavlit also prescribed how to cover important topics, such as anything to do with Stalin.[27] Stalin began to oversee the central press personally at this time. Ivan Gronskii, a member of *Izvestiia*'s editorial staff and editor of the paper from 1931 through 1934, recalled meeting with him almost daily in 1927.[28] From the late 1920s any initiative by *Pravda* or *Izvestiia* required the Central Committee's clearance.[29]

A New Kind of Press

The system's authoritarian logic was implicit in its hierarchy. Elite publications, such as *Pravda* and *Izvestiia,* were distinguished early from "mass" newspapers with a simplified message. Both types originated in Moscow. Key mass newspapers of the 1920s and 1930s were *The Workers' Newspaper* (1922–39), *Working Moscow* (1922–39), and *The Peasant Newspaper* (1923–39), which the Bolsheviks founded after concluding that peasants and workers did not read *Pravda* or *Izvestiia. The Poor* (1918–31), an unsuccessful precursor, served rural activists and officials. Newspapers affiliated with lesser institutions, such as *Labor* (1921–) for the trade unions and *Komsomol Pravda* (1928–) for the Young Communist League (Komsomol), followed elite publications, as did the provincial press. Stalin and his government purged the press in the late 1930s and closed *The Peasant Newspaper, The Workers' Newspaper,* and *The Poor.* As a result, institutional newspapers such as *Labor* and the army newspaper *Red Star* (1924–) gained stature.

Party leaders shaped all modes of expression through the central press, and local publishers reproduced the Party's message. Radio ultimately reached a wide audience, but newspapers retained the chief authority. Radios, including speakers in public places, numbered 7 million in 1940 and 13.3 million in 1950, at a time when the population was nearly two hundred million.[30] In 1940 the circulation of all newspapers was thirty-eight million copies. In 1950, despite a slight decline in circulation, the print news media still exceeded the availability of radio by almost threefold.[31] Even after radio and later television overcame this disadvantage, the press had the final word because it could be accurately cited by officials and activists throughout the empire.

The Bolsheviks wanted more than a conduit for official pronouncements. Newspapers were also to spark discussion, collect information, stimulate public criticism of selected malfeasance, and, to a limited extent, satisfy readers' demands for information.[32] The layout suited these purposes. Journalists produced three largely discrete spheres of reportage. An interpretive sphere included stories that carried overt ideological messages. An interactive sphere allowed for the limited expression of the opinions of sympathetic readers, either authentic or manufactured. Lastly, an informational sphere carried reportage of actual events inside and outside the country. The result was the ability to answer the question, "Who is a good Party member?" according to ideology in an editorial, in terms of an event in a wire service report, and based on character traits such as sobriety and diligence in a reader's letter.

Newspapers owed their visual quality chiefly to the interpretive sphere, which contained the headlines and pictures, editorials, and signed columns that conveyed the official explication of diverse and continuing stories. The subject was not the news but the ideals that animated leaders and some readers as well. In this part of the newspaper authors told the public what to think, as well as what to think about; how to read the news, as well as what news was most important. The presentation was iconographic as well as inspirational. The leaders' speeches often appeared in full, even though readers were known to ignore them.[33] This sphere best served the committed. The interpretive perspective was most intrusive on holidays such as May Day and the anniversary of the October Revolution, when editors of different papers produced nearly identical articles and illustrations.

The informational sphere consisted of stories of events at home and abroad, often from the official wire service. These were more accessible, descriptive, and less jargon-laden than interpretative articles. World news was of interest to many readers. Foreign affairs was the most popular section of *The Workers' Newspaper* according to a 1925 survey, but Party members favored editorials and the section on Party life.[34] Editors slanted the news less overtly in the informational sphere but ignored the calamities and crimes that had figured in the pre-Soviet press. Trotsky complained in 1923 of journalists' unwillingness to report events that excited readers.[35] People were interested in the seamy side of life, he observed, and the bourgeoisie's use of such material to stimulate "an unhealthy curiosity" was no reason to ignore it. Yet the press rarely noted crimes and scandals. When *Working Moscow* reported a mass murder in 1923, the editors crammed the crime, sentencing, and execution into a single moralizing article in which the murderess was described as a glutton and the murderer as a wife and child beater and friend of priests.[36]

The Bolsheviks refused to address popular curiosity. Stories about the private lives of national Party and government leaders were taboo even during Party and Soviet congresses. Inclusion of material considered frivolous violated their conception of the press as instructive. Serialized adventure stories had enlivened popular pre-Soviet newspapers and attracted new readers, but efforts to replicate them came to naught because of the censors' insistence on a political purpose. Thus, in the wake of famine, *The Poor* featured a cumbersome improbable serial in 1923, titled "Bread from the Air (In the Not Too Distant Future)," about flour and meat grown from microbes.[37] What peasant readers, who tended to demand literalness in print, made of such a treatment is unclear.

Newspapers were bland in part because they lacked eye-catching advertisements. The pre-Soviet press had contained a potpourri of entreaties to acquire personal items from perfumes to revolvers. Although advertisements appeared in the 1920s, most involved sales of equipment or material from one institution to another, and there was little to excite the individual consumer. Even filmmakers could not promise entertainment without defying the media's didactic purpose. Advertisements for movies featured illustrations that suggested fun and adventure, but there were no captions spelling out these promises.[38] As a result, newspapers offered limited information seriously, and even this was often dully presented.

The interactive sphere was the innovative part of the early Soviet newspaper, and perhaps the most important. Carefully selected, redrafted, or simply invented letters appeared with commentaries in columns captioned "Party Life" and "Workers' Life" in the 1920s, and "On the Enlightenment Front" and "Soviet Construction" in the early 1930s.[39] Editors often framed the section with a commentary containing advice to readers and citations from letters. Topics usually concerned local affairs, and contributors were often identified as activists.[40] Sometimes a subject of national interest was officially "opened" to people outside the Party elite, for example, the sale of church valuables to buy food during the famine of 1921–22, but in such cases comments varied little.

The interactive sphere depended on local reports of problems and achievements. The more letters, "the more working people will read it," noted the editor of *Working Moscow* in 1923.[41] Editors stressed the whistle-blowing function of reports, and many were sent on to interested agencies, including the police. This was "whistle-blowing" addressed to the state as well as society, however. The editors of *The Workers' Newspaper* celebrated their first year with the announcement that in their letters they had printed "complaints about 'mismanagement,' about petty tyranny and willfulness by all types of authorities, and about a multitude of defects in our order."[42] Editors of *The Peasant Newspaper* claimed that, on the basis of 80,000 letters in 1925 and 1926, they had satisfied 60,000 informational requests, called 673 people to account, and had the authorities bring 948 people to trial, fire 769 from their jobs, and expel 139 from the Party and Komsomol.[43]

The authorities officially treated letters as an accurate reflection of opinion and used them to evaluate policies.[44] When they did so, they confused the letter writers' views with those of less-active citizens who had trouble understanding newspapers, let alone writing to them. The quality of all messages to the center declined during the 1920s, including letters, but there is little evidence that Party leaders were aware of it. Local participation was critical to the Bolsheviks' idea of the newspaper, and Party leaders expected active workers and peasants to contribute. The idea stemmed from the revolutionary past, when workers' letters to *Pravda* were highly prized. The early Bolsheviks formalized and expanded ties with readers through networks of correspondents who were paid for notes and articles on local issues.

The first conference of worker correspondents was held in the spring of 1923, and the ranks of worker, peasant, and army correspondents grew to half a million in 1928.[45] Correspondents were independent and critical of local authorities in the early 1920s, and some operated covertly, signing with a pseudonym or number. They soon lost their adversary role, however, and were urged to act openly and constructively. "You are not informers but organizers of the workers' affairs," an official explained in 1924.[46] "We cannot describe workers' lives in the Soviet Republic as we would in the West," admonished M. I. Kalinin, the "peasant" president of the Central Executive Committee, who officially headed the government. "Among ourselves we must be supportive," he wrote.[47] During the 1920s the press sometimes equated the reports of worker and peasant correspondents with public opinion.[48] The authors were unrepresentative, even with respect to demographics, but they were important in building the new state. Those who wrote to *The Peasant Newspaper* from 1923 to 1926 were mostly unaffiliated peasants under thirty years of age with a primary education.[49] Less than 10 percent were Party members, and one-fifth belonged to the Komsomol.[50] By contrast, 60 percent of correspondents of *The Workers' Newspaper* were Party members in 1924.[51]

Nikolai Bukharin, who edited *Pravda* the first few months after the revolution and again from July 1918 until Stalin forced him out in late 1928, wanted correspondents trained as professional journalists, and a State Institute of Red Journalists was organized.[52] The correspondents were often activists with a stake in the new order. The author of a 1926 handbook for rural correspondents of *The Peasant Newspaper* asked: "Who is the rural correspondent? He is primarily the advanced peasant who clearly understands that Soviet power is his own power; he is not afraid to die for it, and he helps it rejuvenate and remake the village with his labor and advice."[53] Such statements attest to the Bolsheviks' faith in the correspondents and to their increasingly official role.

Professional as well as amateur journalists in this conception served the Party and state, not the public. The rise of journalism as a profession in England and America depended on a measure of autonomy from the state. The Soviet system doubly limited the scope of the profession. Since state or Party service was the main criteria for advancement, journalists had little cause to enlarge civic life or their own importance by criticizing the central government. Nor did they have reason to claim "objectivity," as did twentieth-century American reporters.[54] The fusion of public life with the state left scant room for such a proposition. No Soviet "Fourth Estate" arose, and journalism, like law, lacked many professional attributes. Soviet newspapers commented on public affairs without the self-activated political journalism that lent public opinion its historic meaning in America and Great Britain.[55] There was no Clark Kent to play Superman in Soviet culture, and Soviet Russia's film industry never produced movies about independent journalists such as the American *Front Page* (1931), *Deadline USA* (1952), or *All the President's Men* (1976) in which reporters and editors battle corruption and restore society to its presumed norms.[56] Journalists in these films are heroes of civil society, like fictional private detectives, and Soviet Russia wanted neither.

The liberal democratic press, particularly that of England and America, generally arose independently of the state, although not of politics. The Soviet experience resulted in a near merger of public space with official structures, with little room for openly dissident opinions, even in the more open post-Stalinist era. From the outset Bolsheviks stifled unofficial organizations and tried to place all group activity under government control. This institutional contraction characterized all subsequent systems of a Soviet type. So did the suppression of the discussion and commentary that historians have often identified with the pluralism and "public sphere" of eighteenth-century England, France, and America.[57] For Marx, civil society was simply bourgeois society, a necessary historical stage but one to be superseded when the state and society became one under communism.[58] For Lenin, on the other hand, civil society—that is, liberal bourgeois society—was itself problematic. He stressed the perniciousness of liberalism, and his idea of the press was linked to a desired unity of state and society, even before attainment of the communist ideal.

When read as propaganda, the Soviet press seems akin to that of Nazi Germany. Yet there were differences as well as similarities. Both displayed the "newspeak," "doublethink," and "Ministry of Truth," which George Orwell described in *1984* (1949) and Hannah Arendt cataloged in *Totalitarianism* (1951). Orwell and Arendt wrote of propaganda backed by terror. Orwell imagined a society in which "the proles" stood apart from the political elite and "no attempt was made to indoctrinate them with the ideology of the Party."[59] Arendt, who feared modern mass culture, in contrast, saw fascism and communism as systems in which "the masses had to be won by propaganda."[60] Hitler and Lenin would have concurred with the argument of contemporary sociologist Jacques Ellul that "propaganda is made, first of all, because of a will to action."[61] Yet had they discussed it, they would have disagreed about how to achieve their different ends.

Joseph Goebbels founded *Der Angriff* (The attack) in 1927, and by 1930 it had one hundred thousand readers.[62] His purpose was "not to convey information, but to spur, incite, drive" the reader to action.[63] "Faith is all!" he vowed in a play written in the late 1920s.[64] In *Der Angriff,* faith meant faith in Hitler and in a Germany cleansed of Jews, as evoked by pictures of Hitler and anti-Semitic cartoons.[65] Hate, power, and militarism were the themes; Hitler was the cement that bound them together. "Only a storm of burning passion can turn people's destinies, but only he who harbors passion in himself can arouse passion," wrote Hitler in *Mein Kampf.*[66]

Prerevolutionary *Pravda* (1912–14) differed from *Der Angriff,* although its circulation in October 1917 was similar.[67] Like Goebbels, Lenin saw the press as a collective agitator but sought to nourish the Party's intellectual core, not readers' emotions. Prerevolutionary *Pravda* promoted action through understanding, not by inflaming passions. Nor did it appeal to violence and hatred, as the Nazis did later. Its editors, who believed in the infinite malleability of man in the tradition of the Enlightenment, appealed to reason, albeit reason of a dogmatic sort. *Pravda* in the early years had no cartoons, no cult of the leader despite Lenin's prestige, and no mastermind of propaganda. For early Bolsheviks, Marxism was truth, not a means to beguile the masses. Although this changed in the 1930s, Stalin, unlike Hitler, did not perform on radio or in documentaries and usually relied on the press to convey his words and image to Soviet citizens.

The trajectories of the Nazi and Soviet systems of public information also differed. Hitler and Goebbels built their empire of print on the economic success of Nazi policies and improvements in living conditions. They manipulated the press instead of nationalizing it, and they utilized and expanded an existing rhetoric of anti-Semitism and nationalism that found a powerful resonance among their comparatively well-educated audience. The widespread support the Nazi government enjoyed was reflected in the relatively small size of the Gestapo, which rose from a mere 7,000 officials in 1937 to 7,600 in the expanded Reich on August 1, 1941.[68] By contrast, the People's Commissariat of Internal Affairs (NKVD) had 366,000 employees in 1939, twenty times the German per capita ratio of security police to population.[69]

When Goebbels became Reich Minister for Popular Enlightenment and Propaganda, he tried to unite all Germans except Marxists and Jews. He wanted people to think and act identically and to serve the state unquestioningly.[70] Stalin and his supporters shared this sentiment, but not the Nazis' deliberate irrationality or cynicism. Goebbels showed the pragmatic flexibility of the calculating strategist, not the fanatic ideologue; he muted anti-Semitic propaganda, for example, during the 1936 Olympic games.[71] When faced with the disaster at Stalingrad, he used the defeat to mobilize public opinion against "the hordes from the steppe."[72] He even choreographed news of the capitulation with a Wagnerian opera, stating that the Sixth Army had remained "true to the last breath to its oath to the flag."[73] The Nazis controlled their narrative of events, even as they lost the war. Their rule lasted a little more than a decade, but Goebbels's handiwork served them to the last, motivating soldiers and civilians who fought in the streets of Berlin. The Bolsheviks achieved a different but longer lasting hegemony.

Political Literacy and the Search for Common Readers

Lenin and his followers tried haphazardly to win over ordinary people through rational argument, but the press retained an elitist bias from the outset. This was not as important during the civil war, when mobilization and support of the army were the objectives, as it was afterward, when the authorities governed the devastated country. In 1921 Lenin abandoned the policy of war communism (1918–21)—the effort to control all economic activity and forced requisitions of grain—for the New Economic Policy (NEP), based on a mixed economy and legalized and semi-legalized retail trade. Initially, however, neither the reform nor the earlier military compulsion served to reestablish a strong link between publishers and readers.

A mass audience was accessible, but the Bolsheviks failed to address it effectively. In 1926 literacy among men and women aged nine to forty-nine was 72 and 43 percent, respectively.[74] Yet although many ordinary people could read to some extent, their skills and knowledge were rudimentary. The sixty million rural readers constituted 71 percent of the literate in the country in 1926.[75] *The Poor* was the first publication specifically for peasants, but it was never popular. The name itself conflicted with the aspirations of many new readers, who wished neither to be poor nor to think of themselves as poor. During the civil war three-quarters of all copies were given to the army for free distribution.[76] Later it was handed out in the countryside. Confusion about its audience was evident in the format, which alternated between a tabloid and a broadsheet until the less-popular larger size was adopted. Production rose from fifty thousand copies a day in 1918 to eight hundred thousand in 1921. But when a price was put on it in January 1922, after the limited introduction of a mixed economy under the New Economic Policy, circulation tumbled in a single week from five hundred thousand to two hundred thousand copies.[77] Only thirty-five thousand copies a day were printed in 1923, and one authority estimated only seven thousand individual subscribers.[78] In desperation in late 1923, Party leaders founded *The Peasant Newspaper* for readers who were "not ready for more serious material," and they recast *The Poor* to serve "the advanced stratum" of village society, "who worked in the Party and the Soviets."[79] *The Peasant Newspaper* began as a weekly tabloid and became a biweekly in October 1928.

Circulation neared half a million in 1923, more than a million in late 1928, and a million and a half at the end of 1929.[80] With its simplified language and message, it was the most successful Soviet experiment in mass media during the 1920s.

The Bolsheviks created *The Workers' Newspaper* and local city papers such as *Working Moscow* for workers who did not read the leading newspapers. Editors of *The Workers' Newspaper* described their audience as the politically active "middling worker."[81] *Working Moscow* began in 1922 and had a circulation of 125,000 copies in 1926. Even these tabloids missed many less-educated workers. "The existing network cannot serve the culturally and politically backward strata of the proletariat either in form or content," complained the editors of *The Workers' Newspaper* in late 1926.[82] Five months later they admitted that "neither the existing mass newspapers nor the trade union newspapers have penetrated into the thick of this enormous stratum."[83] They suggested a "mass kopeck newspaper," referring to the prerevolutionary tabloid, but no such paper appeared. Entertainment and sensation, the staples of the penny press everywhere, were taboo. "We cannot avail ourselves of such methods of winning readers' popularity," wrote I. Vareikis, a Party official and publishing boss in 1926.[84]

Many lower-class readers also remained beyond the purview of the press because the political system favored emerging and established elites. The press served as a reservoir of the information people needed to get ahead and demonstrate superiority over others.[85] *Pravda* particularly was a lexicon for aspiring Party members. The Bolsheviks used the phrase "political literacy" to denote a familiarity with ideas and concepts essential to new cadres who wished to distinguish themselves from less-informed brethren. The press was a primer for political literacy. The interpretive sphere, in particular, contained explanations and texts for study. The editors of *The Poor* explained in 1923, "We have decided to present a series of articles on basic questions of political knowledge in order to facilitate the liquidation of political illiteracy among the least-prepared members of the Party."[86] Local Party schools were organized to teach political literacy to new members who joined after Lenin's death in early 1924.

Ordinary readers, however, often found the language and concepts of even mass newspapers baffling. Before 1917 publishers, writers, and distributors had competed to develop a language for newly literate common readers. Bolshevik publishers rejected the old language along with its themes and formulas. They had new information to communicate and few means to gauge readers' responses. The results were disheartening. Publicists wrote with little regard for potential readers' comprehension. Abbreviations, neologisms, and Russifications of foreign words proliferated. Contemporary observers bemoaned "foreignisms."[87] Active readers of *The Workers' Newspaper* grumbled that they needed "ten dictionaries" to read the paper.[88]

A speaker at a Leningrad conference of propagandists in the mid-1920s urged listeners to translate peasant newspapers into familiar speech before reading them aloud.[89] Literate peasants found much of what was published for them in the 1920s "not for us," as one reader put it, and written "not in Russian but in political language."[90] The misunderstandings could be surprising. Grigorii Zinoviev, the Leningrad Party leader who had initially joined Stalin against Trotsky, confused peasant readers with his pamphlet *Lenin: Genius, Teacher, Leader, and Man* by juxtaposing the names Lenin and Ilich, according to one local observer.[91] "The peasants do not understood this, and if they understand, they think it funny," he explained. "'The funeral of Lenin and the Legacy of Ilich.' How can we understand that? Does it mean that Lenin and Ilich are two different people?" A thirty-five-year-old rural Communist explained to an investigator early in the NEP that among the words in the newspaper he did not know were "element" (used in such phrases as reactionary element) and the abbreviation for the Ukrainian Republic.[92]

Propagandists compiled lists of words that were unfamiliar to common readers at trial readings, often in Moscow, or from letters to the press.[93] The lists hardly overlap, suggesting that the words belong to a larger pool of equally unintelligible expressions and usages. Readers did not understand terms central to the Bolsheviks' message, such as *democracy, imperialism, dialectic, class enemy,* and *socialism.* Listeners were baffled by *syndicate, blockade, USSR, budget, deficit,* and *balance.* They were puzzled by scientific words such as *nitrogen* and *microbe* and abbreviations for even familiar organizations such as *Komsomol* and *KSM* (for *Komunisticheskii soiuz molodezhi*).[94] The journalists' determination to use difficult words and constructions despite the havoc this caused seems inexplicable except as an unconscious desire to create an insiders' language.[95] In this way, Bolsheviks perhaps unwittingly raised the price of entry into the body politic and made a certain level of understanding and accommodation to a new language a condition of membership.

The revolutionaries also faced distribution problems. The chaos of revolution and civil war limited circulation as much as the self-imposed censorship. Almost every aspect of publishing declined after the revolution, and newspaper production foundered. By March 1919 there were only two newspapers in Petrograd with a combined circulation of four hundred thousand copies.[96] The six most widely disseminated newspapers reached the circulation levels of the six most popular prerevolutionary newspapers only in 1924.[97] In 1925, however, there were only 107 Soviet dailies compared to 715 Russian-language newspapers in 1915.[98] Even in 1928 the number of dailies was far below prerevolutionary levels, although their combined circulation was considerably higher.

Money nearly disappeared under war communism (1918–21), and deliveries of newspapers were haphazard. The government promoted cottage reading rooms, libraries, centers for the liquidation of illiteracy, and other local institutions of education and propaganda, and their numbers far surpassed those of their pre-Soviet equivalents. Yet anecdotal information suggests that much of what was given away was never read. After the reforms of the NEP, which began in late 1921, readers had to pay for periodicals and books that had formerly been distributed free of charge, and this precipitated new problems.[99] Institutions and individuals had to choose among offerings rather than accept them all. The total national circulation of all newspapers dropped from three million to fewer than one million copies a day by May 1922.[100] A journalist traveling in southern Russia wrote in *Pravda* on August 11, 1923, that newspapers were rare even at large railroad stations.

Figures on printing machines and production of cardboard and paper corroborate the decline of reading.[101] The number of rotary presses, flatbed presses, and lithographic and typesetting machines in operation fell to two-thirds of pre–World War I levels by 1924–26.[102] Paper and cardboard production, in 1920–21, fell to less than 10 percent of the 1913 level, returning to pre-war quantities only in 1928–29.[103] Despite the scarcity of paper and machines, much was wasted on reports of state and cooperative institutions. Confusion and the novelty of state management affected quality. Printers of *Working Moscow* (circulation sixty-two thousand in 1923) apologized for worn-out presses, inadequate typesetting machines, inferior ink, and poor paper.[104]

The collapse of retail networks further hindered distribution. Pre-Soviet publications had been sold through bookstores, kiosks, railroad stalls, and rural general stores, as well as by hawkers at fairs, markets, and in villages. Schools, philanthropic educational institutions, churches, local government, and the military had also distributed printed material. Soviet authorities relied on the Red Army, local government, the Party, the schools, and institutions of adult education. The government nationalized the remnant of the entrepreneur A. S. Suvorin's sixteen hundred kiosks and funneled up to half a million copies of newspapers a week through them during the civil war, but distribution shrank under the NEP.[105] In 1919 and 1920 as much as 40 percent of all newspapers went to soldiers, but many never received them or, if they did, used them for other than intended purposes.[106]

Peasants seeking to buy printed materials suffered from the loss of small rural shops, unreliable mail delivery, and unmotivated sales personnel at post offices and cooperatives. Near the old textile center of Ivanovno-Voznesensk a book cooperative received two thousand copies of *The Peasant Newspaper* each week, but "the newspaper is heaped up right away in bundles on the floor and lies there for months," complained a frustrated subscriber.[107] "The absence of newspapers, literature, instructions, and guidance from above reduces village Communists to such a level of development that it is difficult to distinguish them from non-Communists," complained an observer in *The Poor* in late 1922.[108] The effect may well have been the reverse. The hiatus in the reading experience of ordinary people tended to heighten the gap between those inside and outside the system.

According to official observers of rural Russia, who were inclined to stress the peasants' ignorance, diverse rumors flourished in the absence of reliable information. An investigator in central Russia reported in mid-1923 that in the countryside only Komsomol and Party members read the press. "The rest of the village lives by rumor."[109] In 1923 and 1924, according to reports from an "expedition" sent to study newspaper circulation in the countryside, wild stories were circulating about the overthrow of the Bolsheviks, Lenin's death, revolution in Western Europe, taxes on women, and new "robber taxes" reminiscent of war communism.[110] Particularly colorful were those concerning the fall of a huge meteor in the region of Astrakhan in December 1922. According to the press, peasants believed that the meteor was made of gold and jewels, that only Communists were allowed to approach it, and that taxes would be canceled for two years because the riches of the meteor would be sufficient. "Rumors have replaced the newspaper in the village," Ia. Shafir concluded in 1924, surveying results of the expedition and other studies.[111] "The village as a whole is beyond our influence; the peasants do not receive information from us or with our perspective about what happens in the world outside the village," he wrote.[112]

Nevertheless the Soviet government continued in its efforts to master the material task of producing large numbers of newspapers and distributing them widely. One way in which Soviet publishers circumvented the lack of individual demand was to focus on institutional sales. Distribution to the army during the civil war was a model. Newspaper subscriptions were sold according to "collective demand," and compulsory subscriptions were common at factories until the late 1920s.[113] According to an observer in 1920, only 13 percent of the workers' newspapers (including, one assumes, *Pravda* and *Izvestiia*) were distributed by direct individual subscription, compared to one-third of the newspapers for peasants and national minorities.[114] Purchases by collective subscription declined to 14.5 percent of the total by 1927 and 1928.[115]

Readers were not willing to pay the full cost of the newspapers, and newspapers were not expected to show a profit even under the NEP, although managers were pressured to minimize losses. Only the most widely circulated newspapers, including *Pravda, The Peasant Newspaper, Working Moscow,* and *The Whistle* were profitable in 1928, partly as a result of institutional advertisements.[116] Purchases by Party members were always important. The Eleventh Party Congress made subscription to a newspaper compulsory for Party members in December 1921, and the Twelfth and Thirteenth congresses, in 1922 and 1924, reaffirmed the order.[117] A peasant watchman at a grain depot, when asked in 1924 who subscribed, pointed to a local Party member. "He is one of our Communists; he is a compulsory subscriber."[118] This was an ominous turn.

From the Mass Public to the Exemplary Reader

The Bolsheviks largely abandoned their attempt to use the press to convert common readers to their cause at the very moment when they gained the physical capability to reach this audience. The shift from an imagined mass public to be swayed by rational argument to a narrower and less-critical audience of insiders coincided with the implementation of the great Stalinist coercive projects. These included the First Five-Year Plan (1928–32), which was intended to industrialize the country, and the collectivization of agriculture, which largely eliminated private farming, restricted the movement of the peasant population, and insured the state's near monopoly on the procurement and sale of agricultural products.

As the government turned from common readers, it ceased to study them. The official study of the reader began soon after the revolution with open-ended queries about what people wanted to read. In the late 1920s and early 1930s the enterprise concluded with demonstrative reports on model citizens' reactions to model texts.[119] Typical of the government's early interest was a study of twelve thousand Red Army soldiers during the civil war.[120] The questions were broad. Soldiers were asked, "What do you particularly like to read?" and given ten choices, ranging from "history" or "politics" to "novels and love stories." They reported preferences for agriculture, novels, and adventure stories.[121] Their favorite author was Lev Tolstoy. *The Workers' Newspaper* polled readers in May 1925, seeking information about their social position and preferences.[122] The replies were chiefly from workers (54 percent) and white-collar employees (28 percent), who wanted more attention paid to workers' social problems and economic interests.[123] Few answered a question about whether they had read a supplement with speeches of Party leaders, and, if not, why not.

The Bolsheviks' sponsorship of thousands of such studies indicates that they had not given up on a mass audience. That they were willing to ask open questions was a measure of their optimism about what they offered. As the NEP progressed, however, their interest in open inquiries waned. In 1927 librarians at three mines in the Donbas asked miners how they liked officially sanctioned library books, and the interlocutors passed the answers on to the local Party cell for use in evaluating the borrowers' political views.[124] Sometimes librarians were blamed for the unorthodox tastes of readers under their supervision. As a consequence, official voices predominated, and readers became reluctant to answer anything except anonymous queries.[125] During the late 1920s editors and publishers chiefly solicited the comments of citizens who could be counted on to say what was required. A late attempt to investigate readers' tastes was a study by A. Meromskii and P. Putnik, *The Village Is for Books* (1931). As evidence that "the village is for books," they cited an activist's report that the pamphlet *Tractors and Combines* taught everyone "the usefulness of these machines" and encouraged young people to ride "the steel horse."[126] The State Publishing House gained the exclusive right to study readers' interests in 1930, but few studies were undertaken. Under a monopoly, the investigation of taste is unnecessary.

The effort to study readers ended as the Stalinist government lost patience with the pace of economic and social change. The failure to communicate with people marked a critical phase in the development of the dictatorship of the word. Restricting information meant restricting participation in the political process, the opposite of what Lenin and his allies claimed to seek in 1917. By 1930 a new system of public information had taken shape, with the daily newspaper as its foundation.

When different social groups are thrown together during chaotic times, a society's governing values may change abruptly. The thinking of the lower strata may acquire prestige, and the ideas of the dominant strata may be thrown open to challenge.[127] The Soviet press of the 1920s was a vehicle of such infiltration from below and of percolation up and down social hierarchies.[128] Although many ordinary people found Soviet public culture confusing, some understood it and became an expressive constituency of the press. Such people increasingly staffed the institutions of the new state, including the media. They were serious about learning the language of public life and about acquiring cultural capital in the form of political literacy. The mass newspapers linked the intellectual world of the upwardly mobile common people with that of Soviet leaders.

The managers of the Soviet press both succeeded and failed during the first decade. They succeeded in incorporating into the newspapers voices and concerns of officials and activists. This link between the government and its supporters facilitated the implementation of the First Five-Year Plan and the forced collectivization of the peasantry. Yet the press failed to reach many semiliterate common people who had been accustomed to the cheap, popular, commercial publications that had circulated under the old regime.

Reading newspapers has been a modern habit everywhere, surviving even the electronic media, and Soviet Russia was no exception. Print culture was an incubator of group identities for half a millennium in Europe, and the mass replication of images and rhetoric was the time-tested means for the representation and invention of peoples and nations. The initial break in the reading experience of ordinary people in Soviet Russia thus facilitated the Bolsheviks' control not only over the printed word but over the society's public self-image. This, more than anything, accounts for the ability of members of the ruling Party to represent themselves positively, despite their difficulties, and to spin the fantasies of the following decades. For most people the choice was between new, prescribed public images and no public images. An aged peasant woman from Krasnodar recalled in 1992:

> When the Reds won, they began to name everything—"Red October," "Soldier of the Revolution." When they gave us plots of land after the revolution, one said, "I served in the revolution and want my plot to be called 'Soldier of the Revolution.'" And so they go into the steppe to mow, and say, "Over there is 'Soldier of the Revolution,'" and we do the same.[129]

The Bolsheviks and their supporters not only wrenched the physical controls of Russian society from the hands of the former rulers; they also seized its spiritual and imaginative levers through monopolistic control of the press. What began as an effort to eradicate political opposition developed into a full-fledged seizure of the public imagination. With consolidation of control over the content and distribution of newspapers came a consecutive diminution in the power of the press to include and reach many groups within Soviet society. The leaders' inability to communicate with those in whose name they ruled thus culminated in the shift from persuasion to compulsion in the late 1920s.

Two　————————————————————————————

The First Decade: From Class War
to Socialist Building

WHEN the Bolsheviks emerged from the underground in February and October 1917 they had to describe themselves and their project, that is, present an identity and agenda that they and their supporters could understand. Moreover, they had to reach a broader constituency than the clandestine stalwarts. The huge linguistic operation of the official press was initially driven by the contradictory need for explanations among the committed and the uncommitted. Abrupt political changes and shifts in domestic and foreign policy complicated this dual task for the leaders and journalists. Lenin sparked one reorientation when he replaced the regimen of war communism with the mixed economy of the NEP in 1921, thereby forcing his colleagues to alter their brutal military style of governance and adopt less openly draconian means.[1] The decade that followed featured many such changes following Lenin's incapacity in 1923 and his death in 1924. In the struggle for succession Stalin allied himself first with Grigorii Zinoviev, chairman of the executive committee of the Communist International (Comintern), and Lev Kamenev, chairman of the Moscow Soviet, and then in 1925 with Nikolai Bukharin, who had edited *Pravda* almost uninterruptedly since October. In 1924 Stalin proposed achieving "socialism in one country," and in the following year he and his allies forced Trotsky from his post as commissar of military and naval affairs. In 1927 he destroyed the opposition led by Trotsky, Zinoviev, and Kamenev, sending Trotsky into exile in Alma-Ata. Then in 1928 he broke with Bukharin and advocates of the NEP to launch his own radical program of industrialization and collectivization. Until the end of the decade Stalin and his opponents used the press to ride this political roller coaster.

Under Lenin, newspapers had reported some intra-Party controversies, particularly during Party congresses; Stalin abandoned this practice, using his post as general secretary of the Party and his influence over the secret police to deny the press to his enemies. When Lenin turned against him in late 1922 and early 1923, Stalin tried to contain the leader's criticism. In January 1923 Stalin and his collaborators discussed suppressing Lenin's article on the Workers' and Peasants' Inspectorate, which was critical of Stalin. They even considered printing a special issue of *Pravda* to trick the ailing leader into thinking that the article in question had appeared.[2] Bukharin, who opposed publishing Lenin's original article, printed a modified version less hostile to Stalin. Throughout

1923 Stalin and his allies used *Pravda* to their advantage, and on December 29 Trotsky and others protested to the Politburo against the "falsification and forgery" by which *Pravda*'s editors misled "the public opinion of the Party."[3] In September 1924 Trotsky found *Pravda* closed to him when he tried to publish an obituary of M. S. Glazman, his secretary during the civil war.[4] Later that year, when Trotsky attacked Zinoviev and Kamenev, then Stalin's allies, the press campaigned against him. In 1924 Stalin also used the press to quell rumors of Lenin's "testament," his deathbed characterizations of potential successors in which he warned against Stalin and expressed ambiguous support for Trotsky.[5] Trotsky's American booster Max Eastman published a version of this document, and Stalin ordered Molotov to oversee the circulation of the denials of its existence that were written by Trotsky and Nadezhda Krupskaia, Lenin's wife, under pressure from the Stalinist majority on the Central Committee.[6]

The press continued to slant coverage of exchanges between Stalin and his rivals as long as open opposition existed. Although in late 1925 Zinoviev's supporters at the Leningrad newspaper, *Leningrad Pravda,* polemicized with *Pravda,* Stalin soon silenced them.[7] In 1926 editors of *Pravda* and other central newspapers skewed coverage of Stalin's clash with his foes over the Chinese Communists' cooperation with the nationalist Kuomintang. Stalin defended the ill-fated alliance, Trotsky and others opposed it, and press coverage was largely favorable to the alliance. Similarly, in 1926 and 1927, the editors promoted the developmental strategy based on agriculture and supported by Stalin and Bukharin over the rapid industrialization advocated by the opposition led by Trotsky.

With the press almost closed to them, Trotsky, Zinoviev, and Kamenev adopted underground methods. In 1926 Viacheslav Menzhinskii replaced Feliks Dzerzhinskii as head of the Unified State Political Administration (OGPU), a successor to the Cheka, and proceeded to increase physical harassment of the opposition. In the fall of 1927 the Stalinists prevented their opponents from disseminating their "Platform" for the Fifteenth Party Congress.[8] The opposition took to the streets and suffered further repression. When Stalin abandoned the NEP for industrialization and collectivization, Bukharin, his erstwhile supporter and a determined advocate of the mixed economy, fared no better than Trotsky. Once Stalin opposed him, Bukharin was unable to express his views openly, even though he still edited *Pravda*.[9] He left much unsaid even in his famous defense of the NEP, "Notes of an Economist," which appeared in *Pravda* on September 30, 1928. Trotsky wrote the epitaph for open discussion when, in the mid-1920s, he noted, "The battle of ideas has been replaced by the administrative mechanism."[10] In fact, the Bolsheviks, Trotsky included, had never sanctioned a free flow of ideas.

The issue is not Stalin's polemic with opponents, however, but the more extensive daily flow of commentary on small and large events that shared space with it. This is a different chronicle than that of the ideas and strategies of the

great actors or of the milestones of major events. It is the story of how the changing leadership, the managers of the print media, and the rank-and-file journalists pictured Soviet society and the world, a record of continuities and discon-
tinuities of public expression during the tumultuous first decade of Soviet
politics. It is also an account of the new official culture that expanded beyond
the old Bolshevik elite to encompass Soviet public life and many aspects of
private life as well.

Historically, newspapers have been considered a means of setting agendas
by telling people what to think about, if not what to think. Agenda setting is effective and people take cues from the media when they can fit information into
culturally shaped patterns.[11] Such patterns have been called schemata.[12] Readers use schemata to integrate new information with what they know and seek
new schemata when old ones fail to match information that cannot be ignored.
Although schemata exist in readers' minds, journalists also use them. Schemata
are akin to "media packages" or "frames," that is, combinations of metaphors,
examples, slogans, and visual materials writers use to shape diverse but related
information.[13] The meanings promoted by the newspaper staff under the Party's
direction were vital in the Soviet case because conveying certain understandings was the explicit function of the press, even when the leaders were somewhat divided.

Soviet leaders and journalists expressed the relative openness of the first Soviet decade by employing three overlapping but often contradictory schemata
to describe themselves and their society. First, they used Marx's notion of class
war to frame their struggle for survival from 1918 to 1921, as well as later militant efforts to transform the country. Second, after the introduction of the New
Economic Policy in 1921, they increasingly adopted a more pragmatic perspective, allowing for some diversity of opinion and for reportage of compro-
mises essential to the mixed economy. Lastly, from the mid-1920s, they utilized
"socialist building" to promote Stalin's program of "socialism in one country."
This schema also predominated later, when Stalin broke with Bukharin and
other supporters of the NEP and enacted the First Five-Year Plan (1928–32)
and forced collectivization.

Class War

Metaphors of class war gained sway as the Bolsheviks concentrated power and
resources under the program of "war communism" (1918–21). This entailed
forced requisitions in the countryside, rationing in cities, nationalization of all
enterprises, distribution of goods and services according to class categories,
suppression of dissent, and terror against presumed enemies. According to the
dictates of class war, the Bolsheviks characterized themselves as the "general
staff" of a worker-peasant army. In *Pravda,* in late 1919, Trotsky described the

atmosphere of a Party meeting as "the tranquility of a war council of hardened fighters after one battle and before the next."[14] Lenin told the Petrograd Soviet on November 7 just after taking power, "We possess the strength of mass organization to overcome everything and lead the proletariat to world revolution."[15] Within the construct of class war, society was divided into opposing groups: we, the revolutionaries, and they, the opponents. "The majority of the people are with us," Lenin said on November 18.[16] He could not say "We the People," as did authors of the United States Constitution, because he was unwilling to relinquish the idea of leadership by the avant-garde. He reserved *we* largely for himself and his supporters. "We are the state," he told delegates at the Eleventh Party Congress in early 1922.[17]

Like Lenin, *Pravda*'s editors and columnists used *we* to command.[18] "We need work and organization," wrote an editorialist in 1918.[19] Another explained the government's move from Petrograd to Moscow early in the same year: "To the workers and soldiers of Petrograd we say: for us, moving the revolutionary government to Moscow poses new tasks to guard the revolution with tenfold vigilance" (March 10, 1918). Contributors to the interactive sphere sanctioned this usage by stressing their eagerness to carry out orders. "Before us, Communists, looms a new and urgent task—work among peasant women," wrote a female activist (October 30, 1919). "We need close ties among the organs of the [Soviet] Union," wrote a young Communist (January 4, 1920). Such authors expressed the tension between the press's intended mass appeal and the dialogue about orders and directives between leaders and officials, and supporters.

All societies develop shared explanations of why things happen. How a society represents agency largely determines the way it assigns responsibility for events. Soviet leaders and journalists often assigned agency to the state. But the vague terms and euphemisms they employed, such as *Soviet power, the revolution, the Party,* or *toilers,* tended to obscure responsibility. "All these decrees and decisions of Soviet power are dictated by a striving to raise labor productivity as quickly as possible," noted one *Pravda* correspondent (May 6, 1921). "The Party's Task in the Area of Cooperatives" was a typical headline (April 2, 1921). Even presumed good deeds lost a human dimension. "Soviet power recognized the business of providing for and bringing up children as one of its tasks from the first days of its existence," explained Mikhail Kalinin (February 23, 1921). The result was to camouflage the dictatorship, make decisions appear inevitable, and diminish individual actors.[20] Trotsky warned of this bureaucratization of society in his 1923 pamphlet *The New Course*.[21]

The schema of class war, with society divided into "us" and "them" according to class categories, marked the high tide of Marxism as a public explanation of social life. Following Marx, journalists associated political behavior with class origins and stigmatized prosperous peasants as *kulaks,* literally "fists," a slippery term which after 1917 encompassed more prosperous and usually more literate and industrious peasant farmers, some of whom employed hired labor and lent money.[22] A local organizer wrote of a village: "The wives of Red Army soldiers decided to go to the meeting, then the wives of poor peasants, and last of all the wives of middle peasants."[23] "Wives of kulaks stayed away," she added. All disputes became class conflicts. A journalist described a Cossack mutiny in Krasnoiarsk in 1921 as a bourgeois plot, with no further elaboration, as if other explanations were implausible.[24]

Metaphors focus and fix meaning, and the press used those of class war to assign agency to cryptic authorities.[25] Key words were *front* and *struggle*. Obstacles and problems became enemies, and actions ended in victory or defeat. "We can conquer the dangerous front of disorder, hunger, and cold," *Pravda* editorialized in the terrible year of 1919.[26] Things that were not literally "weapons" became them. The Party became an army, and a good Party member "an honest soldier of the revolution" (February 12, 1919). To join was to enter "our ranks"(October 30, 1919). Industry became "the production front" and slackers were traitors (September 9, 1920; December 21, 1919). A claustrophobic image of an embattled land arose. "The fortress of Soviet Russia is 'the fortress' of the working class; the 'panic' of the Whites is the panic of a 'dying' old world," read one account (January 1, 1920).

The same metaphors governed representations of the wider society, including the arts, but in this case an earlier schema had to be overcome. Bolsheviks with experience in organizing, such as Lenin and Nadezhda Krupskaia, treated literature and art as revolutionary pedagogy. Nevertheless, artists and writers in arms were as natural to this mobilized culture as proletarian and peasant soldiers, and images of art as a weapon abounded. Articles in this vein account for more than half of *Pravda*'s cultural coverage in the first quarter of 1921, a third during the same period in 1924 and 1925, but less than a fifth by 1927, when the schema of socialist building gained sway. "We can and should regard literature as a weapon, and an altogether powerful weapon to affect the reader's consciousness and will," wrote one critic (February 19, 1924). Militants of the proletarian arts associations shared this view.[27] "Film is the strongest weapon in the struggle for communist culture," proclaimed the Association of Revolutionary Filmmakers the same year.[28] The effect was to relegate art and artists to one side or the other of the barricades.

In dividing society into class allies and class enemies, the revolutionaries adopted a rhetoric of violence and reprisal. Enemies figured in almost every editorial during the civil war and in many other articles as well.[29] Two months after the revolution, *Pravda*'s editorialists stressed "the simple self-evident truth" that "this war is carried out by all means and methods."[30] Coverage of repression elsewhere in Europe bolstered the message. Referring to the retribution after the failed Hungarian Revolution in 1919, *Pravda* editorialized: "You wait, messieurs the bourgeoisie! Execute thousands! The deaths of its best sons will be etched in blood in the proletariat's heart. It will remember them with love and sadness. It will know then what must be done."[31]

The Bolsheviks stigmatized their most serious political opponents, the Socialist Revolutionaries, as class enemies in a grandiose public trial, lasting from June 8 through August 7, 1922. The accused, members of the Party's Central Committee, had already spent several years in jail. They were incarcerated despite their observance of an agreement signed in 1919 not to use physical force so long as the Bolsheviks did not kill socialists.[32] In return, the government had excused them from prosecution for activity before February 1919. Nevertheless they were charged with starting the civil war, contesting the peace of Brest-Litovsk with Germany, opposing the government, and spying for the Entente powers. Mass demonstrations were organized to demand the death penalty, and *Pravda*'s editors laid the case before international "proletarian public opinion" as "Russian workers' struggle against the innumerable hordes of capital."[33] The lead editorial on the second day was captioned, "Who Are the Traitors?" (June 9, 1922). Since there were only two sides to class war, treason to the working class was the only explanation for opposition to Bolshevism. "Down with the traitors! Long live the unity of all workers in the struggle against kings, the bourgeoisie, and social democracy," proclaimed Trotsky (June 18, 1922).

The press promoted social cohesion among supporters by counterpoising presumably loyal masses to would-be oppressors. "Remember comrades, there is a thin line of the bourgeoisie and generals against millions of workers and peasants," wrote a columnist in the midst of the civil war (October 30, 1919). "Where the bourgeoisie sees only coal and grain, we see oppressed classes of people, striving for liberation and deserving our support and sympathy," noted another in 1918 (February 7, 1918). The press used class war to justify repression. Denunciations of enemies were coupled with statements such as "The working class well understands" and "Workers and peasants cannot hold two opinions on this question"(December 3, 1918).

The Bolsheviks also drew on Orthodox Christianity to portray selfless soldiers of revolution when they commemorated deceased comrades in *Pravda*. Despite the fact that they themselves often lived in prosperous circumstances, they celebrated self-sacrifice, the disavowal of personal needs and interests, and the denial of homes and families.[34] In 1921 a deceased Party member was recalled as a good comrade, "who never considered himself."[35] By 1925 a deceased Bolshevik could be applauded for asceticism: "Comrade Nesterenko had no personal biography and no personal needs."[36] In 1925 the pseudo-saintly obituaries of Frunze, the ill-starred successor to Trotsky as military chief, illustrated the mix of old ideals and new realities. I. S. Unshlikht, Frunze's deputy and a Bolshevik from 1900, wrote: "Comrade Frunze had no personal life but strove with all his force for common socialist ideals."[37] Even when obituarists did not cite self-sacrifice, they strongly implied it. "His life was torture; he lived only because he believed in the final victory of the working class," observed Kamenev in his funeral speech, with reference to Frunze's experience as a tsarist prisoner. Whereas officials employed such images of service to claim privileges, readers charged them with high living in unpublished letters to newspapers.[38]

The secondary role of women in this hypocritical litany was unambiguous.[39] The press showed them abandoning their families or simply not having them. Women were praised for solicitude for comrades or for the revolution, rather than for their aspirations or achievements. The office manager at the Ministry of Education was lauded for working late and only going home to "rest in order to return again on time."[40] M. P. Ivanitskaia, an official at the Central Executive Committee, who had no family and insisted on living in a tiny, cold room in a communal apartment despite her declining health, was remembered for her dogged devotion to the revolutionary ideals. "During the course of the winter," wrote the author of her obituary, "I tried to convince M. P. to get herself a reasonable room, since the room she occupied was cold and full of smoke, but she answered: 'The majority of workers live in these conditions; why should I have a good room and not they?'" (July 17, 1921).

Leaders and journalists used a military metaphor for their own service. Preobrazhenskii wrote of the revolutionary organizer and head of the miners' union, "Artem" (F. A. Sergeev), who was killed in a train wreck in 1921: "This idiotic accident has removed . . . one of the best soldiers from the ranks of the Old Guard of our Party" (August 14, 1921). "Demian Bednyi stood at his fighting post in the most difficult moments of the revolutionary years," wrote Karl Radek, congratulating the writer on his tenth anniversary as a contributor to *Pravda* (May 24, 1923). The author of an obituary of the old Bolshevik A. G. Shvartz praised him in 1927 for "humility and devotion" to the Party, and concluded, "One more rank-and-file soldier of the revolution has left our workers' family" (January 16, 1927).

The metaphor by which the Party became a surrogate family, though less common than the military metaphor, served to enhance the loyalties and priorities of activists. "It is now the task of old Party comrades to join together promptly in a single united communist family," observed one local correspondent in 1919 (October 30, 1919). Bolsheviks promoted a world in which actual families and homes counted little; thousands of pages of newspapers from the 1920s contain hardly a single picture of a family or of a child with a parent. Parents figured occasionally in the biographical sketches but only as markers of social origins. Children and spouses rarely appeared, and, when they did, their role was largely negative.[41] The Bolshevik elite seldom mentioned families of the deceased when they commemorated comrades. Journalists cited families primarily as obligations or burdens, particularly if premature death made families dependent on the state, as in the case of an official who "left a wife and five small children without support."[42]

Bolsheviks did not have a consistent term for the quality of sacrifice, but the word they often used was *devotion,* with all its religious connotations.[43] During 1921 and 1923 the objects of devotion were the revolution, the working class, the ideals of socialism, and, less frequently, the Party. For example, one author wrote, "The workers' revolution has lost a tested and devoted fighter."[44] In the mid-1920s, the Party became an object of devotion, as evidenced by obituaries of Frunze. Rykov praised the military leader for "devotion to the revolution" and Trotsky recalled him as someone who "served the cause of the proletariat," but Zinoviev said Frunze had given "himself fully to his Party, his class, and the great proletarian revolution" and Stalin wrote simply that the Party had lost "one of its truest and most disciplined leaders" (November 5 and 13, 1925). By 1927 the phrase "wholehearted devotion to the Party" was standard (January 30, 1927).

There were two interactive genres of reportage in which personal characteristics considered worthy of recognition were represented in *Pravda* during the early 1920s. One involved "human-interest stories" by local correspondents and occasional journalists. The other consisted of contests to name the best employees in a particular profession. *Pravda* held two such contests in 1923, one for the best schoolteacher and another for the best factory director. In each case activists were supposed to nominate, and journalists evaluate, the most promising candidates.

Local correspondents and activists imitated their leaders by embracing revolutionary self-denial in reports on exemplary individuals and entries in contests. They praised a factory director, who "completely forgot about himself" and a "teacher-ascetic" (March 29, April 13, and May 4, 1923). Although the lives shown in the interactive sphere resemble those attributed to the Party elite, the object of loyalty often differed. Instead of the Party or the revolution, devotion was often to a locale, a collective, or a workplace. Lizavetushka, an exemplary woman, worked late. "At home, her children and husband await her, but she continues to work" (January 21, 1923). And why? "All her strength, despite her weak health, she gives to social work, forgetting the needs of her own 'personal' life and finding her sole satisfaction in work among the family of workers."

For committed women, children were often presented as an inescapable burden in these reports. "Comrade Kabalina is a widow. She has two daughters on her hands, and hence her life was particularly difficult in the first years of the revolution" (January 13, 1923). Similarly, an exemplary proletarian widow "works with her former energy," despite having "a bunch of children on her hands" (March 8, 1923). Men, on the other hand, were permitted to abandon their families in the name of the cause. A local correspondent nominated a colleague for the honor of best schoolteacher, noting in passing that he had deserted his wife and children. "The German advance and fear of Polish retribution compelled Comrade Sechko to leave his family to the mercy of fate and flee to Borisovskii District, where he was able to establish himself as a teacher," wrote the author of this report (April 28, 1923). "Comrade Sechko is not a Communist," the author explained, "but he is faithful to the proletariat to the depths of his soul."

Local correspondents contrasted the "new" and "old" life, as did Party leaders, but in order to stress obligations rather than entitlements.[45] The authors of obituaries and accounts of contestants and exemplary people cited the evils of the tsarist past to show why citizens should be beholden to the government. For example, a local journalist praised a female textile worker and hero of labor: "She is a non-Party person, but bitter experiences of past exploitation and oppression have made her a staunch proponent of Soviet power."[46] When the leaders complained that young people lacked the experience of living under the old regime, they assumed that this ordeal guaranteed loyalty to the new order.

The idea that ordinary people owed something to the Party and state for the revolution later evolved into the rhetoric of the gift, according to which all good things were bestowed by the Party and Stalin, rather than earned by those who enjoyed them. The elevation of gratitude and dependence as exemplary characterizes the transmutation in which "Soviet power," the Party, and the revolution became the chief actors in society. Stalin was the ultimate beneficiary of this theft of agency from individual citizens, and his supremacy was epitomized in the 1930s by the slogan, "Thank You, Comrade Stalin, for a Happy Life."

Pragmatic Accommodation and the New Economic Policy

The Bolsheviks adopted the NEP at the end of the civil war in response to economic collapse, an uprising at the Kronstadt naval base, and rebellious workers and peasants. At the Tenth Party Congress in March 1921 they introduced a tax in kind to replace forced grain requisitions in the hope that peasants would produce more if they could sell after-tax surpluses. Later they legalized some trade, replaced the tax in kind with a monetary tax, and privatized many enterprises, although not banking or heavy industry. Agricultural and industrial production reached prewar levels by mid-decade and growth continued to 1927, when low prices discouraged peasants from selling grain to the state.[47] Lenin, however, saw the NEP as a strategic retreat in class war.[48] He told delegates of the Communist International, "Until the final issue is decided, this awful state of war will continue. And we say: 'A la guerre comme a la guerre; we do not promise any freedom, or any democracy.'"[49] Yet he allowed that the retreat might be lengthy and did not fully exclude pluralistic representations of society from the press.

Newspapers became a forum, albeit a restricted one, in which certain economic and social grievances could be aired, and the words *question* and *problem* appeared frequently.[50] Such usage echoed debates before 1917 about "the woman question" and "the labor question." Soviet journalists wrote of "questions of production," "practical questions" of the trade union movement, and "questions of daily life."[51] *Pravda* portrayed the NEP as an era of questions without simple answers. Unemployment was a question. Poverty was a question. New capitalists and merchants who got rich in a gray market of grain trading constituted a question. Even foreign affairs, in which the leaders sought recognition and concessions from class enemies, was a question. Authors who wrote of questions in the interpretative sphere accepted some ambiguity and drew back from images of a bipolar world.

This form of presentation mattered. Placing questions before readers, Bukharin and the other editors of *Pravda* made the public an implicit judge of right and wrong. Although appeals to public opinion are familiar in the Western press, they were new in late imperial Russia and also in the 1920s. The image of readers as a "court of opinion" was inherent in the idea of the revolution as a project to be explained rationally to potential beneficiaries. If not in newspapers, then where should leaders argue for their projects and plans? Yet when they did so, even while predetermining the verdict, they inadvertently validated an interlocutor separate from the state. For example, in 1923, while the government still subsidized a few state farms that had outlived war communism, L. Sosnovskii charged, on page 1 of *Pravda,* that state cows produced less than a third of the milk peasants got from their scrawny private ones. "A poor economy was acceptable in 1918–21," he wrote, "but now, under conditions of cost accounting, it is criminal to hide criminal mismanagement."[52] Sosnovskii addressed an imagined public that was rational and judgmental.

Although the practice of questioning was soon curtailed, journalists initially used it to highlight problematic issues and what they considered abuses of authority. Such commentaries were common in *Pravda.*[53] "In the name of truth and justice, remember pensioners before it is too late," wrote a local reporter in 1922.[54] "We say that everywhere the economic situation is still weak," wrote another three years later.[55] These intractable problems differed from the wrongdoing journalists "signaled" in the 1930s. In the 1920s they were something to discuss; a decade later they were something for state or local authorities to remedy. Citing problems the government had ignored, the press inadvertently thwarted the presumed unity of state and society. Such stories proliferated in the NEP but were rare thereafter, although attacks on inept and corrupt managers continued.[56]

The pragmatic sentiment of the NEP also shaped portrayals of outsiders and opponents. Journalists wrote less stridently of class enemies, often portraying them as problems to overcome rather than deadly antagonists.[57] "We must remember that the government's timely intervention can foil the current machinations of village speculators, as it foiled urban speculators' attempts to wreck the monetary reform," wrote an editorialist under the heading "We Will Prevail."[58] "It is not surprising that the worker runs to the private trader when for the same price [as at the cooperative store] he receives high-quality goods," wrote another editorialist, who advised, "We must not complain, but set to work" (August 8, 1924). Authors writing in the interactive sphere likewise expressed confidence that class enemies could be peacefully overcome. A local official complained in early 1925 of kulaks using the cooperatives to buy machines. "This threat is easily liquidated, however, by the policy of refusing to supply the kulaks with tractors," he wrote (February 12, 1925). A worker from the Moscow region in the same year used a measured tone to describe two groups of youths in his factory settlement:

> The first are the Komsomols and Pioneers. Their life is either in the [Party] cell or in the club. . . . The second are young people living with their parents and following them in everything. In daytime they work or study; on holidays they attend church, get drunk, and make trouble. For the time being these groups exist side by side and are of equal size (August 6, 1925).

This softer view of struggle extended, on occasion, to political opponents. In 1924 the press covered the trial of Boris Savinkov, a Socialist Revolutionary lured home from abroad, in the same style as that of the Party's Central Committee two years earlier, but in this case *Pravda* cited his confession and appeal "to recognize Soviet power and submit to it" as grounds for leniency (August 29, 1924). He received a ten-year sentence but fell or was thrown to his death while in jail the following year.[59]

The relative openness of the pragmatic schema during the NEP was more evident in the presentation of science and the arts. In *Pravda*, scientists and engineers were often portrayed as experts whose competence did not stem wholly from the state, and, in the cultural sphere, reviewers frequently evaluated works on their aesthetic merits. In these fields, as was partly true in politics, the press represented authority as rational and legitimized it by expertise and reason rather than the passions of nationalism or class consciousness.

The Bolsheviks were eager to combat religion with science, and *Pravda* ran a bimonthly column titled "Science and Technology" during much of the 1920s in which prominent scientists described their research. Contributing authors, however, validated science as a profession as well as a social value. Typical was a statement by Professor N. K. Koltsov, a pioneer in molecular genetics and later a victim of the charlatan agronomist T. D. Lysenko. Admonishing skeptics about organ transplants from animals to humans, Koltsov wrote in 1924 that "people forget the time when humanity managed without the beneficial intervention of science."[60] The key was intervention. He and other contributors to the column contrasted their expertise with the layman's ignorance. This confidence underlay their accounts of research and prognoses of progress in the early and mid-1920s. "From what has been said, it is clear that science [i.e., not Soviet power] has correctly posed the solution to the question and has already given a series of unequivocally practical recommendations for agriculture," wrote the author of an article on biological pest management.[61]

Scientists and reporters on science and technology validated their profession by references to international science and foreign research, ranging from Einstein's theory to American technologies designed to tap energy from wind.[62] The press often likewise approved participation in world science in accord with the spirit of the NEP. The chemist V. N. Ipatev recalled, in emigration, that after a trip abroad Lenin urged him to write two articles for *Pravda* on economic and industrial conditions.[63] "We ought to examine carefully Western achievements in science and technology and introduce new methods into our chemical factories in conformity with our possibilities," he wrote in *Pravda* in 1927.[64] He defected at a scientific meeting in the late 1930s.

Scientists who wrote for *Pravda* often validated public funding with a utilitarian agenda. "Who does not know crystals and has not admired their orderly geometric forms?" began Professor G. Wolf in an article on the chemistry of crystals; but he concluded by evoking the demands of "our practical age" and explaining that "the significance of the structure of crystals for technology is enormous."[65] Contributors did not have to be professors or academicians to promote the authority of experts. The author of an article in 1926 on air transport stressed the need for expert planning. "The opening of each new air route, as is well known, demands a preliminary land survey, equipping of the landing area, and study of the climatic, geographic, and other conditions of the region," he wrote.[66]

In art, as in science, Bolshevik leaders initially permitted diversity and some independence for those sympathetic to the regime. They codified this position in a Central Committee resolution of June 18, 1925, titled "The Party's Political Line in the Area of Belles Lettres."[67] Although they declared that "art cannot be neutral" while class struggle continues, they accepted competition among literary groups and declared neutrality on style. This opened the way for critics in *Pravda* to evaluate art in its own terms, especially at the peak of NEP in 1924 and 1925, when apolitical commentaries filled a quarter of all space allocated to culture.[68]

Reviewers who demonstrated expertise substantiated professional authority by identifying their subject as something requiring a trained observer. The best example was music, the least political and most cosmopolitan of the arts in the 1920s, although not during the 1930s. *Pravda*'s regular music critic, Evgenii Braudo, often demonstrated his specialized knowledge and ability to judge music on aesthetic terms in commentaries such as one on the former capital's musical decline. "In Petersburg," he complained, "it is impossible to follow the new music, to learn of its latest developments either in the West or here."[69] Literary and film commentators were more political, and regular professional critics were less common. Yet even critics of literature could be apolitical in the early 1920s.

Despite these traces of pluralism, the press of the NEP identified the successful life largely with the state and the Party. This was particularly true in mass newspapers, the task of which was to bring ordinary citizens into the new social order. Although the NEP was intended to provide a legal framework and inducement for small private farmers to increase productivity, journalists implicitly denigrated private farming almost as forcefully as they praised collective enterprises and political organizing. In this respect, the official acceptance of the NEP remained largely formal, with little echo in the cultural media that reached the general public. The government's policies to secure land tenure, rationalize taxation, and encourage peasants to improve their holdings were not effectively communicated. Large sections of *The Poor* and *The Peasant Newspaper* were devoted to arcane tax laws, rules for land use, and regulations concerning various groups of peasants. Moreover, policies changed often and the texts in the press were so confused that at no time during the NEP could a peasant who relied on newspapers for information have confidence that land tenure was secure or that tax policy was stable.

According to official policy at the outset of the NEP, peasants could keep the land they farmed and could invest in it and improve it with confidence. Yet an agronomist complained in *The Poor* in 1922 that the land was like "a girl who sleeps around" and "no one knows to whom today's land will be granted tomorrow."[70] *The Peasant Paper* ran a story in the spring of 1926 about villagers who had established private farmsteads in 1922 and saw their improved land merged with the lands of peasants who had remained in the commune.[71] Fluctuations in policy toward the peasant commune added to the confusion. At times the commune was promoted as a step toward socialized agriculture, and at other times it was condemned as a feudal remnant. In 1922 peasants were granted the right to choose among the traditional commune, private farming, or some sort of collective agriculture.[72] Readers of *The Peasant Newspaper* were warned in the spring of 1924, however, that "the prosperous muzhik is generally the one who wishes to separate," since "there, beyond the eyes of the peasant commune and the authorities, he can do what he wants to the agricultural laborer."[73] By early 1927 families on private farmsteads were enemies of the people, the private farmer "a venomous proprietor."[74]

The NEP was a period of fundamentally ambiguous policy in agriculture, and the press communicated much of this ambiguity. Peasants were encouraged to improve their private production and simultaneously warned against kulaks, those who had the most improved production. Distinctions between "strong," "prosperous," and "rich" peasants, on the one hand, and kulaks, on the other, remained unclear. Nevertheless, the press charged "kulaks" with various sins. For example, as early as the summer of 1922 they were accused of allying with the foreign bourgeoisie and creating famine.[75] By early 1927 they were condemned as "pests of the Soviet village."[76] The half-hearted attempts to soften these threats at the peak of the NEP were probably unconvincing. Although private farming flourished, energy and talent flowed into the public sector.

Kalinin, the only member of the Party's highest ranks from peasantry and a frequent spokesman on agricultural issues, announced in *The Peasant News-paper* in the summer of 1925 that there was no danger from kulaks (July 14, 1925). In a year the line had changed, however, and by March 1926 kulaks were said to present a danger (March 23, 1926). A peasant wrote to *The Peasant Newspaper* also in 1926 that many were afraid to become prosperous because they could lose their vote and see lands they had improved exchanged for forest or scrub (June 1, 1926). In reply, Kalinin reaffirmed the alliance with the poor, adding, almost as an afterthought, that the government had nothing against peasants who became prosperous through their own labor.

The Peasant Newspaper often promised peasants a good crop or, on occasion, a fistful of money if they would farm scientifically. In a story on flax, published in 1925, hands were shown clutching money (May 19, 1925). In another the caption read, "Let Clover Go to Seed and Earn Big Money" (June 23, 1925). Yet in their contempt for money, journalists showed the peril of success outside official hierarchies. They promoted state lotteries but never showed winners enjoying their legal bounty. They occasionally reassured readers that possessing money was not dangerous, but their protestations were more likely to raise suspicions than quiet them. For example, during a campaign in 1926 to increase savings accounts in the state bank, one author assured readers that "a depositor is not a kulak" (March 30, 1926). Similarly in 1928, amid an effort to promote bee-keeping, an author asked: "Is a young person diminished socially or materially if he becomes a horticulturist or a horticulturist-beekeeper? Speaking more openly, does he ruin his life's career?" His answer was "a thousand times no" (May 15, 1928). In each case, even the unsuspicious might conclude that the journalist protested too much.

Conflicting representations of the world abroad also reflected uncertainties of the NEP.[77] The Bolsheviks founded the Communist International in March 1919 to overthrow capitalism, but diplomacy gained sway after revolutionary failures in Finland and the Baltics in the winter of 1918–19; in Hungary and Germany in the spring of 1919; in Poland after the Red Army's advance on Warsaw in the Polish-Soviet War of 1920; and again in Germany in 1923. Diplomatic successes included a trade agreement with Great Britain in March 1921, followed by similar agreements with other countries. The Soviet Union attended the Genoa Conference on the reconstruction of Central and Eastern Europe and in April 1922 signed the Rapallo Treaty with Germany, establishing open economic and secret military relations. In 1924 the country gained de jure recognition from Britain, France, and others, but not from the United States until 1933. This propensity for diplomacy was interrupted by crises conducive to the isolationism of "socialism in one country." These included a near break with Britain in 1923 and the termination of the Anglo-Soviet trade agreement in 1927.

Covering these and other stories, the editors of *Pravda, The Peasant News-paper,* and *Labor* echoed the government's emphasis on events in the West. Articles on foreign affairs occupied roughly a tenth of all space in the three news-papers, and largely concerned England, Germany, France, and America.[78] Beyond these nations, only chaotic China received regular coverage. The press also reflected the ambivalence of the era and the government's dissembling in foreign relations. Soviet editors produced four competing foreign stories in tandem with the three domestic schemata. These revolved around prospects for revolution abroad, peaceful relations with other countries, the bad life under capitalism, and foreign threats. The first two accorded with the relative pragmatism of the NEP, since those who told them identified with the West either as the site of future revolutions or of current trade. The latter two suited a contrary desire to withdraw into the realm of Soviet exceptionalism as befitted Lenin's vision of class war and Stalin's program of "socialist building." Each of the four filled an equal share or roughly a quarter of the cumulative space the central press allotted to foreign affairs from 1921 to 1928.[79]

The Bolsheviks seized power advocating internationalism rather than national distinctness. Stalin and Bukharin, however, began promoting disengagement from world linkages in their dispute with Trotsky during the mid-1920s. They advocated autarchy over ties to the world economy, "socialism in one country" rather than world revolution, and agricultural priorities instead of investment in industry. Each side had its vision of "the West," a term used often in the press. Each had its orientation toward foreigners. Although anti-Westernism came naturally to many Bolsheviks, Stalin advanced this inclination through his promotion of "socialism in one country."[80] Lenin had mentioned "two camps" in March 1920, but in the context of world revolution, not autarchy.[81] Stalin's program meant building communism and guarding against "capitalist encirclement," as Molotov recalled years later.[82]

Stalin and his opponents also differed on foreign trade. Trotsky and the opposition rejected economic isolation as unproductive, but Stalin's faction felt otherwise.[83] "The more our exports and imports grow," Stalin explained in 1925, "the more we depend on the capitalist West and the more vulnerable we become to attacks from our enemies."[84] Both sides ostensibly favored trade, but Stalin, like Lenin, defended the state trade monopoly as protection against spontaneous commercial exchanges with foreigners.[85] Bukharin said much the same in *Pravda* on October 10, 1927: "We do not want to be swallowed up by our deadly capitalist enemies. For this we need a barrier—the monopoly on foreign trade." Trotsky and the opposition toyed with abolition of the monopoly in 1927, but their arguments were suppressed.[86] The Stalinists won and, for the October anniversary of 1927, used the slogan, "The Monopoly of Foreign Trade Is Our Shield against Imperialists' Slave-holding Claims; Yes, Long Live the Socialist Monopoly on Foreign Trade!"[87] They cited threats from abroad to justify abandoning the market socialism of the NEP for collectivization and rapid industrialization. Western trade collapsed in 1931, partly owing to the Great Depression, and Stalin and his colleagues closed the country to foreign investment.[88] Limits on foreign ties and a quarantine on Western trends in literature, the arts, entertainment, and even certain fields of science, followed. These policies paralleled the demise elsewhere of international systems in economics, politics, and culture, but the Soviet turn inward was largely of domestic manufacture, a repudiation of trends of the NEP for what one historian has called "national Bolshevism."[89]

Writing of revolution abroad, however, early Soviet journalists often expressed sympathy for foreigners and foreign causes rather than distrust, even as they denounced capitalism. This distinguished their reports from articles about the bad life under capitalism. "In which country would proletarian revolution be most advantageous from the Communists' standpoint?" asked Trotsky in 1922.[90] His answer was the United States. Even when they chided foreign revolutionaries for failures, they often imagined a conversation among equals. Zinoviev posited a dialogue with German workers in 1922, arguing, "You say that you do not want civil war, that you do not consider yourselves Communists; very well, we will wait and see what happens in a year or two" (March 30, 1922). Journalists also granted respect when they wrote of supporters abroad or Soviet aid to foreigners (April 8, 1924; May 4, 1924). "Massive Dismissal of Revolutionary Workers in the Ruhr," read a headline in 1928 (December 6, 1928); "Brotherly Aid from Workers of the USSR," was the subtitle. Authors showed Soviet people joining others. "There is civil war in China," wrote one in *The Peasant Newspaper* in 1924, "[and] workers of the whole world follow it with sympathy."[91] Yet even in China, revolution was proving a mirage.

As revolutionary prospects faded, Soviet leaders sought accommodations with existing governments. Despite their hatred for capitalism and liberal democracy, they allowed the press to extend the NEP's murky pragmatism to foreign relations. Soviet diplomats sought foreign ties, and journalists chronicled trade, recognition, foreign visits, travel abroad, and foreign science and culture.[92] The authors of brief anonymous informational reports frequently expressed a benign orientation, and even leading Bolsheviks and regular journalists occasionally applauded. A wire-service story from 1922, "On the International Position of Soviet Russia," contained brief quotes from the foreign press, including one that read, "Rumors originating in Germany about unofficial discussions between the French and Russians today were the subject of increased commentary in London newspapers."[93] On January 1, 1924, *Pravda* published a front-page cartoon of a smiling worker receiving offers of recognition from all sides (Figure 2.1). Four years later a columnist speculated in *The Peasant Newspaper* that the British Labor Party's return to power could "save the whole world from disasters that presently threaten it."[94]

Favorable reports on foreign trade also fit this pragmatic approach. In 1922 the Soviet foreign-policy specialist Karl Radek hailed "businesslike" trade discussions with the West and gloried in Soviet negotiations with the great powers.[95] A brief article in *Pravda* a year earlier, captioned "The Opinion of the

Figure 2.1. *Pravda*, January 1, 1924. The Soviet Union portrayed as a worker receiving offers of "recognition."

Italian Press," read in part, "From Rome comes the information that the whole Italian press recommends the renewal of trade relations with Russia as soon as possible."[96] A note in *Labor* in that year on "Goods from Abroad" read simply, "Representatives of foreign firms have arrived in Rostov with goods for exchange with Soviet Russia."[97]

The citation of foreign opinion, which brought foreign voices and judgments into the press and signified foreign validations of Soviet accomplishments, had much to do with the country's long orientation toward the West. It represents a sharp contrast to the experience of, for example, revolutionary China and Iran.[98] Coverage of the Soviet foreign minister's popularity in Germany during the Genoa Conference (1922), when the two outcast nations signed the Rapallo Treaty, was typical: "At the Berlin movie house 'Scala,' which holds three thousand people, the audience gives the People's Commissar an ovation every time he appears on the screen."[99] A tiny unsigned report in *The Peasant Newspaper,* "Foreign Newspapers about A. I. Rykov," which appeared in 1924 soon after Lenin's death, reads simply: "Swedish newspapers call Comrade Rykov an intelligent and careful man. German newspapers call Comrade Rykov an honest and disinterested person."[100] Rykov was an advocate of "socialism in one country" but paradoxically drew authority notwithstanding from the opinions of foreigners.

Comparisons with foreigners were not always to Soviet advantage. Sosnovskii asked in *Pravda,* upon returning from the conference in Genoa, why the Soviet border was "marked by some kind of horrible henhouse, with a torn reddish boot on the roof and a Red Army man inside."[101] Even the Soviet train seemed humiliatingly shoddy: "We build electric stations and trolley lines. Is it really true that the RSFSR [Russian Soviet Federated Socialist Republic] cannot repair five railroad cars? To whom are we displaying such helplessness?"[102] Portrayals of visitors and foreign goods were similarly revealing: "Whoever thinks that Americans first provided themselves with excellent roads and then began to build a million automobiles is deeply mistaken," wrote a *Pravda* columnist in 1927 under the caption, "The American Automobile or the Russian Cart?"[103] Foreign trivia, such as a "Reference Section" in *Labor* in 1928 listing U.S. sports magazines in English and Russian, provided a light touch and brought foreign exposure down to daily life.[104]

The depth of the West's allure to advocates of the pragmatism of the NEP and the ambiguity with which they expressed it was most evident in representations of the United States.[105] America had been important in the Russian press before 1917, and interest continued during the 1920s although the United States did not recognize the Soviet Union until 1933, long after other industrial nations had done so.[106] Despite the lack of formal ties, America was a focus of intense hopes for cooperation among early Bolsheviks who saw in America both a rival path to modernity and a paragon of science and technology.[107] "In America they have invented a machine" became a formula for promoting new technology, and "American machines" meant quality.[108] Hence when journalists wanted Russians to understand that something was useful, they said that "the practical Americans" use it.[109] In fact, the press called diligent workers and peasants "Russian Americans." "Who are 'the Americans?'" asked a commentator on "Russian Americans" in January 1923. "They are people who know how to work with speed and vigor, and under pressure, unlike in old Rus."[110]

Even the leaders were not immune to the passion for American industrial organization and efficiency. Lenin adopted Taylorism but qualified his praise by noting that it combined "the refined bestiality of bourgeois exploitation with the richest scientific achievements."[111] Trotsky told a visiting U. S. senator in 1923, "The words 'Americanism' and 'Americanization' are used in our newspapers and technical journals in an altogether sympathetic way and by no means in the sense of reproach."[112] Stalin also wished to appropriate American efficiency. "The combination of Russian revolutionary sweep and American efficiency is the essence of Leninism in Party and state work," he wrote in 1924.[113] Bolsheviks used the slogan "Fordism" to express their janus-faced fascination. Ford signified "the bad life over there" during the early 1920s as "the automobile king," but when factories reached prewar norms and new construction was planned in the mid-1920s, journalists hailed Soviet Fordism.[114] Fordism then meant the assembly line and conveyer belt, and publicists assured readers that Soviet use would differ from the exploitative practices of capitalism. "There is nothing frightening about Fordism in a Soviet country," wrote one publicist in May 1926.[115]

Ford's system meant order and labor discipline, as Antonio Gramsci noted at the time.[116] Fordism as a set of values was thus consistent with Soviet conceptions of the economic benefit of revolutionary enthusiasm and the increasing emphasis on social control. Yet when those who wrote leads for *Pravda*'s "Workers' Life" column called the best workers and managers "Russian Fords," they communicated cosmopolitan values more in tune with the NEP than "socialist building."[117] But only the leaders and professional journalists adopted the phrase. Local correspondents and occasional letter writers ignored it. The elites had no problem with promoting American techniques and qualities, while condemning America. They felt no simple enthusiasm for foreign things.[118] They hoped to use America to build their own future but rejected an American future for themselves and the world. Within the ambiguities of the 1920s, they could cite America and go their own way.

Socialist Building

The relative tolerance of the NEP was short-lived. The government began to curtail the mixed economy in the mid-1920s and set the stage for a new image of the country and its citizens with preparations at the end of the decade for the

First Five-Year Plan and collectivization. The political system was changing in ways that restricted public discussion and facilitated coercive policies. All unsupervised meetings of organizations and congresses were forbidden in 1925. The *nomenklatura* system of Central Committee appointments by which important positions were centrally allocated arose at this time, merging hierarchies of the Party and state. Meanwhile, the Soviets lost the power to discuss the decisions of these institutions. In the early 1930s the government began submitting lists of decisions to the Central Executive Committee of Soviets for ratification without discussion.[119]

Party spokesmen extolled industrialization after the Fifteenth Party Conference in 1926, and preparations for the First Five-Year Plan began the next year. "Socialist building," which previously had meant institution building and economic recovery, became the catch phrase of a fresh outlook.[120] Unlike the earlier schemata, "socialist building" was used to shape a unified national agenda. Lenin and most other advocates of class war did not dream of constructing communism in backward Russia, with its peasant majority and shortage of proletarians. But when Stalin promoted "socialism in one country" in 1924, a new representation of Soviet society, power, and national identity became necessary. The active internationalism of the civil war and the moderately pragmatic cosmopolitanism of the NEP, expressed in matter-of-fact reports on growing relations with capitalist nations, waned. In their place appeared ethnocentrism and Soviet exceptionalism and, by the late 1920s, public expressions of xenophobia and isolationism.

Official journalists appealed to national pride, and *Pravda* and other leading newspapers denounced Trotsky and his supporters for "sowing disbelief in the proletarian character of our state."[121] Promoters of Stalin and Bukharin glorified Soviet institutions and processes. As one editorialist wrote in *Pravda* in early 1927, "Nowhere in the world besides the Soviet Union do the proletarians and peasants really take part in governing the state."[122] Such pronouncements accorded with Stalin's promise to build socialism in isolation and confounded critics of bureaucracy and the emerging Stalinist state. The trumpeting of accomplishments reached a crescendo in celebrations of the tenth anniversary of the October Revolution.

The endorsement of "socialism in one country" brought a shift in the treatment of foreign affairs. The elevation of national pride brought increased disparagement of foreigners and warnings against their wiles. Counter to the almost reflexive cosmopolitanism of the NEP were stories about the bad life abroad and the hazards there. Commentators drew on old images of venal Germans, dangerous orientals, and bitter religious opponents, as well as World War I and the Russian Civil War.[123] In these terms, as well as Marxist ideology, they denounced a capitalist nightmare in reports ranging from "Serfdom in France" to notes on storms, heat waves, floods, and other foreign disasters.[124] Such articles filled a fifth to a quarter of the space on foreign affairs in *Pravda, Labor,* and *The Peasant Newspaper* from 1921 through 1928. Those who wrote them answered the question "Who are we?" by denigrating life abroad and saying "our wonderful life differs from theirs." The author of "Among Us and Among Them," a column in 1925 about villages on the Soviet-Polish border, described Polish peasants straining to hear discussions and speeches among Soviet peasants across the border.[125] "This is Not England" read the caption of an unsigned article about an English captain who imprisoned a Chinese dock worker for stealing a pack of cigarettes in Vladivostok.[126]

Frightening reports of foreign threats brought the authority and power of the Soviet state into the foreground of the Soviet identity. Articles about hostile and aggressive international behavior occupied a fifth of the space on foreign affairs in *Pravda* and *Labor,* and 36 percent in *The Peasant Newspaper,* where the war scares of 1923 and 1927 received great attention. Yet fascism, the most dangerous threat, was largely ignored after an initial burst of interest. Bolsheviks initially registered its menace as a militant form of capitalism and in 1922 cited fascism in articles occupying 14 percent of *Pravda*'s foreign coverage. Trotsky, Zinoviev, Radek, and others wrote prophetically at this time, but they dropped the issue when the struggle to succeed Lenin began.[127] For the press, the chief danger was invasion or blockade by England, France, and Poland.[128] Such fears recalled the foreign interventions in the Russian civil war.

Reports of repression abroad helped create an environment conducive to Stalin's plans for socialist building. "Glory to the Hero and Death to Provocateurs" was the caption of an article in 1925 on a condemned Polish revolutionary.[129] "Wherever the bourgeoisie rules, the moans of tortured people are heard and in answer to them the sobs and plaints of defenseless children and old people," wrote a columnist on International Women's Day in 1926.[130] Repression was real, particularly in Central and Eastern Europe, but journalists who showed foreign villains cleared the way for nativism and the pitiless treatment of enemies at home. A columnist in 1923 mocked the Italian founder of an Odessa noodle factory under the caption "Without Italians," noting that "Russian gold [earned in the noodle factory] flowed to Italy" until the revolution sent the noodle maker back to "his native Palestine."[131] Isolationism took a xenophobic twist in reports of spies at home. "He did not sell important secret information abroad for English pounds and Finnish marks or silk stockings and Parisian perfumes, but for ideological inducements, out of a conscious wish to harm Soviet power," wrote a columnist in late 1927.[132]

War scares in 1923 and 1927 provided the image of a real enemy that could serve as a foil for a Soviet identity.[133] The British filled this role twice, and two groups of Soviet leaders took the opportunity to assert their legitimacy as defenders of Soviet independence. In 1923 antiforeign rhetoric was largely an ephemeral expedient, whereas in 1927 it was an official policy used to crush domestic opposition. The stated issues in 1923 were Anglo-Soviet rivalry in India and the Near East, British claims to nationalized properties, and Soviet religious persecution, but the problem for Soviet leaders was to shift authority away from the ailing Lenin. A British ultimatum on May 8 charging Soviet meddling in India and the Near East appeared in *Pravda* on May 11. The Soviet diplomat and old Bolshevik V. V. Vorovskii was assassinated in Lausanne on the same day. Lenin's would-be successors seized the opportunity. *Pravda* exhorted in a lengthy headline on May 12: "Workers, Peasants, Red Army men! All honest citizens of the USSR who do not want our country to be under the yoke of foreign capital, raise your voice against the perfidious villains!"[134]

The editors accused Britain of taking advantage of Lenin's illness to make Russia "'a dominion' of his majesty the king of Great Britain, the closest relative of Nikolai Romanov." The next day the cartoonist Dmitrii Moor, the most celebrated Soviet poster artist, portrayed the British Minister, Curzon, together with Mussolini, Poincaré, as a three-headed monster, assisted by Lilliputian Mensheviks; a giant worker captioned "We" punched the monster's head labeled "Curzon" (Figure 2.2).[135] *Pravda* and other papers featured Trotsky, Bukharin, and Georgii Chicherin, the commissar of foreign affairs, but not Stalin, as Russia's defenders: "The Soviet republics will not submit to humiliation" (Chicherin); "England will never convert us into an occupied zone" (Bukharin); and "The word command does not reach Moscow" (Trotsky).[136] "An international gang of incendiaries named "the Entente" is uneasy while the worker and peasant republic lives, develops, and gains strength," wrote the editors of *Working Moscow*.[137] A press campaign for the air force and Air Force Week commenced soon after.

The crisis of 1927 began on May 12 when British police searched the Soviet trading company ARCOS in London. Two weeks later Britain broke relations and trade agreements. Ties had soured after Soviet trade unions aided British strikers in the general strike of 1926. A fanatic killed the Soviet ambassador to Poland on June 7, and the Soviets retaliated by executing twenty conservative prisoners. As in 1923, front pages flamed with headlines and cartoons but this time without quotes from leaders. Stalin was silent for nearly two months while journalists honed their rhetoric.[138] "The dark forces of world reaction threaten to attack the USSR," cautioned *Pravda*'s editors.[139] Voroshilov, the army chief, ordered preparations in the provinces for "an armed attack at any moment."[140] The peasant paper printed pictures of peasants in gas masks. Nevertheless *The Poor* assured its audience of largely rural administrators that no attack was imminent.[141] The press warned of plots to murder Bukharin, Rykov, and Stalin.[142] "Is this the terror of which the White Guard newspapers now speak so often?" asked N. Pogodin, a well-connected columnist and playwright, on June 9.[143] The differential coverage frightened the least knowledgeable and reassured the cognoscenti. Stalin and his allies used the occasion to tar the opposition and distract from policy failures in China and at home.[144] On June 18 Bukharin in *Pravda* accused the opposition of ignoring the danger, and a rain of abuse commenced. The campaign sharpened with the proclamation of Defense Week on July 10 and subsequent trials of spies and traitors.

Figure 2.2. *Pravda*, May 13, 1923. Drawing by D. Moor. Titles beneath the cartoon read: "Mussolini, Poincaré, Mensheviks, Curzon, our Mensheviks, WE." The headline reads in part, "In reply to Curzon's hostile ultimatum and the revolver shots of the murderers of Lausanne, a thunderclap of indignation engulfs our whole country."

Stalin focused the campaign on July 28 with his "Comments on Contemporary Themes" about the danger of war, China, and the opposition's treason. When "terrorists and arsonists are attacking our factories and plants," he warned, the opposition plans "desertion." The speech appeared with his picture on page 1 of *The Peasant Newspaper* as well as other publications. Denunciations, confessions, professions of loyalty, and lists of defectors from the opposition followed.[145] As in 1923, editors encouraged donations to the military and published patriotic letters. "Workers have energetically taken up military studies in order to be ready to meet the class enemy with a gun in hand," read one letter in *Labor* on July 28.

Between the scares of 1923 and 1927, journalists transformed the country from a fighting outpost of world revolution into a space apart. *Pravda*'s visual commentary shows the metamorphosis. Soviet Russia is no more than a worker's fist and a bit of military machinery in Moor's front-page cartoon at the outbreak of the crisis on May 13, 1923 (Figure 2.2).[146] Most of the picture is devoted to capitalist monsters devouring workers. The same artist mocked foreign enemies in 1927, but he pushed them to the side of the picture and had them threaten the thriving country from afar. On June 11 he showed kings and bourgeois gentlemen on a hill, heaving bombs and shooting at crowds framed by factories and a Moscow skyline (Figure 2.3). In early July he showed snarling capitalists, fenced out by an armed worker and soldier behind whom factory smokestacks belch productive smoke.[147] Foreign sympathizers were there but they worked for Soviet Russia, not for revolutions in their own countries.

World revolution faded from the press during both war-scare campaigns.[148] Amid fear of war, foreign causes lost their glamour. The images of the Soviet land that surfaced in 1927 reappeared in altered form in the First Five-Year Plan and during collectivization. The scares served to consolidate a language of isolationism. Fear of ostracism in the face of issues such as patriotism can be a powerful factor in shifts of opinion even in democratic societies, where a vocal minority may intimidate a passive majority.[149] Stalin and his followers employed such intimidation as they took control of the Party and the government apparatus. The ambiguity of varying representations of foreign places and peoples disappeared from the press as the schema of socialist building and the parallel story of heroic builders besieged by foreign enemies took hold.

The effects of this inward turn on the information system itself were substantial. Lenin and the early Bolsheviks expressed public awareness of what was being said in the world around them. As the Stalinist leadership narrowed the permissible range of views about Soviet domestic life, they curtained off the foreign mirror in which they might have seen themselves somewhat differently. This was a reversal of public values far-ranging in its impact on sources of self-knowledge for Soviet society. Its effect on information from without paralleled restrictions on inputs from within. During the civil war Bolsheviks wrote

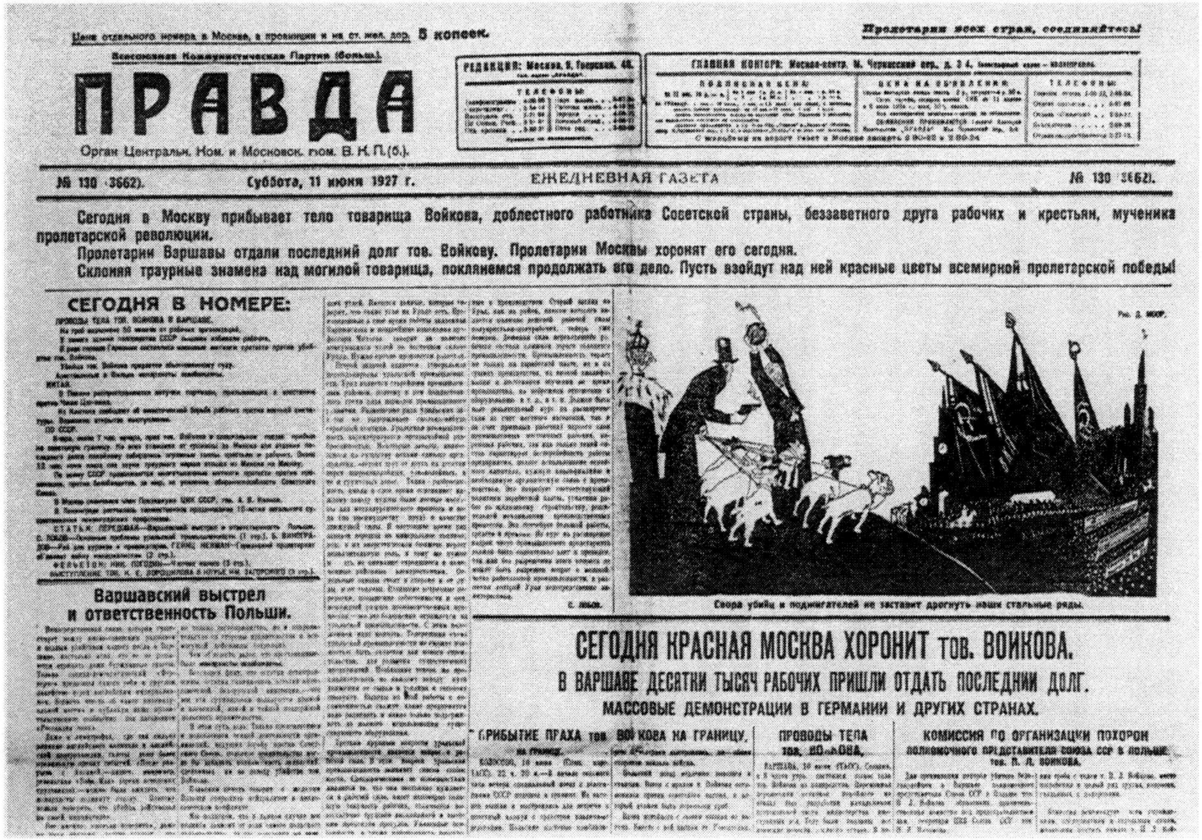

Цена отдельного номера в Москве, в провинции и на ст. жел. дор. 5 копеек.

Пролетарии всех стран, соединяйтесь!

Всесоюзная Коммунистическая Партия (больш.).

ПРАВДА

Орган Центральн. Ком. и Московск. ком. В.К.П.(б).

№ 130 (3662). Суббота, 11 июня 1927 г. ЕЖЕДНЕВНАЯ ГАЗЕТА № 130 (3662).

Сегодня в Москву прибывает тело товарища Войкова, доблестного работника Советской страны, беззаветного друга рабочих и крестьян, мученика пролетарской революции.

Пролетарии Варшавы отдали последний долг тов. Войкову. Пролетарии Москвы хоронят его сегодня.

Склоним траурные знамена над могилой товарища, поклянемся продолжать его дело. Пусть взойдут над ней красные цветы всемирной пролетарской победы!

СЕГОДНЯ В НОМЕРЕ:

Варшавский выстрел и ответственность Польши.

Свора убийц и поджигателей не заставит дрогнуть наши стальные ряды.

СЕГОДНЯ КРАСНАЯ МОСКВА ХОРОНИТ тов. ВОЙКОВА.

В ВАРШАВЕ ДЕСЯТКИ ТЫСЯЧ РАБОЧИХ ПРИШЛИ ОТДАТЬ ПОСЛЕДНИЙ ДОЛГ.

МАССОВЫЕ ДЕМОНСТРАЦИИ В ГЕРМАНИИ И ДРУГИХ СТРАНАХ.

ПРИБЫТИЕ ПРАХА тов. ВОЙКОВА НА ГРАНИЦУ.

ПРОВОДЫ ТЕЛА тов. ВОЙКОВА.

КОМИССИЯ ПО ОРГАНИЗАЦИИ ПОХОРОН ПОЛНОМОЧНОГО ПРЕДСТАВИТЕЛЯ СОЮЗА ССР В ПОЛЬШЕ тов. П. Л. ВОЙКОВА.

Figure 2.3. *Pravda,* June 11, 1927. Drawing by D. Moor. “A Pack of Murderers and Incendiaries Will Not Shake Our Steel Ranks.” The headline reads in part: “Arriving in Moscow today is the body of Comrade Volkov, a valiant employee of the Soviet country, a selfless friend of workers and peasants, a martyr of the proletarian revolution.”

as if they were speaking to one another, but also to workers and peasants. During the NEP they often addressed a vague judgmental public. When they rejected the mixed economy, they turned to an imagined public of officials and enthusiasts more appropriate to the administrative culture of the emerging command economy. Despite the fact that remnants of the NEP lasted into 1927 and even 1928 and Stalin remained allied with Bukharin, a defender of private farming, the press began to conjure up a nation of attentive supervisors and passive employees as early as the mid-1920s.

A new political class and a new social structure arose during the first decade of Bolshevik rule for whom "socialist building" in both its foreign and domestic variants had great appeal. People of common origins joined the Party in large numbers, and some took administrative jobs, competing with better-educated existing elites.[150] The Party had only 23,600 members in early 1917.[151] Membership rose to three-quarters of a million by 1921, fell to half a million in 1922 after purges, and rose to one million four years later.[152] The influx and fluctuations changed the character of Bolshevism. By 1927 less than 1 percent of members had joined before 1917.[153] The Party had become a doorway to success for people with a smattering of schooling.[154] Among those who went on to advanced education were *vydvizhentsy,* worker communists promoted during and after the early 1920s. The image of a participatory public was likely to have appealed to these upwardly mobile officials and activists, as was a new way of viewing the world. In an environment that stigmatized individual ambition, "socialist building" provided a positive context for their aspirations to build careers.

The expansion of the state meant upward mobility and jobs in the public sector. Communicating this message, mass journalists merged the image of the activist with that of the meritorious official rising in a just order. *Working Moscow, The Poor,* and *The Peasant Newspaper* described the country as open to the initiative, talent, and energy of those of proletarian or peasant origins. "The worker-peasant republic can say to its sons: The road to knowledge is open to you," wrote a journalist in 1922.[155] Such reports reminded readers that ambitious people were in demand. A journalist who identified himself as a student at a *rabfak* (a special preparatory school for workers entering higher education) wrote in 1921, "Any peasant straight from the plow can become an agronomist, an engineer, a doctor, or, in general, any kind of scientist or scholar."[156] Opportunity was the message Kalinin spelled out in *The Peasant Newspaper* in 1926 when he offered to trade places with an unemployed former Red Army soldier who complained he had found no worthy job after his service. "To be twenty-five years younger in the Soviet Republic?" he scolded. "What could be more valuable than that? If you do not know how to do something with your riches—then blame yourself."[157] Trotsky argued contrarily that the steady bureaucratization of Soviet society reduced opportunities for ordinary people.[158]

Articles about Party membership and on successful and unsuccessful local cells conveyed the image of a corporation in which local employees and middle management were constantly advancing. Publicists could not cite Party membership as a criterion for success, but they implied it. "Active, Soviet Party and professional employees with a secondary education ought to be sent to the rabfaks" read an article in 1922.[159] Letters from people eager to join, such as one in *The Peasant Newspaper* captioned, "Why I Knock at the Door of the Leninist Family," served the same purpose.[160] In fact, despite warnings that people should join to serve rather than profit, ambition and a Party card were linked even for peasants. Articles about peasant Communists became common in the second half of the 1920s, as in reports such as "A Peasant Straight from the Plow into the Party."[161] The ladder of success was further revealed in stories such as "A Good Secretary—A Good Cell" and "The Bolshevik Shumilova at Work," which meant recognition and perhaps promotion, as well as "The Mistakes of Our Cell" and "Everything Is Not OK with Us," which conveyed the opposite message.[162]

In the press, government employment also signified the pinnacle of ambition. Reports of congresses of Soviets carried glamorous interviews with delegates identified as peasants and workers.[163] I. Gavrilov, a journalist and member of the Central Executive Committee of the Congress of Soviets described himself in 1922 as a poor peasant who began government service in 1918.[164] A series on chairmen of local Soviets in the Moscow region in *Working Moscow* in 1922 showed officials who were ambitious and devoted. "From the first days of Soviet power to the present time Comrade Maslov continuously participated in state building and occupied various responsible posts."[165] In local government, the press stressed opportunities for women. "Anna Vakhrusheva—Chairman of the Local Soviet," read the caption of an article praising an activist.[166] In another story, a local official and former cook explained that her life confirmed Lenin's dictum in *State and Revolution* that "every cook should learn how to govern the state."[167] Leaving families and children to readers' imaginations, the authors of these stories praised women who had no commitments other than to state service.

The press also highlighted opportunities in the public sector of the economy. "He gave up the plow for the city in childhood," read a story in *The Poor* in 1922 about a man who rose from day laborer to factory manager.[168] A story in *Working Moscow* in the same year about the director of a chemical factory featured a picture of the director.[169] Under the caption "Comrade I. S. Pichugin, Hero of Labor," readers could see a prosperous man wearing an enormous hat of Persian lamb and a coat with a puffy fur collar. "Comrade Pichugin was born in a poor peasant family in 1882," the biography began. This image of prosperous and respected state employees contrasted sharply with representations of private shopkeepers, petty traders, and others who tried to "rake in money" from the market economy.[170] On Sundays in 1922 *Working Moscow* ran a cartoon strip satirizing and threatening profiteers. The paper's warning to those who got rich on moonshine was curt: "The moonshiner ought to be punished in the same way as the so-called White Guard or foreign spy caught at the explosion of an ammunition dump or a railroad bridge."[171]

The press promoted the army as well, but less so than the Party or the government as the demobilization of 3.5 million soldiers in 1920–21 and the association with Trotsky limited its appeal.[172] It only regained prominence in the late 1920s when soldiers became collectivizers. Nevertheless promises were made, as in "Be a Commander," an article on the officer corps in *Working Moscow* in 1921.[173] Here education, too, was the lure. "They often enter the military schools without any learning and half-literate but with a burning thirst to study and serve," observed a journalist, who hailed officer trainees as "our own Soviet, worker-peasant intelligentsia" in *The Poor.*[174]

In contrast to government's alleged protection of private farming, the mass press favored public employment in agriculture. Without openly condemning private farming, journalists showed that organizing led to big rewards. For those who set up cooperative enterprises, disseminated political propaganda, promoted improved farming methods, or advocated collective agriculture, vistas opened. "Take the Example of These Three" read the caption of an article in 1924 about three peasants who opened a cooperative shop with the support of the local Soviet.[175] "How We Began to Manage Things in a New Way" was a report a year earlier about an "innovator" from Saratov who taught peasants to farm collectively.[176] Indeed, on the rare occasions when peasants were praised as good farmers, readers were told that they had abandoned farming for organizing.[177] Becoming active in local organizations was a way for peasants to put their feet on the bottom rungs of an officially approved ladder to success. Achieving prosperity on a private farm led in a different direction. Moreover, even in the case of poor farmers, the press showed the state to be the font of benefits.

Despite the failures of collective farming, journalists advanced its heady prospects. "There, where the lord's oats whispered, the village state farm has grown up like a mushroom," wrote one author in *The Poor* in 1922.[178] "If You Want to Escape from Need—Form Agricultural Collectives" was the title of another article three years later.[179] The success of collective ventures satisfied ideological needs, if not economic ones. The press presented such projects in a way that was likely to appeal to rural people in state employment. "Now peasants no longer laugh at collective labor, and they believe that much can be gained collectively," wrote a journalist in *The Peasant Newspaper* in 1927.[180] For those who shared these feelings there was much to glean from the mass press. Yet for most, by 1927, the window of rationality in the public culture was closing.

Editors of mass newspapers discouraged the ambitious from seeking prosperity through farming, yet provided information that seemed designed for that purpose. They crammed their pages with material on agronomy and promoted science, rather than individual economic incentives, as a way to raise productivity. Readers were told that if they farmed scientifically, they would become prosperous. A journalist avowed that if only peasants would take "the path indicated by science, we would quickly restore our economy and catch up with other countries."[181] "Why do the people live poorly in Russia, and why does the *muzhik* manage his farm so badly? The whole reason is that he has no science." That peasants did not take this advice supported those who blamed agriculture's weakness on the peasants' backwardness and intransigence, rather than on a faulty incentive system.

Collectivization, with reduced scope for decisions made by individual peasants, had a strong appeal to those who felt that peasants willfully refused to adopt modern methods and should be forced to do so. A columnist in the spring of 1923 argued that "the business [of farming] can be put right only with the help of the state organs."[182] The same view surfaced in late 1927 on the eve of collectivization. "The peasants live closely together, but they think separately, each one about himself," a columnist complained in *The Peasant Newspaper*.[183] The conclusion that state authorities needed to take peasants in hand suited the mood of socialist building.

Stories about common people who rose in the bureaucracies of early Soviet life or found government a horn of plenty were matched by stories of others who excelled at modest jobs. These were often elderly workers who were honored for superior performance in their allotted station in life. The praise of such people implied that all work had merit and one did not have to rise to win respect. This was a critical lesson at a time when mobility was much in evidence. Such people included model workers. "She served fifty years at the factory, inspiring the young—Glory and honor to this heroine of labor," read one account.[184] Such people were the bricks and mortar of socialist building. Peasants who fit the mold distinguished themselves by producing a prize vegetable or a record harvest on a small piece of land. The press hailed accomplishments such as "150 Poods per Desiatin" and, in one case, "A Hero of the Land," whose yield was eight times the average for his district.[185] Yet farmers were never shown to benefit from their achievements beyond the publicity; neither a prize-winning cabbage nor a remarkable yield made them well-off.

Stories of mobility and honorable service had the effect of legitimizing the new hierarchy. Identifying mobility with merit implied that those who found themselves at the bottom were not there unjustly. Stories about model workers and peasants can be seen as an attempt to soften the dichotomy between the deserving who advanced and those who did not. Stories about dignity in ordinary jobs, about respect for authority, about elders who inspired young people to be proud of their work at whatever rank they found themselves carried values mportant for promoting stability in a time of rapid social change.

The official success story also encroached on the arts. The proletarian poets discussed in *The Workers' Newspaper* were those of the Workers' Spring group, with whom the newspaper had a special relationship. There were fewer cultural articles in rural newspapers, but these usually carried the message that official ties were important. A crude example was an account in *The Poor* in 1926 about a self-taught sculptor, whose search for recognition began in his own village with a statue of Lenin.[186] When asked why he molded Lenin, he explained: "Because he is always before my eyes." According to the story, after he gave them busts of Lenin and Kalinin, district Party leaders sent him to Rostov, the provincial capital, and from there he went on to a Moscow art school. The equivalent story in science was of a struggling inventor who likewise won recognition from local or central authorities.

Largely absent from reportage about individual lives in Moscow newspapers during most the 1920s were the non-Russian nationalities. Although the government invested in non-Russian regions and promoted non-Russian cadres, images of local non-Russian leaders and activists were uncommon during the first decade of Soviet power. A stress on nation building did not fit either the militantly international schema of class war or the largely cosmopolitan and pragmatic formulations of the NEP. In the late 1920s, however, the nationalities gained visibility when journalists began to integrate them into the schema of socialist building. The rediscovery of non-Russian areas fit the nationalist paradigm and Soviet exceptionalism but also the murky longstanding notion of "Eurasianism," the belief that Russia's destiny lay not in the West but in the uniquely multinational empire.[187]

Critical to formulations of "socialist building" and to the increasing incorporation of people of common origins into the administrative apparatus was the use of the word *task*.[188] The metaphoric use of "task" can be traced to the civil war, although it became prevalent later. "The socialist building of life, the creation and strengthening of its economic foundation—that is the main task we ought to resolve during this second interlude" [in fighting in the civil war] editorialized *Pravda* in late 1918.[189] Although "task" had pedagogical connotations, it also connoted hierarchical authority. Its use corresponded to a picture of the state as the manager of economy and society. "The task is assigned, it must be carried out," read a piece from late 1925 about getting manufactured goods to peasants.[190]

The additional metaphors of "the path," "the line," and "building" were all widely employed at this time to emphasize control, purpose, and leadership from above. Most important was "the path," an organizing metaphor for the whole Soviet experience from the time of the civil war.[191] "The path" reinforced the meaning of "task." Lenin had often used "the path" to express his conviction that there was a single way to do things, one strategy, one ideology, and one direction. He did not borrow this construction from Marx and Engels. Although Marx and Engels had imagined linear historical movement from revolution to revolution, they employed vaguer metaphors of development and growth. Lenin spoke of "the path" at the Tenth Party Congress in March 1921 in order to emphasize correct ideology: "Since the peasantry is now wearier and more exhausted, or rather it thinks that it is so, we make more concessions to it in order to obtain safeguards against the restoration of capitalism and to ensure the path to communism."[192]

The metaphor of "the path" also fit the concept of an avant-garde Party, since the visual image implies leaders in front. It was expressed in images of trains and marchers in Soviet posters throughout the 1920s and 1930s.[193] Even the meaning of literacy in the early Soviet years was linked with this image. "The Worker's Press Is a Torch Lighting the Path to a New Life," read one early slogan.[194] "Literacy Is the Path to Communism," reads another.[195] One of the most famous of the early Soviet literacy posters, Aleksei Radkov's "The Illiterate Is also Blind—Bad Luck and Misfortune Await Him Everywhere," shows a blind man who has strayed from the path and is about to step off a cliff.[196] Trotsky dubbed sympathetic non-Bolshevik literati "fellow travelers," literally "those on the path."[197]

Bolsheviks portrayed the revolutionary process as movement toward a future they and their leader had designated. They suppressed information on Lenin's failing health. He died at 6:50 P.M. on January 22, 1924, but *Pravda* announced his death only on January 24. On that day the leaders used various metaphors to celebrate his continuing authority. Bukharin cited him as a teacher and problem solver, and Kamenev pictured "the torch of Leninism in the hands of [the world's] working people." Trotsky, in contrast, stressed discontinuity. "The Party and the working class are orphaned," he wrote. *Pravda*'s front page featured graphic artist Viktor Deni's drawing of Lenin, not as a militant class warrior or a benign fatherly figure but as a quizzical human being in accord with the NEP's ambiguity (Figure 2.4). The leaders subsequently adopted religious phraseology, emphasizing Lenin's "testament." This was particularly true of Stalin, whom *Pravda* cited only briefly on January 27 for his remarks at the funeral.[198] On February 12 N. A. Semashko, the minister of health, exalted Lenin for choosing "straight and true paths, leading to the establishment of the forms of the social order that he foresaw."[199] By the mid-1920s the phrases "on the Leninist path" and "the path to socialism" were ubiquitous.[200]

The use of "the path" changed toward the decade's end as the metaphor acquired the connotation of moving from one planned period of activity to another. Although planning was no more than a statement of faith even after the inauguration of the First Five-Year Plan, this shift had enormous import. "The path" became an agenda-setting metaphor. The thrust was to deny the present except as a means to something else, to restrict public attention to those on the path, and to limit authority to leaders who claimed to know it. On December 18, 1927, an illustrated mass magazine featured a front-page photograph of Stalin addressing the Fifteenth Party Congress, the congress at which he gained full control of the Politburo and began to move against the NEP.[201] The accompanying quote from his speech began, "We are on the correct path."

Figure 2.4. *Pravda*, January 24, 1924. *Pravda* announces Lenin's death. The two lead articles are captioned, "Comrade" and "A Great Rebel."

The metaphor of "the line" was narrower.[202] *Pravda* employed it from 1926 to contrast policies of Stalin's Central Committee with those of Trotsky and his followers. In such cases the authors used it to signify support for the leadership and its "path to socialism."[203] In fact, the two were often used together as when one editor equated "the general line" with the "highway" to socialism in 1926.[204] The metaphor of "building" worked similarly.[205] After military victories in early 1919, Lenin declared the country on "the correct path of socialist building."[206] A columnist wrote optimistically about revised transport regulations in 1920: "The new rules represent an enormous step forward in the area of our socialist building" (September 9, 1920). A half decade later the term had begun to signify issues to be resolved. An editorialist in 1926 questioned whether "the socialist elements of building" were sufficient in cooperatives (February 9, 1926). A year later the liberation of women was described in *Pravda* as "a problem of socialist building" (October 9, 1927).

As the country entered an era of greater planning and administrative control over the economy, portrayals of agency took on features of the mechanical fulfillment of directives from above. Orders from institutions often replaced explanations of behavior, and tasks were described without explanations of their purpose. In the press, the possible range of human actions atrophied, and administrative and government acts were made to appear as inevitable events rather than attributable and motivated action.[207] Class motivation, which had lost its preeminence in *Pravda* during the NEP, was buried by bureaucratic motivation.[208] The country appeared as something to be worked on, moved forward, and perfected.

The change coincided with a worsening view of enemies and outsiders, who were now seen as furtive and malignant obstacles to a utopian enterprise. The metaphors of "building" and "the path," which reinforced images of progress toward perfection, thus merged into a rhetoric of social hygiene. In his long suppressed novella, *The Foundation Pit*, written during collectivization, Andrei Platonov showed the horror of this linguistic process by portraying the "socialist construction" of a bottomless pit and the cleansing of a community by the device of floating expropriated kulaks down a river to the sea.[209] On the tenth anniversary of the revolution in 1927, *Pravda*'s editors communicated the idea of a united country moving ahead and leaving behind one alien element after another: "We raised the country from the depths. We are going quickly ahead. We have strengthened socialist industry. We have commanded the village to follow us. We have squeezed capital and beat the kulak at his own game. Who are we? The masses. Millions. Workers and laboring peasants."[210]

What Lenin had been unable to say, Stalin and his supporters now hazarded. State and society were one. The image of the public as a court of opinion had faded. Science and the arts began to serve socialist building and, in the process, shed many of their former independent qualities. Over the decade in *Pravda* the ruling authority evolved away from its early identity as an elite defined by superior knowledge and shared prerevolutionary heroism. By the late 1920s authority wore a hard hat and spoke for all as it began to supervise the building of socialism. Journalists confronted transgressors with an authoritative *we,* representing themselves, the state, the Party, and a new inclusive public, and they ordered troublemakers off the construction site. An enthusiastic chorus replaced earlier voices of divergent interests. Journalists answered the question "Who are we?" with a voice that bespoke the managerial authority of a new elite. They had deployed the revolutionary "we" Zamiatin found so intimidating to rally the builders of a new social order and to marginalize those who might have questioned its character.

In unpublished letters, peasants and others showed their susceptibility to the press by employing "Soviet power" and other similar constructs. "What is the poor proletarian to do: Support Soviet power honorably or start speculating [i.e., buying and selling in the market] and struggle against it?" an unknown woman asked "Respected Comrade Lenin" in March 1920.[211] In 1927 a peasant with a separate farm, who found himself denied government aid, wrote to *The Peasant Newspaper:* "I still ask Soviet power to look to the peasantry as the state's foundation."[212] A rural correspondent and invalid of the civil war asked for help in 1927: "Comrades, I feel myself free and know that because Soviet power loves workers and peasants who are striving to live, it will never forsake us."

Although correspondents often replaced the official "we" with their own alternatives, they could not fully escape the new language. One complained to *The Peasant Newspaper* in 1926: "We peasants wish to be proud of the words and deeds of 'the worker-peasant authorities,' 'the state,' 'the government,' 'the Red Army,' 'the Worker-Peasant Dictatorship,' and not only the proletariat."[213] Another chided Kalinin in March 1927 that under "socialist building" two classes had appeared: "The first class is workers and peasants who labor; the second is Soviet employees who receive a fine salary of fifty rubles or more."[214] A third correspondent in 1924 began a critical letter about heavy taxes, "We workers and peasants know that our lives should improve since we won Soviet power."[215]

The gravest sign of the inability to resist the cultural onslaught was in responses to the term *kulak.* One author complained in 1925 that "if a peasant succeeds in raising himself from poverty, then they [the Communist Party] slander him as a kulak and consider him an enemy of Soviet power, but there is no peasant who does not wish to improve his farm . . . In other words, no peasant who is not striving to become an enemy of Soviet power."[216] An author from Ulianovsk pleaded in 1927: "Truly, isn't it possible to replace 'kulak' with an inoffensive word, `prosperous,' for example?"[217] As he put it: "What distinguishes the prosperous villager from the pauper is that he is better-dressed, reads newspapers, does not drink."[218]

To ignore the official vocabulary was beyond the power of many common readers of lower-class origins. Most were probably unable to maintain fully two parallel cultural systems, even when one was so much at odds with their long-standing beliefs and practices. Unlike colonized peoples, Soviet citizens could neither stigmatize the encroaching official culture as foreign nor counter it with a reflexive nativism. During the first decade of Soviet rule, neither society nor the press had marched in lock-step toward the world of the 1930s, but, by the great turnabout of the First Five-Year Plan and collectivization, political power, society, and the public culture were sufficiently aligned for Stalin and his supporters to promote socialist building without effective opposition. Although the social order still lacked the sacralization and ritualistic practices it subsequently acquired, the lights in the theater of Soviet public life were dimming. An extraordinary political performance was about to begin.

Three

The Performance Begins

ON MAY DAY, 1939, *Pravda*'s editorialists compared enlightened humanity's discovery of the Soviet Union to Christopher Columbus's sighting of America: "Now all advanced humanity says of our country—the Union of Soviet Socialist Republics—'There it is, the promised land of communism!'"[1] In the 1920s the Bolsheviks vowed to remake an imperfect world. The press presented the First Five-Year Plan and collectivization in 1928 and 1929, respectively, as supremely rational programs to do just this, insisting in almost Benthamite terms that these measures would bring the greatest happiness to the greatest number. As the plan neared completion, Stalin and his supporters declared victory, denying the dichotomy between what they had promised and what they had wrought. In their management of the press, they began a new kind of reportage, an official celebration of accomplishments that lasted decades and colored the imaginations of millions of people.

The Plan and Collectivization

During the NEP, leaders and chief journalists frequently wrote as if they anticipated a diverse response from readers. In contrast, their successors in the 1930s expressed themselves as if they alone could question and interpret public speech. They began to issue official directives as befitted an economy based on planning, and they dramatized their authority by portraying the giving and receiving of orders. Simultaneously, the press augmented its pedagogic tone by prescribing correct behavior through ritualistic commendations and reprimands. Differences between explanatory, informational, and interactive articles shrank, and all authors began to repeat the same laudatory phrases.

As public questioning diminished, Soviet Russia diverged from its inspiration in the Enlightenment and the European socialist tradition.[2] The rift that opened was not with Rousseau's notion of a government that transformed people but with the canon of reason, a commitment to rationalism, and the assumption that leaders could and should argue with citizens about the state's agenda. If the Enlightenment and romanticism are two poles of European culture, then Stalin and his colleagues now inclined toward the latter and thus toward the rule of imagination rather than that of reason. The workers and peasants whom editors had often courted in the 1920s were supplanted in the press by officials and enthusiasts, and the large-scale studies of common readers carried out so assiduously during the NEP virtually ceased.[3] Rarely did journalists address the public as impartial judge of right and wrong, as they had on occasion earlier.

By 1932 the government's failures to fulfill past pledges were empirically observable, although what contemporaries saw is unclear. The capital investment program was so wasteful and collectivization so disastrous that living standards tumbled. The government introduced rationing in order to distribute resources selectively.[4] Workers' real wages in Moscow dropped to 52 percent of their 1928 level in 1932, and meat and dairy consumption fell.[5] Although urban conditions improved in 1934, rationing lasted another year, and consumption norms of the 1920s went unsurpassed in the 1930s despite a gradual recovery.[6] Collectivization devastated agriculture. Eight to ten million people died in the famine of 1932–33, mainly in Ukraine, but also in the Volga Basin, the Urals, Siberia, and Central Russia. Estimates of deported *kulaks,* a term inclusive of all peasants prospering in the market, ranged from a few million to ten million.[7] The calamity culminated in 1933, the decade's worst year for "excess deaths" and also the year Hitler came to power.[8]

The plan was intended to raise living standards and achieve national self-sufficiency in capital equipment. These objectives were not attained, although there was considerable progress in machine building and expansion of industry into new locations.[9] Substantial self-sufficiency in heavy industrial goods was attained by 1941. National income, including public investment, grew through 1931, declined in 1932, and then resumed growth, but living standards fell since a shrinking share of national income was devoted to consumption.[10] Nevertheless the country achieved a rough equivalent to the success of American and European managerial capitalism in the production of chemicals, metals, electrical equipment, machinery, and transportation, as well as education— what is sometimes called the "Second Industrial Revolution."[11]

Stalin's supporters and beneficiaries could point with pride to construction and social mobility. "The country changed before our eyes," the writer and war correspondent Konstantin Simonov recalled long afterward, explaining his support of Stalin in this period.[12] The millions who moved from manual labor to white-collar jobs in industry, agriculture, the Party, the Komsomol organization, trade unions, and other institutions had personal motives to explain their support for the system. More than 750,000 worker-Communists were promoted into the professions and skilled white-collar jobs by 1933.[13] The Communist Party was transformed by recruitment in 1927 and purge in 1929. In 1930, 850,000 of the 2 million Party members were new, and by 1933 more than 700,000 members and candidate members were peasants.[14] Numbers of Party members and candidate members fluctuated wildly as a result of purges, but the total rose from 920,000 on January 1, 1938, to 2.4 million on January 1, 1939, and to 3.9 million two years later.[15] The collective farms alone had 2 million administrative slots by the mid-1930s and 10 million minor non-field posts ranging from guards and firemen to bookkeepers.[16] Such jobs, according to one account, provided up to 30 percent of a farm's able-bodied male population with non-field work and a corresponding rise in status.[17]

Leaders and journalists pledged abundance when they introduced the plan and collectivization. *Pravda* announced in late 1927 that the country had entered a "period of building foundations," auguring prosperity for ordinary people. The paper published speeches about planning and a manifesto of the Central Committee recounting past successes and promising future triumphs. "The victorious solution to the most difficult questions of economic policy," they noted, "became possible when the October Revolution created the basis for the PLANNED LEADERSHIP OF THE COUNTRY'S ECONOMY."[18] They pledged a seven-hour day, improved workers' housing, a better life for poor peasants, and, in a word, to make Russia "a socialist country." Such promises were reiterated over the next few years, but in 1931 the government also began to stress defense. Patriotic and military themes were opportune at a time when the benefits of collectivization and the plan went largely to administrators and activists, and workers faced lower wage scales and tightened managerial authority. The foreign threat was also real, as seen in the Japanese invasion of Manchuria, as well as the Nazi movement. Defense outlays doubled in 1931 and grew rapidly thereafter, after rising slowly during the 1920s.[19]

In 1928 a socialism of economic power and plenty was largely aspiration. Journalists dwelled on past victories, the start of a few big projects, and the promise of things to come, but they did not fully picture a new socialist order. *Pravda* greeted the eleventh anniversary of the October Revolution in 1928 with a quarter-page picture of Lenin surrounded by the iconography of planning—power plants, oil wells, grain elevators, and housing construction.[20] The editorialist wrote: "Although we are a beggarly and backward country, every day we move forward in projects such as the Dnieper site, which are literally transforming the life and character of whole regions.

Four years later in October 1932 *Pravda* grandly welcomed the completed Dnieper Dam (Figure 3.1) as a new socialist reality in a new world, with new people, and a new mode of action—all counterpoised to a new set of enemies. The project was evidence of promises fulfilled and held enormous symbolic significance, since other evidence was scarce. A quarter-page picture showed the curve of the great dam with foaming water rushing through it. The header was partly in uppercase letters, sandwiching a paranoid aside between two layers of exultant rhetoric:

THE DNIEPER HYDRO-PLANT—THE GREATEST HYDROELECTRIC STATION IN THE WORLD, THE BEAUTY AND PRIDE OF THE FIVE-YEAR PLAN—BEGINS OPERATION TODAY AS PART OF SOCIALIST INDUSTRY. Neither the frenzied opposition of class enemies, nor the base work of

Figure 3.1. *Pravda*, October 10, 1932. The headline reads in part: "The Dnieper Hydro-Plant—The Greatest Hydroelectric Station in the World, the Beauty and Pride of the Five-Year Plan—Begins Operation Today as Part of Socialist Industry."

opportunist agents can halt the victorious expansion of socialist industrialization.
THE GENERAL LINE OF THE PARTY IS WINNING AND WILL WIN! THE
WHOLE PARTY, THE WHOLE COUNTRY, GREETS THE SUBJUGATORS
OF THE DNIEPER, THE WORKERS AND ENGINEERS OF DNIEPROS-
TROI, THE HEROES OF A BOLSHEVIK PACE [of work].[21]

Pravda hailed the plant as "the greatest victory of the general line," Stalin's
metaphor for his policies. "Every new electric lightbulb, every new turbine,
every new electric station," they wrote "is the fulfillment of Lenin's testament
and brings the triumph of communism closer." A passage in bold type began:
"The Soviet country has firmly strengthened itself by moving on the socialist
path."

An antiworld of enemies and hostile foreigners complemented this image of
the new order. The anonymous author contrasted the flourishing Soviet Ukraine
with life across the border in Poland.

> Need we compare what takes place today on the banks of the Dnieper with con-
> ditions in the Western Ukraine, where working people groan under the unbearable
> oppression of the landowner, the kulak, and the unbridled militarism of Polish im-
> perialism? Need we contrast the pitiable hovels of western Ukrainian peasants with
> the bright, clean, new city that sprang up with the electrification of the left bank of
> the Dnieper?

Publication of these words in 1932 while a famine induced by government
policy decimated the Ukrainian population was a lie that showed how com-
fortable leaders and journalists had become with the press's accounts of socialist building. The suppression of news at this time was, in part, an act of political control. The control ranged beyond the political, however, and became
an effort to shape the public memory and imagination, with long-lasting consequences.[22] As George Orwell observed, theocracy must rearrange the past
because "its ruling cast, in order to keep its position, has to be thought of as
infallible."[23] A witness to the famine recalled after World War II:

> The grief of the Leningrad blockade is "legal," and many write of it but of this no
> one can write. Yet people remembered and discussed it among themselves. A dis-
> tant relative could not forget and constantly cursed Soviet power, as if it "ate up
> her brother."[24]

Many prominent Soviet public figures participated in the denial of facts of
Soviet life that contradicted the general line. In the same issue as the editorial
on the dam, the writer Maxim Gorky greeted "the Creators of the Dnieper Plant"
and compared Soviet Russia to the world of capitalism:

> The capitalists of bourgeois Europe and the USA have accumulated tens of mil-
> lions of unemployed workers and beat them when they ask for bread and work.

Not one capitalist state can create for itself anything like that which the proletariat, master of the Soviet Union, has created to enrich its land, strengthen its power, and spread its influence to the working people of the whole world.

A report from managers of the project to state and Party authorities accompanied Gorky's apologia and announced their completion of the assignment. Stalin congratulated the managers on the same page. With tasks assigned, fulfilled, and lavishly lauded, the new socialist order had arrived in the public media, where it attained a fuller realization than was ever possible in the more complex experience of actual Soviet life.

Stalin's Charisma

The charismatic aura of Stalin's manufactured persona anchored the new order. The grounding of a new social order in charisma is unremarkable. Charismatic persons have often been imbued with "supernatural, superhuman, or at least specifically exceptional powers or qualities" and identified with the overthrow of existing norms and the inculcation of new ones.[25] Moreover, such leaders can provide a society in flux with a symbolic center.[26] Yet this was not an easy role for Stalin to assume, however much he may have aspired to it. He had failed to distinguish himself either in 1917 or the civil war, and he cut a decidedly unheroic figure thereafter. Since he could not legitimately draw on revolutionary feats of heroism or on the traditional Russian sacred order that had sustained the tsarist monarchy, his transition from administrator to charismatic leader had to be something of a ruse.[27] When he gathered the reins of state power into his hands, he was able to use the monopoly on the press and other media to put himself in the center of a new symbolic order.

Stalin and his supporters defeated Trotsky, Zinoviev, and Kamenev in 1927 and Bukharin and other defenders of the NEP in late 1929. They denied the press to their opponents, and *Pravda* ceased to be the "free tribune" for influential Party members that it had been earlier in the decade.[28] Bukharin remained working editor throughout 1928, and formally until April 1929.[29] In late 1929, when Emelian Iaroslavskii, a leading official and early Stalinist, became de facto editor, Stalin disparaged him in a letter to Molotov for "not seeing beyond his nose."[30] "There is no editor there, only a board," Stalin subsequently declared at a plenum of the Central Committee on July 13, 1930.[31] Later that year L. Z. Mekhlis, chief of the press section of the Central Committee, took over and made the paper Stalin's mouthpiece. After he became chief of "political enlightenment" for the Red Army in 1937, *Pravda* passed into the hands of Stalin's shadowy personal secretary, A. N. Poskrebyshev, in effect his court chamberlain, who edited the newspaper from 1937 through 1940.[32] Khrushchev later dubbed him "Stalin's faithful dog."[33] Stalin also at-

tended closely to *Izvestiia*. Ivan Gronskii, who became editor in 1932, long afterward recalled consulting with his new boss almost daily, reading and reread-
ing editorials over the phone for approval.[34]

When the Central Committee celebrated Bolshevism in its October 1927
"Manifesto" on the plan, it did so without a charismatic leader. Over the next
decade newspapers featured Stalin in this role, despite his clumsiness as a
speaker and his unimposing physical appearance. By the mid-1930s an aura of
authority and almost magical power had settled around him. The writer Kornei
Chukovskii noted in his diary the almost erotic effect of Stalin's appearance at
a congress of the Komsomol in April 1936:

> And HE stood, a little weary, pensive, and stately. One could feel the tremendous
> habit of power, the force of it, and at the same time something feminine and soft.
> I looked about: Everyone had fallen in love with this gentle, inspired, laughing
> face. To see him, simply to see him, was happiness for all of us.[35]

Yet despite Stalin's aura, and in sharp contrast to Nazi and fascist journalists,
Soviet publicists did not eroticize his public persona or, for that matter, Lenin's.
The Nazis and fascists, who invested their leaders with masculine authority and
power, had images of dominant men and submissive women at their disposal
from popular culture and their political traditions.[36] The Soviets, on the contrary, were constrained by Marxism and the lack of a consumer culture of
desire. This did not prevent them from idolizing Stalin, however.

Unlike Lenin, Stalin became the living protagonist of an almost sacred cult.
The press had allotted Lenin a modest and largely ideological role on his fiftieth birthday in April 1920.[37] Journalists writing as late as 1928 vested authority in the Party, the working class, Soviet power, the October Revolution, the
Central Committee, the leadership, or simply *we*. Sometimes they weighted
their words with citations of Lenin and Stalin but usually only parenthetically.
Glavlit specified the details for the promotion of Stalin's fiftieth birthday in
1929, including the photos to be used.[38] His official date of birth was December 21, 1879, but he had actually been born a year earlier and had changed the
date in April 1922, when Lenin appointed him general secretary of the Party.[39]
Whether he wished to match the age of his arch-rival, Trotsky, or had some
other reason, the fiction served him well in 1929, when he elevated himself in
a way that would have been difficult a year earlier.

Pravda hailed him on his official birthday as "the organizer and leader of socialist industrialization and of the collectivization of the Soviet country; the
leader of the Party of the proletariat building socialism in one-sixth of the
world."[40] The editorialist greeted him as "friend," initiating the incorporation
of personal feelings into the cult. Such terms of affection became a common
device to humanize his authority. "The Communist Party, working class, and
world revolutionary movement today celebrate the fiftieth anniversary of their
leader and chief, friend and fighting comrade, Comrade Stalin." In response to

these tributes Stalin pledged in large type at the top of *Pravda*'s front page "all my strength, all my ability, and, if need be, all my blood, drop by drop" to the cause.[41] [A diarist named I. I. Shitts cited a wag's reply, "Why so slowly?"][42]

Other newspapers followed *Pravda*. *Izvestiia* filled the top quarter of the front page with a picture and greetings, printing Stalin's thanks to well-wishers in bold print.[43] *Komsomol Pravda* gave him two pages and a large picture.[44] *The Peasant Newspaper* featured a special issue with iconlike illustrations and testimonials from institutions and prominent people. The heading above his picture began "To the beloved leader, the truest pupil and comrade-in-arms of Vladimir Ilich Lenin."[45] Stalin created a series of legends to support the derivation of his authority, and most important of these was his closeness to Lenin. Yet when Stalin cast himself as the ideological descendent of Lenin, drawing on Lenin as a quasi-traditional source of authority, he substituted himself for his predecessor. Khrushchev recalled how Kaganovich in the early 1930s pleased Stalin by suggesting that the slogan "Long Live Leninism" be replaced by "Long Live Stalinism."[46]

The graphic artists at this point made Stalin larger, more solid and imposing and Lenin paler and less prominent. On January 1, 1931, *Pravda* published two drawings by graphic artist Deni (Figure 3.2).[47] In one, Stalin appeared in his military tunic and black civilian coat, hands in pockets, against the background of a factory and grain elevator, with flags reading "Lenin," "Industrialization," "Complete Collectivization," "Socialist Competition," "shock work," and "Carry Out the Industrial Financial Plan."[48] Beneath it, bourgeois generals and statesmen manned a cannon and held a flag reading "Intervention." Here were two worlds: Stalin's kingdom, in which Lenin appeared only on a flag, and that of the hated enemies. *Pravda* and other papers published similarly imposing pictures of Stalin on other holidays in the early 1930s, while Lenin was dematerializing. On the October anniversary in 1933, *The Peasant Newspaper* showed a silhouette of Lenin in the background beside pictures of happy collective farmers and farm machinery in action (Figure 3.3).[49] In subsequent illustrations Lenin was relegated to statues, pictures on banners, a name on slogans, and, in the late 1930s, he often vanished entirely. On May Day, 1938, *Pravda* showed Stalin leading a huge procession with Lenin on a poster in the background.

Lenin continued to figure in fake historical scenes in which Stalin appeared as his best pupil and chief associate, but even here the successor effaced the original, standing while Lenin sat, speaking while Lenin listened, and pointing to maps and plans while Lenin looked on. *Labor,* on November 7, 1936, showed Lenin and Stalin planning the revolution in October 1917. Sometimes Lenin vanished even from historical scenes, as on November 7, 1938, when *Labor* counterposed a picture of people storming the Winter Palace, labeled "1917," to another, captioned "1938," of people marching with flags; between the two was a picture of Stalin.

Figure 3.2. *Pravda,* January 1, 1931. Drawing by Deni. Captions of two cartoons read, "The general line." Flags read, "Lenin, industrialization, complete collectivization, socialist competition, shock work" and "Exceed the Industrial Financial Plan." Below, in second picture, the flag reads, "Intervention." The bold headline reads: "Life has given us two sets of historical facts. Behind are the first two years of the five-year plan. Ahead is the decisive third year, the year of laying the foundation of a socialist economy, the year of the victory of the Party's general line."

Figure 3.3. *The Peasant Newspaper,* November 6, 1933. "Long Live the Sixteenth Anniversary of October, Long Live the Proletarian Revolution in the Whole World."

While editors and journalists surpassed one another in paying homage, Stalin presented himself as the nation's schoolmaster and later "father," both evoking the founder's authority and obscuring it. During the war scare of 1927, he instructed oppositionists who accused him of wrecking the Chinese Revolution: "I think that due regard for the tactical principles of Leninism is an essential condition, without which a Marxist verification of the Comintern's line in the Chinese Revolution is impossible."[50] He developed this pedagogic posture during the first plan, lecturing on Leninism in *Pravda* and peppering "reports" to the Central Committee with remarks such as "here is what Lenin says on this score" and "here is what Lenin says in another passage."[51] This stance was so important that with the country near chaos in early 1930, he carried out "a conversation" in *Pravda* with students from Sverdlov University, captioned "The Questions of the Sverdlov Comrades and the Answers of Comrade Stalin."[52] The exchange was a list of questions and answers, a kind of catechism, in which Stalin's reply followed each query.[53] It began:

> 1. In the theses on the tactics of RCP(B) [Russian Communist Party—of Bolsheviks] adopted by the Third Congress of the Comintern, Lenin spoke of the existence of two main classes in Soviet Russia.
>
> We now speak of eliminating the kulaks and the new bourgeoisie as a class.
>
> Does this mean that in the NEP period a third class has taken shape in our country?
>
> *First question.* Lenin spoke of two *main* classes. But he knew, of course, that there was a third, the capitalist class (the kulaks, the urban capitalist bourgeoisie).[54]

By quoting and even correcting Lenin, Stalin affected mastery of the founder's canon and asserted his own leadership. He initiated a dialogue that presupposed an unquestioning listener, who, like a pupil or child, could be expected to hang on his every word.[55] Stalin thus assumed an eminent role in Russian tradition, that of writer-teacher. Dostoevsky and Tolstoy had spoken as sages or seers, and by 1917 writers rivaled generals and saints in almanacs and cheap prints.[56] God himself welcomed Tolstoy to heaven in Iakov Protazanov's film, *The Departure of a Great Old Man* (1912).[57] Labor journalists lauded writers; Lenin and Trotsky wrote on literature, and literary talent was prized in the European Social Democratic tradition. Stalin matured in this atmosphere, wrote poems, and acquired literary ambitions.[58] He became a writer-teacher, while authors of his day were assigned a lesser role at the Writers' Congress of 1934, which embraced his teaching on literature. His interventions in literary life were legendary. "I sat and marveled," wrote Ilya Ehrenburg, of a session held with writers in 1940.[59] "The war was coming, and was Stalin really so sure of our might that he had time for literary criticism?"

Stalin enhanced his persona with public commendations, demonstrating his authority to grant boons and recognition. He issued anniversary greetings in late

1928 to the Komsomol and to women workers. Soon afterward he began thanking people and institutions for completing assigned tasks. *Pravda* featured his first "blessing" of the plan era in late 1928, to participants in socialist competition: "Fraternal greetings to workers of the Red Profintern Factory. I congratulate you on accepting the challenge of workers of the "Katushka" and Yartsevo factories. I wish you success in the Soviet election campaign."[60]

Other *Pravda* "greetings" followed, two in 1930, nine in 1931, and nine in 1932. Over time Stalin grew more authoritative, issuing orders as well, thus making people personally responsible to him. Using *Pravda*'s editorial space, he commanded the head of the film industry, Boris Shumiatskii, in early 1935 to make films like the Vasilev brothers' 1934 hit, *Chapayev,* about the civil war hero: "Soviet power expects new successes from you, new films like *Chapayev.*"[61]

Stalin made himself the legislator of a new normative order and benign creator of the wonders the press displayed. On January 1, 1933, *Komsomol Pravda* showed him smiling on a miniature collective farm dotted with tractors and combines. "The results of the five-year plan have shown that it is quite possible to build a socialist society in one country. The economic foundations of such a society have already been laid in the USSR," he declared a week later.[62]

Pravda's editors cited Lenin as an authority in fewer than a fifth of the lead editorials from 1921 through 1927 and Stalin in equal measure from 1928 through 1932, but from 1933 through 1939 they mentioned Stalin in more than half.[63] The press extolled leaders such as Molotov and Kaganovich, too, but their mini-cults were peripheral to the story of Soviet success. From 1936 Stalin did everything, knew everything, and took credit for everything good in Soviet life. When he promised in the late 1930s to "make all workers and peasants cultured and educated," *Pravda* declared, "That is what Comrade Stalin said; that is what will be!"[64] The press affirmed the most dubious triumphs. "On the Stalinist Path to a Prosperous Life," was *Labor*'s caption to news of the end of rationing in September 1935.[65] *Komsomol Pravda*'s editorialists concluded on the October anniversary in 1936: "The Soviet people know to whom they owe these great attainments, who led them to a happy, rich, full and joyful life. . . . Today they send their warm greeting to their beloved, dear friend, teacher, and father."[66]

Stalin codified his accomplishments in 1936 by presenting a draft of the new "Stalin Constitution," "the constitution of socialism."[67] When he introduced it to the Extraordinary Eighth Congress of Soviets in late November, *Pravda* pictured him surveying Moscow like a lord of creation, and Nikita Khrushchev, the city's Party leader, described the reconstruction of "Stalinist Moscow" (November 25, 1936). A day earlier the newspaper printed court artist A. M. Gerasimov's depiction of Stalin standing with the document in his hand, beside seated colleagues (November 24, 1936). Readers learned that the text came from "the pen of the greatest master of socialist building—Comrade Stalin," although in fact it was written by Bukharin and in part by Radek, both of whom Stalin would soon put to death (December 6, 1936).[68] *Komsomol Pravda* emblazoned each page of the ratified text with a medallion of Stalin's head. "The Constitution of the USSR was written by the hand of Stalin, the greatest living human being," wrote *Labor* the same day. What writer could claim more? "Last night Stalin's new constitution was adopted. I won't say anything about it; I feel the same way as the rest of the country, that is, infinite delight," Galina Vladimirovna Shtange, an activist and wife of an engineering professor, wrote in her diary.[69] Yet enthusiasm cut two ways. In 1940 people angry about a decree increasing penalties for lateness and absence from work cited the constitution. One wrote, perhaps disingenuously, "The decree enserfs the workers. Where is the personal freedom given in our constitution?"[70]

The cult reached its apex on the leader's sixtieth birthday in December 1939, with World War II under way and the USSR invading Finland. Coverage of the birthday drove foreign news from the press. Journalists blended metaphors in use since the mid 1920s—of war, family, building, the school, the task, and the path—to sing Stalin's praises as "the great driver of the locomotive of history," "the Lenin of today," "genius of communism," "inspirer of inventors," "the friend of science," "the great thinker," "the creator of the people's happiness," and "friend of humanity."[71] Praising Stalin and applauding his wisdom and power, participants depicted consensus and social harmony, and explained away failures and troubling questions. "Stalin's life is our life, our beautiful present and future," editorialized *Pravda* in 1936.[72]

His near deification, in effect, answered a question typical of creation myths: How did our universe arise? A less personalized creator, such as the Party, could also have served. "The Party" as an answer might have been more rational and comprehensible, since it would have expressed in shorthand the statement that active participants in Soviet society had created a new order through collective action. Instead, the press emphasized Stalin as the agent of creation, reinforcing the mythic nature of the cult and lending it almost magical power.

Stalin's Charisma as Political Theater

Stalin's cult and its embellishments in representations of Soviet life had the classic attributes of a primitive ritualistic drama: recurrent themes, stereotypical characters, and symbolic settings. The political theater of high Stalinism drew in all the active elements of Soviet society, engaging them at once in participation and complicity. How can this extended performance involving so many people be explained? Scholars have explored its apparent religiosity, and one can argue that Stalin filled a void created by the suppression of religion.[73] Parallels have been drawn to peasant life, particularly the patriarchal authority of the household and the peasants' traditional respect for the tsar.[74] The cult has been identified with Russian political traditions, the autocracy and the Muscovite past, and the suggestion has been made that it filled the void left by the destruction of old institutions.[75] Stalinism has alternatively been seen as an extension of Marxism as well as Leninism.[76] The Soviet style of governance has even been linked with modernist artists and intellectuals who sought to control and transform the world as an aesthetic environment.[77]

Such parallels are reminders of the nearness of the past, but not full explanations of what followed. The Bolsheviks employed Marxist terminology to advance their own agendas, not Marx's. Images of a personal ruling authority extend far back in Russian culture, but Stalin's persona was largely his own. Moreover, the rhetoric of aesthetic modernism permeated Russian public culture before and after 1917, and it would be odd not to find traces of it in the Stalinist era. Soviet Russia was a land of peasants and former peasants, and they may indeed have sought a father figure to replace the patriarchal authority of household and monarchy or even found spiritual satisfaction in an ersatz religion of politics.[78] The traumas of the five-year plan and collectivization, as well as purges and persecutions, may have created a crisis of self-perception among beneficiaries of Stalin's programs. Such favored people were likely to be better educated and more mobile than similar groups of the 1910s and 1920s, but they endured tremendous geographic and social disruption.[79] Perhaps, under such conditions, some were inclined to crave a tsar-patriarch, but why?

The suggestion that the upwardly mobile cadres who succeeded in Stalin's Russia may have drawn on the tsarist past for lack of other usable traditions is a good but partial answer.[80] A full understanding of the cult as public culture must encompass its contemporary context and function, as well as its parallels in Russian traditions. Stalin explained the cult to a German sympathizer, Leon Feuchtwanger, in an interview in 1937 that Stalin had translated and published in a large edition. According to Feuchtwanger, Stalin tolerated the cult because of "the naive joy" it accorded those involved in it, and he blamed "inappropriate" practices, such as the display of his portrait at a Rembrandt exhibition, on "people who were slow to accept the regime and tried to express their devotion with redoubled zeal."[81] In this way, Stalin allowed for innovations from below in the cult's performance and for the cynical participation of unbelievers. He also showed his awareness of the contradiction of an authoritarian cult in a socialist country.

Stalin and his circle were known to be contemptuous of peasants and peasant beliefs, and they themselves may have acted to satisfy what they considered to be expectations of ignorant functionaries and supporters. Bolsheviks had justified Lenin's cult and mummification in this way over objections by Krupskaia and others.[82] At the time, according to one account, Stalin in particular urged attention to "the Russian conception of love and veneration of the deceased" and a need to satisfy "certain of our comrades in the provinces."[83] The minicult of the feeble Kalinin as "all-Russian peasant elder," complete with his photograph in peasant dress at "his" village or holding court at the House of Peasants in Moscow was another such an invention.[84] Interpreted this way, as theatrical costuming by participants both high and low, vestiges of old traditions seem less a revenge of the past than a purposeful and calculated appropriation to smooth a very rough system of authority. A local Party official urged in 1936 that more be done to promote patriotism "by cultivating the utmost love for Comrade Stalin."[85]

The Soviet press adopted elaborate rituals of theater to tell a story about the Soviet experience, to legitimate the social order, and to promote a politics that revolved around Stalin's ceremonial role. Did Stalin actually believe that this grand show, which depended on his acquiescence if not personal direction, would bring about a national consensus based on his personal and near mythic authority? If so, he anticipated the theories of some modern social scientists about the function of political theater and sacred ritual in drawing an audience together and dispelling disbelief.[86]

Such accord was far from certain in the Soviet case. Stalin's government had the power to command the appearance of belief but not necessarily belief itself. In political theater, forms of behavior matter most, and therefore it may be, as one historian of China has argued with respect to late-imperial Chinese rites, that correct performance, rather than belief, was most important to Soviet authorities.[87] The significance of correct performance may explain why people were punished for small mistakes, such as printers' errors. Alternatively, such slips may have been punished as evidence of covert feelings or beliefs. In any case, as a former Trotskyist later noted, "Strict observance of verbal formulas was one of the characteristics of Stalinism."[88] Although this feature of the performance may owe something to an Orthodox religious tradition in which details of the service were important, Stalin's cult can hardly be said to have embraced the spirituality of the religious tradition. The widespread acceptance of the cult may nevertheless owe something to the population's familiarity with ritual and display.

It is probable that many accepted the performance and participated because they craved some kind of legitimate order, Marxist or not. Others may have simply recognized its brute power and opportunistically joined rather than opposed. Herbert Marcuse explained the seemingly magical features of official Soviet communication in the 1930s as an attempt to enforce rationality in the face of "the absurdity of a historical situation" in which "new productive forces are used as instruments of repression."[89] This inverted rationalism also suggests a longing for order among those knowledgeable enough about Marxist doctrine to try to reconcile it with experience. The crisis years of the plan and collectivization provided a context in which such a longing could develop. In the popular culture of Imperial Russia, order and authority were long counterpoised to freedom and anarchy.[90]

The employees and managers of the organizations and institutions of the Soviet state benefited from Stalin's programs. Even if they had few personal complaints, daily they had to confront the deficiencies of the new order. How could they explain shortfalls to themselves and others, particularly after Stalin's "Dizzy from Success" article of March 2, 1930, in which he blamed others for the disastrous results of collectivization. Nikita Khrushchev recalled thinking, "If everything has been going as well on the collective farms as Stalin has been telling us up until now, then what's the reason for the 'Dizzy with Success' speech all of a sudden?"[91] Perhaps even if old Bolsheviks doubted that he was making progress to socialism, younger members may have accepted his claims.[92] Doing so, they had to ignore what did not fit the performance.

Not all participants in the Soviet press may have agreed about what was taking place in the country, but the state prevented the disruption of the prevailing official view and provided an overriding motive for participation.[93] In this respect, Lenin and his colleagues launched the performative culture in 1917 when they established the monopoly on information. Once the monopoly was in place, no enlightened naif could stop the show by proclaiming that the emperor had no clothes. The nature of the performance led to a particular kind of reflexivity; that is, the performers and much of the audience were aware of the performance as a performance. Participants projected an image "onstage" that they could use for other purposes "offstage," even if they did not fully accept the performance. By joining official rituals and ceremonies, active citizens could demonstrate inclusion in the Soviet project.

Such behavior is not restricted to political drama. Participants in habitual everyday situations internalize the logic and forms of familiar rituals, and can thereafter innovate and improvise to sustain the expected sequence of behavior.[94] The mundane performances of daily life work well precisely because participants assume that others will understand what it is they are doing, will innovate in order to maintain the necessary consistency, and will act swiftly to resolve deviations from the norm.[95] The same may be said of the official rites of Soviet culture, although the price for disruption was infinitely greater. Like those of daily life, the routinized and highly structured performances of Soviet culture were open not only to persons who unconsciously understood "the facts" but also to those who had consciously mastered this knowledge in order "to pass" as good faith participants.[96]

The Mythic Dimension of the Performance

Soviet political theater acquired a mythic dimension in the mid- to late 1930s, when Stalin cast himself as father of the nation.[97] Earlier in the decade the nation had been the fatherland, but now it became the homeland or motherland in implicit union with the great father. The press of the late 1930s showed Stalin in a familial pose among women and children. As pointed out in the prologue, the trade union paper even featured him as Grandfather Frost, the Russian Santa Claus, on December 30, 1936, showing him laughing and clapping at children dancing around a "New Year's tree" decorated with schools, buses, planes, and other such "gifts" (Figure 3.4). The tree, permitted for the first time a year earlier, signified the substitution of New Year's Day for the Orthodox Christmas.

Stalin appeared in photographs as "the friend of children." One by M. Kalashnikov, "Comrade Stalin and Gelia Markizova," shows him taking flowers from a small girl in a sailor suit at a Kremlin reception in 1936 for delegates from the Buriat-Mongolian Autonomous Soviet Socialist Republic (Figure 3.5). *Pravda* published it months later on "the holiday of a happy childhood," and millions of copies circulated as a poster.[98] "Ringing voices strike up a song about youth, the homeland, and Stalin, whose care has won our children a joyful, happy, and steadfast life," read the editorial beside the picture. The girl's father was later shot as an enemy of the people, and her mother committed suicide.[99] On New Year's Day, 1937, *Pravda* featured an engineer, his wife, and a son whose life was saved by Stalin's intervention. The story that Stalin dispatched a doctor by air to the Chuvash Republic in response to the desperate father's telegram confirmed Stalin's power to intervene at his own discretion and exercise his supreme will through acts of kindness or mercy like a god or a tsar. Stalin's acceptance of this view of himself and his powers is apparent from his efforts to intervene personally in almost every aspect of Soviet life.[100] Citizens registered their accord with his presumption in letters they wrote to him, whether or not they hailed his miraculous powers.[101]

Pravda greeted the anniversary of the Party's youth league, the Komsomol, in late 1933 with flowers, children, and smiles of happiness in a photomontage of young people around Stalin and Lenin.[102] "With the inauguration of the Second Five-Year Plan in 1933, 'Keep Smiling' became the motto of the day," recalled Markusha Fischer, wife of correspondent Louis Fischer.[103] By 1935 flowers figured in Stalin's portraits, and even in military displays, as on New Year's Day 1937, when *Pravda* showed Stalin smiling at a flower-bedecked procession walking beside a tank (Figure 3.6). On May Day, 1936, *Pravda* featured a huge portrait of Stalin flanked by girls holding flowers amid a smiling crowd. On November 7, 1939, *Pravda*'s front page showed a display above the gathered dignitaries at the Bolshoi Theater in which a banner with a huge head of Stalin and a small one of Lenin hung over a mountain of flowers.

The amalgam of flowers and fatherhood enhanced Stalin's near magical persona in the performance, his power over life itself. Flowers have signified royalty, paradise, and rites of passage, particularly of love and death, throughout Eurasia.[104] Flowers had many of these functions in Imperial Russia, as its advertising and packaging attest.[105] The early Bolsheviks, with their severe style, reduced the presence of flowers in public life for more than a decade, although Lenin's death prompted the appearance of wreaths and other floral displays.[106] The reappearance of flowers in Stalin's portraits, and then in representations of

Figure 3.4. *Labor,* December 30, 1936. Drawing by P. Vasilev. "The whole country exalts, laughs, and gleams with merriment / because children live joyfully / the country is marvelous for them / and each hour, whether study or leisure / has become unusually joyful / because, for us children / our great Stalin is our best friend."

Figure 3.5. *Pravda*, June 29, 1936. "Comrade Stalin and Gelia Markizova."

Figure 3.6. *Pravda*, January 1, 1937. Drawing by V. Deni and Nikolai Dolgorukov. "Happy New Year, Comrades!" The banner reads, "Long Live the Stalin Constitution." The editorial is titled "The Great Helmsman Leads Us."

the populace, symbolized happiness and authority but also served to divide the flowery realm of the press's official theater from daily life.

Modern plays and similar events can be compared to primitive sacred dramas that entail a journey into a realm of spirits.[107] In a play, actors and audience briefly leave the quotidian world to enter a special arena of time and space. To describe this realm of the "betwixt and between" in which wishes or dreams hold sway, one can employ the concept of "liminal," that is, a threshold between sacred and profane, a transitional zone that participants in a ritual must enter in order to leave the everyday world. Arnold van Gennep, who introduced the notion in his classic 1908 study, *The Rites of Passage,* postulated three phases of ritual drama: (1) *Separation* from the ordinary world; (2) a liminal phase of *transition*—from *limen* meaning threshold in Latin; and (3) *incorporation* or *reaggregation* into society on a new "postliminal" basis.[108] The liminal phase is thus a kind of limbo in which social norms momentarily dissolve, only to reappear in new forms. It is characterized by its hypothetical character and wishfulness, and in this way is similar to the unreality of performance. And like performance, the liminal phase serves as a venue for the introduction of new values and practices.[109]

The Soviet press set apart a special space and time for the cultural performance midway between modern theater and sacred ritual.[110] This performance can be read as a rite of incorporation, a transition through which participants acquired new values and new social standing. The process of creating a special space began during "the great break," when Stalin's government destroyed private property through collectivization and nationalization. The press shrank private space still further during these years by enlarging and sacralizing public places and structures. Even housing, which journalists represented as a gift from Stalin, often appeared public, just as Stalin's gifts of buses and schools on *Pravda*'s New Year's tree were public. The press constructed a public space, and its sacred separateness was made explicit in the law of August 7, 1932, "on safeguarding the property of state enterprises, collective farms, and cooperatives, and strengthening public (socialist) property," which has been attributed to Stalin himself.[111] According to the new law, sentences of death by shooting and confiscation of property were assigned for theft of even small quantities of goods. "Public Property Is Holy and Inviolable," read *Pravda*'s editorial."[112]

This was the era of model farms and factories, rendered not only in the press but also in films, literature, and art. Such burnished images were also displayed to gullible foreigners. V. M. Berezhkov, later Stalin's translator, recalled no qualms about giving foreigners a peek at the "bright future" rather than showing them the sorry state of ordinary farms, since he believed that "our country would [soon] become the richest country in the world."[113] "A 'show' of the country was always made for foreign Communists," wrote Svetlana Alliluyeva decades later.[114]

The greatest "show" and also display of the leader's power was the All-Union

Agricultural Exhibition, which opened in August 1939 on the tenth anniversary of collectivization. The exhibit highlighted Soviet exceptionalism but also, conversely, Soviet universalism. It was equivalent to England's Great Exhibition of 1851, but whereas the Crystal Palace was enclosed in glass, the Soviet display was set apart on 136 hectares, with working models of farms and factories.[115] *Pravda* dubbed it "an audit of the collective-farm order"; Molotov called it a "demonstration of the great victory."[116] The paper gave half its front page to Sergei Merkurov's huge gloomy statue of the leader, which visually dominated the exhibit. "Collective farmers make the display, and the whole people observe it," wrote the prominent columnist David Zaslavskii, whom the émigré historian Boris Nicolaevsky praised for style and condemned for lack of "principles."[117]

The exhibit can be called a liminal space in the sense that those who passed through it were supposed to be transformed. *Pravda* called it "a great school" and "springboard" for future progress.[118] Journalists also drew readers' attention to the presence of the new official heroes of Soviet life. *Pravda* wrote that "among the participants at the exhibition are many of those people whose initiative has led to the great success of the collective-farm order."[119] The paper went on to list them, including such champions as Mariia Demchenko—"one of the important people of the splendid movement of collective-farm women for a big harvest of sugar beets"—and Ibragim Rakhmatov, who "bravely raised the flag of struggle for breaking the world record for cotton yields."

The Agricultural Exhibit was a long-delayed celebration of empire, "a holiday of peoples."[120] Non-Russians had hardly figured in *Pravda*'s editorial commentaries during the NEP, appearing in less than 6 percent of its editorials from 1921 through 1927.[121] During 1928–32 the figure rose to 11 percent, but from 1933 through 1939 it jumped to almost a third. The definition of a sacrosanct space extending to the country's geographic borders began during the First Five-Year Plan, when journalists described the empire largely as a zone of building sites and collectivized agriculture. The press produced map after map with new factories, plants, and "collective farm giants." *Pravda* greeted the October anniversary in 1932 with a photomontage of projects in Central Asia, Ukraine, and Siberia.[122] On January 2, 1933, the Party paper hailed the plan's completion with a map of projects on which Magnitogorsk, the Siberian steel center, was larger than Moscow.

Newspapers began to show nationalities mingling at public events. When *Pravda* covered the First Congress of Collective Farm Shock Workers in February 1933, pictures of non-Russians accounted for just over a third of the photos and roughly an equal share of the space allotted to such illustrations.[123] During the Second All-Union Congress of Collective Farm Shock Workers in February 1935, these figures reversed, and pictures of Central Asians, Ukrainians, and other non-Russians accounted for two-thirds of the graphic representations of the congress. Deni and Nikolai Dolgorukov prominently featured a

Central Asian woman with braided hair and a traditional hat in their New Year's illustration for 1937 (Figure 3.6). Although similar pictures had occasionally appeared earlier, their prominence now accentuated a new rhetoric of identity and nation in which the imagined land itself was further sanctified.

Hitler had spoken of an anti-Bolshevik crusade for "living space" in the East, and, now that he was in power, Soviet leaders and journalists replied with a patriotism encompassing all nationalities and particularly areas threatened by Germany. Stalin claimed in his speech introducing the constitution in 1936 to have produced a "multinational state" based on "the brotherly cooperation of peoples."[124] The sacred always inclines to the universal and stressing the multinational state was one way of universalizing the Soviet Union as a family of man. Two years later *Pravda* editorialized on citizenship:

> Great Russian people, Ukrainians, Belorussians, Azerbaidzhany, Georgians, Armenians, Tadzhiks, Uzbeks, Turkmen, Kazakhs, Kirgiz, and also many others joyfully and in a friendly fashion erect the great building of socialism. Each one loves his homeland, his people, his language—and all together as Soviet citizens are selflessly devoted to the common motherland of the great Soviet country.[125]

For the nationalities, this patriotism meant a return to Russian chauvinism. The government in the 1920s had spurred a Soviet multiculturalism as a vehicle of nation building among non-Russians, promising economic and cultural development, as well as the use of native languages, while retaining central control.[126] These policies suited a negative view of the tsarist empire as a "prison of peoples." Stalin in the 1930s in contrast repudiated multiculturalism for Russification, the glorification of the past, and the superiority of Russians as "big brothers" of other Soviet peoples.[127]

Stalin identified himself with "our socialist fatherland" in a 1931 speech in an issue of *Pravda* devoted to the fiftieth birthday of his crony, the military leader K. E. Voroshilov.[128] There he made his famous prediction that Russia had a decade to overtake its rivals. "We are fifty or a hundred years behind the advanced countries," he wrote. "We must make good this distance in ten years. Either we do it, or we shall go under."[129] Just as he effaced Lenin while capturing his aura, so he now recast Russian nationalism by denying its past legitimacy while at the same time drawing on its authority. Although nationalism was implicit in "socialism in one country," Stalin's invocation of "fatherland" in 1931, and later "homeland" and "motherland" when he became "father,"[130] were innovations in Soviet rhetoric, borrowed from the prerevolutionary past: "In the past we had no fatherland, nor could we have had one. But now that we have overthrown capitalism and power is in our hands, in the hands of the people, we have a fatherland, and we will uphold its independence."[131]

The press accordingly began to enhance Soviet and Russian pride. After Hitler took power in 1933, the need for such borrowing may have become obvious to Soviet leaders. Popular nineteenth-century Russian writers had glorified generals, such as Napoleon's nemesis Field Marshal Kutuzov; poets, such as Lermontov and Pushkin; and even tsars, such as Peter the Great and, to a lesser extent, Ivan the Terrible.[132] In the mid- to late 1930s Soviet publicists promoted various historical figures ranging from the much-beloved, early-nineteenth-century poet Mikhail Lermontov to the half-forgotten educator K. D. Ushinskii (1824–1870).[133]

The performative aspect of these appropriations was apparent in the centennial of Pushkin's death, which in 1937 followed the great purge trial of Karl Radek and others accused of forming an "Anti-Soviet Trotskyist Center." The hysteria of the trial colored the poet's commemoration, and editors of the peasant paper attributed his death in the famous duel to a plot by "a gang of nobles."[134] The press made Pushkin an opponent of serfdom and autocracy but also an ally of Stalin. A contemporary joke had sculptors planning his monument beginning with a statue of Pushkin reading Byron and ending with one of Stalin reading Stalin.[135] The anonymous pundit conveyed the message of the cult and the centennial; Stalin appropriated the mantle of Russia's literary heroes, and his supporters coupled his name with theirs. "I have already read Engels and Sholokhov, Stalin and Pushkin," boasted a champion miner from the Donbas in a 1935 interview with a journalist.[136] Covering the centennial, the press linked the two idols in a roster of accomplishments worthy of Russian pride. "The dream of the great genius has been realized," editorialized *Pravda,* referring to the poet.[137] "The people have thrown off their age-old slavery and found the path to real freedom and culture."

The Sacralization of Time

The press created its own time. Time in late Imperial Russia was largely synchronized with the rest of the industrial world, as it was in early Soviet Russia, which adopted the Western calendar in 1918. During the NEP the country sustained the relatively free movement of labor and capital over time and space on which the market economy was predicated. Also during the NEP reliance on money increased; money served as a store of value over time and allowed intertemporal arbitrage. The country likewise shared the formal grid of interchangeable fixed units of time—clock time, railroad time, and airplane time— that fit over the world and in which time and space were interchangeable as hours or kilometers, in contrast to the more localized time and space of seasonal routines.[138] Russia also partook publicly, to a degree, in the search for personal pleasure and the enjoyment of the ephemeral, expressed in advertising and aesthetic modernism elsewhere in the industrial world.

The xenophobia of the late 1920s and the monopoly over foreign trade undermined this international temporality. Moreover, the command economy as imagined in the press increased the state's geographic and temporal control over labor and capital, while devaluing money and spawning an alternative system of value and prestige. During the 1930s the promotion of a new national time from above left little room for public recognition of private time. The press seldom featured private time since most Soviet citizens were expected to forgo present consumption for future benefits. The new official time was analogous in its special separateness to the carnival time M. M. Bakhtin described in his famous study of Rabelais, which he began during these years. Whereas the sixteenth-century French carnival, as Bakhtin described it, was a mockery of official norms, the Stalinist "theater state" ceaselessly confirmed them.[139] The Soviet genre was the morality play, not the carnival, but its temporality was also distant from daily life.

The Stalinist conception of time as a path facilitated a reordering in which the past and future eclipsed the present. The German Communist, Wolfgang Leonhard, who grew up in Moscow, recalled delight and then confusion when, in 1935, he and his mother bought a replacement for their outdated 1924 city map only to find that the new map was dated 1945 and included projected improvements for the next decade. "We used to take both town plans with us on our walks from then on—one showing what Moscow had looked like ten years before and the other showing what it would look like ten years hence," he wrote.[140] What had vanished or, more exactly, become compressed between two dream worlds was the present.

Official spokesmen who took the rostrum at the Pushkin Centennial of 1937 placed the poet in a netherworld of time and space, extending from past to future. Stalin's court poet Demian Bednyi proclaimed:

> He is ahead. Therefore we say "Forward to Pushkin." Centuries hence when communism has already long been established throughout the whole world, the slogan of communist humanity will be: "Forward to Marx, to Engels, to Stalin! Forward Comrades!"[141]

An anonymous editorialist in *The Peasant Newspaper* likewise wrote of Pushkin so as to fuse the wished-for present with an idolized past:

> He is alive, he is ours, he is with us now. Is it really possible to consider him a man of that dark and evil time in which he lived? . . . He is our person, our contemporary, our comrade and friend, our shining singer. His burning truthful words about freedom and reason are our Soviet words, bolstering a living cause.[142]

Thus Pushkin, who gloried in aristocratic freedom, was mobilized on behalf of a culture he would have fully detested. Stalin's enthusiasts used the past to reinforce a fantastic present and made Pushkin their surrogate.

The Short Course of the History of the All-Union Communist Party (of Bolsheviks) served the same end. *Pravda* serialized the text in the fall of 1938, and it overshadowed the Munich crisis. Whether or not Stalin wrote it, and many think he did, he appears as Lenin's equal, architect of victory in the civil war, founder of the socialist economy, and scourge of the Party's enemies.[143] The old Stalinist Iaroslavskii urged "the younger generation, which has not passed through this school [of Bolshevism]," "to study" *The Short Course*.[144] The effect was to make the past a book to be opened or closed at will. "The heroic pages of the Bolshevik Party's struggle to prepare for the dictatorship of the proletariat unfold before readers in all their fullness and diversity," editorialized *Pravda* after several chapters had appeared.[145] *The Short Course* concluded with a quote from Stalin in which the aging leader compared himself and other Bolsheviks to the mythological Antaeus, the son of Poseidon and the goddess of the earth, who was invincible and hence immortal so long as he touched the ground, a secret Hercules used to kill him.[146] Stalin asserted:

> I believe that the Bolsheviks resemble the hero of Greek mythology, Antaeus. They are strong like Antaeus when they retain their link with their mother, with the masses, who gave birth to them, fed them, and educated them. And while they keep their link with their mother, with the people, they have every chance of remaining unbeatable.[147]

The gaps between past, present, and future vanished in the press's near mystical account of Soviet life. Time became a path through the present, not to the present, which explains the official obsession with commemorative dates and the "historic." Record-breaking flights were "historic"; the Stalin Constitution was a "historic fact"; and the Soviet invasion of Poland was the "historic resolution" of an old problem.[148] "Under Stalin there was no clear distinction between the historical and the contemporary," as art historian Matthew Cullerne Bown has observed.[149] Nor was there a sharp demarcation of the future. This was more than a convergence of real and ideal, as in the tradition of American exceptionalism. It was an attempt to force past, present, and future into a single magical continuum. On January 22, 1940, the anniversary of Lenin's death, *Pravda* featured a picture of Stalin and his government standing before a portrait of the founder which rested on a mountain of flowers, as if in the flowery realm the living and dead were truly one. A decade earlier, this link between living and dead immortals was made explicit in the architecture of the Lenin Mausoleum, which allowed living Party leaders a platform directly over the sarcophagus of the founder.[150]

In the world of the performance Stalin appropriated time, as evinced by the decision to complete the First Five-Year Plan in four years. At the Sixteenth Party Congress in mid-1930, he raised targets in some cases by as much as 100 percent and announced the completion of collectivization in two or three years instead of five.[151] *Pravda* and other newspapers adopted the slogan "Five Years in Four," applying it not only to the plan but to the country's complete transformation, and children displayed the slogan on banners.[152] This promise was an expression of near absolute power.[153] The government introduced a continuous work week on August 27, 1929, requiring four days of work followed by one day of rest. The system lasted until 1940, when Sundays again became holidays as elsewhere in Europe. Although the four-day week and the slogan "Five Years in Four" may seem an attempt to accelerate work on a par with the Taylorism and time-motion ideas that fascinated Lenin in the early 1920s, the rejection of the constraints of time was broader and deeper.[154] Valentin Kataev began his novel *Time, Forward!* (1931) by quoting Stalin's famous 1931 speech giving Russia ten years to complete the work of a century. "This is a building site, not a stunt," his hero repeats, as if to convince himself that the Magnitogorsk metallurgical plant in the Urals can be completed.[155]

The managers of the performance enriched the new Soviet time with the promise of science and technology, particularly after the First Five-Year Plan and collectivization. Whereas *Pravda* devoted only seventeen lead editorials to science and technology from 1921 through 1927, it allotted fifty-four from 1928 through 1932, and eighty-four from 1933 through 1939. The newspaper's size remained roughly six pages, but space given to science and technology tripled from three pages a month from 1921 through 1927 to nine from 1928 through 1939.[156] The phrase "technical reconstruction of the Soviet economy" became synonymous with the plan during the late 1920s and early 1930s. "We Are Liquidating Our Technical-Economic Backwardness," read an editorial in early 1929.[157] The word *tekhnika,* meaning engineering or, broadly, technology, worked as a mantra in slogans, such as "We Must Liquidate Our Technical and Economic Backwardness" (January 11, 1929). The press defined collectivization as science in practice, asserting that mechanization, seed treatment, crop rotation, land improvement, and irrigation "can [only] be achieved by the unification of separate peasant farms" (March 4, 1928). *Pravda* promised, in November 1930, a "technological revolution in agriculture" that would bring "economic improvement to many millions of poor and middle peasants" (July 11, 1930).

The press employed science and technology in a truncated continuum in which the future and past overrode the present. "Yesterday nothing; tomorrow everything," was the way the disillusioned André Gide summed up this attitude on returning from a visit to the Soviet Union in 1936.[158] "We are becoming a country of metal, a country of automobiles, a country of tractors," Stalin stated in late 1931.[159] Official representatives of Soviet science expressed this enhanced present by emphasizing practice, as did Trofim Lysenko, who gained sway over agronomy and biology with promises of instant results.[160] The press made Stalin a nexus between science and society, and technology's heroes paid tribute on completing their feats, as did scientists in public appearances. The explorer-mathematician O. Iu. Shmidt, perhaps the most popular figure of Soviet science in the mid-1930s, at the Seventh Congress of Soviets in 1935 described his work as "a victorious song in honor of Comrade Stalin."[161]

During the 1930s journalists infused the metaphor of "the path" with an imminent future. The author of an editorial in 1935, "To the Heights of World

Technology," stated: "Our country has covered a long path of economic development, which under capitalistic conditions would require many decades. We ought to be able to end our technical and economic backwardness in the shortest time and attain a place in the world that befits us."[162]

Editorialists gradually insinuated this performing time into their New Year's Day remarks. The threshold of a new year is an occasion for prognostication in many societies, but Soviet journalists under Stalin did more than prognosticate. In 1928 there was no commemoration in *Pravda,* nor had there been any to speak of in previous years. On January 1, 1931, however, the editors turned to the future: "The coming year will bring new attainments, great new successes in socialism's struggle with capital." By 1933 the New Year's commentary was a regular feature in *Pravda* and other central newspapers, but instead of a prognosis it became a statement about a luminous and desired present. On January 1, 1933, *Pravda* praised 1932 as the greatest year in contemporary history and concluded: "We cross the threshold of the new year as the masters of a new life."[163]

The mood depicted was time in the subjunctive, specifying what might be, what should be.[164] "We ought to usher in the plan year with 100 percent fulfillment," *Pravda* editorialized in late 1930.[165] Toward the end of the decade New Year's editorials had a special quality. *Pravda*'s lead editorial on January 1, 1937, began:

> Truly, our great country goes boldly into the new year of 1937. We know it will be a year of great labor and intense struggle; it will be a year of new and splendid victories. It will bring us closer to the cherished objectives: to the building of a communist society, to the victory of proletarian revolution and socialism in the whole world.

The authors of such statements did more than promise great accomplishments. By calling up a cherished future, they further diminished the neglected present. The editorial for 1939 had a still sharper flavor. "Every year that passes brings the socialist state of workers and peasants newer and newer victories."[166] The implication of this perspective for doubters was devastating. Lysenko explained in a speech in *Pravda* damning critics of his fantastic proposals:

> Really, comrades, to have possibilities such as those that the collective-farm order offers our agricultural science and not to move this science ahead at a pace unheard of in the history of biological science—this means not to participate in socialist building, not to live in the epoch of socialism, which is taking our society to the bright dream of humanity—to communism.[167]

Stalin's legitimacy depended on the faultless projection of the Soviet project forward and backward in time, which explains why he so emphasized the future as well as the past in the performance. The writer Michael Ignatieff points out, "It was the central metaphysical conceit of the totalitarian state that its functionaries would never answer to any other future than the one which history, the Party, or the leader had preordained."[168] The press reinforced this conceit by appropriating time itself.

The Apotheosis of the Leader

The cult was eternal; to imagine a ruler besides Stalin was unthinkable. The slogan "Long Life to the Great Stalin" in birthday greetings and at the Agricultural Exhibit bespoke near immortality as well as longevity, as did the photographs of him with adoring children.[169] A journalist for *Izvestiia* recorded a conversation at the Agricultural Exhibit between collective farmers from Ukraine and Georgia in which one exclaimed: "Stalin. He is always with us. And now he sees us and rejoices in our friendship."[170] As sociologist Edward Shils has noted, "The bearer and the adherents of charismatic authority . . . tend to think of their norms as legitimated by a source remote in time or timeless, remote in space or spaceless."[171] Stalin had become such a legitimating agent in the press's performance.

People who participated and lived these years in public life later recalled the theatricality of their experience. "In the time of my youth," wrote comedian and film star Arkady Raikin, "everyone around me sang that everything is open to us young people, and I sang along with all the rest."[172] D. A. Tolstoy, son of popular Soviet historical novelist Alexei Nikolaevich Tolstoy, ascribed his father's survival to "acting talent."[173] For such people, silence was not an easy option. "For his silence would have been too eloquent," his son explained.

Newspapers of the 1930s probably had a greater impact on participants than the more argumentative publications of the 1920s. This was true despite what seems in retrospect to be the banality of the rhetoric, the function of which was probably more incantatory than explanatory.[174] The leaders, journalists, and others represented the world and themselves in a performance that continued without a break, encompassed all aspects of public life, and was the only show in town. As the writer Vasily Grossman later observed, "The state which had no freedom created a stage complete with parliament, elections, trade unions, and a whole society and social life."[175]

The Economy of the Gift: "Thank You, Comrade Stalin, for a Happy Childhood"

A NEW CAST of high achievers with new scripts joined the performance during and after "the great break." In story after story, journalists showed that these super citizens, as well as ordinary people, owed their lives and all the goods and services distributed in Soviet society to Stalin and the state. According to the logic of the performance, great champions might defy time, science, and human endurance, but none of their accomplishments could constitute full repayment for the benefits they had received. The enlargement of the ruler and the state, which suited the logic of the command economy and Stalin's dictatorship, diminished the individual as creator and initiator of value in economic life. Lenin had fostered this moral economy of the gift when he made his vanguard party society's benefactor. Stalin and his government enlarged it by claiming to have created a socialist society.

In one respect, the Stalinist economy of the gift was a sharp departure from what had transpired earlier. Until the completion of the First Five-Year Plan in 1932, the press had emphasized self-sacrifice. Behind the schemata of class war, the pragmatism of the NEP, and even formulations of socialist building was the presumption that citizens were forgoing consumption so that they or their descendants would benefit in the future. Although the lie behind the image of self-sacrificing elites was palpable, the appeal to sacrifice was a powerful one. This changed after 1932, when the press hailed the plan as a success, praised the quality of Soviet life, and trumpeted grandiose rewards for achievers in various professions, from factory workers and peasants to artists and scientists. The ethos of self-denial for a cause prevalent in the 1920s gradually gave way to perpetual indebtedness. The former had, to a limited extent, empowered individuals, since they were the ones choosing to sacrifice. The latter denigrated individuals by making them objects of the leader's beneficence. Achievers were rewarded on a grander scale but nonetheless remained dependent and subservient.[1]

The anthropologist E. E. Evans-Prichard opined on introducing Marcel Mauss's classic *The Gift* in 1967, "How much we have lost, whatever we may have otherwise gained, by the substitution of a rational economic system for a system in which exchange of goods was not a mechanical but a moral transaction, bringing about and maintaining human, personal, relationships between individuals and groups."[2] Stalin and his compatriots developed a society in which public allocations of resources were officially presented as moral transactions, and performers who publicly thanked Stalin validated personal ties to the leader. Alongside the formal moral economy arose a well-developed practice, rooted in Russia's past, of private exchanges ranging from expressions of friendship and affection to bribes that undercut the rigidities of the command economy. The official enfolding of economic transactions into the moral economy of the gift implicitly undermined both public and private commitment to more straightforward economic transactions and markets. It also provided a rationale for attributing personal success and achievement to Stalin and the state. Stalin himself validated the moral economy by personally picking recipients of important state prizes.[3]

Gifts are often reciprocal, but the press depicted even heroes as people powerless to recompense the immensity of their debt. "What more can I give the homeland to repay her as a true daughter for my training and for all her attention and love?" asked the prize-winning collective farmer, Mariia Demchenko, a Don-Cossack winegrower and student of agronomy.[4] Most citizens were still less able to reciprocate benefits allegedly conferred on them, and therefore "gifts" to them from Stalin and the state were inherently demeaning.[5] How could the school buses and buildings on *Labor*'s New Year's tree for 1937 ever be repaid? How could citizens not be grateful for oranges, sausages, smoked fish, and other scarce goods that appeared in major cities before the holiday?[6] It was as difficult to recompense the country and Stalin for "gifts" of goods and services as it was to meet the production quotas of the era. Recipients of gifts, that is, normal wage-earning citizens, were thus permanently in debt. The performers' expressions of appreciation confirmed their indebtedness and the shortfall of their efforts, as in the slogan, "Thank You, Comrade Stalin, for a Happy Childhood."[7] The performance solidified the official order by justifying hierarchies and concealing an elaborate system of rewards that was not readily justified. The symbolic incentives of the moral economy also reinforced behavior required by the performance.

The explicit moral economy had another strength. The Israeli philosopher Avishai Margalit has argued that people can lose self-respect and humiliate themselves while nonetheless retaining a sense of achievement and self-worth. As he explains, "Grovelers humiliate themselves in order to achieve other advantages at the cost of their self-respect—advantages that may well serve their self-esteem."[8] Those who abased themselves before Stalin in the performance gained prestige from proximity to him. Those who felt powerless before overweening authorities could take consolation in seeing their own obsequiousness mirrored on the public stage by powerful heroes who groveled before the leader. Yet perhaps the ritual was ambiguous even with regard to Stalin. "Humiliating others, you humiliate yourself," reads a Russian proverb.[9] Hegel argued in his dialectic of master and slave that it is self-defeating for a master to demonstrate absolute power over a slave by demanding that the slave recognize his power, since a slave's approval is worth little.[10] In fact, in the mid-1930s, a disgruntled worker was reported as having made this very observation by asking, "Is Stalin happy because there are many fools who write 'the Great Stalin' during his lifetime?"[11]

As the media abandoned argument for fanfare, notables became increasingly important. The press had celebrated workers and peasants collectively during the NEP, but by the 1930s *Pravda* featured them individually as heroes of the morality play.[12] Outstanding workers were first called shock workers, a title conferring prestige but little material advantage; later the appellation "Stakhanovite" brought real benefits to those who acquired it. The movement began inauspiciously in the summer of 1935 when a Donbas coal miner named Alexei Stakhanov exceeded his quota by a factor of fourteen in a local propaganda stunt. *Pravda* published the story on its last page a month later, but Sergo Ordzhonikidze, commissar of heavy industry, seized on it to raise norms, reward enthusiastic workers, and shake up management.[13] Although the economic contribution of the Stakhanovites was uncertain, the government paid them more than ordinary workers and granted a few prominent super-achievers huge salaries, cars, and other perquisites.[14] The title was soon extended to select collective farmers and even to soldiers, and the press joined local Party leaders in showing that Stakhanovites increased production. A memoirist from the lumber industry recalled that after his enterprise had raised production, a reporter asked for a list of their Stakhanovites. He quoted his boss as exclaiming, on learning that their production figures were broken down by shifts, not by individual workers: "Well, all right. I will settle this somehow with the Party organizer . . . We'll find some Stakhanovites."[15]

Stakhanov confirmed Soviet technological power as well as his personal obligation to the leader when he told *Labor* in September 1935 that his record was "an answer to our STALIN's call to use technology fully."[16] Two months later he thanked Stalin. "To him, to the great Stalin, we are all obliged for the happy life of our country, for the joyfulness and glory of our beautiful homeland."[17] Accordingly, the columnist Mikhail Koltsov, who was later famous for his coverage of the Spanish Civil War and then murdered in the wake of the great purge trials, discounted Stakhanov's part in his own success, attributing all his power to the influence of Soviet society:

> Yesterday a peasant, a sullen poor peasant, today he is remade in the Bolshevik crucible into an advanced worker, the pride of his class and country—he has become before one's eyes a strong person of tomorrow, the reliable friend of his still constrained brothers abroad, whose productive strength is paralyzed by the mindless capitalist order.[18]

Pravda's photographer showed Stakhanov on November 7, 1935, marching in front of other miners from the Donbas, smiling, jackhammer in hand (Figure 4.1).

Figure 4.1. *Pravda,* November 7, 1935. Alexei Stakhanov leading other Donbas Miners.

During the NEP *Pravda* had enlarged the symbolic power of the state by highlighting negative experiences before 1917. Now the newspaper extended the bad times to include life before the plan and collectivization, effectively shifting the rite of passage to the experience of living through Stalin's reforms of "the great break."[19] The paper published an article in 1933 about an exploited farmhand reborn after collectivization, shown smiling broadly in an accompanying photo (Figure 4.2).

Look at Moshurov! From a cowed agricultural laborer he has become the literate brigadier of the best collective farm in the region, who fully understands compli-

МОШУРОВ, бригадир бригады колхоза
им. Сталина, Богучарского района, ЦЧО,
делегат всесоюзного с'езда колхозников-
ударников.

Figure 4.2. *Pravda,* February 14, 1933. "Moshurov, brigadier of the brigade of the
Stalin Collective Farm, of the Bogucharskii District in Central-Blacksoil Oblast, and
delegate to the All-Union Congress of Collective Farm Shock Workers."

Figure 4.3. *Pravda*, January 1, 1935. "A Bolshevik Greeting to Male and Female Shock Workers of the Great Country of Soviets, to Advanced Masters of Technology."

cated computations. Ivan Sergeevich Moshurov is now a Party member; he is his own boss on the collective farm, and he strides ahead with the collective farm.[20]

The press made such people's obligation strikingly apparent, as in *Pravda*'s front page on January 1, 1935, which featured a drawing of Stalin at a podium, with diminutive shock workers proffering bouquets of flowers (Figure 4.3). Thus in the press, personal moral ties to Stalin replaced bonds to family, friends, colleagues, the community, and ultimately to society itself. The workers' dependence on Stalin and the state was particularly evident in the case of the Stakhanovites. Stalin cited Stakhanovites in 1935 as evidence of the prosperity he promised, and announced, "Life has become better, life has become merrier." *Pravda* excerpted and printed his words on its masthead, below "Proletarians of All Countries Unite!" It read:

> The founding of the Stakhanovite movement served most of all to improve radically the material condition of the workers. Life has become better, Comrades. Life has become merrier. And when life is merry, work goes quickly. Hence high norms of production. Hence heroes and heroines of labor. This most of all is the root of the Stakhanovite movement.[21]

Thus proletarian and peasant notables acted out rituals of the gift and celebrated their miraculous rebirth as new people with a special relationship to their benefactor. Many behaved in the press as if they belonged to a family headed by Stalin and addressed him in the familiar (*ty*), usually reserved for family, close friends, and children. For example, a front-page letter to Stalin in *Pravda* from shock workers on a collective farm in late 1933 read in part: "We want to tell you (*tebe*) how honorable shock labor has already earned us a prosperous life during this year."[22]

The authors of letters to Stalin displayed their virtue and the system's fairness. The promotion of "socialist competitions" between enterprises had a similar import.[23] The effect was a circle of obligation, effort, entitlement, and reward including all publicly recognized segments of the population. Many no doubt rejected this message, but few could disregard it. Witness a factory foreman who is reported to have complained in April 1938, "The ordinary person makes such speeches ['Hooray, we have reached a happy, joyful life'] like a street newspaper-seller," but his wife "reproaches him that today she has been torturing herself in queues and did not get anything—there are no suits, no coats, no meat, no butter."[24] A more common reaction was probably the offhand joke, "Oh, you Stakhanovite, lets have a smoke."[25]

Women and Family in the Shadow of the Cult

Early in the performance, the press extended the theme of rebirth to women. Bolsheviks had promoted loyal women from the first, but *Pravda* only began to portray women prominently in the 1930s.[26] Whereas journalists of the NEP recounted women's struggle for liberation, commentators of the mid-1930s treated the issue as resolved. "Peasant Woman, daughter of labor and care! Today we celebrate the day of your future emancipation," read *Pravda*'s headline on International Women's Day in 1923.[27] This was the first time the paper celebrated the holiday. Yet aside from the brief header on page 1, the editors relegated the story to inside pages, where leading Bolshevik women such as M. Frumkina and Krupskaia explained, "The building of a new life cannot be completed as long as our country is surrounded by capitalists." A year later the press declared March 8 a holiday, but struggle remained the key theme: "Women have already attained much in the country of Soviets under the leadership of our Party, but they ought to attain still more," *Pravda* noted on March 7, 1926.

The paper became self-congratulatory only in 1928, claiming women as active contributors to the new order: "We count thousands and thousands of promoted female proletarians in the posts of red factory directors, in the management of cooperatives, in workers' clubs, in special courses for workers and in high schools, in the GPU and the Red Army, and in administrative and Party work," read an editorial from that year.[28] The paper concluded: "We firmly set off on the path of the complete emancipation of women from all oppression." With the end of the first plan and collectivization, this victory was announced in a *Pravda* editorial on international Women's day in 1934: "Women have equality not only in law but in life."[29]

Journalists increasingly featured youthful, vital, and attractive women, and by the late 1930s female figures constituted a third of the exemplary people portrayed in *Pravda* and *Labor*.[30] There were female pilots, athletes, and Stakhanovites in industry and agriculture. This new presence coincided with a change in government policy. The early Bolsheviks had tried to liberate men and women from the institutions of family and church, and this was the intent of the first family code in 1918 and legalized abortion in 1920. The revised code of 1926 protected women and children from abandonment, while preserving the earlier legislation's emancipatory features. The press featured women as active participants in collectivization and the First Five-Year Plan but gave them increased visibility only later in the 1930s, when official policy became paternalistic, pro-natalist, and family-oriented.

The shift came in May 1936 when the press printed a discussion of new family legislation, which was adopted a month later without major changes.[31] The change coincided with the promotion of Stalin as paterfamilias of the nation. *Pravda* emphasized the criminalization of abortion and the primacy of the family unit as evidence of "Stalin's concern for mothers and children: "We need a healthy, unmaimed mother; we need healthy children who are replacements for the builders of socialism; we need a strong socialist family!"[32] The next day the paper proclaimed the "Holiday of the Happy Child," beginning a promotion of motherhood and children that was to last almost as long as communism.

The prominence of women in the press coincided with changes in representations of the body. Newspapers began to feature eroticized images of men and women, lightly dressed participants in sporting events and in parades. At roughly the same time homosexuality was banned, as it was in Nazi Germany.[33] On Constitution Day in 1936, seventy-five thousand athletes "demonstrated the force and happiness of youth in the Soviet land."[34] *Pravda* showed them spelling out Stalin's name in the parade and also dancing and marching, the men bare-chested and the women in close-fitting clothing.

Despite the accent on family, the press favored attractive female Stakhanovites, athletes, and pilots rather than established homemakers. Several days before the new family legislation was announced, the press covered the "Congress of Wives of the Commanders of Socialist Industry," which met in the Kremlin with much fanfare. "Delegates to the congress are the best representatives of that large strata of women of our country who are not satisfied with managing their homes when they can manage the country," editorialized *Pravda* on May 10, 1936. A few weeks earlier, on International Women's Day, female shock workers gathered at the Bolshoi Theater and cheered Stalin. *Pravda* captioned the women's letter to the leader "From the Working Women of the Soviet Capital to Comrade Stalin," using the familiar to address him. Like other champions of the Soviet order, they, too, accommodated themselves to the economy of the gift. They wrote:

> What more is there to ask when there is Soviet power; when exploitation, oppression, lack of rights, and slavery have been abolished forever; when there is the Party of Lenin-Stalin, a worker-peasant government, which exists only to make a rich, joyful, and happy life for millions of working people—the men and women of the new socialist society.
>
> We are obligated to you, our own dear Iosif Vissarionovich, for the great respect, honor, and love women receive in the Soviet country and for the recent concern and attention of the Party and government for our children. (March 11, 1936)

The women promised to bear "champions," "new detachments of Stakhanovites in production, female engineers, scientists, flyers, sailors, and snipers proficient in all weapons." A few months earlier, on November 22, 1935, the paper had published "The Report of Khristina Baidich," a harvester at a beet farm who came to Moscow with other rural champions. She appeared in an accompanying photo with a look of reflective satisfaction (Figure 4.4). The text read in part:

> Three years have passed since Comrade Stalin told collective farmers: You will have a prosperous life. Then our collective farm labor day [the unit of payment] was worth a half kilogram of grain and some did not have enough grain. But Stalin saw further than all and said the prosperous life will come. . . .
>
> And now look at us. We are all well-dressed, we have good shoes, we are hap-

Figure 4.4. *Pravda,* November 22, 1935. Khristina Baidich.

py and healthy. Look at our horses, how sleek they are, our machines, our construction, our whole economic order.

In the performative culture of the 1930s the press resolved the tension between self-interest and revolutionary selflessness, between private and public life, so evident in the 1920s. Private rewards and enjoyment were public goods that came from Stalin. Actors on the public stage no longer abjured family and home but were thankful for these boons. Stakhanov mentioned his wife and children in *Pravda* on November 15, 1935, crediting his happiness to Stalin—"To him, to the great Stalin, we are all obliged for the happy life of our country." On November 3, 1932, *Pravda* described "visiting Ivan Nikitich Kuchma," a worker at the Dnieper Dam, with a wife who was a homemaker, one daughter in the Komsomol and another in the Young Pioneers, the official organization for younger children. Their cheerful apartment resembled a stage set: "A big bright room flooded with light, a table covered with a white cloth, a couch, and many flowers. There is another smaller room, for Vera and the pioneer Viktoria. The kitchen is clean and bright." After describing the family's improved circumstances, the author concluded: "Ivan Nikitich was recently chosen as a member of the factory [Party] committee and therefore he has a lot of work. But tomorrow is a day off, and he is free. If the weather is good he will go fishing; if not, to the movies." Thus when the press reintroduced private life into the morality play, it did so not to encourage genuine privacy but to open a hitherto little recognized domestic domain to occupation by the cult.

The Nationalities in Their Assigned Roles

The non-Russian nationalities also crowded on stage in the mid- to late 1930s, and their increased prominence coincided with a turnabout in policy.[35] Throughout the 1920s Stalin had promoted a policy of encouraging the cultural development of nationalities summed up in his slogan: "Socialist in Content; National in Form."[36] Toward the end of the decade he rejected this policy. The government soon curtailed its program of nation building in non-Russian regions, began to promote the Russian language, and prohibited criticism of the tsarist empire.[37] In the mid-1930s Stalin overthrew the "Pokrovskii school" of Russian history, which saw the empire as a prison of peoples and the tsarist government its jailer. He had privately expressed his dislike for Pokrovskii as early as 1925. In his speech in 1931, warning that Russia had a decade to catch up to the advanced countries of the West, he effectively treated the Russian and Soviet past as one.[38] In March 1938 Russian became compulsory in all non-Russian schools and the sole language in the Red Army.[39] The official revival of Russian nationalism suited Stalin's promotion of himself and hence of Moscow as the center of Soviet life.

During the First Five-Year Plan editors had represented outlying regions largely as construction sites. *Pravda* noted the Uzbek Republic's fifth anniversary on February 20, 1930, in a tiny article on page 7 about new factories. Soon, however, the press loudly proclaimed the nationalities' obligation to the dictator and to Russians. The leaders of Azerbaijan wrote in *Pravda* in 1936 on the fifteenth anniversary of the establishment of Soviet Power in their republic: "You, Comrade Stalin, were the brain of the Baku proletariat."[40] "The Friendship of the USSR's Peoples Is Alive and Flourishing," *Pravda* editorialized in late 1936. The editors continued, claiming: "The Great Russian People, first among equal participants of this brotherly union of peoples, provided enormous help to the weaker nations in the years of heroic struggle against counterrevolution and intervention, and in the years of great building."[41]

Coverage of nationalities swelled in the mid-1930s with the publication of greetings to Stalin and testimonials on national issues.[42] *Pravda* reported comments from a factory in Kiev on the trial of Zinoviev and Kamenev, charged in 1936 with trying to kill Stalin. According to *Pravda*, the workers proclaimed: "They aimed a revolver's barrel at the Party's beautiful heart; they wished to kill the one who leads the multinational Soviet Union to genuine human happiness."[43] Ukrainian youth leaders wrote on the front page of the paper in 1936: "To You, great leader and teacher, best friend of youth, the first word of deep love and greeting from us, delegates to the Ninth Congress of the Komsomol of Ukraine" (April 4, 1936). *Pravda* published an accompanying picture of five happy delegates (Figure 4.5).

The press recorded the non-Russians' fawning compliments. Suleiman Stalskii, the folk poet of Dagestan and a promoter of the cult at the writers' congress, praised Stalin at a Moscow meeting of shock workers in early 1936 as the sun who "illuminates the world" (February 16, 1936). Later that year he expressed regret to Stalin in *Pravda* at his inability to attend the Eighth Congress of Soviets: "My own wisest and most beloved leader! During these joyful days when the whole country reaches out excited hands to Moscow, from which rises a new inextinguishable sun that you have set aflame, I cannot attend the congress personally" (December 4, 1936). It was ironic but fitting that someone so servile should represent so rebellious a people. Yet even Stalskii was sometimes outdone. At the "Congress of the Wives of the Commanders of Socialist Industry" a delegate from Baku claimed: "Just as the moon takes its light from the sun, so do we, speakers of Turkic languages, reflect the light of our great genius Stalin. Thank you, Comrade Stalin, for our free, bright, and smiling life" (May 13, 1936).

Early in the 1930s exemplary representatives of the nationalities had celebrated Stalin's achievement; later they embodied the transformation of their peoples. Russian and non-Russian delegates to the First Congress of Collective Farm Shock Workers in February 1933 hailed collectivization similarly in interviews and testimonials. "Under the leadership of the Communist Party and the Central Committee, and primarily of Comrade Stalin, we have attained the

Figure 4.5. *Pravda*, April 4, 1936. Delegates to the Ninth Congress of the Komsomol of Ukraine.

greatest successes in socialist building," affirmed a farmer from the Collective Farm "Radio" in the Bashkir Republic (February 19, 1933). Two years later, with Hitler in power, delegates to the Second Congress of Collective Farm Shock Workers noted the benefits of empire. A Ukrainian farmer contrasted his fortunate condition to that of Poles across the river, "Everyone certainly knows from newspapers and books how they farm there and how they live in poverty, and we see it" (February 11, 1935).

Gorky in 1934 urged writers to seek in folklore the cultural riches of ordinary people who accomplished so much under Soviet power. Folklore soon became an instrument of the cult and a medium for the nationalities' participation in the performance.[44] One expression of this was the press's coverage of a series of festivals of different nationalities, held in Moscow from the spring of 1936 until the war. These *dekady* (literally, a ten-day period) were an occasion for the display of officially sanctioned non-Russian identities.[45] Simultaneously the State Committee on the Arts began preventing theatrical and musical companies in the republics from accepting foreign invitations.[46] Ukrainian, Kazakh, and Georgian festivals were held in Moscow during 1936, and an Uzbek theater festival the following year was front-page news.[47] Nationalism raged in Europe, and German rearmament, the Spanish Civil War, and conflict in the Far East were reasons to promote national unity. *Pravda* praised the festivals as "new and irrefutable evidence of the success of the Leninist-Stalinist nationality policy of our Party" (June 1, 1937).

Expressions of indebtedness confirmed the economy of the gift and the Russians' preeminence. The press presented the *dekady* as offerings to the state and Russian people, and, in that sense, as a consumer good. TASS's reporter noted of the Uzbek festival, "Uzbekistan supplies the country with beautiful cotton textiles and other goods. Now Uzbekistan has given us something else—beautiful art." The official sanctioning of national performances locked non-Russians into the social order. They, like Stakhanovites, could be nothing outside the system. *Pravda* commended Uzbeks but ascribed their success to the state rather than to indigenous pre-Soviet Uzbek traditions. "With what marvelous speed the Uzbek theater has flourished and blossomed under the gentle sun of Soviet nationality policy!" (May 26, 1937). Praise for the festival was capped by the distribution of awards to theaters and performers.

Although this language implies reciprocity, it was an asymmetric reciprocity. Uzbeks outdid one another to affirm their obligation to Moscow. "We owe all our success to the Party, the government, and, most of all, to Comrade Stalin," stated Karimov, chairman of the Uzbek Republic (June 1, 1937). A performer noted, "We will report to our people that Comrade Stalin applauded Uzbek art." Other festivals came to Moscow during the late 1930s—from Tadzhikistan in late 1937, Azerbaijan in 1938, Kirghizia and Armenia in 1939, and Azerbaijan, Tadzhikistan, and Belorussia in 1940.[48] A. Danielian, an "honored artist" of the Armenian Soviet Republic and a deputy to the Supreme So-

viet of Armenia, described her arrival by train: "Dachas flashed by, the last sub-
urbs, and there she is, Moscow, our own beloved, which has prepared a marvelous unexpected greeting for us."[49]

The roles the press assigned to individuals and groups in the Soviet performance were ritualistic and confining. Cultural critic Vladimir Papernyi argued
that Stalinist architecture served "to tie people to their spaces, to settle them
down," unlike structures of the 1920s.[50] The performative culture of the press
served a similar purpose. "The unity of interests of society and the separate person, of the state and each citizen, is one of the most remarkable characteristics
of the Soviet order," explained *Pravda* in late 1936.[51] *Pravda* editorialized
about the delegates to the Extraordinary Eighth Congress of Soviets, which approved the new constitution: "One after another the chosen among the happi-
est people in the world rose to the platform to say with complete justification—
we are the state!"[52] Yet full citizenship was limited to active participants in the
performance. *Pravda* editorialized in 1938:

> It is a great honor to be a Soviet citizen, to bear this high title. It is a great joy
> to be a participant in socialist building in the Soviet country. Great is the pride of
> living and working in the Soviet country, the first citizen of which, the most
> beloved, is Comrade Stalin.[53]

Enter Scientists, Pilots, and Explorers

The press displayed flamboyant heroes, particularly scientists, pilots, and explorers as exemplary Soviet citizens. Early Soviet leaders expected science to
supplant religion and transform society, and the Soviet Union invested heavily
in science and technology during the 1930s.[54] Yet, as if to demonstrate the arbitrary power to raise up and cast down, Stalin and his government elevated
charlatans, mediocrities, and timeservers to share the limelight with the truly il-
lustrious.[55] Soviet scientific celebrities included internationally recognized figures such as I. P. Pavlov and the space visionary K. E. Tsiolkovsky, as well as
loyal Bolshevik allies, such as the plant physiologist and popularizer of Darwin
A. K. Timiriazev, the biochemist and functionary A. N. Bakh, and the geologist
A. P. Karpinskii, president of the Academy of Sciences from 1917 to 1936.[56]

The Soviet Union was to become a genuine power in science and technology, but in the press three dubious figures overshadowed all others. These were
I. V. Michurin, a plant hybridizer; V. R. Williams, a fanatical advocate of planting grass as a cover crop; and Trofim Lysenko, an unscrupulous quack and promoter of vernalization, a means to stimulate plant growth by treating seeds to
reduce the dormant period. Each confirmed Stalin's oft-repeated dictum: "What
millions of honorable people in capitalist countries have dreamed of and continue to dream of is already established in the USSR."[57] Each was shown to
have traversed what amounted to a rite of passage to become a public figure

empowered to achieve marvelous things. For the older figures, Michurin and Williams, the rite involved surviving the alleged horrors of the old regime. In this case, a career in Soviet science erased their otherwise unacceptable social origins. For younger people, such as Lysenko, the rite consisted of growing up in the Soviet system and acquiring its blessings.

Michurin seems an unlikely candidate for official honor. The story of his life resembled that of the ephemeral inventors of the 1920s. Born a nobleman in 1854, he grew up as an impoverished autodidact and tried for many years with limited success to develop new commercial species of fruit trees.[58] Journalists of the 1930s nevertheless made him into a powerful figure whose lonely struggle encapsulated the official story of the Soviet order. *Pravda* applauded him in its feature "The Country Should Know Its Heroes" when he won the Order of Lenin in 1931, and acclaimed him in 1934 as "The Great Gardener," a title sometimes conferred on Stalin himself.[59] When Michurin died in 1935 the paper contrasted his supposed isolation and suffering under the old regime with the benefits he derived from the Soviet system and hence his unequivocal indebtedness to the Soviet state. The author of the lead obituary noted that after the October Revolution, "he was among the first . . . to say: 'I am with you, I want to work for the new authorities'" (June 8, 1935).

Williams was another orphaned professional who allegedly suffered under the old regime but won laurels under Bolshevism. *Pravda* dubbed him "the Professor-Bolshevik" in 1933, after he won the applause of radical students at the Timiriazev Agricultural Institute. On November 15, 1933, the paper quoted him approvingly when he brusquely dismissed previous soil scientists, explaining that "to put soil science and agriculture generally on a truly scientific basis, one must recast this whole science anew." *Pravda* cited him on his eightieth birthday, on April 3, 1935, for taking soil science beyond "fat books covered with dust." Williams was an exemplary contributor to the performance and a zealous promoter of purges in agricultural science.[60] "Williams," the dissident Russian historian Zhores Medvedev wrote in the Khrushchev era, "was a cabinet theorizer, dreamer, and fanatic who, under the cover of loud phrases about the fatherland and socialism, concealed the aim of establishing the supremacy of his own ideas in science and in practice by all available means."[61] In a birthday tribute, Zaslavskii summed up the official story of Williams's life of neglect under the old regime and concluded, "And now it is our Williams, the Soviet Williams, the Bolshevik Williams, a world scientific luminary and pride of Soviet science."[62]

Trofim Lysenko, the chief villain among these official heroes, was a loner of common origins who became a symbol of the Soviet scientific professions. He used his power to destroy Soviet genetics and hamstring the country's agronomy for generations into the future. *Pravda* congratulated him in 1927 for planting peas in Azerbaijan in winter and thereby saving fertilizer.[63] Seven years later he was famous, and the paper cited "the names Michurin, Tsiolkovsky, Lysenko" as proof of Soviet scientific accomplishment.[64] The editors printed his harangue at a meeting of agrarian activists in 1935 in which he urged the rejection of "the old science" for "our science" and appended Stalin's famous interjection—"Bravo, Comrade Lysenko, bravo!" (February 15, 1935). A year later he was the chief spokesman for a science that lent its full prestige to Stalin and the state and which confirmed a rosy image of collectivized agriculture.

Konstantin Tsiolkovsky, "the Russian Edison," was a legitimate scientist, but it is easy to see why promoters of Michurin, Williams, and Lysenko liked him as well. A reclusive autodidact, he was also a Soviet discovery. *Pravda* praised him on his seventieth birthday on March 11, 1928, and again four years later (September 18, 1932). When he died in 1935 the paper contrasted his prerevolutionary life as a neglected schoolteacher with his miraculous inclusion in the Soviet family: "After living sixty years in terrible poverty, amid total indifference, mockery, and oppression, the great scientist felt himself among his own with the arrival of Soviet power" (September 20, 1935). Shortly before his death he allegedly told Nikita Khrushchev, "I am immeasurably grateful to the Party and the Soviet government" (September 21, 1935).[65]

Two aged officials, the geologist and president of the Academy of Sciences A. P. Karpinskii and A. N. Bakh, an administrator and specialist in fermentation honored during the 1920s, were also included among the Soviet scientific pantheon. Although neither made great discoveries, both were revered as geniuses, presumably as a result of their longtime service. *Pravda* honored Bakh with a huge front-page picture on his eightieth birthday in 1937, extolling him as "a model scientist."[66] "Who in the USSR does not know Academician A. N. Bakh, the oldest scientist-revolutionary?" asked a commentator a year later.[67] Karpinskii received a state funeral in 1936, with front-page testimonials by Molotov and Stalin, and *Pravda* showed the dictator himself holding the coffin.[68]

The formula of Michurin's life also served to induct Pavlov and the deceased Mendeleev into the performance. *Pravda* portrayed both as lonely researchers, neglected in tsarist times. Although Pavlov received less attention than others, the paper praised him on his eightieth and eighty-fifth birthdays as a luminary of world science and on his death in 1936 as "a true son of his Soviet homeland."[69] The government honored the hundredth anniversary of Mendeleev's birth in 1934 with an international gathering of scientists.[70] *Pravda* called it a "holiday for all Soviet science," adding, "Yes, of Soviet science! For Mendeleev was truly valued only by the power of the working class, the interests and path of which fully coincides with the interests and path of the development of science." In 1937 one author wrote simply, "Mendeleev dreamed of the flowering of science, and the USSR became the center of world scientific thought."[71]

Soviet science, as revealed through these chosen heroes, was partly an old man's sphere. The image of the scientist as aged wizard was appropriate to the dreamworld of the performance. They embodied a science that promised a rapid and magical transformation of material life. Akin to alchemists, they often looked the part with their beards, wrinkles, and eccentricities. They were able to accomplish in the performance what Stalin and his government were often unable to do in actuality: to manipulate the world of man and nature and to claim predicted and desirable results. Moreover, they achieved their triumphs within the explanatory frame of the gift. Miracles were possible, even obligatory, in the performative culture, and the role of scientists was to deliver them.

This view of science as the handmaiden of the state was not uncontested. Some scientists challenged it and survived.[72] Even in *Pravda,* on rare occasions, specialists invoked independent scientific objectives and external international standards. For example, in late 1934 Professor Iu. B. Rumer, a physicist soon to be sent to the GULAG for twenty years, used Mendeleev's hundredth birthday to argue publicly for the importance of quantum physics, citing Bohr, Heisenberg, and others in the process, despite the official emphasis on the primacy of a national Soviet science.[73] Similarly in 1936, an era of inflated claims, manipulation of data, and groundless rhetoric, the physicist P. L. Kapitsa praised Pavlov, on his death, for the exactitude of his research:

> The glory of Pavlov as founder of a whole new area of physiology is exceptional. For us physicists it is difficult to evaluate all the depths and specifics of his work, but one aspect of it is linked with our branch of knowledge. In our science we cultivate quantitative and exact methods of measurement and see in them one of the most important means to determine the essence of the phenomenon being studied.[74]

In contrast to the mostly elderly scientists, *Pravda* also promoted young pilots and explorers, conquerors of space as well as time, who were likewise indebted to the official order. The paper devoted nearly two-thirds of its editorials on science and technology from 1933 through 1937 to record flights and geographic expeditions.[75] The darling of the decade was the flyer V. P. Chkalov, who was acclaimed for sensational flights in 1936 and 1937, and died in a crash in 1938.[76] *Pravda* saluted his first feat with a composition by the artist Deni showing the route, Stalin, and photos of the pilots. The paper also announced medals and an award of thirty thousand rubles to Chkalov and twenty thousand to his copilots, nearly twice the yearly earnings of a skilled miner.[77] Chkalov's wife expressed to Stalin her "limitless feeling of gratitude, my gratitude as a wife and mother."[78]

After Chkalov's second flight a year later, from Moscow to Oregon by way of a Soviet polar station, the paper printed a picture of the pilot explaining his itinerary to Stalin and the army leader Voroshilov before he left (June 21, 1937) (Figure 4.6). In the same issue a columnist described Chkalov's thoughts: "It seemed that he himself had still done little, too little for the country, for the Party, for Stalin, who raised him and to whom he owed everything, as did [his

Figure 4.6. *Pravda*, June 21, 1937. Drawing by Vasilev. "Hero of the Soviet Union Comrade Chkalov expounds the plan for the nonstop flight Moscow—North Pole—United States of America. In the picture (*left to right*): Comrade Voroshilov, Stalin, Kaganovich, Molotov, and Ezhov. Beside Chukalov stand Comrades Baidukov and Levanevskii, who participated in the discussion of the plan on May 25 of this year."

fellow pilots] Baidukov, Beliakov, and thousands of others." As the editors wrote: "It is the great power of the Soviet state that has made this fairy tale come true, has conquered the North Pole, and has made it possible to use the Pole's conquest immediately to plan a flight across the Pole to America." *Pravda* had Chkalov exclaim, with respect to Stalin's concern for his safety, "the person is always the very dearest thing in Stalin's eyes."

The writer Konstantin Simonov recalled Stalin's public link to these heroes: "We felt that Stalin stood behind the organization of it all, behind all these brave undertakings; they came to him and they reported to him."[79] The press demonstrated the tie frequently in the late 1930s. On June 26, 1937, *Pravda* published a front-page photo of Stalin kissing Otto Shmidt, a bearded academician and explorer who had just returned from the arctic (Figure 4.7). The kiss symbolized Stalin's blessing on the performative science, as well as science's partial repayment of the state's gift. *Pravda*'s photographer, by making the diminutive dictator appear slightly taller than the explorer, who was more than six feet, five inches tall, confirmed the rule that none could stand above Stalin.[80]

Shmidt, a successful but unexceptional mathematician, a Party member since 1917, had won glory in late 1933 and 1934 when his arctic expedition team on the ship *Cheliuskin* became icebound in the arctic and was rescued by air.[81] "The Country Rewards Its Heroes," was *Labor*'s headline when the Central Committee awarded the rescuers the title "Heroes of the Soviet Union" in April.[82] The same day *Pravda* printed a huge front-page photomontage of the heroes beside their shattered ship and mountains of ice. "All our work in the North is a victorious song in honor of the great Party, a victory song in honor of Comrade Stalin," Shmidt exclaimed in *Pravda*.[83] Despite the public enthusiasm, there was some covert mockery, including an underground poem picturing Shmidt and his colleagues gorging on sausage, butter, and jam while awaiting rescue.[84]

Stalin became paterfamilias to heroes of science and technology. They, too, acted out the ritual of the gift and celebrated their miraculous birth as Soviet citizens. Newspapers even published letters from parents, crediting Stalin and the Party with their sons' accomplishments. "With all our hearts we thank the Party and our beloved Comrade Stalin, who raised our son as a proud falcon of the country of socialism," wrote one couple.[85] Columnists used the pedagogical metaphor to emphasize dependence. "We are Bolsheviks and Stalin's pupils," *Pravda* editorialized on May 20, 1935. "Get an 'Excellent' on the Technological Exam" was the caption of an editorial on technology (December 18, 1933). When things went awry the culprits were accused of ignoring the headmaster. "Evidently, Bolsheviks of the Urals still have not managed to extract all necessary lessons from Comrade Stalin's comments about the Urals' backwardness in the Stakhanovite movement," *Pravda* noted on January 4, 1936.

Stalin expressed "collective intentionality."[86] Citizens were shown to care about him, and he, in turn, about them. "Stalin is our brain, our heart, our spirit,"

Figure 4.7. *Pravda*, June 26, 1937, At the Central Frunze Airport on June 25. Stalin kisses commander of the northern expedition O. Iu. Shmidt. On the tribune (*left to right*): Comrades Dmitrov, Molotov, Stalin, Voroshilov, Molokov, Kaganovich, Chubar, and Shmidt. Hero of the Soviet Union, Comrade Vodopianov, speaks.

read a caption in *Pravda* in 1936.[87] He was the agent of good intentions. "Embarking on this difficult expedition, we felt the warmth of Comrade Stalin's truly humane attitude toward those fulfilling the tasks of the Party and government," remarked Shmidt in *Pravda*.[88]

There was perhaps something personal in Stalin's and other aging leaders' identification with these honored heroes. The youthful vigor of pilots and Stakhanovites matched the scripted vitality of elderly scientists. *Pravda* described Pavlov at eighty-five as swimming every morning, then playing games with his pupils, and finally "romping" with his favorite lab monkeys, before conducting experiments.[89] Stalin was over fifty in 1929 and over sixty on the eve of World War II. Many in his entourage were of the same generation. From this vantage point, the fixation on young pilots, explorers, and shock workers, together with older scientists in full possession of their powers, may suggest not only the urge to dispel a powerlessness before economic and social problems but also a yearning to achieve, if not immortality, at least the exuberance of youth. "Kitsch is a folding screen set up to curtain off death," wrote Milan Kundera.[90]

Pravda's editors set death at a distance after 1933 by printing fewer obituaries.[91] Those published during the First Five-Year Plan retained something of the individuality of the NEP, but even among these there was a growing attempt to deny aging and to minimize the fact of death. "Despite tsarist repression and many years of exile, prison, and emigration, Comrade Skvortsov-Stepanov preserved the full energy of a fighter and builder of socialism until the very end of his life," remarked a group of comrades in late 1928 of an old revolutionary.[92] A decade later Voroshilov and others wrote in one of the obituaries of the famous pilot, Chkalov: "To the very last minute Chkalov, the best citizen of the Soviet Union, gripped the controls of his fighter, to the very last he honorably served his homeland, which will never forget his compelling image as a true Bolshevik and people's hero" (December 16, 1938).

The press tried to show that death held no terror for the new people who had been transformed by the Soviet experience. A. Enukidze, himself a future victim of the purges, wrote in 1930 of a former member of the Cheka: "He lived for work and wanted to live for it, but did not fear death" (March 17, 1930). The tireless Zaslavskii in 1935 compared the dying Tsiolkovsky to Lev Tolstoy's Ivan Ilich, noting how the tsarist official had rejected life, whereas the expiring Soviet scientist turned his mind to the Party and Stalin:

> His last thoughts were about his work, the people who worked together with him, the country in which he lived, the people for whom he expressed his thoughts in the long years of solitude, the Communist Party, the leader of the Party and country, Comrade Stalin. So he looked death fearlessly and calmly in the face, and deep wisdom penetrated his last words, great wisdom and great love. (September 20, 1935)

In the world of the press the great heroes derived enormous comfort from their service in the repayment of the gift. This was true not only for scientists and pilots but also for others, including writers, who had traditionally played such an important moral role in Russian society. They, too, were cast into new roles in the official morality play.

gift of socialism?

fear of Death

Five

Literature and the Arts: "An Ode to Stalin"

AT THE FIRST CONGRESS of Soviet Writers in Moscow in August 1934, an ensemble of cultural personalities added their voices to the official choir of approval. It was a time when the leaders may have felt they needed additional powers of persuasion in view of the greatly depressed living standards that resulted from the five-year plan and collectivization. In fact, on June 4, 1934, two and a half months before the congress opened, the Central Committee, when delegating duties of its apparatus among Party secretaries, granted Stalin "Cultural Enlightenment," a responsibility he retained until November 27, 1938, when it was passed on to Andrei Zhdanov.[1]

The writers met in the lull between the Seventeenth Party Congress in January 1934, where opposition to Stalin surfaced, and the assassination of Sergei Kirov in December of the same year, which commenced a wave of repression that engulfed many of the delegates to these two gatherings. The indications of political resistance added urgency to the portrayal of a society unmarred by dissent or doubt.[2] The Stalinist government insisted that writers and artists adjust their idiom accordingly. When the congress began, Zhdanov warned Stalin of "serious dangers."[3] Two weeks later, when the congress was nearly over, he wrote again to his chief, congratulating himself on its success and not concealing his contempt for participants: "They tried to outdo each other in their ideological spirit and ability to pose deep creative questions, and their speeches had all the extra flourishes."[4] "I remember the congress as a big wonderful holiday," recalled Ilia Ehrenburg years later, adding that he prepared "like a girl prepares for her first ball."[5]

Pravda published speeches and summations of them, as well as editorials, commentaries, interviews, and illustrations. The paper claimed undisputed authority to define legitimate cultural activity, and an unsigned article was tantamount to an official pronouncement.[6] "A Holiday of Soviet Culture" read the paper's headline on opening day, and beside the headline Stalin and Gorky grinned at each other in artist Deni's quarter-page drawing (Figure 5.1).[7] The contrast with the paper's previous coverage was striking. Literature and the arts had occupied only 1 percent of *Pravda*'s total space or a third of an issue a month in the era of the New Economic Policy and well into 1929.[8] This amounted to barely a page per month in the early and mid-1920s, a page and a

Figure 5.1. *Pravda*, August 17, 1934. Drawing of Stalin and Gorky by Deni.

half at the decade's end, and two and a half pages in each of the first four months of 1933 and 1934. But *Pravda* granted fifty pages of coverage during the two weeks of the congress. In fact, the paper's size grew on some days from four or six pages to eight or ten, and occasionally as much as half this space went to the congress. And *Pravda* was not alone in its coverage. *Izvestiia, Labor,* and even the tabloid peasant newspaper, which appeared every other day at this time, all gave the congress nearly full front-page exposure from start to finish.[9]

Socialist Realism

The congress adopted the term *socialist realism,* with endorsement by the committee that had formed the writers' union in 1932. Once approved, the term was attributed to Stalin, who had told writers and others meeting at Gorky's house in Moscow on October 26, 1932: "The artist ought to show life truthfully. And if he shows our life truthfully, he cannot fail to show it moving to socialism. This is and will be socialist realism."[10] *Pravda* printed a definition from the statutes of the new union on the eve of the congress:

> Socialist realism, the basic method of Soviet artistic literature and literary criticism, demands truthfulness from the artist and a historically concrete portrayal of reality in its revolutionary development. Under these conditions, truthfulness and historical concreteness of artistic portrayal ought to be combined with the task of the ideological remaking and education of working people in the spirit of socialism.[11]

On the face of it, socialist realism seemed to concern the proper subject and method of portrayal. Of course the authorities had previously prodded artists and writers for positive portrayals, but only haphazardly. Ilia Ilf and Evgenii Petrov mocked these prescriptions in their famous sketch of late 1932 about a writer whose editor insists that he create a truly Soviet Robinson Crusoe, with a party committee and the masses on the island.[12] By 1934 the terms *correctly* and *truthfulness* entered the press's narrative as measures of artists' and writers' success in accommodating themselves to the official portrayal of Soviet life.[13] Meanwhile censorship tightened, and it was often referred to by euphemisms such as *oblit* and *gorlit* for provincial and city bureaus, respectively, while the censors became "inspectors."[14]

Pressure on writers to celebrate Soviet society had increased even before the formal adoption of socialist realism. F. I. Panferov, the sole author *Pravda* reported addressing the Seventeenth Party Congress, urged fellow authors to portray peasants' joy at collectivization.[15] That writers and artists joined this fraud attests to their de facto acceptance of the performance as a higher truth governing public expression. This was, in fact, how officials presented it. P. F. Iudin, a bureaucrat whom the Central Committee added to the organizational bureau of the new writer's union in August 1933, explained that since "truth" was found in life itself, the artist had only to represent it faithfully, for "life" was "more interesting than it is made to be in artistic literature."[16] The truth to which he referred was that of the performance.

Gorky, despite a falling out with Stalin and resulting restrictions on his travel, advertised socialist realism as a creative reflection on the best of Soviet life.[17] "We live and work in a country where feats of 'glory, honor, and heroism' are becoming facts so familiar that many of these are already no longer noted in the press," he wrote.[18] He also blamed writers for being too negative and for seeing life through the prism of the old critical realism rather than its Soviet successor. Long-time resident and sympathizer Louis Fischer later explained socialist realism as follows:

> The Soviets knew the hypnotic effect of the great dream, and as the promised future faded into the past they strove to keep alive the trust in delayed benefits. Among other things they ordered all writers, in the middle of the 1930s, to treat the present as though it did not exist and the future as if it had already arrived.[19]

Socialist realism in 1934 belonged to the performance. It was neither a literary tradition nor simply the tool of a dictatorship.[20] The leaders and supporters of the Stalinist system used it to enlarge the domain of their moral and intellectual claims. Even if one were to find a secret order from Stalin or Zhdanov or Gorky explaining that socialist realist novels would have to include a positive hero, heroic acts, optimism, references to Stalin, and so forth, the meaning of these constructs depended on the larger public performance which was beyond the power of any one of the leaders to articulate or fully shape. Over time, socialist realism became associated with aesthetic conventions and literary formulas, but it always represented a grossly unequal arrangement in which writers worked under the authority of cultural bureaucrats to promote the government's changing agenda. Accordingly, Stalin and his colleagues oversaw the redefinition of each element of a literary work—subject matter, author, and audience.

The press presented socialist realism in conjunction with its presumed subject matter: the exemplary figures whose names called up a heroic depiction of contemporary Soviet life. *Pravda*'s editors and commentators had shaped the image of heroism with coverage of "feats" since the beginning of the plan and collectivization.[21] These accounts had little to do with a new aesthetic or, for that matter, "positive heroes" of the nineteenth-century literary tradition, who, regardless of their other qualities, were heroes of civil society. On the day of the congress, a local correspondent hailed the three "best shock workers" who produced the seventy-five-thousandth tractor at a Kharkov plant. *The Peasant Newspaper* greeted the congress with a map of the country on which faces of "outstanding" workers from collective farms were superimposed. The caption read: "Our great country is remarkable, our people are remarkable. Write remarkable books about this."[22] In effect, the writers were urged to amplify the press's coverage of heroes and heroines, and hence to blur the boundary between the imagined and the observed.[23] They were to embellish an ongoing performance, not initiate one, and they were often expected to follow the journalists' lead. The implicit message was that this is what they owed the state.

The big news in the newspapers during the spring and summer of 1934 was the aerial rescue of Shmidt's expedition on the *Cheliuskin.* On the second day of the congress, the paper printed a large front-page picture of the "heroic flyers" and the rescued "Cheliuskinites" in Red Square holding flowers and waiting to shake hands with Stalin.[24] "Is it necessary to repeat the names of the seven heroes who plucked hundreds of Cheliuskinites from icy captivity after half the world had written them off as doomed?" read *Pravda*'s editorial (August 18, 1934). The *Cheliuskin* rescue, together with great industrial projects, were models of heroism at the congress. "For us," *Pravda* explained on the same day, the second of the congress, "the main figures, the main characters in Soviet literature, consist of people from the Magnitogorsk Construction Site, the Dnieper [Dam] Project, the *Cheliuskin,* the builders of a new life." Some of these people, including Shmidt, the leader of the *Cheliuskin* team, as well as champion workers whom *Pravda* identified by name, such as "Nikita Izotov, Stepanenko, Kaushnian, the best miners of the Donbas, holders of medals," were present at the congress (August 18, 1934).

With the introduction of socialist realism, writers also became actors in the performance.[25] The headline over poster-artist Deni's picture of Stalin and Gorky on the opening day of the congress read, "To the Advance Detachments of Soviet Culture, 'Engineers of Human Souls,' Writers of Our Great Homeland—an Enthusiastic Bolshevik Greeting." The creative intelligentsia had been largely peripheral to the press for the decade after 1917, with the exception of the Party favorite, Demian Bednyi, whose doggerel appeared regularly. The sudden prominence of literati on front pages beside explorers, airplane pilots, and government leaders let it be known that authors now belonged to the public drama. On the first day of the congress, writers appeared in photographs inside the paper and in Kukryniksy's drawing of "The Literary Parade" on page 3.[26] These cartoonists, later famous during World War II, portrayed Gorky, Zinoviev, Bukharin, Radek, and several other cultural bosses reviewing a literary lineup that included Isaac Babel on a scrawny nag, civil war cap and spectacles askew. Although the caricaturists made writers appear eccentric, the newspaper's headlines, captions, and commentaries conveyed the message that they were an integral part of the performance.

To be a writer now meant to participate. *Pravda*'s editorialists produced a statement on the congress's first day in which the odd usage of Aleksei Maksimovich Gorky, instead of the familiar Maxim Gorky (pseudonym for Aleksei Maksimovich Peshkov), accorded with the pomposity of the performance:

Today, in the capital of our state, the All-Union Congress of Soviet Writers opened. Today, from the tribune of the congress sound the words of the great pro-letarian writer Aleksei Maksimovich Gorky, summing up the flowering of Soviet literature and pointing out its path of further development.

The country honors its artists of the word, "engineers of human souls," the pow-erful detachment of the builders and creators of Soviet culture with a flurry of greetings and good wishes. (August 17, 1934)

The editors stressed that writers could no longer sit on the sidelines: "It is important that the overwhelming majority of writers, the creators of spiritual values, unanimously and unconditionally join with the party of Lenin-Stalin, the proletariat, the people of the Soviet country."

The word *devotion,* with its religious connotations, came into play at this time, as it had earlier in biographies and obituaries of exemplary people (August 24, 1934).[27] From the late 1920s the press had cited heroic figures for selfless devotion to the Party. By 1934, however, Stalin also figured in this equa-tion, and telegrams to the leader sometimes accompanied news stories about heroes. *Pravda* published a telegram from a group of flyers whose round trip from Vienna to Moscow was covered on the opening day of the congress. An-other telegram from writers appeared on the next day below the picture of the rescuers of Shmidt's expedition on the *Cheliuskin.*[28] It read in part: "Our own dear Iosif Vissarionovich, accept our greeting, our full love and respect for you, as a Bolshevik and a person, who with brilliant intuition leads the Communist Party and the proletariat of the USSR and the whole world to the last and final victory."[29] At this point Isaac Babel is reported to have told Shmidt, who was present at the congress, "If it goes on like this, we shall soon have to declare our love through a megaphone like umpires at soccer matches." [30]

Writers such as Babel who were not enthusiastic supporters of the system could thereafter only be designated as public enemies. The union's organizer, P. Iudin, summed up this view in a speech printed on September 4 as a conclu-sion to the congress:

In their works, with their books and at their first congress, Soviet writers affirm openly before all the world that they are proponents of the communist worldview, that they are firmly behind the positions of Soviet power, and that they are ready to give their whole lives as active fighters for the triumph of socialism in the USSR, for the victory of the proletariat in the whole world.[31]

Pravda prominently displayed the phrase "engineers of human souls" on the congress's opening day, and thereafter it became ubiquitous. It signified, as David Joravsky has pointed out, a "job category, an administrative slot."[32] Sta-lin made this clear in a 1934 interview with H. G. Wells.[33] Who could read *en-gineers* in 1934 without recalling the Shakhty trial of 1928 and the arrest of half the engineers and technicians of the Donbas, or "the industrial party affair" of

1930 that devastated the technical intelligentsia and marked its full inclusion in the Soviet project?[34] These "affairs," with their xenophobic overtones, undermined the independence of the professions and served notice that standards in all fields would be set nationally from above. Equally damaging for the professional standing of experts were Stalin's widely promoted slogans empowering cadres over specialists, "The Bolsheviks Should Master Technology" and "Technology Decides All in the Period of Reconstruction."[35] To equate writers with engineers under these circumstances was simply to bring literature into line with other reconstituted occupations.

The author of the lead editorial used the oddly sounding "master craftsman" and "apprentice" of the printed word to express perhaps the anachronistic character of literary work in the age of Soviet industrialization (August 17, 1934).[36] An engineer emphasized accountability: "We are demanding and strict. We accept every book from you just as they accept a machine from us—only when certain that it will bear the maximum load" (September 4, 1934). Yet the phrase "engineers of human souls" was disingenuous in another respect: Although the word *engineers* aligned the arts with the construction industry, *souls* implied a spiritual function. As chief engineer, therefore, Stalin also implicitly commanded Soviet spiritual life. The effect was to enlarge not literary authority but that of the leader, the Party, and the state. This shift was explicit in the attribution of the term *socialist realism:* "Our Party and Comrade STALIN chose socialist realism as the path for Soviet literature and art," *Pravda's* editors explained two weeks before the congress opened (July 28, 1934). Gorky was the only writer on the "Honorary Presidium of the Union," which was otherwise composed exclusively of Party and Comintern officials, including Stalin. The writers did gain stature in one important sense at the congress, however. For the first time they joined other heroes and heroines of the performance. This was the aspect that Ilia Ehrenburg recalled most fondly, hobnobbing with Shmidt and champion shock workers.[37]

When writers and artists joined the performance, the schemata of the 1920s, which had served to represent literature as a profession, a means of education, and a weapon of class war, faded from the central newspapers. The official culture of the 1930s was not an outgrowth of the Bolsheviks' association with modernism but a repudiation of it.[38] The press of the 1930s redefined professionalism and "correctness" in the arts. The metaphors of pedagogy and war that had empowered some artists during the NEP dimmed, and the arts became a product of the administrative command economy with Stalin as architect and schoolmaster. The multifaceted battle against capitalism, with room for diverse allies, was now displaced by a narrower struggle for construction. Journalists employed new metaphors of growth, of building, and of the artist's "path" to full collaboration with the state.[39] "Task" and "assignment" now prevailed, though military metaphors of "front" and "struggle" lingered on with new meanings.[40] The front became one-sided as barricades became construction sites and warring sides metamorphosed into builders and wreckers.[41] "If we look to the development of literature in the past year, then a simple question arises: Is our literature growing? Can we speak about regular achievements in this area?" wrote a critic who viewed the profession as an expanding structure.[42] Writers, like other heroes, produced a quantifiable product: "He wrote twenty volumes and more than 150,000 lines of fighting verses," wrote A. Efremin about the political poet Demian Bednyi.[43]

There was little room in the performance for the self-judging function of professional criticism. Its end came gradually, without the startling trials that terminated the engineers' independence. There were two types of cultural reporters during the 1920s: those who commented occasionally and those who wrote regularly on one art form or another. The occasional critics produced editorials and otherwise shaped the interpretive environment for the arts. The custom of inviting prominent public figures to discuss the arts was part of the Russian cultural tradition, and the unchecked executive power of the Soviet system lent such commentators immense authority. Lenin, Trotsky, Bukharin, and other leaders pontificated freely on literature, art, and film, hardly distinguishing their personal tastes and judgments from official policy. The Communists' intervention began in 1917 and continued nearly until the system's demise, but Stalin oversaw its golden age. As critic in the Kremlin, he condemned and praised, rewarded and punished, added and deleted works from the repertoires of theaters and lists of publishing houses, and ordered changes and revisions in individual works.[44]

When the editorial *we* replaced regular identifiable critical voices in the press, literature and the arts were no longer portrayed as occupations in which respected professionals determined quality and set trends. The new, frequently anonymous commentators of the late 1920s and early 1930s often affected a bullying tone and wrote as if they had a monopoly on truth, which, in their eyes, they did. "We judge Mayakovsky's suicide like any withdrawal from a revolutionary post," rebuked one commentator in 1930.[45] "But we have the right to demand more from [I. P.] Utkin," wrote another after praising the poet's first book.[46] *Pravda* of the early NEP had been but one authoritative word among many, whereas in the mid-1930s the newspaper was commonly assumed to express Stalin's voice.[47] "We have often and justly spoken about the fact that our artistic literature, especially drama, has fallen behind life and does not satisfy the growing needs and demands of the working masses," wrote the editorialists welcoming the Writers' Congress in 1934.[48] Writers could not challenge such official pronouncements; they could only interpret them.

Journalists further undercut literature as an autonomous occupation in their depictions of non-Russian writers at the congress.[49] *Pravda* gave non-Russians 20 percent of the articles on the congress and 12 percent of the space, and *Izvestiia* also featured them prominently.[50] The Party paper showed writers whose status depended almost exclusively on the Soviet state rather than on their works or any national public. For example, the illiterate official folk poet of Dagestan, Suleiman Stalskii, appeared in both a large article and a picture beside Gorky, who welcomed him with the words, "I am simply happy that I see a real singer of the people."[51] *Pravda*'s reporter described him as "one of the country's great talents" (August 20, 1934). The poet himself proclaimed in the same issue: "From this congress I bring my people hands full of literary fruits grown by the great gardeners of life—Stalin and his Party." Other designated notables displayed similar credentials. "We have one task: to fulfill the brilliant instructions of the leader of the Party," explained the poet-functionary and head of the writers' union of Belorussia, M. N. Klimkovich (August 24, 1934). *Pravda*'s coverage thus served to sanction a particularly slavish literary role.

Press coverage of the writers' congress reflected the recasting of Soviet policy toward the nationalities. By showing people of other nationalities, and especially remote and exotic ones, in the same roles that Russian activists had performed throughout the late 1920s and early 1930s, the press showed the official Soviet practices and mores as truly multinational. When Uzbeks and Ukrainians, Belorussians and Turkmenians, made the same kinds of statements that Russian activists and enthusiasts had been making throughout the late 1920s and early 1930s, they demonstrated the openness of the performance to all peoples. Moreover, they showed that there was no public space for nonparticipants of whatever nationality.

During 1934 and 1935 the government cut back on its support for non-Russian traditions, cultures, and languages, and instead encouraged assimilation.[52] Russification and the glorification of Russia became the order of the day. At the congress, some of the non-Russian writers were shown to express great deference to Russian culture and pledged to follow Moscow's guidance in future development of their national cultures. Ukrainian and Byelorussian writers promised to overcome nationalism and promote, in the words of one, "a full and open orientation toward proletarian Moscow."[53] A Tatar writer, K. G. Tenchrin, announced, "We playwrights from the national republics are learning from our older [Russian] comrades and experienced masters of art" (August 30, 1934). The press showed non-Russian writers adopting a Russified national identity, as befitted what would become the "family of peoples" in which Russians were elder brothers (January 14, 1935). Here, too, socialist realism meant collaboration and performance on a special stage. "No, it is not only writers who have gathered at the congress," editorialized *Pravda* at the end of the first week of the congress, "it is the peoples themselves of the multinational Soviet Union who have gathered as if to give a first accounting of their cultural development" (August 23, 1934).

The Peasant Newspaper and *Labor* paid little attention to non-Russian writers but cast proletarian and peasant authors in similar supporting roles. The peasant paper, in its special issue on the congress, reduced the literary community to Gorky, Demian Bednyi, Zhdanov, Bukharin, Radek, and writers of tracts with titles such as *The Sound of Tractors, How We Became Prosperous,* and *The Harvest Is in Our Hands.*[54] On the congress's opening day, *Labor* juxtaposed front-page photos of a dozen "worker authors" with a picture of Gorky and Stalin.[55] "These are only examples from the thousands of talented representatives of the proletariat who are creating a new socialist culture," read the text. Inside were reports on Bolshevik stalwarts D. Bednyi, A. Novikov-Priboi, A. Serafimovich, and V. Mayakovsky.

Socialist realism, in its contemporary context, required not only performers but also a new audience of participants. This was not "a new class" or a social group but a wishful representation of the body politic that was acted out by actual people. The performing public included a range of heroic figures, from the Stakhanovites to minor officials and government leaders. All joined Stalin in a celebration of the Soviet order. Isaac Babel invoked the dreamlike quality of this public when he retreated into the risky silence that may have cost him his life. In his tortured speech at the congress, he confessed that he respected the reader so much that he had stopped writing. The beginning of the passage is famous; the end is less so but more revealing.

> I feel such boundless respect for the reader that I am mute from it and fall silent. Well, I keep quiet. (Laughter) But if you imagine yourself in some auditorium of readers, with about five hundred district Party secretaries, who know ten times more than all writers, who know beekeeping and agriculture and how to build metallurgical giants, who have traveled over the whole country, who are also engineers of souls, then you will feel that you cannot get by with conversation, chatter, high school nonsense. There, the discussion ought to be serious.[56]

Babel did not have to imagine this audience; those who claimed to embody it were present at the congress, both among the thousand guests on the first day and later in still greater numbers. *Pravda* portrayed local chiefs and activists from around the country who sat near the writers at the opening session, together with the Moscow elite and a few dozen sympathetic foreigners. The editors described the proceedings: "Beside the masters of Soviet artistic word, beside 'the engineers of souls' in the hall sit hundreds of readers, the best of readers. These are the outstanding people of the nation, the shock worker heroes."[57] Ehrenburg recalled that the crowded hall reminded him of a theater.[58]

The newspapers produced many images of these readers during the course of the congress. *Pravda* depicted a gathering in which the writers faced twenty-five thousand "readers" who were all representatives of institutions situated in Moscow.[59] Commentators frequently identified the new public with the masses, but the meaning of this transference was never in doubt. The leaders and activists in this drama attributed their own wishes to the masses. As *Pravda* put it:

Millions of readers and viewers want the highest images of art; they avidly wait for their life and struggle, for the great ideas and deeds of our century to be shown in artistic works of great force and passion, in works that will enter the history of socialist culture, filling and organizing the thoughts and feelings not only of contemporaries but of future generations. (August 17, 1934)

A. I. Stetskii, chief of the Central Committee's Department of Culture and Propaganda (of Leninism) and a member of the presidium of the writer's union, urged writers to attend to the new readers: "They came to this tribune and said: We love you, Soviet writers, we respect you, but we are waiting for you to give us new songs, new works in which new feelings and thoughts flow" (September 1, 1934). Both Stetskii and *Pravda*'s editorialists pinpointed the writers' dilemma: They were to be teachers and pupils, both to instruct readers and learn from them. Babel slyly alluded to this when he explained his silence before the five hundred Party secretaries. Writers and artists sat before this imagined public like pupils at school. "The time when the writer sat for an exam for critics alone has passed," wrote V. G. Lidin (pseudonym for Gomberg). "Now he sits for an exam before the whole country, before an enormous reader" (August 24, 1934).

The congress reverberated with demands for writers to engage in "constant deep study," explained the Ukrainian writer I. U. Kirilenko, a member of the union's secretariat (July 26, 1934). In his words, all school metaphors pointed to the teacher of teachers, "the great man, the giant of Bolshevism, the friend and teacher of Soviet writers, Comrade Stalin."[60] The moment Stalin and the Party became the schoolmasters, writer-pupils lost stature. As *Pravda* explained midway through the gathering, "The first days of the congress showed that this force [literature], under the wise leadership of the Party and Comrade Stalin, serves the historic purpose of educating the working masses in the spirit of communism."[61] This was presumably the role Stalin had in mind when he had officials impress writers with the pedagogic function of literature in the months leading up to the congress. "I attempted to express Comrade Stalin's views on the educational significance of literature," I. Gronskii, a Central Committee spokesman, reported to Stalin and other leaders about a meeting with writers in early June 1933.[62]

When *Pravda* showed writers and artists addressing a public of selected workers, peasants, *intelligenty,* activists, officials, Party cadres, and the leaders themselves, including Stalin, they enshrined an exemplary body politic shaped by nearly two decades of soviet power. This group of performers was representative of society but highly exclusive. As "outstanding new people," they stood apart from ordinary collectivized peasants, factory workers, white-collar employees, and many others who made up the majority of Soviet society. The press had traveled a long distance from its relatively open-ended queries to readers on matters of public policy during the early 1920s. By the decade's end, the atrophy of the public was nearly complete. In A. Iar-Kravchenko's pseudo-historical painting of 1941, "Gorky Reads his Fairy Tale 'The Maiden and Death' to Stalin, Molotov, and Voroshilov on October 11, 1931." Only the great chiefs are listening.[63]

The heroes celebrated by the press during the 1930s were representative of the official public. On the eve of the congress, the influential columnist D. Za-slavskii concluded an article about the Ossetians with the demand that writers look at "the new socialist economy of the country, its culture, literature, and new people."[64] The following day M. Koltsov, another leading journalist, wrote in *Pravda*, "Never were there in our country such people, such listeners, such brother readers."[65] To write about these characters was to glorify not only the heroes themselves but also "the performing public" as a substitute for the nation as a whole.

Pravda presented the writers at the congress bowing to an overweening authority, camouflaged with the phrase "Soviet power." The Russian novelist L. N. Seifullina declared: "Should we teach how to write or speak about our devotion to Soviet power? Soviet power cannot doubt this devotion because being writers of the Soviet country, we cannot be hostile to this country."[66] Her confusion was understandable. Behind all formulations lurked Stalin as the reader of readers. Nadezhda Mandelstam described what she considered to be her husband's effort to placate the dictator in 1937, "To write an ode to Stalin, it was necessary to get in tune, like a musical instrument, by deliberately giving way to the general hypnosis and putting one's self under the spell of the liturgy which in those days blotted out all human voices."[67] Although the poet himself may have intended to insult Stalin rather than praise him, she conveys the power of the performative ethos as she perceived it.

Pravda and the central press in 1934 showed writers and artists interacting on the stage of public life with a presumed public that ranged from enthusiastic activists and Babel's local Party secretaries to Stalin himself. This audience differed from the ordinary people surveyed in the early and mid-1920s, despite claims that it embodied "the masses." The audience instead was largely coterminous with the actual state authority that sent artists and writers to industrial projects and collective farms to study and perform, and others, as yet largely peasants and political opponents, to die in prisons and camps.

The Nationalization of the Arts

A new process of labeling and categorizing Soviet classics and outstanding Soviet writers paralleled the rise of the new public. In the early and mid-1920s commentators discussed nineteenth-century Russian classics but were restrained with respect to contemporaries. Zeal for the plan, however, sparked interest in contemporary production in all fields, including the arts. *Pravda* honored Dmitry Furmanov, author of the novel *Chapayev*, later a famous film, on the fourth anniversary of his death in 1930. Mayakovsky's suicide a month later brought a flood of tributes, largely silencing his old enemies.[68] "A great revolutionary poet has died, a master of the writer's craft has died; a tireless stonemason of socialist construction," wrote one enthusiast (April 15, 1930). Soon living artists won equal attention. There was a string of celebrations in early 1933, including the seventieth birthdays of the director K. S. Stanislavsky and the writer A. Serafimovich. *Pravda* hailed Stanislavsky with considerable pomp, but Serafimovich's birthday was grander. "Bolshevik, *Pravda* Columnist, Writer" was the paper's headline (January 20, 1933). Although he had written only some stories and a short novel on the civil war, *The Iron Flood*, Serafimovich soon starred in the performance as one of "the founders of socialist realism."

For designated classics and their authors, *Pravda*'s commentators had unbounded praise. One reviewer, on January 13, 1934, cited Nikita Gurianov, hero of Panferov's novel of collectivization, *Bruski:* "Panferov brought him to life as Goncharov brought his Oblomov, Lev Tolstoy his Platon Karataev, Maxim Gorky his Pavel Vlasov and Klim Samgin." Writers joined the game by naming colleagues. Konstantin Paustovskii praised Alexei Tolstoy, the historical novelist who had pleased Stalin by writing about Peter the Great. "Alexei Tolstoy is for us not only the greatest master of the new socialist times," Paustovskii wrote, "but the bearer of high traditions, from Pushkin, Gogol, Chekhov, Gorky" (January 27, 1939). Nevertheless classical Russian cultural figures often proved more durable than Soviet counterparts, whose names could easily fall from grace.

The inclusion of prerevolutionary luminaries in a Soviet canon depended on a shift in policy toward the tsarist past and the nationalities. In the early 1930s the rejection of "the Pokrovskii school" of Russian history, which denigrated imperial Russia, opened the way to link Soviet and prerevolutionary classics in a continuum of greatness. While Stalin began to envisage himself as an empire builder in the spirit of Ivan the Terrible and Peter the Great, the press started to treat the Soviet and Russian arts as the arts of empire, which they remained until the collapse of communism.[69] The notion of *narodnost'*, sometimes translated as nationality or official nationality but expressing the idea of a people, particularly the Russian people, arose here as well. It meant the incorporation into the arts of an official concept of national worth. As the correspondent Zaslavskii wrote in 1936, "*Narodnost'* is one of the most important aspects of the art of socialist realism."[70] A member of a Ukrainian opera company divulged his feelings on performing in Moscow: "Moscow! The heart of our great homeland."[71] Such views could hardly have been unwelcome to the Soviet managerial class, whose livelihood often depended on great projects in the hinterland that were directed from the capital.

Jubilees, memorials, and anniversaries of Russian cultural figures were important in the late 1930s. During the first third of 1936, *Pravda* published twelve large articles on the radical critic Dobroliubov's hundredth anniversary and many scattered reports on Pushkin and others. In the first two months of 1938, at the height of the terror, the paper printed eleven articles on Nekrasov's birthday and seven on Stanislavsky's. Prominent columnists and the leaders themselves joined the commemorations. The resilient Zaslavskii saluted Dobroliubov and Gogol in 1936 and Nekrasov in 1938. Culture boss Zhdanov wrote on Dobroliubov in 1936 and on Gogol in 1939. Khrushchev, already a leading functionary, brought Shevchenko into the pleiad. Editors used classical figures to convey political messages. *Pravda* observed the sixtieth anniversary of Nekrasov's death with letters from grateful collective farmers. "Reading it, I recalled my earlier life, when grain hardly lasted to the new year; the collective farm order delivered us from bitter need," wrote a correspondent in 1938 about Nekrasov's poem, "Who Lives Well in Russia?"[72]

The apogee of commemorations was the hundredth anniversary of Pushkin's death in 1937, when the whole country turned out to honor the poet in an affair reminiscent of tsarist festivities.[73] A journalist noted a year later how the Pushkin Committee managed the jubilee. The writer's works appeared in more than eleven million copies in 1936 alone and were translated into fifty of the nationalities' languages. There were readings in factories, collective farms, and schools; a show at the Bolshoi for the Party and government; a meeting of the Academy of Sciences; a plenum of the writers' union; and speeches at statues in various cities. "One can boldly say," wrote the author of this report, "that never in history has one people so honored its poets."[74]

The canonizers of Pushkin and others invoked a Russian past that prefigured Soviet triumphs. The artistic director of the Bolshoi Theater S. Samosud, in 1939, called Glinka's "patriotic opera," *Ivan Susanin,* "one of the peaks of human culture."[75] "Like Pushkin in Russian literature," he wrote, "Glinka lay the foundation for a great Russian music." Similarly, a critic described Mussorgsky in the same year as "a genius and artistic innovator, a true son of a great people, vitally tied to his country."[76] Just as the history of the Party shrank to a list of heroes who died timely deaths, either accidentally or otherwise, such as Frunze and Kirov, the arts also diminished in richness. The canonizers turned Russian and world cultural history into a museum of selective displays with many closed wings. They excluded not only aesthetic modernism but also religious, spiritual, and other elements of Russian culture. Stanislavsky became the genius of modern theater, displacing the soon-to-be-murdered Meyerhold and other modernists; Gorky dimmed memories of Leonid Andreev and Alexander Kuprin; Taras Shevchenko obscured artists more identified with Ukrainian nationalism and independence.

This radical reduction of modern culture was probably alluring to upwardly mobile activists and facilitated their participation in the performance. Those with limited education valued the appearance or certification of learning, and a simplified canon served their needs.[77] At a time when hundreds of thousands of semieducated people took jobs of prestige and authority vacated by victims of purge and persecution, emblems of cultural status were highly valued as a means to legitimate social mobility. Zaslavskii, in 1938, described a Ukrainian peasant poet's home: "Portraits of Stalin, Molotov, and Kaganovich hang on the walls of the room. There are also pictures drawn by her son [a tenth grader]. Books by Gorky, Pushkin, Shevchenko, and Ukrainian writers are on the bookshelves."[78] The author of the passage uses the writers and leaders to enhance one another, suggesting the simultaneity of past and present and the timelessness of the current government. The linkage of generations from son to poet confirms the lesson.

Foreign authors and writers held a prominent place in the simplified literary canon. The diversity, complexity, and richness of modern European culture may have been alien to the Soviet political class, but the press incorporated select recognized geniuses from the past, such as Beethoven and Shakespeare, into the performance. Music critic Braudo promised, in early 1929, that Wagner's operas "cannot fail to reach" the working class, just as "the symphonies of Beethoven and other inspired works of art reach them."[79] These remarks of the late 1920s, echoing early hopes for the diffusion of culture, differed only in part from later dedications of Beethoven or Chopin performances to Stalin.[80] The conceit of a grandiose new public of exemplary people who appreciated serious culture was the underlying theme.

The choices the authorities made in canonization were at least partially influenced by sensibilities they shared with constituents. Certain writers and artists could not be left out of the canon, even if portions of what they wrote went unread and unpublished, because even semieducated people expected them to be included, as they had been in the popular canon before the revolution.[81] Dostoevsky could be largely excluded because his credentials had been challenged in the radical milieu before the revolution, but Lev Tolstoy was included, although his ideals clashed equally sharply with the Stalinist ethos. Gogol was included despite his mystical and reactionary writings, and Chekhov, too, found a place, irrespective of a humanism that was truly seditious in a Soviet context.

Pravda often engaged in campaigns in the late 1930s to promote specific new works. In 1936, boosting the film *We Are from Kronstadt*, *Pravda*'s commentators reported crowds in Moscow and mass viewing elsewhere, and they did the same for other Stalinist classics such as *Party Card*.[82] Typically in 1939, one author chronicled Soviet cinema in the Third Five-Year Plan by listing the number of viewers of the film *Chapayev*, seen by fifty million people.[83] Another described watching *Lenin in 1918*, a classic of the Stalin cult, with old factory hands who excitedly recalled those times (April 9, 1939).

Canonization brought a convergence between the cultural and the political narratives. These were years of terror against the intelligentsia and the Party, and journalists who wrote about art incorporated official demands in various ways. A film reviewer praised *The Great Citizen,* Fridrich Ermler's 1937 classic about the purge trials, which the author revised according to Stalin's precise instructions: "*The Great Citizen* teaches vigilance, it teaches how to distinguish enemy from friend and friend from enemy" (February 17, 1938).[84] In Iu. Raizman's review of the film version of Alexei Tolstoy's novel *Peter the Great* in 1939, he described Peter's ill-fated son Alexei, whom the tsar tortured to death for opposing his policies, in terms imported from the purge trials.[85] Zaslavskii praised the nineteenth-century populist poet Nekrasov for instilling "a passionate hatred for enemies of the people and the country and a love for the homeland and the people."[86] Such remarks suggest how deeply persecutions of the era marked the image of the arts.

Journalists augmented the canon by promoting an anti-canon, a catalogue and description of condemned works. Keynote speakers at the writers' congress of 1934, Gorky and Zhdanov, damned modernist literature, as did Karl Radek and others in speeches printed in *Pravda.* Yet editors did not turn fully on their cultural enemies until 1936 when the paper led an attack on Russian and international aesthetic modernism.[87] The composer Dmitry Shostakovich was the first target in two articles, "Muddle instead of Music," about his opera *The Lady MacBeth of Mtsensk District,* and "Balletic Falsity," about the ballet *The Limpid Stream.*[88] Until then, music and, to a lesser extent, art had been more sheltered than literature. "The article on the third page of *Pravda* changed my entire existence," Shostakovich told Solomon Volkov. "It was printed without a signature, like an editorial—that is, it expressed the Party's opinion. But actually it expressed Stalin's opinion, and that was much more important."[89]

A campaign of personal vilification followed, with meetings and declarations to which, like to the articles themselves, Shostakovich could make no reply. The first commentator charged the composer with *formalism,* a term used pejoratively since the early 1930s to describe an emphasis on formal aspects of a work of art such as color or line in painting.[90] "Talent for good music to captivate the masses was sacrificed to petty bourgeois formalist contortions for the pretense of creating original examples of cheap cleverness," the author wrote.[91] "The composer," he continued "evidently did not pose for himself the task of heeding what is expected, what the Soviet audience seeks in music." Instead, he added, "*Lady Macbeth* succeeds with a bourgeois public abroad." In fact, one unstated complaint against *Lady Macbeth,* in which a young woman kills her old husband, may have been sexual mutiny, which offended the elderly male purveyors of the cult, as well as the promoters of the sanctity of the family.[92] Shostakovich later recalled his feelings during the tirade against him:

> If you were smeared with mud from head to toe on the orders of the leader and teacher, don't even think of wiping it off. You bow and say thanks, say thanks and bow. No one will pay any attention to any of your hostile rejoinders anyway,

and no one will come to your defense, and, most sadly of all, you won't be able to let off steam among friends. Because there are no friends in these pitiable circumstances.[93]

Pravda's editors used the articles to launch an antimodernist campaign, condemning the composer and pressuring others to do so. Soon architects, film directors, writers, and dramatists found the articles germane to their fields.[94] *Pravda* denounced "cosmopolitanism," "antirealism," and hence "formalism" in the works of Cézanne and Matisse.[95] "We are against the 'complicated' chaos of Shostakovich's opera and ballet," wrote journalist Iu. Iuzovskii in February 1936. "We are for Shakespeare's and Beethoven's complicated richness."[96] Critics juxtaposed the canon to its opposite, and *Pravda* led the antiformalist campaign.

In mid-March the newspaper noted the formation of a committee of the chiefs of main theaters, directors, and major composers whose chairman, P. M. Kerzhentsev, a likely author of the attack on Shostakovich, urged composers "to accept fully in their work suggestions in *Pravda*'s articles about questions of art."[97] The government's own arts committee, chaired by the same Kerzhentsev, chided those who ignored the articles.[98] Two days later the paper reported on a meeting at which Pasternak and others were accused of "formalism."[99] Ritualistic denunciations followed. "This winter there was a discussion in the papers about formalism," Pasternak wrote to his long-time friend, Leningrad literary scholar Olga Freidenberg, in October 1936. "It began with the article about Shostakovich and was extended to include the theater and literature (with the same sort of insolent, sickeningly unoriginal, echolike, arbitrary attacks on Meyerhold, Marietta Shaginyan, Bulgakov, and others)."[100] Freidenberg herself was attacked in *Izvestiia* at this time. "*Izvestiia* is an official Party newspaper," she recalled in her retrospective diary after the war.[101] "Its every word has official significance, the practical results of which (or, as was then the phrase, the 'organizational implications' of which) cannot be overestimated." Pasternak, who wished to help but feared to worsen her situation, lashed out against the persecuting pundits in a letter to her: "There are certain miserable and completely cowed nonentities who are driven by the force of their own mediocrity to hail as the style and spirit of the times that obsequiousness to which they are condemned by the absence of choice—that is, by the poverty of their intellectual resources."[102]

An official condemnation of the modernist high culture of democratic Europe and America was almost inevitable. Modernism was an international movement that depended on exchanges of information across national boundaries and acceptance of international trends and values. The modernist arts were individualistic, egotistical, and open to multiple viewpoints. Their practitioners, despite frequently leftist inclinations, were politically capricious. Stalin and his government required obeisance. Gorky, in a possibly apocryphal conversation in 1929, compared contemporary writers to Shahrazad who each night won the right to life with her storytelling.[103] Most Russian modernists adapted poorly to this situation, continuing to shock, mimic, and parody authority. They sought new modes of expression in a society that prized repetitive predictability, and they were ambiguous when simple formulaic meanings were valued. Most of all, they did not discard their quirky effrontery. "Negation," as T. J. Clark put it, "is inscribed in the very practice of modernism."[104] A tragic Russian example was Osip Mandelstam's private mockery of Stalin as "the Kremlin mountaineer" in the poem that probably cost him his life.

How could officials organizing new hierarchies and allocating rewards and privileges for services rendered not take offense at the effrontery of creative people whose standing in their fields depended not on the state or their success in the official performance but on other artists and spontaneously formed "publics" at home and abroad? How could writers and artists infused with romantic notions of the self adopt the badges and ribbons of the performance as the sole measure of their worth? Film director I. Raizman recounted in his glasnost memoirs how his friend Mikhail Romm ran to him after getting a medal in 1937, shouting, "I got the Order of Lenin; they will not arrest me now."[105] In fact, medals were hardly a guarantee of safety. Of the 571 writers and officials who took part in the writers' congress of 1934, 180 suffered in the repressions of 1937–39.[106]

Tensions between leading cultural figures and the state unfolded in various scenarios of collaboration and resistance. With the opening of the writers' congress in August 1934, the government inaugurated the system of assignment of dachas, including the famous "dacha village" at Peredelkino, and other perks for cultural figures that would persist until the end of Soviet Communism. The short list of those designated for the first country houses included literary functionaries as well as writers. Among the writers were Babel, Pasternak, Panferov, Shaginian, Seifullina, Serafimovich, and Ehrenburg, who was later to become famous as a war correspondent.[107]

What began with some artists' voluntary, if self-interested, participation in the revolutionary project became enforced conformity to the rules of the performance in the 1930s. By the mid-1930s in the Soviet Union, as in Nazi Germany, the arts had lost many of the independent attributes associated with the professions in the liberal democracies. Yet, in the performative culture, Soviet leaders and journalists invoked the image of the arts as professions and displayed them as a feature of a Soviet civil society whose interests and objectives were identical to those of the state. This invocation explains the public attention given to various unions in the arts and to the proceedings of academies in the sciences, including the Academy of Sciences, the All-Union Lenin Academy of Agricultural Sciences, and the Academy of Medical Sciences, as well as parallel academies in the various republics. *Pravda* was at the center of this transmutation of public values, and Soviet authorities used the newspaper and other media to manipulate "the symbolic order and the power of naming" with an eye to the taste of their supporters.[108]

The Covert Literary Response

By the time of the writers' congress of 1934, the leaders' monopoly of the means of public expression was virtually complete. The efforts and inclination of writers and others to contest this monopoly were necessarily circumscribed and halting. Some critics had continued to comment on the arts as art, particularly music, into the late 1920s and occasionally in the early 1930s. The old intelligentsia, however, reacted privately to the new official canon. Pasternak wrote to his father on December 25, 1934, soon after the writers' congress and Kirov's murder, to explain that he had come to his "senses" and that "nothing I have written exists." He continued: "It would be bad if I did not understand this. But happily I am alive, my eyes are opened, and I am hurriedly remaking myself into a prose writer of a Dickensian type, and then, if my strength suffices, into a poet—of the Pushkin type."[109]

Pasternak chose a literary world that predated aesthetic modernism, but the notion of the intelligentsia was itself incompatible with the new order. "Society" and "intelligentsia" were hierarchical as well as oppositional concepts, suited to a situation in which a "self-perpetuating, sempiternal corporation" of professionals, in the phrase of Frank Kermode, fixed literary value for an educated elite.[110] It was therefore as hard for writers to discard their professionalism as it was for cultural bureaucrats to recognize that they had done so. Yet the meaning of the Russian and world cultural heritage changed so markedly when the government appropriated its treasures that some intellectuals risked challenging it, albeit mostly privately. This may explain Mikhail Bakhtin's passion for Dostoevsky and Rabelais, and Pasternak translating *Hamlet* at his dacha at Peredelkino in 1939 and finding something of "incomparable preciousness."[111] The critic, children's writer, and translator Kornei Chukovskii, despite his active participation in the performance, asserted his own and others' literary authority more openly writing in *Pravda* on Pushkin, Shakespeare, and Nekrasov.[112] These and other transgressions of the official culture, which were peripheral at the time, figured eventually, much later, in the collapse of that culture and the discrediting of its hierarchy of values.

In the 1930s, writers and artists confronted compelling, politically charged official images of their presumed subject matter, of themselves as creators, and of the audience to whom their work was addressed. In response, a contrary veneration of the artist as witness, victim, and preserver of memory emerged. This is the tradition to which Mikhail Bulgakov's *Master and Margarita* belongs together with Pasternak's *Doctor Zhivago*. Although wellsprings of the counter-cult of the persecuted writer go back to the early revolutionary era, the tradition acquired new moral force during the 1930s.[113] In clandestine protest of Stalin's usurpation of the writer's role, Bulgakov made his writer-hero a Christ-like figure, as did Pasternak.[114]

Stalin himself acknowledged the power of writers as moral witnesses. According to one account of his famous phone call to Pasternak, he asked whether Mandelstam was a "master," thus inadvertently accepting a limit on his power to confer the honor.[115] Mandelstam, as if to answer the question himself, had written a poem in 1935 titled "What Is the Name" which begins "What is the name of this street? Mandelstam Street," a wry rebuff to the pretensions of the leader for whom everything was named.[116] Mocking official rhetoric with an outcast hero whose cap is embroidered with the letter M for Master, Bulgakov insisted on the divinity of talent. So did Anna Akhmatova in "Requiem," when she cast herself as recorder of eternal grief in reply to a question whispered in a line outside a Leningrad prison in the late 1930s: "Could you describe this?"[117]

Russia's greatest writers did more than risk their lives secretly to overthrow official images of the artist. Writing "for the drawer," they invoked a world more sacred than that of the performance, with rival immortals and a rival time. In "Requiem," Akhmatova compared herself to wives of mutineers against the tsars—"Under the Kremlin's towers I shall howl"—and called on Christ and the Christian time of the crucifixion: "The heavens were on fire, and he / Said, "Why have You forsaken me, oh Father?"[118] Pasternak appropriated Christian imagery in *Doctor Zhivago* and reshaped the official metaphor of the path to lead not to communism but to the last judgment. The final line of the novel, in the poem "Garden of Gethseman," reads: "So shall the centuries drift, trailing like a caravan, / Coming for judgment, out of the dark, to me."[119] In *The Master and Margarita* Bulgakov created his own sacred time and his own immortals—not Lenin and Stalin but the devil and his suite. Bulgakov's immortals threatened literary bureaucrats and hacks rather than "enemies of the people." His "great ancestors" were not the tsarist general, Suvorov, and the official Pushkin but Christ, Kant, Dostoevsky, and their like. Bulgakov, Akhmatova, Mandelstam, and other writers engaged in a subversive though largely solitary and secret counterperformance in which they venerated the artist, the creative act, and a personal and intimate dimension of life. The subversive tradition paradoxically drew sustained power from the performative culture that opposed and repressed it, and it remained extraordinary until the official culture became moribund.

Six

Honor and Dishonor

EVERY society sets boundaries to identify insiders and outsiders. The genesis of a new society in 1917, and the presumption of its newness, required strict definitions of who did and did not belong. The early Bolsheviks drew boundaries according to a Marxist cartography. Stalin and his supporters first reinforced these lines of division and then largely replaced them with ascription of honor and dishonor as a means of demarcation. The honor they deployed was social honor, the honor bestowed by Stalin and the state on those who fulfilled official expectations by their achievements.[1] This kind of social honor differed from personal self-referential honor or individual pride. Honor defined in this way rewarded merit in the performance and demonstrated the state's arbitrary power to raise up some individuals and cast down others.

Honor has a long history in Russia, as personal honor, "honors" dispensed by the state and ruler, and corporate honor—codes of honor among the upper classes, the intelligentsia, the professions, and the military.[2] The key words are *chest',* which was linked with personal honor as in "debt of honor," and *pochet,* as in "honorary title."[3] Both terms were used in the 1930s in lieu of personal and professional honor. The performative culture had no room, however, for the type of honor that upper-class men defended by dueling in nineteenth- and early-twentieth-century Europe, including Russia. Social honor in the Soviet system was explicitly egalitarian and gender-neutral, despite its inherent biases. Its value was derived from party membership and state employment even in the mixed economy and relaxed atmosphere of the NEP, when money and professional reputation regained some independent legitimacy. After the promulgation of the First Five-Year Plan and collectivization, money and professional standing again declined in value. Privilege and position became more completely the true coin of the realm, and the urge to acquire social honor inspired some of the vigor of the performance.

The government conferred honor in the form of orders, ranks, and commendations, and the press displayed it.[4] The most prestigious state honors were the Order of the Red Banner of Labor, which was established in the Russian Republic in 1920 and made an all-union order in 1928, the Order of Lenin (1930), the Order of the Red Star (1930), and the Badge of Honor (1936).[5] Ranks and titles in the arts appeared in the late 1920s and early 1930s, and in 1939 the Stalin literary prizes were established and sometimes awarded by Stalin himself.[6] Military ranks reappeared in 1935, and formal titles surfaced in other fields as well. The press published lists of prizewinners, for example, a list of builders of the Moscow Metro in mid-1935, including Khrushchev as first secretary of the city Central Committee. "These are the best fighters and commanders of the glorious army of metro builders," *Pravda* editorialized.[7] By the late 1930s rosters of more than a thousand were common.[8] "Practically every reception or festival culminated in the mass awarding of orders of the USSR to leading workers or veterans," wrote the Russian historian Roy Medvedev in his study of Bukharin's last years.[9]

Stalin's American biographer, Robert C. Tucker, referred to these notables as a "service nobility" similar to the elite members of Peter the Great's table of ranks.[10] Yet there was a difference. Peter's table specified honor and order of precedence for a tiny minority. Stalin used honor and awards more generally to divide society into the worthy and unworthy. He wrote angrily to Molotov in 1930 to contrast those who "labor honorably" with the "irresponsible and transient" who "enjoy the same privileges of vacations, sanatoriums, insurance, and so on."[11] *Pravda* noted the honor acquired by those who fulfilled official obligations, such as "honorable Soviet doctors," "honorable Soviet specialists," and "honorable collective farmers."[12]

Social honor conferred by the state replaced professional honor previously bestowed in part by peers. Honor in this regard resembled the ancient Roman *fama,* a mark of good repute, earned by citizens who conducted themselves properly.[13] When a highly praised shock worker exclaimed in *Pravda* in early 1935, "I did not dare to dream of such honor," she expressed her pride at inclusion in this system of externally conferred esteem.[14] The honorable as a group during the 1930s were sometimes designated partly or wholly as "non-Party Bolsheviks," "outstanding people," or simply "trusted people." Nadezhda Mandelstam recalled that in the mid-1930s, "everybody holding a good job was referred to in this way [non-Party Bolsheviks] and behaved accordingly."[15] "We will choose Party and non-Party Bolsheviks capable of raising high the banner of the Party of Lenin-Stalin," read *Pravda*'s comment on elections to the Soviets in late 1939.[16] In his 1939 painting, *Outstanding People of the Country of Soviets,* V. P. Efanov shows Stalin and honored citizens backed by a mural of more honored citizens under blue sky piled with cumulus clouds.[17] There are red flags, statues of Lenin, children, flowers. Stalin is flanked by a white-bearded Central Asian and a young Russian couple. The line between people in the mural and the foreground blurs, as if the painter wished to show that imagined heroes were becoming real.

Soviet society obliged honorable citizens to contribute to the best of their ability because, according to the moral economy of the gift, they were indebted to the state for everything they had. "We will repay the coal debt to the country," was the legend on G. Klutsis's famous poster from 1930 of marching coal miners.[18] Thus the linkage of honor, gifts from the state, and debt to society placed Stalin's builders of communism in a capitalistic predicament. Like the

Micawbers of Charles Dickens's creation, they were bound to labor to discharge debts from which they could never be free. The system that indentured them included a set of values so compelling that even some who were cast out remained under its spell. When the Leningrad poetess Olga Berggolts was arrested in September 1939 she wrote in her journal, "I am with you now, my own comrades! I sob for you, I believe in you, and I yearn for your freedom and for the restoration of your honor."[19]

After the Sixteenth Party Congress in June–July 1930, at which Bukharin and other defenders of the NEP lost power, Stalin appeared the unchallenged leader of the country, the initiator of the plan and collectivization, and the purger of aliens. The editors of *The Peasant Newspaper,* whose circulation approached three million, superimposed Stalin's picture on that of a tractor on the front page during the congress (Figure 6.1). The caption read, "Report to the Sixteenth Congress of the All-Union Communist Party (of Bolsheviks), the Fundamental Turn of the Village toward Socialism Has Been Achieved. Long Live the Central Committee of the Bolshevik Party and Its General Secretary Comrade Stalin." Several months earlier, on February 25, Deni pictured Stalin on *Pravda*'s front page, puffing a wrecker, a nepman, and a kulak from his pipe in a swirl of cleansing smoke (Figure 6.2). The editors would hardly have printed the picture had he not wished to take personal responsibility for the persecutions in progress.

The secret police protected honor and apprehended dishonor, though they themselves sometimes suffered as a result. Stalin's first chief of the OGPU, V. R. Menzhinskii, "died in 1934 and was replaced by Genrich G. Yagoda, an old Bolshevik, who had served in Dzerzhinskii's Cheka. The OGPU was abolished the same year, and the NKVD (Ministry of Internal Affairs) acquired its functions. Yagoda was removed in 1936, arrested in 1937, and shot in 1938. His replacement, Nikolai Ezhov, a political commissar during the civil war, served during the great show trials and oversaw the murder of many of Yagoda's assistants. He in turn was arrested in 1939 and shot in 1940. His successor, Lavrentii Beria, who had begun police work in his native Georgia, was executed after Stalin's death.

The press used two sets of linked metaphors to facilitate the stigmatization of social aliens. The first depended on a metaphor of social hygiene mandating the purification of society through the expulsion of misfits, who were represented, as in Lenin's time, as rodents, vermin, and insects.[20] In the Stalinist construction, the vermin were "wreckers" and obstacles on "the path" to communism, in contrast to honorable builders. A second metaphoric system, which overlay the first and owed less to early Bolshevism, flourished during the show trials of 1936–38. In this system society split in a Manichean fashion into heroes and villains, lightness and darkness, Christ and Judas. At the end of the 1930s the USSR invaded and annexed the Baltic countries and parts of Poland, Romania, and Finland, and the press haphazardly applied both metaphoric systems to inhabitants of the newly absorbed territories.

Figure 6.1. *The Peasant Newspaper,* June 27, 1930. "Report to the Sixteenth Congress of the All-Union Communist Party (of Bolsheviks), The Village's Fundamental Turn toward Socialism Is Guaranteed. Long Life to the Central Committee of the Bolshevik Party and Its General Secretary, Comrade Stalin."

Figure 6.2. *Pravda*, February 25, 1930. "Stalin's Pipe." In Deni's illustration, Stalin is expelling "a wrecker, a nepman, and a kulak" through his pipe. Instead of the common word *nepman*, the demeaning variant *nepach* is used.

The stigmas the press conveyed with these metaphoric systems—class, treason, and Jewishness—had a deadly finality. Although Gorky and others found redemptive qualities in the forced labor used to build the White Sea–Baltic Canal, there was an immutability to the regime's accusations. Nothing showed this more than the identification of enemies as Jews. Anti-Semitism flared on both sides during the civil war and later during Stalin's struggle with Trotsky (Bronstein), Kamenev (Rosenfeld), and Zinoviev (Apfelbaum), all Jews.[21] A joke recorded in October 1926 typifies the undercurrent of Stalin's struggle. "How is Stalin like Moses? Moses got the Jews out of Egypt and Stalin got them out of the Politburo."[22] This was part of Stalin's message when he contrasted his "faith in the Russian proletariat" and the ability to achieve "socialism in one country," with Trotsky's emphasis on Russia's backwardness and the need for Western revolutions.[23] Official anti-Semitism briefly waned during the antifascist campaigns of the early and mid-1930s but reappeared with the show trials and the pact with Hitler.[24] Thereafter it remained present and had a particularly malignant power when combined with the Stalinist penchant for dividing society into insiders and outsiders, the honorable and dishonorable. During purge trials, leaders and journalists employed images of contamination and blood that owed much to the historic fear of Jews.

The Hygienic Impulse

Metaphors of social hygiene appeared in the press during collectivization and the First Five-Year Plan. Kulaks, engineers educated under the old regime, nepmen, that is, those who profited from the mixed economy of the NEP by buying and selling scarce goods, and many others were in the wrong place at the wrong historical moment. Independent farmers did not belong in the new order, nor did private merchants or autonomous professionals. Since these outsiders had no place in the future, society could safely cleanse itself and strengthen unity by casting them out. In a 1931 poster, captioned "We Will Purge the Soviet Apparatus of Elements Alien to the Proletariat," a worker and a peasant pluck class enemies like rodents or bugs from log buildings of a rural Soviet cooperative.[25] The people so stigmatized were not guilty of acts against society; they simply did not belong. As Mary Douglas wrote of Jews in medieval England, "Their real offence is always to have been outside the formal structure of Christendom."[26] Soviet social aliens were not dishonored, since they never had enjoyed official esteem. Nor had they received "gifts" of the state. Yet they were devalued according to the moral economy of honor because they were cut off from the chief public system of valuation. They did not belong in the Soviet city of God.

When the state took on the job of remaking the economy, it assumed an obligation in the minds of leaders and activists to remake and purify society. The vulnerability that newly arrived insiders felt about their positions and about the entire Stalinist project was expressed in a fear and hatred of those who did not fit the "new life" or who challenged its image. The activists' desire for state intervention against those they perceived as nonbelievers or rivals is palpable in their appeals and complaints in the press. A Siberian commentator in late 1928 described a social order vulnerable even to accidental destruction by outsiders:

> Tobolsk Okrug stretches far and wide. Work here is difficult. We are only a handful of proletarians. The multinational peasant sea surrounds us. The center is far away. The party organization is weak. Experienced workers are few. The situation is ripe for any perversion or outrage.[27]

This image of the lone activist looking to "the center" and worrying about "perversion" and "outrage" is a telling one. The non-Party majority was perceived to have power to pervert the social and political order simply by its existence. The press's images of enemies accorded with these fears and with the vulnerability expressed by local correspondents. Following the introduction in February 1933 of internal passports, the local paper of the new industrial city of Magnitogorsk advocated cleansing the city of parasites. "The class enemy is stretching out its hand to snatch a passport!" the newspaper declared. "We must strike that hand."[28] Under the Soviet system, which was much more restrictive than the tsarist, peasants were denied an internal passport and were therefore bound to their collective farms; former capitalists and other "disenfranchised" citizens were likewise excluded and hindered in their movements.[29]

The heightened violence against stigmatized groups that began to rock the country in 1928 required government instigation and authorization. Stalin had sought to exclude capitalist "elements" as early as the war scare of 1927. "Our country is confidently and rapidly proceeding toward socialism, pushing capitalist elements into the background and gradually ousting them from the national economy," he remarked at the Fifteenth Party Congress in December of that year.[30] Seven months later he theorized that as the country moved to socialism, class struggle would sharpen. "It never has been and never will be the case," he explained, "that a dying class surrenders its positions voluntarily without attempting to organize resistance."[31] In late 1929 he launched the policy of "eliminating kulaks as a class" in a piece in *Pravda* on agrarian policy, and the press took up the cry.[32] "We Are Liquidating Kulaks as a Class," was the headline in *The Peasant Newspaper* on January 27, 1930.

Pravda mentioned enemies in roughly half its editorials on domestic subjects each year from 1928 through 1932, except in 1930, when they appeared in nearly three-quarters of the editorials. This represented a substantial increase over such references during the NEP.[33] The editors of *Pravda, Izvestiia, Labor,* and the more lively *Komsomol Pravda* included enemies in 20 percent of their front-page illustrations on holidays.[34] *The Peasant Newspaper,* however, devoted more attention to natural pests, such as insects and drought, than to kulaks and other human enemies. Denunciatory articles appeared but negative images comprised only a fraction of the visual material, with the exception of the trials of "enemies of the people," which were covered prominently.

Fear of encouraging sympathy for the millions of victims may explain the lack of visual material on enemies, particularly kulaks. In August 1930 Glavlit prohibited publication of "drawings and photographs illustrating the actual process of dekulakization (for example, a kulak with children leaving a home that had been seized or kulaks leaving a village in a convoy, and so forth)."[35] It encouraged editors to print "all drawings and photographs showing the collective farms' use of the kulaks' homes and means of production in the building of collective farms (for example, the former home of a kulak in which a school has opened or the former inventory of a kulak now being used by collective farmers, and so forth.)."[36]

There was no such delicacy regarding members of the intelligentsia, who were vilified at the public trials of the late 1920s and early 1930s. The attack on engineers came at the end of 1928, with the "Shakhty affair," the trial of specialists in the Donbas mines accused of sabotage and connivance with the former owners. In early 1929 natural scientists suffered similarly in the purging and restaffing of the Academy of Sciences.[37] These public dramas prefigured the Manichean vision of the later 1930s. The editors of *Pravda* wrote at the outset of the Shakhty trial:

> Reading the conclusion of the indictment, one is involuntarily startled at what enormous obstacles stand in the victorious path of the proletarian dictatorship; what diabolical inventiveness foreign imperialism and its bootlicking agents inside the USSR are capable of in the struggle against the country building socialism![38]

Nevertheless the accused were not credited with doing much harm. The diarist Shitts noted the ludicrousness of the situation in which the accused testified to Soviet accomplishments for which they were partly responsible, while at the same time admitting that progress might have been still greater had they not committed acts of sabotage.[39] At this stage, even alleged enemies were not allowed to undermine the leaders' promises.

Stalin personally blamed wreckers and enemies for problems, and as the disastrous first harvest of collectivization materialized in the fall of 1930, the press began to shift the blame to various enemies.[40] The OGPU prepared a case along these lines against alleged saboteurs in the food industry, who were accused of destroying hundreds of thousands of cattle and large quantities of other food. Stalin instructed Molotov to publicize the arrest and execution of the culprits, and the Politburo specified that the chief newspapers should give the story a page and half.[41] On September 22, 1930, in accord with Stalin's request, *Pravda* featured a three-column lead editorial, "No Mercy for the Conscious Organizers of Difficulties in Food Supply." Pages 3 and 4 were devoted entirely to the alleged plot. *Pravda*'s editorial on September 26, "A Blow for a Blow," following the executions, began thus: "The broad masses welcomed the shooting of wreckers who tried to organize a famine in the country of Soviets with unanimous satisfaction." Several of the accused had Jewish names, and the next day *Pravda* published a front-page cartoon by Deni, showing a wrecker with a hooked nose struck by lightning. It was one of the few frightening illustrations of an enemy of the people to appear, but the public already knew the villains were dead.

The government also employed scapegoating in trials of the "Industrial Party" from November 25 to December 7, 1930, and of Mensheviks in March 1931. During the trial of 1930, the press fanned fears of Polish and French intervention in a fashion reminiscent of 1927. On November 26 the paper printed confessions and charges that these "agents of French imperialism" tried to wreck the economy and, having failed, sought foreign intervention.[42] The editors assured readers throughout, however, that despite sabotage, "we are victoriously overcoming our economic difficulties, moving rapidly forward with socialist building, and daily strengthening the defensive capabilities of the country (November 27, 1930).

In the Menshevik case, the charge was slowing the distribution of goods to cities (March 8, 1931). In *Pravda*, Deni pictured a giant hand holding a small angry Menshevik, with papers titled "Wreck the Five-Year Plan," "Power to the Capitalists and Landowners," and "Intervention" falling from his briefcase (March 4, 1931). Although the indicted were usually represented as too pathetic to cause much harm, scapegoating struck a chord with citizens fed up with corruption and bureaucracy.[43] An anonymous correspondent informed Trotsky's *Bulletin of the Opposition* that workers supported the trial of the "Industrial Party" and even urged harsher sentences than the ten years they received. Trotsky concurred.[44]

Pravda in 1929 divided the population into builders and wreckers. The editors wrote, after the Shakhty case: "Having eliminated the consequences of wrecking, the building of the socialist economy of our country goes on confidently and firmly."[45] Those who used this language virtually ruled out the possibility of specialists who were neither enemies nor enthusiasts. An editorialist noted soon after the sentencing that even "sincere" bourgeois engineers could not understand planning, find a "common language with the broad proletarian masses," or engage in the "Soviet public activity, without which it is impossible consciously to build socialism."[46] Only true Soviet specialists could accomplish these tasks.

The enemies denounced in the 1930s differed from earlier opponents because they had no place in society. Previous enemies could not be fully excluded because there was no cleansed social space from which to expel them. *Pravda* and other central newspapers now constructed this space, and the law of August 7, 1932, "on the safeguarding of the property of state enterprises, collective farms, and cooperatives, and the strengthening of public (socialist) property" confirmed it by declaring all property to be within the official public sphere.[47] *Pravda* greeted the law with an editorial, warning that whoever "infringes" on public property "infringes on the foundations of the Soviet order and should be considered an enemy of the people."[48] The image was graphic. The author celebrated "the factories, enterprises, state farms, collective farms, stores, cooperatives, warehouses, railroads, homes, new housing settlements . . . created with the labor of millions of working people," and cautioned: "The class enemy looks on all this with envious eyes."

Thus the threat extended far beyond the intelligentsia, for amid the public's gratitude for an abundance of material goods and hosannahs about state property, many citizens stole from collective farms, factories, and other state institutions in order to secure a bare minimum of food and clothing. In the first five months after the promulgation of the law on protecting socialist property, fifty-five thousand peasants were convicted and more than two thousand were sentenced to death.[49] Whether the "thieves," who in the countryside were largely women, children, and old people pilfering or gleaning fields, saw themselves as the opponents of the state system, they suffered a double stigma, under the economy of the gift, as ingrates as well as potential public enemies.

Despite the scope of the persecutions, there was no composite stereotype that included kulaks, bourgeois engineers, clergy, rightists, leftists, bureaucrats, nepmen, and old peasant women. Even in the case of kulaks, nothing approximated the Nazi image of the powerful and dangerous Jew. Kulaks appeared short and tall, fat and thin, bearded and clean-shaven, well-dressed and shabby, alone or in groups.[50] Nor was there yet the unwavering fixation on "the enemy" that one might expect of a society in which millions were brutally victimized. The indistinct character of the victims is evident in Deni's drawing of Stalin puffing enemies from his pipe in 1930 (Figure 6.2).

Animal, Tectonic, and Directional Metaphors

The culture of the performance rested on the belief in an ideal order to be created by expunging evil and alien elements from Soviet society.[51] The portrayal of enemies as buffoons reduced the power of the alien element to a level that could be mastered. In the prevailing atmosphere of vulnerability among newly promoted Party members, it was important to diminish opponents' perceived strength. The press had willingly frightened readers with terrifying images of foreign powers during the war scares of 1923, 1927, and 1930, when the actual dangers were minimal. The threat to the symbolic order during and after collectivization and the first plan was potentially less manageable, and a palpable fear comes through in contemporary accounts. The words most commonly used to identify enemies during the 1930s were "vermin" (*vreditel'*), which in political usage meant "wrecker," and "double-dealer" (*dvurushnik*). Both implied stealth and subversion. Enemies were also referred to as "evil spirits" (*nechist'*), literally "the unclean," although the word, with its powerful religious connotations, is also sometimes translated as "scum" or "vermin."[52]

The anonymous author of *Pravda*'s first report on the Shakhty trial in June 1928 asked how wreckers "existed illegally for six years side by side with Soviet power and under the eyes of trade union and Party organizations of the working class."[53] The next day the editors praised the trial:

> It shines a clear light on the secret back rooms and "the underside" of our construction, on the criminal labyrinth of filth, baseness, greed, and bloodthirsty passion, on the labyrinth in which little white-monarchist reptiles have arisen who are spreading fire and poison in the proletarian milieu, infecting the Soviet air with the miasma of treason.[54]

The press situated these images of pollution in the present or recent past, counterpoising them to an increasingly pure society progressing along a linear path to a bright future. The emphasis on "periods"—"the period of laying foundations" and then, in late 1930, "the period of socialism"—served this purpose.[55] Stalin pronounced in 1930: "The kulaks are doomed and will be liquidated. There remains only one path—the path of the collective farm."[56]

The "path" and other directional metaphors reinforced the schema of socialist building and the image of a new order during the first plan. The guiding constructions of the NEP period—the path, the task, and the construction site—were now adapted to an environment in which society was ever more savagely divided against itself. These were supplemented by "the line," as in "the general line" or Party line, and "the front," borrowed from the civil war. The press used new and refurbished metaphors to bolster authoritarian voices in the economy and society; to shift agency from individual citizens to institutions and, ultimately, to Stalin; and to create an imagined historical continuum in which every effort constituted a step toward future goals. These metaphors provided an image of a community of "doers," officials and enthusiasts who were on the path, completing tasks, following the line, and moving forward on "fronts" the press described. A writer and correspondent for a peasant newspaper wrote privately of his experience confiscating the property of "kulaks": "I took not because I had to for myself, my family, or close friends; I took because that was what the Party said, because the Party sent me to take—to take an advance in the name of a future that the person giving me this advance would never live to see."[57]

Metaphors that worked well to uphold the symbolic order also served to expel aliens from it. The "path" and the "line" served to consign all who blocked it to oblivion and gave those on it a sense of collective destiny. The "task" subordinated current measures to a greater goal and reduced the temporal and moral significance of atrocities. The "construction site" suggested that some

Figure 6.3. *Komsomol pravda,* June 26, 1930. Drawing by G. Roze, "On the General Line. The Electric-Express Is Going Full Speed Ahead." The tram is labeled "XVI to Catch and Overtake. All-Union Communist Party of Bolsheviks." The figure on the right says, "For God's sake, don't squash the kulak." The sign on the left reads, "Left Dead End."

people were essential material and others "refuse" to be discarded. Military metaphors served to identify outsiders as enemies, rightfully subject to attack.

The editors of *Komsomol Pravda* welcomed the opening of the Sixteenth Party Congress in June 1930 with a photo of Stalin.[58] There was also an illustration by G. Roze showing a trolley rising over a hilltop, bearing the sign, "XVI to Catch and Overtake," echoing Stalin's slogan (Figure 6.3). "On the General Line," reads the heading, and then in the caption: "The Electric-Express Is Going Full Speed Ahead." People holding a sign that reads "Left: Dead End"

Figure 6.4. *Pravda*, March 8, 1930. Drawing by K. Rotov on International Women's Day. "The Great Alteration." The sign reads, "Collective Farm." Note the cross underfoot.

are knocked out of the way, while to the right, a Bukharinlike figure tries to change the trolley's course. Trotsky screams in the distance. An effete man in a suit and spectacles cries, "For God's sake, don't squash the kulak!!!" Two engineers, labeled "wreckers," try to block the trolley's wheels. A priest and a kulak flee in terror. A clergyman, manipulated by a smiling god, waves a cross and a gun, while Jesus grins in the background and bejeweled capitalist hands hold the ensemble aloft. Most remarkable is the anonymous driver, whose face is shrouded but who wears a cap such as Stalin sometimes wore. Beneath the cab windshield is the abbreviation for the Central Committee and beneath that the abbreviation for the Party. No passengers are visible.

On International Women's Day in 1930 *Pravda* featured a young peasant woman walking a well-marked path to a collective farm, thrusting aside pitiful priests and bourgeois rascals (Figure 6.4).[59] Stepping on a cross on her way to a tractor, she epitomizes the promise that collectivization would bring women prosperity through science and technology. On the anniversary of the revolution in the same year, *Labor* showed an enormous gleaming dirigible marked "USSR," the very image of science for that era, soaring over a crowd of tiny

Figure 6.5. *Labor,* November 7, 1930. "The fourteenth trip. Out with the ballast."

angry foreign capitalists, dumping three ludicrous figures, an engineer, a small snarling kulak, and a timid "double-dealer" (Figure 6.5). The caption reads— "Out with the Ballast."[60]

The Judicial and Manichean Phase

A second phase in the assault on enemies began after the murder of the Leningrad Party chief, S. M. Kirov, on December 1, 1934. The change coincided with the establishment of the performance as a regulator of public expression, and brought with it new ways of defining the boundaries of acceptable and unacceptable behavior. At this point, enemies were credited with doing substantial damage. "The enemy deeply wounded our people," concluded Kalinin.[61] Previous domestic opponents had rarely been granted such power. Promoters of the terror that followed seized on the assassination as proof of danger and a reason to take action against enemies. They also used Kirov's death and the charges leveled at the opposition and others during subsequent trials and persecutions to explain difficulties and failures. Hardly any other mechanism in the political culture served to explain the shortfalls and unfulfilled promises, which were increasingly difficult to ignore.

The economy stagnated in the mid- to late 1930s, and slipshod construction and other errors resulted in terrible accidents in industry and transportation.[62] The government shifted blame to the opposition, or simply "the enemy," for these calamities, as well as for the deaths of prominent people, some of whom, like Kirov and Gorky, were probably killed on Stalin's orders.[63] The oppositionists thus became scapegoats, something kulaks and, to a certain extent, even engineers, were not.[64] As scapegoats, the opposition members at this point underwent not only exclusion but ritual sacrifice within the performance, drawing evil into themselves through confession and subsequently purifying society by sacrificial death.[65] In this respect, their role was to demonstrate the beneficial effect of their own extinction.

After Kirov's murder, cries for vengeance supplemented the rhetoric of social hygiene. *Pravda* printed a statement from the Central Committee in place of its regular editorial on December 2, 1934:

> The Central Committee believes that the memory of Comrade Kirov, the bright example of his fearless, tireless struggle for proletarian revolution, for the building of socialism in the USSR, will inspire millions of proletarians and all working people to struggle further for the triumph of socialism, for the final eradication of all enemies of the working class.[66]

The next day the paper published testimonials to Stalin, and oaths and tributes to Kirov. Editorialists vowed on December 4 that "for every drop of Sergei Mironovich Kirov's blood, enemies will pay dearly."[67] The press's coverage culminated in Molotov's "oath" and warning that "the country will settle with the White Guard scum."[68] Two weeks later *Pravda* reported charges against Zinoviev, Kamenev, and other former "oppositionists," among them many prominent old Bolsheviks. The indictment included self-incriminating statements by several of the defendants.[69] "We stuck to ourselves, poisoned by the venom of our confederates' counterrevolutionary views and convictions," the old Bolshevik G. E. Evdokimov affirmed. "The Party is completely right on the question of the political responsibility of the former anti-Party Zinoviev groups for carrying out the murder," confessed Zinoviev. The reference to poison was consistent with the rhetoric of social hygiene and further showed the progression from mere exclusion of enemies to death.

The crimes of the political opposition entailed dishonor through betrayal, and thus exceeded those of the earlier outsiders: kulaks, engineers, and others. The display of dishonor was a distinctive feature of persecution during the purges. The press devalued enemies as human beings through verbal abuse and by the coerced and concocted confessions. The ritual of humiliation, public shaming, and dishonor became a regular feature of the performance. In late 1934 and early 1935 "workers" and "peasants" condemned the accused as "predatory beast[s]," "reptiles," "base traitors and deserters," "scoundrels," and "refuse."[70] "We demand that the murderers be shot; shame and curses on them."[71] The accused "have lost the appearance of human beings," *Pravda* concluded (December 24, 1934). "Thrice contemptible!" was the paper's epithet, echoing Christian rituals of excommunication (December 22, 1934). The press had begun to deploy a metaphoric system characterized by scapegoating, Manicheanism, and anti-Semitism.

The sins of Stalin's opponents multiplied during the three great trials—that of Zinoviev, Kamenev, and others in August 1936; of seventeen principals including Piatakov, Radek, and Sokolnikov in January 1937; and, finally, of Bukharin, Rykov, Rakovskii, and their associates in March 1938. In 1934 Zinoviev, Kamenev, and others had been accused of spreading poisonous ideas that encouraged a murderer. In 1936 they were charged as scapegoats for organizing Kirov's murder; declared fascist agents seeking to kill Stalin, Voroshilov, Zhdanov, and other Soviet leaders; and accused of encouraging a war against the Soviet Union. The headline read: "YESTERDAY THE TRIAL OF THE TROTSKYITE-ZINOVIEV GANG OF KILLERS BEGAN." The article concluded with a call to action: "Squash the vermin! Shoot the members of the Trotskyite-Zinoviev gang!" (August 20, 1936). In testimony that followed, the accused confessed to these crimes and more.

In the second trial, Radek, Piatakov, and others were charged, along with Trotsky, with causing disasters, planning to dismember the country, and plotting to restore capitalism. A year later Bukharin, Rykov, Krestinskii—each of whom had sat on Lenin's Politburo—were accused of crimes, along with Christian Rakovskii, a leading Soviet diplomat, and Yagoda, Ezhov's predecessor as head of the secret police. The charges included murdering Soviet personalities, such as Maxim Gorky, Gorky's son (Maxim Peshkov), Valerian Kuibyshev (an early Stalin supporter and leader of Gosplan), Menzhinskii (Yagoda's predecessor as chief of the secret police), and Kirov. *Pravda* editorialized on February 28, 1938, a few days before the trial opened: "These murders were part of a diabolical plan to enslave our country to capitalist predators" (February 25, 1938).

The indictment of three physicians—I. N. Kazakov (Menzhinskii's doctor and alleged poisoner) and L. Levin and Dmitry Pletnev (also accused of a role in murdering Gorky, Gorky's son, and Kuibyshev)—fit earlier allegations that enemies of the people were impairing the nation's health and foreshadowed the Doctors' Plot of 1953.[72] The inclusion of doctors confirmed the inversion of good and evil and the monstrosity of the crimes.

Pravda set the stage for the trial of "the doctor poisoners" with a remarkable report on June 8, 1937, of personal charges against Pletnev.[73] "Professor— Rapist, Sadist" was the caption of an unsigned three-column article published five days before the announcement of the arrest and the execution of Gen. M. N. Tukhachevskii and other military leaders. "Soviet society gives doctors a respect and trust that bourgeois society has never given and can never give," the author began, foreshadowing the monstrosity of the alleged crime. The author denounced Pletnev for attacking and biting the breast of a patient several years earlier and included the patient's letter cursing him for disfiguring her. He avowed that although such things could occur in bourgeois societies, "this cannot happen in our country." Charges of blood lust, bestiality, and dishonor reinforced the officially promoted persecution mania. Since blood accusations had long been leveled at Jews, the undercurrent carried a charge of anti-Semitism, even though, of the accused doctors, only Levin bore a Jewish name.[74]

Shaming also figured in the vilification of military leaders. "For Spying and Treason to the Homeland—Execution by Shooting," was *Pravda*'s leader on June 12, 1937. "Shoot the Spies, the Contemptible Servants of Fascism, Traitors to the Homeland," was the headline. "We pronounce the names of the Tukhachevskiis and Iakirs [I. E. Iakir, also a leading general] with disgust and loathing," wrote soldiers and officers in a letter in *Pravda* to Marshal K. E. Voroshilov, People's Commissar of Military and Naval Affairs.[75]

There was more here than a cry for vengeance. This frenzied phase of the persecutions was driven by a dichotomous vision of good and evil, and by the promise that a final battle between the two would yield a perfect, cleansed society. This aspect of the performance resembles what one historian has recently identified as Hitler's "redemptive anti-Semitism," according to which he promised that merciless persecution would free the world from evil.[76] The Soviet presentation of parallel legends of good and evil culminated in the serialization in *Pravda* of the *Short Course*. "*The Short Course of the History of the All-Union Communist Party* shows the treasonous path of the capitulators and opportunists—Zinoviev, Kamenev, Rykov, Bukharin, Trotsky, Piatakov," wrote its anonymous authors in a passage serialized in *Pravda* in September 1938, after the trial of Bukharin, Rykov, and others had concluded.[77]

In covering the great purge trials, the press again employed the metaphors of social hygiene. The demand to cleanse society was embellished with the danger of contamination and with repeated allusions to poisoning and blood. "They, the Trotskyites, needed the people's blood, a sea of which they wanted to spill in order to force their way to power with the bayonets of foreign fascists," wrote *Pravda*'s editors in January 1937.[78] "Get the bad apple out of the barrel," a "worker" was cited in *Pravda* as saying.[79] "We will finally and mercilessly sweep the Trotskyite fascist filth from the beautiful soil of our beautiful homeland," the paper concluded when death sentences were announced in the 1936 trial.[80] In the context of the performance, such cleansing insured the future of society. As *Pravda* editorialized when the sentence on Piatakov and Radek was announced in January 1937: "The true means to provide for the growth and strength of the USSR, to secure full victory, to guard our socialist national economy and our leaders, workers, Red Army soldiers, and children from bites of hidden Trotskyite fascist insects was to pull these insects' stingers!"[81]

The press multiplied Stalin's enemies as it enlarged his glory. During the first weeks after Kirov's murder, *Pravda* and other newspapers were crowded with photographs of the deceased and testimonials to his heroic role in the civil war, beginning with celebrations of the fifteenth anniversary of the Red Army's victory over A. I. Denikin in Ukraine.[82] By 1937 the contrast between good and evil was fully developed, and the forces were personified in the supreme hero and the supreme enemy. Trotsky was assigned the role of Judas, and Stalin, by implication, that of Christ and God combined. *Pravda*'s editors employed this contrast during the second purge trial in January 1937, and it suited the anti-Semitic undertone of the campaign against Trotsky in particular and the trial in general.

> **Judas**—this synonym for the blackest treachery was struck as if branded on the forehead of Trotsky by Lenin more than a quarter century ago.
> The mark of Judas from that time was boldly and clearly stamped on all the deeds of Trotsky and his followers.[83]

The creation of this monstrous double within the performative culture provided a rich foil for Stalin's aggrandizement within the cult. Khrushchev wrote in *Pravda* of "Judas Trotsky" and the others who were accused that "raising a hand against Comrade Stalin, they have raised it against the very best that humanity possesses, because Stalin is hope, Stalin is aspiration, Stalin is a beacon for all progressive humanity."[84] "There are many Jews in this trial, because the Jewish nation loves power" and "the Jews are responsible for everything, and Trotsky should have been killed long ago" were comments on the trial recorded by Party officials.[85]

Ritualistic denunciations of enemies necessitated a new role for participants in the performance. At the end of the second purge trial, *Pravda* featured a photograph of crowds in Red Square with a banner reading, "Shoot the Rabid Fascist Hounds" (Figure 6.6).[86] The first denunciatory letters from prominent people were published in these years and remained a feature of public life up to the Brezhnev era. In 1936 newspapers printed condemnations by public figures as well as anonymous workers. On the eve of the trial of Zinoviev and

Figure 6.6. *Pravda*, January 31, 1937. "Meeting of Moscow Working People in Red Square, January 30, 1937." The front banner reads, "Shoot the Rabid Fascist Hounds." The editorial is titled "The Country Welcomes the Just Verdict."

Kamenev, in August 1936, *Pravda* published the statement by the president of the Ukrainian Academy of Sciences, that "for the collective of the Academy of Sciences there can only be one answer to the announcement of the Office of the Public Prosecutor about the unmasking of the gang of terrorists—severely punish the enemies."[87] Such comments soon became common. One of the most famous, captioned "Wipe Them from the Face of the Earth!" was signed by the writers Fedin, Leonov, and others, including Pasternak without his consent.[88] "The bullet aimed at Stalin was aimed at our heart. It ought to have passed through millions of hearts, for Stalin is our common property, our glory and our honor," they wrote.

The expression of such sentiments, both tribute to the leader and denunciation of his enemies, was essential to the performance. The redemptive promise that the extermination of enemies would bring about a better world became a key tenet of Soviet ideology, and all the pedagogical force of the performance worked to encourage the pretense and actuality of such conviction among the participants. The syncretic character of Stalinism was reflected in the mixed images of its enemies, who were stigmatized according to class, religion, education, employment, and political beliefs. The absence of a single image of the internal enemy equivalent to the Nazis' image of Jews did not, however, mean that the official stigmatizing was ineffective in arming and mobilizing the perpetrators, and in isolating and dehumanizing their victims.

There was a huge administrative apparatus to promote and carry out the attack on domestic enemies: Without it the persecutions on the scale of the 1930s would have been more difficult. Soviet figures on the size of the camp population indicate 175,000 prisoners in 1930, 334,300 in 1933, 965,700 in 1935, 1,196,000 in 1937, 1,672,000 in 1939, and 1,660,000 in 1940.[89] Estimates of the number of peasants deported as kulaks during collectivization range from four to ten million, and of their deaths from less than a million to nearly five million.[90] Estimates of victims of the officially promoted terror vary.[91] According to official data, nearly four million citizens were charged with counterrevolution from 1921 through 1954, and, of these, 642,980 were shot, 2,369,220 sent to prison or the camps, and 765,180 sent into exile.[92] There may be no way to determine the casualties with exactitude. The Soviet government provided excessive and irrelevant detail for favored statistical indicators but neglected indicators considered unimportant. Officials and local activists who either sought a "hygienic" solution or believed the Manichean rhetoric may have acted impulsively without calculating. Since victims were valued to a degree for their labor, perpetrators probably had little incentive to record accurately executions carried out on the spot, and they also might have understated the number of deportees in transit to avoid blame for excess deaths en route.

How much did this fixation on enemies derive from Lenin's and Trotsky's notions of class struggle and how much from Stalin's influence and subsequent tensions of Soviet life more generally? Lenin confidently labeled and punished people according to their social origins. Stalin and his colleagues took the process further and tried to eliminate outcasts altogether. Yet the linguistic tools for exclusion existed from the first days of Soviet culture. The early Bolsheviks had formulated a rhetoric of social hygiene, and their successors used that rhetoric against all opposition, including that of the old Bolsheviks themselves.

The linguistic constructions of insiders and outsiders were probably more meaningful to participants than to nonparticipants, but even those who ignored the press's account of Soviet life lived amid the performance and may have borrowed its images despite themselves. The diarist Andrei Stepanovich Arzhilovskii, an energetic peasant and religious believer arrested several times, reversed the official image of the path as a train when he wrote despondently in early 1938, just before his final arrest: "Life is a speeding train. The ones who have a ticket ride, the others stand and watch them pass by. I used to have a ticket, and I was speeding through life on that train."[93]

The critical public of the 1920s shrank in the early 1930s, but Stalin and his journalists maintained a one-sided dialogue with imagined critics. Stalin, in his *Political Report to the Sixteenth Party Congress* of June 1930, chided comrades who were "skeptical about the slogan 'The Five-Year Plan in Four Years.'"[94] A year later he protested that "only those who are rotten to the core can content themselves with references to the past."[95] Journalists used the same tone when addressing resisting readers. Editorialists complained of "all sorts of conversations" and "arrogant conversations" in 1930 and 1932.[96] "Right opportunists, proponents of a right 'left' bloc do not understand or do not want to understand the specific difficulties of this year's fall cycle of [field]work," wrote one editorialist in 1930.[97] The managers of the press also imagined a hostile oral culture that included kulaks. An editorialist suggested in 1929 that kulaks had changed their "slogan" from "Don't Join the Collective Farm" to "Join the Collective Farm without [Bringing] the Means of Production."[98] By the mid-1930s the press largely disregarded such hostile readers and their presumed demand for explanations about either foreign or domestic affairs.

The antithesis of dishonorable outcasts and enemies was the honorable community of participants. Lenin had identified the fate of the revolution with loyalists whom he often incorporated in the pronoun *we,* and during the decade after his death the press had used the phrase "active Soviet public" to portray the enthusiasts who followed his inspiration.[99] After Stalin gained control the words signified those obligated to act for the state, as in A. I. Mikoyan's demand in 1928—"all forces of the active Soviet public should help work with savings banks."[100] By 1931 the press specified the tasks to which "the whole active public ought to turn its attention."[101] But the phrase lost much of its meaning and faded from view as actors in the performance became the public.[102]

During collectivization and the First Five-Year Plan, in place of "the active Soviet public," the press increasingly used *we* to represent honored supercitizens. During 1929 *we* appeared in 84 percent of *Pravda*'s editorials, roughly a third more than during the NEP.[103] Only the brutal year of 1918 during the civil war approached this figure. Journalists used *we* from 1928 through 1932 to group readers who now became a "link" in a chain of command.[104] "We ought to drive all alien elements from the procurement apparatus," the paper editorialized in early 1929. "We ought to remember Comrade Lenin's caution that we should not become dizzy with success on reaching great heights," a columnist explained later that year, six months before Stalin used the same expression to disavow problems of collectivization.[105] "It is simply utopian to think that we can peacefully build socialism under a proletarian dictatorship without affecting the class interests of capitalist elements, of the kulak," another wrote in early 1929, condoning the assault on prosperous peasants.[106]

Journalists deployed *we* and *us* with menacing authority. Mikhail Koltsov wrote in 1930 of a shortfall of paper—"Comrade papermakers. You have stolen fifty boxcars of paper from the cultural front! You have to answer to us for it."[107] Anonymous authors in *Pravda*'s inner pages were peremptory. "We ought to drive all alien elements from official organizations," wrote the author of an article about collective farms in 1929.[108] Even local journalists could be intimidating.[109] "We hope these promises of workers at the Red Star [Factory] will be fulfilled in a Bolshevik fashion," threatened one.[110] The earlier distinction between the guiding avant-garde and the general public gave way to a unity of performers. The givers of orders and those responsible for fulfilling them were bound together in the inclusive *we*.

Editors used the constitution to demonstrate the fusion of state and society. On the eve of its approval, *Izvestiia* editorialized, beside a picture of a pipe-smoking Stalin: "What is good for the state is good for each working person."[111] Trotsky and his followers, in *The Bulletin of the Opposition* in Paris, questioned the power relations implied by the official *we*. They seized on Stalin's statement explaining the role of the secret ballot in the new constitution—"And therefore we wish to give Soviet people full freedom to vote their choice"—and asked rhetorically: "Who is this *we* who can give or not give the freedom to vote?" Their answer was "that stratum in the name of whom Stalin speaks and acts: the bureaucracy."[112] The opposition, of course, spoke from outside the performance and were not heard within it.

The pronoun *we* acquired a new resonance after "the Great Break," and editors and columnists often reserved it for pontifical statements.[113] "We cross the threshold of the new year as masters of a new life," *Pravda* noted on New Year's Day, 1933.[114] In such cases the referent was the nation of participants, with Stalin as "first citizen."[115] Koltsov defined *we* in 1934 in a series of statements that began, "We—it is the rural correspondent and Komsomol member Petia," and ended, "We—it is the great Stalin, the constructor and engineer of the non-class socialist society, the leader of the Leninist party, the bold and solicitous educator of the peoples of our country, teaching us to go further and further ahead."[116]

Izvestiia editorialized in 1936 on the day following the approval of the constitution: "We have taken human history to the highest level of its development. . . . With what triumph and pride sounds the title 'citizen of the Country of Soviets.'"[117] This usage of *we* encompassed a new patriotism. *Pravda* editorialized in early 1937, amid the terrible purges: "Yes, we are patriots of our great country; to us, Soviet workers, peasants, and intelligentsia, belong the richest mineral wealth, the rivers and seas, mountains and plains."[118]

The power of this usage was evident to participants. Critic and children's writer Kornei Chukovskii cited it in his diary in 1934, soon after the writers' congress adopted socialist realism. Noting problems with censorship, he explained *Pravda*'s acceptance of his article on the nineteenth-century realist painter Ilia Repin, a member of the Wanderers, who was soon to be lauded as a precursor of socialist realism. "In my opinion I wrote about Repin from the least interesting point of view—an uninteresting one—but *necessary* for Repin's glory in the USSR—the theme is "Repin is ours!"[119] Two years later, in early 1936, he employed the device in a sketch in *Pravda* about a child's trip to the zoo.[120]

> "Whose elephant is that?" [asks the boy.]
>
> "The state's," she [the mother] answered.
>
> "That means it is partly mine," he announced with great satisfaction.
>
> This phrase delighted me. Can one express more exactly and more distinctly the sense of socialist property that has become characteristic of millions of children in the USSR in recent years?
>
> I have not (until now) noted that many older children express joy at the possession of state property. For example, a boy stands at a map during a geography lesson and, pointing a finger at the Soviet tundra, says in a proprietary voice: "Peat, we have so much there, and we have dug up so much."[121]

With Repin, the elephant, and the peat, Chukovskii confirmed the communal property rights of the community of performers. This was the thrust of the Pushkin centennial, when *Pravda* editorialized "Pushkin is ours," as it had been two years earlier when the paper hailed Williams as "our Williams."[122] *Izvestiia* captioned its editorial on Stalin's sixtieth birthday in 1939 simply "Our Stalin."[123] For those outside the performance, the intimidating exclusiveness of the pronoun was only too clear. "The word *ours* was for me first a political term—I was raised in a home where grown-ups cursed *ours*," recalled a memoirist who grew up during the famine in Ukraine.[124] Some workers and peasants likewise opposed equating rulers with common people. As a wag put it during the 1937 elections to the Supreme Soviet, "Whoever was in power will be again; we won't get in."[125] Others, however, loyally contrasted wreckers and builders. "They wreck, and we restore with our backs," complained a collective farmer in the late 1930s.

The press used selected foreigners to universalize Soviet values and show the Soviet order's ubiquitous appeal.[126] *Pravda* honored the French novelist, pacifist, and humanitarian Romain Rolland in a front-page editorial on his seventi-

eth birthday in 1936 as "a generally recognized participant in the great proletarian cause," although he was not a Communist.[127] He wrote "To My Soviet
Friends" in the same issue: "When visiting you in the past year, what struck me
most were the letters with greetings I received from all corners of the USSR,
the heartfelt cry: 'Comrade Romain Rolland, how truly happy you must be
among us, where you see all the dreams of your life fulfilled.' It is true, Comrades. I am happy." *Pravda*'s editors coupled his letter with this salutation from
the writers' union: "As an ardent, wise, and truly great writer, your name is pas-
sionately and loudly repeated in our country, which, under Stalin's leadership,
achieves the regime of human happiness of which you always dreamed and to
which you always appealed as a true engineer of human souls."[128] A year earlier, when covering the International Congress of Writers in Defense of Culture
held in Paris, *Pravda* published front-page pictures of Rolland with Stalin and
also with Gorky.[129]

Rolland, like other foreign sympathizers, was blinded by enthusiasm for a
world that seemed to flourish while the West suffered the Great Depression. He
wrote to a skeptical friend in 1931, while "dekulakization" raged, "There is certainly nothing idyllic about it," but then he added, "It is the only country in the
world at this moment where thousands of men and women—the youth—joyfully sacrifice themselves to build, at the very least, the foundations of a better
world."[130] Later, like many other foreign advocates, he concealed misgivings
and denied publicly and in correspondence with critics what he suspected to be
true about Stalin's rule.[131] Stephen Spender, similarly charmed by his role as
Soviet advocate, later wrote, "I allowed myself to be forced into the position of
feeling guilty not only about my own indecisions but about the very virtues of
love and pity and a passion for individual freedom which had brought me close
to communism."[132] Andre Gide, who soon became disillusioned with the Soviet experiment, wrote equivocally in the mid-1930s, "It too often happens that
the friends of the Soviet Union refuse to see the bad side or, at any rate, refuse
to admit the bad side; so that too often what is true about the USSR is said with
enmity, and what is false with love."[133]

The effect of foreigners' self-censorship was to broadcast Soviet performative culture abroad. Soviet sympathizers shaped international culture in the
1930s and in the half-century that followed, not only for themselves but also
for critics and skeptics who honed their ideas and opinions against what they
considered falsehoods. Among the most difficult feats of self-deception for both
foreign and domestic intellectuals was the denial of the persecution of political
figures and colleagues who had once befriended them. Equally appalling was
their denial of the Soviet treatment of ordinary people, which contradicted the
most basic tenets of their public faith. Lending their names to this deception,
foreign sympathizers enlarged the performative culture, which, despite its
crudeness, became the public lens through which official Russia saw itself and
presented itself to the outside world.

Foreign Affairs and Foreign Enemies

As radical right-wing movements advanced, Soviet journalists showcased domestic achievements. Although *Pravda* had devoted nearly two-thirds of its editorials to foreign affairs from 1924 through 1927, the percentage dropped to
one-third in 1928 and 1929, to less than one-fifth from 1930 through 1933, and
then to almost zero for the rest of the 1930s.[134] During 1939 and 1940 foreign
affairs were usually consigned to the fifth or sixth page of a six-page issue. In
1940 and early 1941 *Pravda* devoted hardly a single editorial to foreign affairs.
The editors' disregard for the outside world was not surprising since the Bolsheviks had systematically reduced the presence of educated elites in all fields.
Lenin's government attacked class enemies and political opponents, and Stalin
enlarged the target with campaigns against bourgeois specialists, opponents in
the party, and all those with ties abroad. Higher education was always scarce in
Russia, and although 80 percent of the population was literate in 1939, only 9
percent had attained secondary schooling and only .7 percent a higher education, including technical education.[135]

The composition of the government reflected these policies. From December 1934 until February 1941 not a single full member of the Politburo had a
higher education.[136] Perhaps as a result, when several officials were given *Mein
Kampf* to read in the mid-1930s, none completed it.[137] Khrushchev, who received a copy, recalled, "In his book *Mein Kampf*—which disgusted me so
much that I could never finish it—Hitler spelled out the aggressive designs he
had on the world and the misanthropic philosophy that motivated him."[138]

In accord with its inward turn, the press refocused reports about foreign
workers and peasants away from their own goals and toward their admiration
for the USSR. "In China, in Spain, in Austria, in the underground in fascist Germany, throughout the whole world, millions of working people are drawn with
love and hope to the flag of the Soviets," wrote *Pravda*'s editorialist on the anniversary of the revolution in 1934. "The world's eye has moved East, toward
the Soviet Union, toward Moscow."[139] According to this official conceit, foreign working people thought more of the Soviet Union and its defense than
about bettering their own lives. On International Women's Day in 1933 *Pravda*
devoted page 2 to oppressed foreign women.[140] A young Hungarian woman
wrote of appallingly long work days and no opportunity to study, ending, "I
cannot even believe . . . that there is a country where women are given the possibility to study and develop. Above all, I envy your opportunity to rest in a
human fashion and also to study." In this lens, antifascism was simply another
way to admire the Soviet Union, as in *Pravda*'s statement on the promulgation
of the Stalin Constitution, on December 6, 1936: "The oppressed of all the
world look on us with rapture and love."[141]

When Soviet journalists covered Europe, they often stressed the bad life
abroad rather than antifascism. The depression suited this approach, and the

united front against fascism in the mid-1930s did not wholly undermine it. Viewed simply as a display of the bad life, the capitalist world acquired a deceptive sameness. An antifascist poster from 1935 showed a worker's fist smashing fascist columns labeled, respectively, Finland, Romania, England, Poland, Germany, Italy, and America.[142] The captions read, "The Imperialists Prepare Fascist Bands for Intervention against the USSR" and "We Will Bring Millions of Working People to the Defense of the Homeland of the World Proletariat." Marshal Voroshilov, people's commissar of defense, told the February–March Plenum of the Central Committee in 1937, "The whole world is against us."[143]

In *Pravda* and *Izvestiia*, Hitler's appointment as chancellor on January 30, 1933, did not merit front-page notice, although each printed a small report in the back pages. Each paper featured the burning of the Reichstag in February 1933 and, more prominently, the so-called Enabling Act in March, giving Hitler dictatorial powers, but news of the First All-Union Conference of Collective-Farm Shock Workers soon crowded out Hitler's revolution. *Pravda* featured no lead editorials on German developments for months, although the paper did report the terror against Communists. Whereas Hitler's rise made the Soviet Union seem a bastion of democracy to some Western intellectuals, the impact on the Soviet self-image was insignificant.[144] Editors had long warned readers of horrors abroad, and therefore, except for the destruction of the German Communist Party, they portrayed Hitler's appointment and repressive policies as unsurprising. "Fascism extended the historical lie of the bourgeoisie to its limit: The glorified bourgeois 'kingdom of reason' became a kingdom of medieval obscurantism and prehistoric barbarism," *Izvestiia*'s editorialist gloated in December 1936, at the height of the Spanish Civil War and on the day of ratification of Stalin's Constitution.[145]

Pravda editor L. Z. Mekhlis secured Stalin's personal permission, also in 1936, to send Koltsov to Spain to cover the Spanish Civil War.[146] Koltsov, who was executed at the end of the great purges after Stalin had marked Spain as a breeding ground for traitors, was a flamboyant and successful reporter.[147] Spain figured briefly on *Pravda* front pages in reports of rallies for the republic, but attention soon flagged.[148] Koltsov vented his fury in his first Spanish report in mid-August 1936, almost as much against anarchists and Trotskyites as against fascists.[149] By the time he discovered the Communist organizer "La Passionaria," coverage of the purge trials precluded interest in all else.[150] Although Spain reappeared in the news, it never regained its prominence. More trials followed, and these, together with the feats of Soviet test pilots and other domestic news, were more than enough to crowd out Spain, despite a flurry of excitement during the defense of Madrid in November 1936.

Ironically, while European and American intellectuals linked communism with antifascism and European Communists advocated a popular front against fascism, *Pravda* and other central newspapers promoted a Soviet identity in

which the country's opposition to Hitler, Mussolini, and Franco was largely irrelevant. The press portrayed a bipolar world, divided into the spheres of home
and abroad, rather than of fascism and antifascism. Soviet leaders may have
learned from fascism and borrowed from it, but the press largely ignored this
parallel assault on liberal democracy. If these violent twentieth-century twins
shared in a self-reflexive relationship, as some historians have argued, the Soviet press suppressed most traces of it.[151] Although the leaders no doubt informed themselves about fascism, the nature of this movement was not an issue
in the press.

As "The Great Patriotic War" approached, editors ignored foreign affairs
more than ever before in Soviet history. They briefly noted the Japanese invasion of China in early July 1937 but soon refocused on test pilots celebrated as
"Stalinist champions."[152] The Munich crisis interrupted this trend in late September 1938, when it briefly overshadowed domestic news, including the serialization of the hallowed *Short Course of the History of the All-Union Communist Party. Pravda* even allotted a full front page to the foreign minister
Maxim Litvinov's speech at the League of Nations promising Soviet aid to
Czechoslovakia and featured an editorial warning the British and French that
by negotiating with aggressors they were "playing with fire" (September 21,
1938). Yet after Munich, foreign affairs again slipped from the news.

The press reported the Nazi-Soviet Pact tersely on August 23, 1939. *Pravda*
had hardly commented on the initial trade agreement, which the editors cited
in a brief editorial as simply "natural" (August 21, 1939). At the time the Party
paper printed no pictures and gave scant attention to any advantages of the pact.
Although *Pravda* welcomed the nonaggression pact with a picture of Stalin and
Molotov smiling at German Foreign Minister Joachim von Ribbentrop and Dr.
Friedrich Gaus, the chief of the German Foreign Office's legal department, the
accompanying editorial was also restrained. The next day the editors turned
their attention to the production of vegetables (August 24 and 25, 1939). In contrast to *Pravda*'s report, Goebbels's *Der Angriff* (Attack) clamored: "The world
is faced with the towering fact." William Shirer sardonically recalled the Nazi
press's display as "wonderful to behold."[153]

The Soviet press covered the Nazi invasion of Poland, an event foreseen in
the secret Nazi-Soviet protocols, with an article on page 5 titled simply "Military Action between Germany and Poland."[154] The sole indication that something big was happening was a lead editorial two days later titled "The Joyful
and Holy [Military] Obligation to the Homeland," followed by a full page of
commentaries on the legendary civil war hero Chapayev.[155] England's declaration of war on Germany on September 4, 1939, merited fifty lines on page 4.
Pravda's editors remarked confidently in the late summer of 1940 in a rare commentary on foreign policy, "The great Stalin skillfully pilots our ship of state
by all reefs and submerged rocks; his genius predicts the flow of events and
knows in advance the thoughts of bourgeois politicians and governments."[156]

Figure 6.7. *Pravda,* September 22, 1939. Poster by V. Koretskii of a former Polish citizen, in a shirt embroidered in the Ukrainian style, kissing a Russian soldier. The accompanying article is captioned, "Unforgettable Meetings." The editorial is titled "The Friendship and Brotherhood of the Peoples of the USSR."

An unwavering official faith in a Soviet-centered universe informed these commentaries.

Despite *Pravda*'s subdued coverage of the Nazi-Soviet Pact, Soviet censors were quick to expunge remarks unfavorable to Germany from the media. On March 3, 1940, N. Sadnikov, chief of Glavlit, cited the inclusion in his past year's work of "the great political events stemming from our relations with Germany and the events in Poland."[157] Nor were friendly images of the Nazis completely lacking. Three months after the signing, *Pravda* published a chummy photo of Hitler beside Molotov.[158] This turnabout also involved special attention to Jews. Whether to avoid provoking Hitler or to deprive the Nazis of a future propaganda weapon, in early September 1937 the Central Committee informed the editorial boards of central periodicals that Jews should take Russian pen names. According to one account, this was in response to Hitler's attacks on Jewish Bolshevism.[159]

Realpolitik had long been the byword of Soviet foreign policy, as evidenced by the Anglo-Soviet Trade Agreement of 1921 and the Rapallo Treaty with Germany of 1922. Nevertheless Stalin may have been more concerned than the Nazis with preparing "public opinion" for this diplomatic "revolution."[160] Khrushchev, for one, recalled the difficulty of squaring the treaty with public expectations.[161] If such expectations existed, they had been nurtured by antifascist columnists such as Koltsov and Ehrenburg. On reading that with the signing of the pact the true Russian-German friendship could now flourish, the outraged Liubov Shaporina, founder of the Moscow Puppet Theater and wife of the composer Yuri Shaporin, wrote in her diary: "That photograph in *Pravda* tells it all: On the right the stupid, bloated snouts of Stalin and Molotov, and on the left von Ribbentrop standing like Napoleon with his arms folded across his chest and a smug grin on his face. Yes, we've lived to see the day."[162] Police reports indicate that such dismay was widespread.[163]

Despite the pact, the government prepared for war. Investments in armaments increased, soldiers appeared on the newspapers' front pages, and commentators discussed military preparedness, without, however, identifying a potential enemy. Yet this was as much in accord with the Stalinist line of two camps as with antifascism. Memoirists recall a sense of the approaching war, but Stalin had been warning of attacks for more than a decade. Writing off the pact with Hitler as a mere interlude, Sakharov recalled, "Our people had been psychologically geared up year after year for what seemed an inevitable war with fascism."[164] Yet in retrospect, one may agree with the first half of his observation and question the second. Stalin and the press had argued for more than a decade that all capitalist states were potential enemies. The militarization of public culture coincided with an expansionist foreign policy, which, while haphazardly articulated, was hardly antifascist.

New Enemies, New Stories

The press's neglect of foreign affairs foreshadowed its irresolution in describing the expansion and defense of the empire on the eve of World War II. During the interval between the purge trials and the Nazi invasion, the Soviet Union fought two bloody engagements with the Japanese, a short war with the Poles, and a longer and costlier one with the Finns. There was also the Spanish Civil war, which involved several thousand Soviet advisers and lasted until January 1939. In addition, the country annexed Bessarabia and Northern Bukovina from Romania on June 28, 1940, and seized the Baltic Republics on August 1–6, 1940. Editors and journalists covering these events did not forge a consistent image of the enemy. Nor was there a coherent rhetoric of either national expansion or communist liberation. Instead, journalists wavered in presenting explanatory motivation for the engagement. The performance with the cult as its center had worked well to concentrate state power and stigmatize domestic enemies, but it was less effective in the foreign arena.

The Red Army rebuffed a Japanese incursion at Lake Khasan (Changkufeng) on the Soviet-Manchurian border in mid-1938, with Russian losses of 717 killed and 3,279 wounded, and fought a short war near the river of Khalkin Gol from May through August 1939 in which 6,831 Soviet soldiers died and more than 16,000 were wounded.[165] *Pravda* stressed insulted national pride rather than social revolution in reporting the initial Japanese demand for the hill over Lake Khasan.[166] *Pravda*'s coverage of Soviet meetings and resolutions held in response to the clash resembled the war scare of 1927, but now Stalin became the emblem of pride and determination. "We rally even more closely around the Communist Party and the beloved leader of peoples, Comrade Stalin," read a statement from a Leningrad factory on August 2. A meeting of seventy thousand in Alma Ata heard a poem by Dzhambul, "beloved bard of the Kazakh people," praising Stalin as the "chieftain of ages, the unbeatable chieftain" (August 2, 1938).

The government had reasons to minimize the clashes with Japan in the aftermath of the *Anschluss* and Hitler's entry into Vienna. *Pravda* reported Soviet losses at Khasan of only thirteen dead and fifty-five wounded, and emphasized that the Red Army had respected the border (August 2, 1938). Editors and journalists nevertheless used the memory of the battle to strengthen the military dimension of the cult and the economy of the gift. To broadcast news of the fighting the following year at Khalkin Gol would have been impolitic just after Munich and during negotiations for the pact with Hitler, which was followed by the German invasion of Poland. Yet as tensions rose during the spring and summer of 1939, the press wrote enthusiastically about the victory at Lake Khasan (July 14 and 23, 1939). This lesser-known engagement was the origin of the slogan "For Stalin, for the Homeland," later incorrectly identified with World War II.

On the anniversary of Khasan on August 6, 1939, A. N. Poskrebyshev, Stalin's factotum who had replaced Mekhlis at *Pravda* in 1937, printed a front-page montage of Soviet troops carrying a banner with the legend, "For the Homeland, for Stalin, for Communism!" "'For Stalin'—with this slogan the battalion made seven bayonet charges," affirmed Colonel M. Bochkarev, a ro of the Soviet Union." The slogan appeared sporadically until the Nazi invasion and was identified with self-sacrifice, as befitted the economy of the gift.[167] Aside from a few brief notes on "provocations," however, *Pravda* was silent about the struggle that continued. The paper concluded the nonstory of Khalkin Gol with a terse announcement of an agreement on September 16.

The next day the Red Army invaded Poland, which had already been over-run by Germany from the west, with limited casualties.[168] Soviet leaders and the press appealed to ethnic unity as well as communist liberation. Molotov announced on September 17 that the army acted to "protect the life and property of the population of western Ukraine and western Belorussia." *Pravda,* on September 22, published V. Koretskii's famous picture of a former Polish citizen, wearing an embroidered shirt in the Ukrainian style, kissing a Russian soldier (Figure 6.7). The paper also stressed class unity. "Millions of people worn out by heavy slavery under the Pan and left to their fate by their brutal and cow-ardly government see the red banners as a symbol of the great truth of social-ism, freedom, and a happy life," read an accompanying comment. There was room for the cult as well. "The inhabitants often asked about Comrade Stalin, and their faces expressed great love for the leader of the people," read another article in the same issue. Reports on the benefits of "the new life" continued for several months with accounts of the allocation of the landowners' lands and the holdings of the Catholic Church to peasant committees, the opening of schools, and the promotion of Ukrainian and Belorussian languages.

The press gave the invasion of Finland a defensive turn. "The Naked Provo-cation of the Finnish Military," read *Pravda*'s header over reports of demon-strations and resolutions condemning the Finnish government on November 27. The paper's cartoonist showed an armed Finn grabbing for Leningrad on No-vember 30. The Red Army attacked on the same day, and the formation of a "People's Government of Finland" was announced on December 1. Its head was O. Kuusinen, a Comintern functionary who remained in Moscow. "Wipe the Brazen Finnish Bandits from the Face of the Earth," was *Pravda*'s header. On December 2 the paper promised "the long-suffering working people of Finland" liberation, and the Kukryniksy, the group of poster artists later famous during World War II, showed a rat firing at a giant ship labeled "The People's Gov-ernment of Finland," while other rats leaped into the water.[169] On December 4 the paper cited the questioning of a Finnish soldier, who allegedly expressed confusion at seeing "so many [military] vehicles." Stalin, who was soon to cel-ebrate his sixtieth birthday on December 21, may have counted on a victory to embellish the festivities. If so, he was disappointed. The Finns did not accede to Soviet demands until March 1941, and the press suppressed the awkward story. *Pravda*'s editors returned to the theme of protecting Leningrad in de-scribing the final agreement.[170] On the Soviet side, nearly four hundred thou-sand were dead, missing, or wounded in the war with Finland.[171]

The press wavered between nationalism and communist liberation in covering the seizure of Bessarabia and Northern Bukovina from Romania and the occupation of the Baltic Republics. "Henceforth Bessarabia, torn from the Soviet Union (Russia) by force in the beginning of 1918 is again united with its mother country, with its Soviet land," editorialized *Pravda* on June 29, 1940. "Thank you, thank you, Comrade Stalin," stated a Bessarabian delegate in Moscow a month later.[172] On August 3, 1940, the paper presented the occupation of the Baltic Republics no less ambiguously. "The Foreign Policy of the Great Country of Socialism," was the title of *Pravda*'s editorial on the acquisitions, but the text stated that "the peoples of the Baltic countries have established the power of the Soviets and realized the cherished dream of all peoples of the world."

The expansion of Soviet territory was accompanied by an effort to extend the persecuting rhetoric of the domestic commentary to new subjects. The hunt for enemies in new regions began in Spain, with persecutions of Trotskyites and anarchists. In July 1938 *Pravda*'s star foreign reporter, Koltsov, transposed domestic scapegoating when he blamed "too many traitors" for the loss of Bilbao to Franco's forces (July 18, 1938). The frenzy of domestic persecution had peaked, however, when the new territories were acquired, and *Pravda* featured little more on the subject. In writing about lands seized from Poland and the former Baltic Republics, journalists stressed enemies' irrelevance but not their fate. A columnist in October 1939 described the mill workers' request that the Soviet commandant free their miller: "Without him we are lost; who will give us work?" (October 1, 1939). Readers learned that the mill workers were grateful to their Soviet "liberators" for a "lesson in political literacy," but the miller's fate was not disclosed. Likewise, reports from the Baltics in the late winter and spring of 1941 noted seizure of property from landowners and kulaks, but without explaining what became of the former owners (February 20, 1941).

Whether commentators were restrained by concern for foreign opinion or an inability to focus on an indistinct foe, the lack of current commentary did not hinder the murderers of 14,700 captured Polish officers and 11,000 prisoners in western Ukraine and Belorussia or the brutal sorting of friends and enemies in occupied areas.[173] The perpetrators had been exposed to years of repetitive denunciations of enemies of all sorts. Deportations and executions from areas seized from Poland from September 1939 to late June 1941 reached well over a million, and the tiny Baltic republics lost more than 150,000.[174] In the Finnish region and that seized from Romania, many fled before the Soviet advance, but more than 30,000 former Romanians were deported.[175] The lack of attention to foreign enemies may also have been a reflection of a general confusion about policy goals. *Pravda*'s editorialists ceased to use the pronoun *we* as frequently as they had previously. In 1937 they used *we* in more than half their columns, but usage fell thereafter to 40 percent in 1938, 23 percent in 1940, and only 12 percent from January 1, 1941, until the Nazi invasion on June 22.

What Stalin's plans were in the last few months before the German invasion is subject to dispute. Some historians have argued, with considerable evidence, that he was preparing to attack Germany.[176] In May and June 1941 Soviet leaders met and discussed an attack on Germany. Stalin told graduates of the military academy on May 5 to prepare to take the initiative, and orders were given to propagandize the idea.[177] One of those who attended the meeting noted in his journal a few days later, "Ahead is our move to the West, ahead is the possibility of which we long dreamed."[178] On May 6, 1941, Stalin was declared head of the government in a decree of the Presidium of the Supreme Soviet; previously he had only been the general secretary of the Party. *Pravda* printed the announcement beneath a half-page picture of him dressed in a simple military tunic but without commentary, and the editorial concerned railroad transport. Whether such activities reflect defensive maneuvers, efforts to foil a German attack with a preemptive strike, or planning for a true offensive in the West is still unclear. Yet whatever the case, the government's public-relations efforts lacked consistency.[179] *like everything*

The press increased coverage of the army and printed slogans about offensive capabilities, but such initiatives were hardly effective. Criticism of Germany had been disallowed since 1940, and, given the press's official character, an abrupt shift would have been tantamount to a declaration of war. Therefore a press campaign such as the government had employed in the past to mobilize the population was impossible. Yet the covert messages the authorities printed were unlikely to mobilize a population immured in rituals of the performance. The government's conundrum was apparent on May 9, when the press printed TASS's announcement that foreign reports of concentrations of Soviet troops on its borders were false. It was still more apparent on June 14, when Tass confirmed the government's continuing commitment to the pact and denounced as "absurd" reports that Soviet troop maneuvers were directed against Germany. This confusing last-minute flurry of contrary information did not prepare the country for the Nazi attack, to say nothing of a surprise offensive. Utter unpreparedness was evident in the summer of 1941 when the Germans and their allies invaded.

Seven

Many Wars, One Victory

ON JUNE 22, 1941, *Pravda* printed the ordinary domestic news. The next day the paper headlined Vyacheslav Molotov's radio address announcing the war and evoking the dual themes of Soviet patriotism and Marxist liberation. Molotov, chairman of the Council of Ministers since 1930 and foreign minister since 1939, had negotiated the Nazi-Soviet Pact less than two years earlier. He now urged Soviet citizens "to rally around our glorious Bolshevik Party, the Soviet government, and our great leader, Comrade Stalin." He spoke of a "patriotic war for homeland, honor, and freedom," but reminded listeners, "This war is thrust upon us not by the German people, not by the German workers, peasants, and intelligentsia, whose suffering we well understand, but by a bloodthirsty clique of German rulers."

P. N. Pospelov, the seasoned functionary who had replaced Poskrebyshev as *Pravda*'s editor in 1940, offered patriotism and Stalin's cult on *Pravda*'s entry into the war. Stalin's face filled the front page, although the leader would remain silent until July 3. The phrase "Great Patriotic War" capped a commentary by Iaroslavskii, a member of *Pravda*'s editorial board. "The day of June 22, 1941," he wrote, "will go down in history as the start of the great patriotic war of the Soviet people against fascist Germany." The phrase echoed the historical canonizations of the 1930s, when heroes such as M. I. Kutuzov, Napoleon's nemesis, were frequently lauded.[1]

David Ortenberg, editor of *Red Star,* the army newspaper, credited the well-connected poet and lyricist Vasilii Lebedev-Kumach, a member of the board of the writers' union, with first using "holy war" and "people's war" on June 23— "the following day we repeated them in *Red Star*'s leader: 'The Soviet people have raised the banner of a *holy* patriotic war for the homeland, for its honor and freedom.'"[2] The phrase "Great Patriotic War" headed reports of public meetings on page 2. Lebedev-Kumach wrote:

> Rise up enormous country,
> Rise to the struggle of life and death
> Against the fascist forces of darkness,
> Against the cursed horde!
> Let the noble fury
> Boil up like a wave,

> The people's war has begun,
> The holy war!

Writers were immediately in demand. On the first day, Ortenberg sent his cultural specialist to fetch "obligatory" poets and others from Peredelkino, the writers' colony where Pasternak, Chukovskii, and others lived.[3] He hired Vsevolod Vishnevskii, who wrote "The lessons of History" for the first wartime issue.[4] Vishnevskii traced Russia's struggle with Germans from Alexander Nevsky's defeat of the Teutonic knights. "No free Russian, no son of the victors of Chudskoe Lake," he wrote, "will live under the fascist heel; no Ukrainian, no son of Zaporozhskye Cossacks will live under the cursed Baron's heel." Later, in 1941, editors evoked Slavic unity, and Alexei Tolstoy and others followed suit.[5] Stalin spoke of patriotism and "great ancestors" at the Moscow Soviet on November 6, 1941, and in Red Square the next day. "We often called it 'holy,'" Ilya Ehrenburg wrote in *Red Star* in 1943. "Indeed, is it not better to say it is a holy war for the human being."[6]

Within months of the invasion, the war had spawned a plurality of intertwined narratives and a range of perspectives. The press abandoned its single-minded effort to center all Soviet identity on Stalin. The American correspondent Alexander Werth, who covered the war for the *Sunday Times* and the British Broadcasting Company, captured something of the change when he wrote in his *Moscow War Diary* in 1942: "There is no longer a dividing line between 'Soviet' and 'Russian.'"[7] Yet there was more than a simple commingling of Soviet Communism and Russian nationalism. An assortment of narrators with differing viewpoints—poets, writers, literary correspondents, local reporters, regular journalists, officials, and Stalin himself—began to use the press in different ways to advance one objective: victory over the invaders.

The new concatenation of images, stories, voices, and personages did not mark an institutional revival of civil society, but for a time journalists displayed a world in which Stalin said little and in which some authority shifted to others. Stalin's face continued to appear, but in *Pravda* it was often a frame from a documentary film rather than a photograph of an event of the previous day. Thus, on February 15, 1942, *Pravda* featured a picture of Stalin addressing the parade in Red Square on November 7, 1941, from a film about the defense of Moscow. While Stalin became more remote, literary war correspondents, such as Ehrenburg and Konstantin Simonov, gained respect within the press and outside it. During the early part of the war, they and others projected the image of a society and a social order more open to diversity than during the 1930s. Nevertheless the Stalinist state managed the wartime effort, ran the economy, and headed the administrative structure that achieved victory. The Soviet Union outproduced Nazi Germany in planes, tanks, and artillery in part because patriotism and initiative were sustained by the patriotic public culture of which the press was a part. The Red Army had the spirit and moral edge to defeat its opponent for much the same reason.[8]

The Credibility of the Press

As is often the case in war, the first casualty was truth. *Pravda* reported on June 23, 1941: "Our brave army, fleet, and falcons of Soviet aviation dealt the aggressor a crippling blow."[9] The leaders soon knew better, but the press still claimed victories. Many people later recalled Stalin's words on July 3 on the radio and in newspapers: "Comrades! Citizens, brothers and sisters! Fighters of our army and fleet. I turn to you, my friends!" The form of address was new, the phrase "my friends" startling, and in saying "brothers and sisters" he dropped his patriarchal role. "How could it happen that our glorious Red Army would give up a series of cities and districts to fascist troops?" he asked. Defending his pact with Hitler and blaming German success on surprise, he explained: "Despite the Red Army's heroic opposition, despite the fact that the enemy's best divisions and the best part of his air force are already destroyed and have gone to graves on the battlefield, the enemy continues to move forward, throwing new forces into the front."[10]

Marshal Zhukov, at the time chief of the General Staff and vice minister of defense, later recalled the speech as one of three appeals "to the heart of the people" and compared it to the November 7, 1941, parade in Moscow's Red Square and the salute honoring the liberation of Orel and Belgorod.[11] He credited Stalin with telling "the truth about the danger hanging over our country." Ehrenburg recalled people staring "gloomily" at a map displayed at *Izvestiia*'s offices.[12]

All sides understated losses. When the first big city, Minsk, fell in late June, the Soviet Information Bureau—the official source and regulator of all military news for domestic and foreign consumption—reported victories.[13] "In the direction of Minsk [a euphemism used at this time to conceal the fact that Minsk itself was lost] Red Army troops continue their successful struggle with enemy tanks, blocking their movement to the east," the bureau announced on June 29. On July 2 it had the army inflicting "significant defeats." On July 3 the bureau reported air victories and on the fourth "significant [enemy] losses"—"The enemy cannot bear the bayonet thrusts of our troops."[14] On July 5 the bureau denied German claims of "a fantastic number of prisoners" but made no mention of Minsk.

The following facts were not reported in the press: During the first month, 28 of the 170 divisions opposing the German advance were destroyed; 70 were reduced to half strength; thousands of heavy weapons and 3,468 planes were lost, including 1,200 on the first day.[15] Many guessed the truth from accounts of battles well to the east of Minsk. A nineteen-year-old poet from Iaroslavl, Iurii Baranov, who died a year later, wrote in his diary on July 18: "Losses are certainly very great on each side, but greater on ours! However, I do not know it. Reports say the opposite, but one need not always believe them."[16] Perhaps, as in this case, many found the press's rosy picture reassuring, even if not fully credible.

As land was lost and soldiers captured, the Information Bureau ceased to cite specific battlefields, and journalists were compelled to do likewise. By mid-July spokesmen and journalists avoided cities and noted only northwestern, western, and southwestern "directions." Reportage changed with the unreported loss of the "Smolensk pocket" in August during which twenty-five Russian divisions were captured or destroyed. "After a resolute struggle, our troops left Novgorod," wrote a reporter later that month.[17] "After a resolute battle our troops left the city of Chernigov," wrote another on September 13. Even these euphemistic formulations offered little comfort when Kiev fell in late September with the loss of nearly half a million soldiers.[18] Stalin had denied Colonel General Kirponos's plea to withdraw, and he covered his error by ordering editors "to provide no particulars" on the city's capture.[19] After citing fighting "chiefly near Kiev" for several days, the Information Bureau offered a single line on September 22: "After a bitter battle of many days, our troops left Kiev." Other papers did likewise, and Kiev vanished temporarily from public discussion.[20]

Pasternak's friend, Olga Freidenberg, soon to be trapped in besieged Leningrad, wrote in her diary: "We were abandoning one city after another. The reports, so avidly, so anxiously awaited, grew more and more laconic. The more each of us worried about the news, the less of it we were given. Rumors began circulating."[21] Civilians were disoriented by the lack of information. A teenager digging trenches near Smolensk remembered questioning soldiers: "We greedily inquired about the front. We thought it was still far away, far from the Dnieper. How could we know how rapid the fascist advance had been? In early July we asked soldiers on the road what was happening at the border, but by that time Minsk had already fallen."[22]

He noted how only days later he and other evacuated children walked "peacefully, even merrily, along the highway" with no idea that the Germans were close behind.[23] A reluctance to report defeats imperiled defenders and civilians alike. "We certainly did not know then that thousands of tanks and tens of thousands of weapons had been lost in border battles in the terrible encirclements of Belostok, Minsk, and Kiev," recalled a mobilized civilian who wondered at the obsolete weapons he was issued.[24]

The press overlooked Moscow's peril in September and early October, covering only Orel and Viazma.[25] "After many days of bitter battle in which the enemy suffered huge casualties in people and weapons, our troops left Viazma" (the last town before Moscow), wrote a reporter on October 14. "We could not consider Moscow until the Information Bureau reported it," Ortenberg recalled.[26] *Pravda* warned finally on the fifteenth: "The bloody Hitlerite hordes are reaching toward Moscow." Editors did not report the panicky official exodus on October 16, and on October 21, on Stalin's orders, printed a photo of Gen. G. K. Zhukov planning the city's defense.[27] Zhukov later told Ortenberg: "Although I assured him we would not lose the capital, he was not fully persuaded. So he wondered on whom he should load the guilt in case of defeat."[28] Nine days later *Pravda* declared, "The State Committee of Defense and its head, Comrade Stalin, are in Moscow and planning the country's defense. This communiqué inspires Moscow's defenders to glorious new feats."[29] The author borrowed rhetoric of the 1930s to motivate defenders with the image of Stalin rather than patriotism or self-interest.

Stalin told the Moscow city council in the Mayakovsky subway station on November 6 of Nazi casualties of 4.5 million as opposed to Russian losses of 378,000 and 1.2 million wounded.[30] In fact, during the past six months, Germany took approximately 3 million prisoners, and as many as 1.5 million Red Army soldiers were dead—this against Nazi losses of .75 million, including 200,000 Germans.[31] By the war's end, Soviet deaths—mostly Russians, Ukrainians, and Belorussians—numbered roughly 26 million, as well as 18 million wounded.[32] There were between 13 and 15 million casualties among civilians living in Soviet prewar borders.[33] According to data collected by Stalin's government, the invaders murdered 11.3 million civilians in occupied territory, 16 percent of the population.[34] Nearly 9 million Soviet citizens were interned in concentration camps, as well as 3.9 million prisoners of war. In addition, 4.2 million civilians were sent to Germany as forced labor. Whether or not editors and reporters wished to report this cataclysm, they were constrained to understate losses not only during the war but afterward as well. Stalin gave an official figure of 7 million in February 1946.[35]

Soviet leaders wanted atrocities shown, however, and many came to light when the Germans withdrew from the environs of Moscow. In January 1942 *Red Star* noted the damage to Lev Tolstoy's estate and efforts to obliterate Russian culture.[36] In February editors described retreating Germans razing villages and driving the population west in cold and snow (February 6, 1942). In March E. Gabrilovich wrote of murdered civilians (March 17, 1942). In June Mikhail Sholokhov described victims: "One especially sticks in my mind. She was about eleven, evidently going to school; the Germans caught her, dragged her to the vegetable garden, raped her, and killed her" (June 23, 1942). In August editors showed captured photos of massacres, and in the same month Ortenberg printed a letter from a sergeant about a Russian girl held in Germany (August 6, 1942). "The German monsters have turned our girls into slaves and sell them; I cannot keep silent," the sergeant wrote (August 11, 1942). On November 6, a year and a half after the invasion, Stalin finally described the threat: "They rape and murder the civilian population—men and women, children and old people, our brothers and sisters. . . . They decided to enslave or exterminate the population of Ukraine, Belorussia, the Baltics, Moldavia, the Crimea, and the Caucasus."[37]

Jews in particular had little warning of their special risk. Nearly three million lived in territory that was occupied, two-thirds in lands the Soviet Union had annexed in the pact with Nazi Germany, and most died.[38] Before the 1939

Nazi-Soviet Pact, the press had reported Nazi repression of workers, Communists, and Jews as features of capitalism and fascism, but the pact had stilled fears. By June 1941, as Ortenberg recalled, "wrathful expressions such as 'fascist beasts,' 'fascist brigands,' and 'occupiers' had long vanished from our newspapers."[39] The chief of a military hospital wrote to Ehrenburg of atrocities in 1942 at Essentuki, a Caucasian spa that took on evacuees: "My wife Galina Lvova Aizenberg and ten-year-old son Aleksandr perished in Essentuki. I learned from survivors among the local population that Jews were naive and did not expect Germans to commit such a perfidious and monstrous massacre of innocent people."[40]

The government organized a meeting of intellectuals on August 24, 1941, to ask American Jews for aid, and *Pravda* and other papers excerpted remarks by the Yiddish actor S. M. Mikhoels, Ehrenburg, Eisenstein, and others, but information remained scarce. A. Erusalimskii depicted Hitler's views in *Red Star* in mid-1942 but skipped his anti-Semitic phobia.[41] K. Goffman cited plans for "resettling peoples" but did not mention Jews.[42] Nikolai Tikhonov wrote of "German sadism" on October 3, 1942, though not of anti-Semitism. Ehrenburg depicted Nazi atrocities in November 1941 but in a small article on page 3 of *Red Star.*[43] In any case, the invaders gave Soviet citizens little time to flee, and unreported defeats doomed many regardless of what they expected. Stalin muzzled the press after huge German victories on the southwestern and southern fronts in May 1942, and the Information Bureau noted "no activity."[44] Since he had insisted on the spring offensive, his interest in hiding its ruinous result was obvious.

Stalin Draws Back and Literary Journalists Come Onstage

As cities fell and explanations failed, Stalin drew back. *Pravda*'s editorialists and journalists still referred to him constantly as they had in the 1930s, but often as if alluding to a hero in the wings.[45] Two examples suffice. On January 12, 1942, after Moscow's successful defense, the editors wrote, "The guards units, flower of the Red Army, born on the field of battle, educated by the great captain Comrade Stalin, will multiply the glory of Soviet arms daily, smashing and destroying the robber hordes of German aggressors." On May 19, 1942, citing Stalin's order on May 1 to destroy the fascist armies and liberate the country within the year, they wrote, "Our country, people, and Red Army now fight to fulfill Comrade Stalin's May 1 order about the final destruction of the fascist scoundrels in the current year of 1942." In neither case did Stalin actually appear; in neither case did he do anything in the immediate quotidian world of the press. Such citations, however, were no substitute for an active appearance in the news.

Stalin's presence also diminished visually. During the year and a half before the invasion, *Pravda* featured him in thirty-one front-page pictures, of which all but three were contemporary news photographs at holiday celebrations, government meetings, the signing of treaties, or together with colleagues.[46] By contrast, the paper printed only twenty-five pictures in the first two and a half years of war, of which nine were current photographs that specified place or situation. Most were simply drawings or photographic portraits, which the paper used even when he issued military directives, such as that of May 1, 1942. On November 7, 1941, *Pravda* printed a dramatic picture of Stalin speaking in Red Square, but other occasions passed without a portrait, as his order to defend Moscow on October 19, 1941. Moreover, the press never showed Stalin, then or later, visiting army units, checking war damage, or meeting with generals. What Ehrenburg wrote later may well be true, namely, that "Stalin knew he had to lie low."[47]

There were other indications as well. In the 1930s *Pravda*'s editorialists had often shown him as a historical actor, but from June 23, 1941, until the end of 1943 they rarely devoted an editorial to his pronouncements or decisions.[48] Nor did journalists make his name the clarion it was later. They employed the famous prewar slogans—"For Stalin, for the Homeland" and "Where Stalin Is, There Is Victory"—briefly at the outset, only to abandon them until the war's end.[49] *Red Star* hailed the successful defense of Moscow on December 13, 1941, without mentioning his name:

> The valiant troops of our western front won a glorious victory in the battle for Moscow. The heroes of this victory are our Generals Zhukov, Lelishenko, Kuznetsov, Vlasov, Rokossovskii, Govorov, Boldin, Belov, and Golikov, who skillfully led their troops with iron hands through the fire of battle. The heroes of this victory are our fighters, commanders, commissars, and political workers, who fought the enemy selflessly, stoically, and without fear of death. The victory's heroes are the Moscow working people, who selflessly aided the front with their heroic labor, vigilance, calm, and support.[50]

Only pictures of the generals, Zhukov in the center, appeared on the front page (Figure 7.1). Similarly, on June 23, 1942, the Information Bureau summed up "the political and military results" of a year of war in *Pravda*'s editorial space without citing him. On July 30, when the fortunes of the Red Army reached their nadir, in part because of Stalin's insistence on a spring offensive, *Pravda* published his famous order—"not a step back"—which was read to troops on the same day. Although this was understood as Stalin's order, *Pravda*'s editors printed the words beside the masthead without attaching his name.[51] Nor did they credit him in the editorial, although they quoted his remarks from the civil war and the outset of the invasion. The passage read in its entirety:

> Soviet troops! Not a step back! Such is the homeland's appeal, the Soviet people's demand. The homeland lives through difficult days. Our task is to deflect the threat hanging over the Soviet country, to stop, throw back, and destroy the enemy at whatever cost.

Figure 7.1. *Red Star,* December 13, 1941. Center picture: "Commander of the Western Front, General of the Army, G. K. Zhukov." The editorial is titled "Our Victory in the Battle for Moscow."

Although *Red Star*'s editors cited him, urging, "Not a step back!—That is the demand of the People's Commissar of Defense, our leader and commander, Comrade Stalin," neither paper had his picture.[52] Each devoted its front page to new medals named for Alexander Nevsky, Alexander Suvorov, and Mikhail Kutuzov; the first a prince and Russian Orthodox saint, the others tsarist generals.

Stalin nevertheless asserted his familiar role and resented any seeming transfer of glory to others. "You've printed enough on Konev," he snapped on the phone and hung up, after Ortenberg featured Gen. I. S. Konev's attempted counterattack in the first week of war."[53] He struck Zhukov's name from a list of 135 commanders and officers awarded orders and medals after the Battle of Moscow on January 2, 1942. "We at the editorial board [of *Red Star*] were furious," noted Ortenberg, a friend of Zhukov's from the war with Japan.[54] The next day the caption "General Zhukov's Troops Press the Enemy" appeared on page 2 instead of the usual "troops on the central front press the enemy." "I do not know whether anyone noticed this tribute from *Red Star* to the commander of the front," Ortenberg noted, "but among us such headings counted most."[55]

The war correspondents also enjoyed a taste of the celebrity Stalin was loath to share. At the outset S. A. Lozovskii, assistant chief of the Information Bureau, gathered writers and told them to promote the war. The literati, Ehrenburg recalled, wanted to scrap "stock phrases" and "address readers in their own voices."[56] Lozovskii sympathized, but A. S. Shcherbakov, head of the Information Bureau and a true insider, told Ehrenburg not to get "too clever." He could have saved his breath. Writers began to feel their power.[57] Ortenberg recalled Iosif Utkin replying "with a proud smile" in July 1941 to a query about the receipt of a promised poem: "Well, you know, no poet will tell you that [when a poem will be ready for publication]."[58] Instead of writers wooing editors, editors wooed writers. Ortenberg recalled his eagerness to sign Alexei Tolstoy, whose historical novels so pleased Stalin.[59]

The nature of power did not change, however. Ortenberg claimed implausibly that on becoming assistant editor of *Red Star* in 1938, he learned only that former editors had vanished: "Why they left and where they went was unknown."[60] In fact his predecessor was shot in 1938, as was the chief of the section on Party affairs.[61] The secretary of the editorial board had received ten years in the camps. His successor left soon after Ortenberg arrived. Ortenberg became chief editor, with Stalin's approval, at the age of thirty-six on June 30, 1940, thanks to L. V. Mekhlis, his old boss from *Pravda*, who headed the Red Army's political administration.[62]

Militarization brought civilians to military newspapers and officers to civilian ones. More than three-quarters of the sixty-two employees who joined *Komsomol Pravda*'s editorial staff from 1936 to 1940 held military ranks.[63] Ortenberg, a military journalist, who had a great affinity for writers, gave *Red Star* a literary cast. He hired Simonov, Ehrenburg, Vasilii Grossman, Fedor Panferov,

Alexei Surkov, Alexei Tolstoy, and Nikolai Tikhonov. Other editors were jealous. When Moscow was bombed and *Red Star* joined *Pravda* on Pravda Street in late 1941, *Pravda*'s editor, Pospelov, poached Ortenberg's favorites.[64] L. Ilichev, the paper's secretary, checked *Red Star*'s galleys, and if he found a piece by Alexei Tolstoy, he demanded to publish it in *Pravda*. "It was impossible to refuse," Ortenberg recalled.[65] When the Nazis were driven from Moscow, *Red Star* returned to Chekhov Street, but the rivalry simmered. In May 1943, according to Ortenberg, Pospelov snatched Sholokhov's short novel *They Fought for Their Country*, although Sholokhov was working for *Red Star*.[66] Both papers published it simultaneously.

Ortenberg hired once persecuted writers at *Red Star* with Stalin's consent. One was Aleksandr Avdeenko, whom Stalin had damned as "incorrigible" in August 1940 for his refusal to admit errors in his film *The Law of Life* and other sins.[67] Ortenberg wrote to Stalin at the urging of Nikolai Tikhonov, who covered Leningrad, where Avdeenko was stationed. "I think that in the Patriotic War Comrade Avdeenko has atoned for past faults, and I ask permission to print his essays in *Red Star*." Stalin replied: "You may print. Avdeenko has atoned for his fault."[68] In late 1941 Ortenberg hired Panferov, who lost favor for refusing a military assignment, sent him into battle, printed his report, and then called Stalin (53). "He did not ask anything, curse me or praise me for hiring Panferov without approval and sending him to the front, but said only two words: 'Print Panferov,'" Ortenberg recalled. "I realized he approved of our decision" (53). Ortenberg also hired the one-time "kulak agent," Andrei Platonov, at twelve hundred rubles a month, no mean sum when public-sector employees earned three to four hundred rubles and workers in key industries two hundred more (24–31).[69] "Stalin did not curse us and said nothing," he noted.[70]

The literary war correspondents enlarged their voices by emphasizing the first-person singular and investing *we* with new meanings. Simonov began a column in October 1941 about German abuse of Russian prisoners of war: "During four months of war I saw much horror. I saw corpses of children mutilated by the Germans, the remains of Red Army soldiers burned alive, burned villages, homes destroyed by bombs."[71] He wrote in late November 1941 of a raid in the far north: "It was already dawn when we came ashore from the cutter and crossed the city, very chilled but merry" (November 23, 1941). Some adopted a confessional style. A photographer for *Red Star*, S. Loskutov, joined a group of partisans behind German lines, and the paper serialized his story when he returned. The last installment included his picture (Figure 7.2) and a note about how he became a writer.

> I sat in the editorial offices eight hours later and told my story. They advised me: Describe all of it, and we will print it. Describe it? How to convey the events and thoughts of all these stormy days. How to begin, how to end? The fact is, I am not a journalist but a photographer.

Фотокорреспондент «Красной звезды»
С. Лоскутов.

Figure 7.2. *Red Star,* December 4, 1941. "*Red Star* Photo Correspondent S. Loskutov."

I thought, wondered, and then decided. I will write what really happened without embellishment.

Voicing the nation's concerns, literary journalists began to recover the moral authority of Russian and early Soviet literature. Ehrenburg was almost biblical in making cities "speak" and using parables. "First Kiev the beautiful speaks: 'I have covered my head with ashes, the ashes of burned homes," he wrote in mid-November 1941.[72] "It is good when the wolf begins to bleat! It is splendid music to our ears," he wrote when the Nazis were driven back from Moscow.[73] Simonov later wrote: "While the style of Ehrenburg's articles might not appeal to every soldier, their force reached everyone because no matter how much

Ehrenburg wrote he was never stingy, he always shared his heart with the reader, and the reader felt this."[74]

Simonov had his own style in which he thrust himself into the story of the war as exemplary witness:

> Great and enduring is the Russian people. Great and enduring but at the same time fearful in anger. I have driven along devastated roads, through burned-out villages, through places where the cup of suffering is overflowing, and all the same I have seen few tears. When one hates very much, one has few tears.[75]

These sermons had a history. In late August 1941 Ortenberg discussed with Alexei Tolstoy and Sholokhov Soviet soldiers' naive friendliness toward Germans.[76] The prewar Soviet propaganda had succeeded in convincing many Soviet citizens that ordinary Germans, unlike their capitalist and episodically war-mongering leaders, were friendly to the workers' state. Even when these ordinary Germans appeared in uniforms as aggressors on Soviet soil, they were not initially perceived as the enemy. The writers agreed that they had to change this view in order to win the war. Ortenberg remembered their conversation:

> "There is only one remedy for placidity," Tolstoy said, "and that is hatred—such that one cannot sleep or breathe. We must write more of this, sharply and constantly." Then we heard words that became one of our mottos: "One cannot defeat the enemy without learning to hate him with all the force of one's soul."

Ortenberg recalled Tolstoy's article from August 31, 1941, "The Face of the Hitlerite Army," which appeared in *Pravda* and *Izvestiia,* as well as *Red Star.* Tolstoy reported eyewitness accounts of atrocities by German soldiers and civilians.[77] Stalin cited soldiers' attitudes in his public "order" on May Day, 1942: "The placidity and indifference to the enemy that fighters felt in the first months of the patriotic war has vanished." He credited the change to German atrocities but cited Tolstoy's motto: "They understood that it is impossible to beat the enemy without learning to hate him with all the force of the soul."[78]

Ehrenburg and others were later accused of equating Nazis with Germans, but they generally raged at perpetrators, rather than civilians. He wrote in early 1942 when Nazis destroyed the Borodino Museum and nearby villages: "We are not speaking of revenge but of justice. We do not want to shoot sixty-two-year-old German schoolteachers. We will not bother twelve-year-old girls."[79] "I recall how necessary Ehrenburg's articles were for us. Hatred was our support," wrote the writer D. Granin.[80]

Speaking as Old Testament prophets, literary correspondents regained for literature and themselves an authority lost in the 1930s. Whereas Stalin on November 6 and 7, 1941, appealed to "the great ancestors" celebrated in the 1930s, writers emphasized morality and humanism. "We Soviet writers and citizens fight for truth alongside our Red Army," Tolstoy answered Radio Berlin in August 1941.[81] Ehrenburg compared Germany to Sodom and Gomorrah, and

Figure 7.3. "In the Days of the Battle of Stalingrad." David Ortenberg and Konstantin Simonov. Ortenberg is closest to the camera. From Ortenberg's collection, printed in *Literaturnoe nasledstvo: Sovetskie pisateli na frontakh Velikoi Otechestvennoi voiny* vol. 1 (Moscow, 1955), 275.

warned of "the sword of justice."[82] Tikhonov wrote from besieged Leningrad: "'The mill of fate grinds slowly but it grinds finely,' as is written in an old book. The Germans will be ground to dust. Nothing will save them. The retribution that hangs over their heads will not pass by or spare them."[83] Writers who made such statements were aware of their role. Simonov wrote in the spring of 1943 in correspondence with the poet A. A. Kovalenkov: "Not all newspaper editors typically understand the nature of a writer and the writer's real duty before the country."[84]

Ortenberg, Ehrenburg, and Grossman, three Russianized Ukrainian Jews, brought a special quality to the narrative. Each found ambiguous the Soviet promises of 1917 to end prejudice; each witnessed horrors of Stalinism; and each developed his own complex and difficult relationship with the overbearing power of the state. Ortenberg, the most guarded, fought in the civil war and became a journalist during the NEP (Figure 7.3). His debut in *Pravda* in 1936 was marred by the need to adopt a Russian pseudonym. He choose Vadimov (from his son's name, Vadim), and kept it at *Red Star.* Mekhlis later recalled that Stalin had demanded the adoption of non-Jewish pseudonyms ("No need to excite Hitler"); "All the 'bergs' and 'steins' vanished from the newspapers," he remembered bitterly.[85]

Grossman was younger. He grew up in the town of Berdichev, a center of Jewish life in Ukraine. His father used the name Semyon Osipovich, rather than Solomon Iosifovich, presumably to conceal his Jewishness, and Grossman himself was well aware of anti-Semitism both before and after the revolution.[86] He first published during "the great break," won literary spurs in the 1930s, and in 1937 joined the writers' union and acquired its perks.[87] Several family members and friends went to the gulag during the years he built his literary career.[88] In 1938 he saved his wife and her children of another marriage by appealing to the feared N. Yezhov, chief of the NKVD (People's Commissariat of Internal Affairs).[89]

Ehrenburg grew up in Moscow where his father managed a brewery before the revolution (Figure 7.4). He met Bukharin, joined the Bolsheviks at age fifteen in 1906, and went into exile in Paris, where he became a writer.[90] He returned in 1917, criticized the Bolsheviks, and was briefly arrested by the Cheka. He was freed with Bukharin's help, worked a few months at the Ministry of Education, and in 1921 returned to Paris, again with Bukharin's help. A cosmopolitan patriot, he became *Izvestiia*'s foreign correspondent in 1932 and de-

Figure 7.4. Ilyia Ehrenburg (in hat without flaps) with David Ortenberg on the Western front in 1941. From Ortenberg's collection; printed in *Literaturnoe nasledstvo: Sovetskie pisateli na frontakh,* 605.

nounced fascism with passion. Bukharin, the editor in 1934, promoted him, but he flourished even after his friend's demise. "I am a Russian writer," he stated at the Jewish rally in August 1941. "But the Nazis have reminded me of something else; my mother's name was Hannah. I am a Jew."[91] He and Grossman joined the Jewish Anti-Fascist Committee set up under the Information Bureau in December 1941 to win the support of American Jews.[92] The two also worked on *The Black Book,* a compendium of information on the murder of Soviet Jews, for which publication was eventually denied.[93]

German propaganda and the war stirred anti-Semitism, particularly in occupied Ukraine and Belorussia. Ehrenburg and others countered with stories of Jewish valor and suffering, and downplayed Jewish exceptionality. When the government tried Nazis and collaborators after Kharkov's liberation in late 1943, Ehrenburg stressed the variety of victims and the inclusiveness of the tragedy. He wrote: "More than thirty thousand people of Kharkov perished, tormented by Germans. Among them were Russians, Jews, Ukrainians, teachers, workers, doctors, students, young girls, pregnant women, nursing babies, and the aged."[94]

Grossman also bore witness to the holocaust. His mother and aunt died in a massacre similar to that at Babi Yar, of which he learned only late in the war. His estranged wife and daughter escaped.[95] Unable to say all he wished in *Red Star,* he nevertheless wrote in October 1943 "of the organized execution of millions of children, old people, women, captured and wounded soldiers."[96] From Poland in mid-1944 he described the "mechanized murder" of Jews and educated Poles.[97] To this horror he counterpoised kindness and courage. When the war broke out he volunteered as a soldier but was told to work for *Red Star.* In late 1942 Ortenberg urged him to compare Stalingrad and Tsaritsyn, the civil war battle Stalin claimed to have won. He wrote the piece but resisted the opportunity to ingratiate himself with the leader and cited Stalin only once in referring to the name of the city. Ortenberg captioned the story "Tsaritsyn-Stalingrad."[98] Grossman prized love and individual expressions of humanity. He wrote in *Red Star* of an old colonel greeting a wounded medic: "Only a father could meet a daughter this way; the love and faith in each other worked a miracle."[99] In his novel *Life and Fate,* a crazy old man holds "an absurd theory of morality"—"I believe in human kindness."[100] *Red Star* published his picture early in the battle of Stalingrad (Figure 7.5).

Many reporters, both Jews and gentiles, may have cast off shameful memories in the heat of war and assuaged their guilt as survivors of the 1930s. Pasternak spoke for the intelligentsia years later, when he wrote, "And when the war broke out, its real horrors, its real dangers, its menace of real death were a blessing compared to the inhuman reign of the lie, and they brought relief because they broke the spell of the dead letter."[101] Grossman distanced himself from Stalin more than Pasternak did. His friend Semyon Lipkin later recalled, perhaps with hindsight: "This war in his [Grossman's] opinion washes all the Stalinist muck from Russia's face. Its holy blood cleanses us of murdered kulaks'

Figure 7.5. *Red Star,* August 12, 1942. "V. S. Grossman" (during the
Battle of Stalingrad).

blood and the blood of 1937."[102] Yet even these narratives, like those that rivaled them at the end of the war, concerned victory most of all. Grossman wrote
afterward in *Life and Fate* of the shifting balance between stories of a nation in
arms and those of Stalin and the triumphant state: "What had been crucial in
Stalingrad and during 1941 was coming to be of merely secondary importance.

The first person to understand this change was the man who on June 3, 1941, had said: 'My brothers and sisters, my friends.'"[103]

The rhetoric of the past did not simply vanish even in 1941 and 1942, however. "Proletarians of all countries unite," remained on *Pravda*'s masthead, as it had since 1917. Flyers were still sometimes called "Stalin's falcons," as they had been in the 1930s, and occasional oaths and letters to Stalin still appeared.[104] The press continued to print formulaic statements such as "The Party of Lenin-Stalin, the Soviet government, and personally Comrade Stalin give serious attention to the repair and renewal of military equipment," which appeared in March 1942.[105] It also continued to commemorate historic moments of the official past. On December 1, 1941, with the Nazis a few miles from Moscow, the editors allotted most of *Pravda*'s first two pages to Kirov's memory on the seventh anniversary of his death. Tikhonov even contributed a poem, "Kirov Is with Us," in which the dead Party boss helped to defend Leningrad. Yet this reportage coexisted with a multiplicity of other narratives, some of which readers presumably found more affecting.

New Characters and New Narratives Appear

The war, as Grossman and Pasternak later recalled it, allowed journalists a breath of air fresher than the stultifying atmosphere of the late 1930s. Although their actual independence was limited, some tentatively displayed aspects of a civil society. The official narrative fragmented under pressure of defeats.[106] The concept of time changed as the immediacy of struggle preempted other considerations. Journalists discovered diverse explanations of accomplishments and defenders' motivations. The Information Bureau usually issued several daily reports, which appeared as morning and evening notes on local action. In 1941 and 1942 these were often remarkable for the absence of Stalin and the Party, silences readers could fill in or leave blank. The press showed soldiers acting but gave no motivations, leaving readers to imagine the heroes' thoughts. One such story in *Pravda* on July 9, 1941, read in its entirety:

> The other day N unit attacked superior enemy forces. The battle ended with the enemy's defeat. There were 267 dead and 130 wounded German soldiers left on the battlefield. During the battle Comrade Dovzhikov, a soldier, burst into a group of German officers and bayonetted three while the others fled. Junior political officer Comrade Petrov killed six fascist soldiers in a few minutes.

Another on May 3, 1942, was only a few lines: "A group of enemy bombers tried to bomb the military formations of one of our infantry units. Sergeant Poliakov's machine-gun crew opened fire on the enemy and with a few salvos downed two German bombers."

In a contrasting account, Major General Golubev claimed on January 4,

1942, to be "fulfilling Comrade Stalin's instructions to destroy the German-fascist occupiers." He concluded: "Comrade Stalin's practical plan establishes a basis for greater defeat of the enemy. The Maloiaroslav operation is only part of the brilliant commander's general plan." Likewise, *Pravda*'s editorialist wrote on November 11, 1941: "At a meeting of fighters of Lieutenant Pushkin's regiment, Red Army soldier Kuzin said: 'My heart was overjoyed when I heard Comrade Stalin's voice and exciting words. His speech bolstered my certainty of our own victory.'" Such statements were rarer in 1941 and in much of 1942 than later in the war. Instead, authors stressed patriotism or revenge as motives, inviting readers to invest the absence of Stalin and Party with their own meanings. A *Red Star* reporter described how a teacher shot a German officer who vandalized her school and then tried to win her affections. "Shooting the fascist officer was not only an act of self-defense. It was an act of revenge—revenge for herself, for her children, whose letters were trampled, revenge for Soviet women mocked by German rapists."[107] Grossman wrote to Ehrenburg after a sojourn on the southwestern front during 1941 and 1942: "People became different, more lively, more independent, braver."[108]

During the 1930s the press had granted Stalin and the state full authority over social honor and dishonor, but this, too, changed during the war. Molotov avowed on June 22, 1941: "Our courageous army and fleet and the brave falcons of Soviet aviation will fulfill their duty to the homeland and the Soviet people with honor."[109] The same day *Pravda* described the war as a struggle "for homeland, honor, and freedom!" On July 3, 1941, Stalin urged citizens to "defend their freedom, honor, and homeland."[110] The press also linked honor with professionalism. Ukrainian playwright Aleksandr Korneichuk dramatized the issue in his play *The Front,* serialized in *Pravda* in August 1942.[111] Its publication was an event that has often been associated with Stalin's effort to promote a new generation of commanders. The plot was simple. The hero opposes a civil war general who "learned to fight in battles, not in academies." The old warrior sputters: "We will lick any enemy, and not with wireless communications but with heroism, valor." But his brother, head of an airplane factory, warns, "We must know how to fight in a modern way." Stalin promoted the play, and Korneichuk used an offstage Stalin to validate his hero and professionalism.[112] *Pravda*'s editors likewise celebrated skill on October 22, 1942, when they equated "a commander's honor" with professionalism, not the "personal fearlessness" of a soldier's "honor."

The community also conferred honor in the press's reports. "Does it not upset and distress every honorable person who loves his native land to see the armored Nazi monster crawl toward Moscow?" wrote a *Red Star* reporter during the winter of 1941.[113] In the same paper a year later Simonov praised an officer from the Far Eastern region who destroyed fourteen tanks. In the grainy photograph that accompanied the story, Lt. I. Shuklin stands with binoculars on his

НА ДОНУ. Артиллеристы, уничтожившие 14 немецких танков. В первом ряду (слева направо): командир батареи лейтенант И. Шуклин, красноармейцы: Ю. Каюмов, Н. Лончаков; второй ряд: М. Панин, В. Шлонов и К. Вяткин. (Смотри очерк К. Симонова «Единоборство»).

Снимок нашего спец. фотокорр. В. Темина.

Figure 7.6. *Red Star,* August 9, 1942. "On the Don. The artillery men have destroyed fourteen German tanks." (Lieutenant I. Shuklin stands with binoculars on his neck beside soldiers from his unit.)

neck beside soldiers from his unit (Figure 7.6). When thanked by his commander, in Simonov's account, he thinks only of family and friends:

> He suddenly remembered recent events not having anything to do with the war, his mother and father living in the far off town of Oirot-Tura and comrades in the Komsomol from that town, where he was a member of the bureau of the Komsomol's Raion Committee, and also about the girl Valia Nekrasova.

Simonov, who had worked the Komsomol theme into his story, concluded:

> And I hope that after having read this issue of the newspaper, Shuklin's father and mother feel proud of their son, that Komsomol members of Oirot-Tura [his home town] remember their comrade whom they ought to emulate, and the girl Valia Nekrasova knows she loves a really fine fellow with the true eye and strong hand of a Russian soldier. (August 9, 1942)

Simonov was silent about Stalin but validated the official Soviet world of Komsomol together with that of society and private life. He wished Shuklin the respect of family and friends as well as the applause of the state youth organization and, as a writer, extended his own esteem. Although reporters rarely used the word *honor* (*chest'*), they conferred it. Ehrenburg wrote of Jews during the battle of Stalingrad: "Jews became soldiers. They did not give away their right to revenge to anyone" (November 1, 1942).

Journalists also displayed dishonor and made revenge a virtue. "My home is defiled by Prussians; I am tormented by the roar of their drunken laughter," wrote the poet Surkov in the terrible summer of 1942 (August 12, 1942). "We will take revenge not only for destroyed cities; we will take revenge for the deadly insult," Ehrenburg wrote in late 1941 (November 25, 1941). "At last that difficult time is over when we were retreating before those swine and convulsed with shame," read a letter Tolstoy quoted on May Day 1943 (May 1, 1943). "Am I to speak German—kneel on trembling knees, throw my head back in fear before the fat mug of a Hitlerite police agent who roars fiercely in the Berlin dialect and shoves a threatening fist in my teeth?" Tolstoy asked during the battle for Moscow (October 18, 1941). His answer was, "No, better death! No, better death in battle! No, only victory and life!" And no one was exempt. Gen. I. S. Konev told Simonov that Stalin shouted hysterically during the battle of Moscow: "Comrade Stalin is not a betrayer, Comrade Stalin is not a traitor, Comrade Stalin is an honorable man; his only mistake was that he trusted too much in cavalrymen."[114] The cavalrymen were his civil war cronies, K. E. Voroshilov and S. M. Budennyi. He executed as scapegoats Gen. D. G. Pavlov and others whose forces were overrun.[115]

Graphic artists also raised a mirror of shame and honor. The most famous wartime poster was I. Toidze's "The Motherland Calls!" dating from the defense of Moscow in 1941 and showing a stern woman in red holding up the text of the soldier's oath. Equally famous, however, was V. Koretskii's 1942 poster of a terrified woman and child cowering before a bloody bayonet marked with a swastika and titled "Soldier of the Red Army, Save Us."[116] The contemporary viewer might have asked: But where is Stalin? Toidze represented honor as a strong woman. Koretskii identified it with a weak one, shielding a child. In each case honor is constructed around an image of the nation, not its leader.

The acclaimed poster team, the Kukryniksy, developed the theme of dishonor during the first two years of war, and particularly in the summer of 1942. In "Take Revenge!" they portray a dead child in the ruins of a cottage and a woman dragged off by German soldiers (Figure 7.7).[117] The popular children's author, S. Marshak, who often wrote anti-Nazi propaganda during the war, provided the text: "Until recently smoke curled from the stove pipe / the wife baked bread in the stove and children ran about / for this child's corpse beside the cottage, any retribution is cheap at the price." In another, a booted German in a cart whips a young woman, an old man, and a child, who are pulling him along.[118] "Free Us!" is the caption. "Vengeance, bloody vengeance on the dirty fascist

Figure 7.7. *Pravda,* July 19, 1942. Drawing by Kukryniksy, "Take Revenge!" The text by S. Marshak: "Until recently smoke curled from the stove pipe / the wife baked bread and children ran about / for this child's corpse beside the cottage, any retribution is cheap at the price."

dogs for assaulting mothers, desecrating motherhood, and dishonorably insulting Soviet women," urged *Pravda*'s editorialists on International Youth Day, September 28, 1941.

The appeal to men to save women from sexual violation and children from mistreatment is one the most powerful and personal constructions of honor. It had been lacking in Soviet official culture since 1917. Its appearance validated men's wartime roles at the expense of women's. It also undercut Stalin, who had proved unable to protect those over whom he had ruled as "father." Cartoonists did not portray him, nor did they show the wreck of the great constructions of the 1930s, which might have impugned the state's honor. Rather, they pictured poor villages, simple cottages, and plainly clothed people. They rendered women as victims as dictated by honor, although women fought beside men and were sometimes also cast as avengers in the press. They showed Nazis humiliating families and villages, not the state, the Party, or the leader. Literary correspondents told this story to soldiers and civilians, fostering revenge in the name of individuals and communities, as well as the nation.

The Reimagination of the Audience and the Nation

Red Star was popular with civilians as well as soldiers. It benefited from its identification with the army and from its literary cast. The paper circulated widely among soldiers not only in its original edition but also through a network of front-line newspapers, tiny news sheets produced and handed out among fighting units. The editors of these publications borrowed liberally from the newspaper and often reprinted columns by Ehrenburg, Grossman, Tolstoy, Simonov, and others.

Ortenberg was a general, and those who wrote for *Red Star* held military rank. Reporters, including the writers, carried weapons, fought, and shared the army's tragedy, shame, and glory. Simonov, Grossman, and others first wore green quartermaster's uniforms similar to those of medics, but since they felt odd wearing them, Ortenberg soon got them the more desirable uniforms of commissars and political officers, even though some were not Party members.[119] Nevertheless the writers evoked the ordinary people of the nation in their most impassioned comments. In the fall of 1942, Simonov wrote:

> I have seen much on the roads of war, but I will never get used to the spectacle I see now. Perhaps some day a great artist will want to show the depths of the people's grief, the horrors of this war, and will paint a picture to show the burned out hearth, the darkened brick chimney, fragments of burned out planks, scattered with the remains of the things of the people living there—the stove pierced by bullets, the curved back of a bed, bits of rag. And in addition to all this he should draw an old woman.[120]

Platonov also evoked a suffering nation. The first piece he gave Ortenberg was a fable of an old man who promises the narrator a formula for "impenetrable armor." In the story, which appeared on September 6, 1942, the two cross Germans lines to Kursk to find the hidden formula, but the old man dies and the narrator, observing his courage and that of others, realizes that the "impenetrable armor" is the people's spirit. Platonov, whom Ortenberg made a captain, wrote again about soldiers who drew strength from ordinary people during the massive Kursk tank battle of 1943. The hero of "Home Hearth" sees a hearth between two smashed German "tiger" tanks.[121] "And near that still intact stove, an old peasant woman trampled clay with bare feet to repair the hearth of her home while her old man cut logs to build in the shadow of the dead 'tigers.'"

Correspondents shared authority and emotion with readers. "Writers came to the newspaper as if mounting a rostrum," Ehrenburg noted.[122] "Who among us will forget the day the Germans attacked? We each had our own lives, our own joys and sorrows," he wrote in mid-1942.[123] "A burned-out house appeared round the bend, then a second and a third. We drove into a completely incinerated town," wrote E. Gabrilovich in *Red Star* in late 1941.[124] During the Soviet counteroffensive in late 1941, while living at the hotel Moscow, Ehrenburg wrote: "The Germans very much want to get to the hotel Moscow. They write home about it. We won't let them into either the hotel Moscow or the city of Moscow."[125] As literary journalists invested the pronoun *we* with their own feelings, *Pravda*'s editorialists used it less often to express the faceless power of the state. *Red Star*'s editorialists used *we* in an inclusive, often intimate sense twice as often during the early years of war as did *Pravda*'s.[126] The sense of *we* as the nation in arms was now accepted even by some who had hitherto resisted the official Soviet identity. The memoirist O. V. Kalintseva, whose parents had long counterposed "our family" to the official Soviet *we,* wrote in her diary on February 4, 1943, when she witnessed the Red Army's recapture of Kharkov, "Today Aniutka and I met ours!"[127]

Ehrenburg, Simonov, and Grossman did not personally identify people they described as fully as did American correspondents such as Ernie Pyle, but they received the same kind of letters.[128] Thousands wrote to Ehrenburg, and he claimed to have answered "all, without exception; they are all my friends."[129] He helped those who wrote to him and excerpted their letters in his columns.[130] In 1943 he chose a hundred letters for a book but was not allowed to publish it. "This is not [19]41," a Soviet editor told him.[131] Censors had reason to ban it; the values it expressed had become subversive.[132] Ehrenburg had proposed a format in which an article of his from *Red Star* would be followed by several letters. "I beg you to tell me where my son has been buried and to mark his grave," wrote a mother in 1942 (17). "If possible, help me find my son Igor," wrote another (43). In the letters, people addressed Ehrenburg with requests as if he personally had the power to help them. A soldier, who had promised to avenge atrocities perpetrated near his home, wrote: "I told you in my letter that I would take revenge on the Germans for my ruined village and all the suffering they caused our country. Today I am happy to have been decorated with a medal 'for feats of arms.' I have kept my word" (87). Ehrenburg's request to publish in this format in 1943 collided with the reassertion of the power of the state over that of individuals.

Journalists early in the war developed a narrative of family and private life in which suffering was embodied in individual loss and personal relationships. "The collective farmer Kopelev lives here. Two German soldiers came into his cottage and raped his eighteen-year-old daughter, a Komsomol member," wrote a correspondent in October 1941.[133] "I looked. Children were walking about Viazma; naked, hungry orphans," wrote another in September 1943 (September 4, 1943). In "The Dedov Family," Ehrenburg, in 1942, described a sister who urged her brother to avenge a brother's death. "The fighter Mitrofan Dedov," he wrote, "sent me a letter from his parents and sister from a collective farm in Irkutsk oblast" (August 7, 1942). A year later, in "The Fate of One Family," he described an old man whose children and grandchildren had been killed. "I did not invent what I now recount," he wrote. "It is an account of the Pavlov family's fate" (April 6, 1943). Mother now meant not only Mother Russia, but particular mothers. "And how many people on the front suddenly remembered how much they loved their mothers?" asked Ehrenburg in 1942 (August 8, 1942).

Although there was a "guards' family" and a "family" of Soviet peoples, reporters depicted a military family as well (October 2, 1942; August 21, 1943). A soldier's letter in *Red Star* in early 1942 was addressed: "To Red Army Soldier Ivan Petrovich Burtakov." The author wrote almost biblically: "Comrade! I was in your village, spoke with your mother. She blessed me since, like you, her son, I was in a gray coat. She poured water for me, fed me warm bread, and looked at me lovingly as she would have looked on you" (January 11, 1942). The reemergence of warm human family relations contrasted remarkably with the disregard of family in the press of the 1920s and the stress on proper, unidimensional, honorable families from the mid-1930s.

Journalists also wrote of an international antifascist family and a family of humanity. "The Siberian understands the grief of Greece, the Ukrainian understands what France has endured; the suffering of the Norwegian fisherman is close to that of the Belorussian peasant," Ehrenburg wrote in late 1943 (November 11, 1943). "If Germans have excluded themselves from the common family, it is not our ideas that are responsible, but the Germans' atrocities," he explained near the war's end (January 1, 1945). After seeing Dachau in mid-1944, Simonov wrote a three-part commentary on "this crime against humanity by the Germans" (August 10–12). "What I have decided to write about is too enormous and terrible to comprehend," he began. He did not say the majority were Jews, but he implied it. "What is most terrible," he observed, "are the tens of thousands of pairs of children's shoes" (August 11, 1944). The Yiddish partisan poet A. Sutzkever, later a friend of Ehrenburg's, wrote a poem in the Vilna Ghetto in 1943 titled "A Wagon of Shoes," with the lines: "All children's shoes—but where / Are all the children's feet?"[134] An awareness of Nazi atrocities and later of the Holocaust helped to sustain the image of humane Soviet defenders, and later of Soviet avengers.

In the press, people were shown to thank one another personally, without mentioning Stalin. *Red Star*'s photographer, Loskutov, described an old woman's arrival at the cottage where he and his partisan friends were staying.

> The old woman went up to the table and quickly began to take out of her basket wool socks, mittens, and scarfs.
>
> She hastily said:
>
> "The women knitted these for you a while ago, but never knew where to find you."
>
> "Thank you, Grandma!" said the commander of the detachment and embraced the old woman.[135]

Reporters expressed the idea that soldiers were fighting on behalf of specific people who were indebted to them for their sacrifices. Typical was *Pravda*'s report on January 4, 1942, about a unit that liberated a village. "A village boy, having already managed to decorate his cap with a Red Army star, follows the fighters with joyful eyes," the author wrote. The boy runs to the commander, shouting: "That is our house, it is warm. Are you coming to our house?" *Pravda* displayed the bond between soldier and civilian in a report on March 11, 1943, of a soldier who braved enemy fire to place defensive mines: "And his commander was correct when, in response to the thanks of the liberated inhabitants of the village, he answered: Bow down to Zakharov, he is our hero." The same story was told in one liberated village after another. "Thank you, dear fighters, for our liberation from terrible servitude as prisoners of the Germans," women who had been scheduled for deportation to Germany as slave laborers wrote to *Red Star* from Smolensk.[136] Grossman, in mid-1943, described Ukrainians who clung to stories of their liberators. "Now ten days after the arrival of the Red Army," he wrote, "the old peasant women and the younger ones as well love to tell about that first meeting with our troops."[137]

Civilians, too, were thanked, as Simonov wrote in his famous poem "Wait for Me," which appeared in *Pravda,* and ends:

> By waiting here for me
> It was you that saved me.
> Only you and I will know
> How I survived—
> It's just that you knew how to wait
> As no other person.[138]

One way to interpret this turnabout in which soldiers and civilians suddenly congratulated each other is as a change in the quality and object of sacrifice. To celebrate their presumed selflessness, early Bolsheviks had drawn on confluent traditions of Orthodoxy and the intelligentsia. Portraying themselves as martyrs, they had invoked what Nicholas Berdyaev has called one of the "stable attributes" of the Russian spirit, namely, "the ability to endure suffering and to make sacrifices for the sake of its faith, whatever that may be."[139] The official ethos of sacrifice weakened during the 1930s. The Stalinists claimed to have created a near-perfect world, and they announced that all the deserving could be rich and happy. Hard work under these circumstances was, in part, represented as intelligent self-interest.

In covering the war, some journalists rediscovered suffering. They infused people's sacrifice for one another and for the homeland with a spiritual quality, what the persecuted Russian philosopher Alexei Losev called, soon after the invasion, "something elevated and thrilling, something ennobling and heroic."[140] The editors of *Red Star* sounded this note on October 24, 1941, describing a soldier who set off a rocket to warn of approaching German tanks. "Personal danger meant nothing to him. The threat to Moscow blotted out everything. For victory, for Moscow's defense, he defied death." Ehrenburg invoked this feeling when, on October 28, 1941, he wrote: "We bravely look ahead; to grief and also to victory." A battalion political officer on the Finnish front described a dying Soviet sniper: "He opened his eyes and saw familiar native faces. These were his comrades, who were as ready to give the homeland all of themselves, to the last drop of blood, to the last breath, as was he Zuev and [his friend] Lebedev, who had died heroically."[141]

"War has its own set values," wrote Simonov in his postwar novel *The Living and the Dead*.[142] He might have added that such values often diverged from official ritual. War redefined the "enemy," hitherto so critical to the public culture. Persecutions continued, but the press rarely featured them. As *we* and *they* acquired new meanings, official Russia relinquished some of its power to stigmatize. Metaphors changed. War became the "teacher," and Stalin relinquished that metaphorical position.[143] Battles became military, and the real military front dwarfed metaphorical pseudo-fronts such as the ideological front. Building ceased to be an issue, and the "path" was the "path of our troops" and the "path to Berlin"—"The great path traversed by our Red Army."[144] A cartoonist for *Red Star*, in March 1945, even appropriated the train and portrayed the war effort as a locomotive decorated with British, American, and Soviet flags, and without Stalin as engineer (Figure 7.8).[145] Time and narrative were recast. Wartime narratives had definite beginnings and endings. Has Smolensk fallen? Has Minsk been recaptured? Such questions punctuated stories with urgency. The present came alive and was no longer tenuously suspended between a richly embellished past and an imminent future. This was true even in 1944 when all commentaries converged on the approaching victory. Language, too, changed. References to class struggle faded, and journalists used the word *kulak* (fist) to urge "clenched fists," rather than the murder of innocent peasants.[146]

Stalin on Center Stage

Although Stalin receded from public view, he and the apparatus did not vanish. Victories on the battlefield and in the economic war to outproduce the Nazis were achieved through an authoritarian command structure. The army's triumph was also that of the state and the Stalinist administrative system, though not theirs alone. Mekhlis and Shcherbakov constantly scrutinized the press with Stalin in mind, and one or the other met with him several times a week.[147] By contrast, Ortenberg had a rare link by phone. In 1942 Shcherbakov told him to call at any hour with questions about copy, and he recalled how Mekhlis worked over one of his editorials: "He not only painstakingly read it but began to edit it from habit as an old *Pravda* hand."[148] When Stalin introduced a single command structure by placing political commissars under the authority of military commanders in October 1942, Mekhlis told Ortenberg not to mention it. "I did not begin to argue," he recalled. "I knew Mekhlis wrote the regulation and that

Figure 7.8. *Red Star,* March 15, 1945. "The Way Is Blocked!"

Stalin also worked on it."[149] Stalin intervened constantly and arbitrarily. He initially ordered that A. Tolstoy be kept safely in the rear.[150] Legend has it that he championed the partisan martyr known as Zoia Komsomolka (Kosmodemianskaia) after he read in *Pravda* that her captors had asked her, "Where is Stalin?" and she had replied, "Stalin is at his post."[151] A story in *Red Star* by the film director Aleksandr Dovzhenko pleased Stalin in 1942, and he had G. M. Malenkov, a secretary of the Central Committee, tell Ortenberg to give Dovzhenko "Stalin's thanks."[152] Later, when he read Ukrainian nationalism in Dovzhenko's story and film scenario, "Ukraine on Fire," he forbade publication of the writer.[153]

While the tide of battle turned from defeat to victory, Stalin reasserted his public persona, and another narrative of the war arose. As the victory at Stalingrad approached, the press began publishing patriotic declarations addressed to Stalin. In December 1942 the press printed letters promising contributions to the war, accompanied by Stalin's thanks, and soon afterward letters thanking him for liberating particular towns. In 1943 Stalin adopted the formula of announcing victories by publishing "orders" to his generals, as if the military action had been taken under his direct command. Soon after Stalingrad, the press praised his military genius and hailed "the Stalinist school of military thought." In 1944 his picture became even more common. *Pravda* showed him on the front page nineteen times that year, twice as often as in 1943. The press showed him meeting with foreign diplomats and attending official gatherings. In March 1943 he took the title of Marshal, and in 1945 of Generalissimo. In 1945, when Konev and others at the Politburo suggested that he adopt the title of Generalissimo, he allegedly exclaimed: "Comrade Stalin does not need it. Comrade Stalin has authority without it."[154] Yet he agreed, and photographers showed him in ornate uniforms. "Nothing that Stalin ever did was an accident," Khrushchev noted.[155]

Stalin again became the font of recognition and honor. *Pravda* marked his brief speech to the Moscow Soviet on November 6, 1942, in which he mentioned that the German advance had halted at Stalingrad, with a front-page letter from the city's defenders that began, "Comrade Stalin, feeling your concern for us, your leadership of the whole Stalingrad fight, we are stubbornly defending every spot of our land." The paper followed with a tribute from the Soviet in which delegates recalled Moscow's defense and took an oath to "our beloved father and leader."[156]

In early 1943 the publication of Stalin's "orders" to generals began.[157] On January 26, 1943, just before Field-Marshal Paulus capitulated at Stalingrad, Stalin issued an "order" praising officers and armies for victories. "I declare my gratitude to the commanders and valiant troops, who destroyed the Hitlerite army in the trenches of Stalingrad," he wrote. A list followed. A week later, on February 3, 1943, generals on the Don front publicly reported their victory to him as if he had ordered it. The front-page report read: "Fulfilling your order, the troops of the Don front at 16.00 hours on February 2, 1943, finished the rout and destruction of surrounded enemy groups." Signatures included Colonel-General Rokossovskii, Lieutenant-General Malinin, Artillery Marshal Voronov, and General Major Telegin. "I congratulate you and the troops of the Don front for the successful liquidation of the surrounded hostile troops near Stalingrad," read Stalin's reply.

After Kharkov's liberation in the fall of 1943, *Pravda* featured Stalin's "order" to General Sokolovskii, commending him. Below was a letter to Stalin "from the working people of the city of Kharkov." It read in part: "Thank you dear Marshal for our freedom, for children's happiness, for life!"[158] Such orders were also read on the radio. Noting the "Stalin order" of August 6, 1943, which he took for the first, Werth recalled: "The deep voice of Levitan, Moscow Radio's star announcer, now uttered for the first time phrases that were to become like sweet and familiar music during the next two years."[159] Victories were "sweet," but the sweetness was tempered by the loss of the plurality of narratives.

Other rituals of the cult also reappeared and crowded out rival stories as the fortune of the war turned. In late 1942 *Pravda* printed occasional letters to and from Stalin. On December 6 the paper published a report from metal workers of Magnitogorsk promising to fulfill their assigned tasks. On the ninth the paper featured a letter from farmers in Tambov donating forty million rubles for tanks, and Stalin's reply to the Tambov Party secretary. A front-page report about the donation appeared the next day. *Pravda,* on December 18, printed a letter from the chairman of a collective farm in Saratov who donated his life savings. "Soviet power made me a prosperous collective farmer, and now when the homeland is in danger, I have decided to help it all I can," he wrote. Stalin replied the next day: "Thank you, Ferapont Petrovich, for your concern about the Red Army and its air force. The Red Army will not forget that you gave all your savings to build a military airplane."[160] The pages of the central press were soon crowded with letters from local Party officials, followed by Stalin's thanks. Ortenberg, Pospelov, and Rovinskii, editor of *Izvestiia,* asked Shcherbakov if exchanges between local officials and Stalin could be published in papers from regions where they originated since they were crowding out war news. "Aleksandr Sergeevich [Shcherbakov]," Ortenberg recalled, "looked at us as madmen not to print a letter with Stalin's signature."[161]

After Stalingrad, the press also began printing letters thanking Stalin for particular victories.[162] *Pravda* made the recapture of Voronezh in January Stalin's personal triumph.[163] On February 15, after Von Paulus surrendered, the Stalingrad Soviet praised Stalin in *Pravda* as "the organizer of victory." When Rostov was liberated a few weeks later, the ritual became more lavish. The head of the Party committee and chairman of the executive of the Soviet wrote in *Pravda:* "We have no words to express our love and gratitude to you, our father, and to the soldiers and commanders who have given us back freedom and happiness. Great heartfelt thanks to you from all our soul! Thank you for liberating us, for liberating life!"[164]

As Stalingrad was won, Simonov in *Red Star* began to reinvent the past for himself and others, reading Stalin back into the early narratives of defeat:

> I remember the forest beyond Mogilev and the radio reporter reading Stalin's speech—"My friends!" There were several of us. We listened to the reporter's voice shaken by emotion, and though he spoke and it was his voice we heard, it nevertheless seemed to us that Stalin himself spoke to us. He related bleak news, demanding the greatest sacrifices a person can and should make. He spoke to us of the homeland's fate, Russia's fate, Moscow's fate.[165]

Ehrenburg also brought Stalin back. "In this triumphant hour I think of our Great Comrade," he wrote in late 1943 when the Donbas and Smolensk were liberated (September 25, 1943). He returned to the theme a month later, noting that on crossing the Dnieper, "a lieutenant shouted through a megaphone: 'Comrade Stalin's order! The Red Army has liberated Smolensk'" (October 23, 1943). Ehrenburg wrote of Stalin's "military genius" in early 1944, on the eve of the Soviet spring offensive: "Stalin gave battle to the Germans when and where it was to the Red Army's advantage. Hitler thought he was storming Stalingrad's last redoubt, but actually he was wasting his last storm troopers" (February 24, 1944). Late in the war the impetus to praise was very great. By September 1944 Nikolai Tikhonov, who covered Leningrad for *Red Star,* wrote simply: "The genius of Stalin is the genius of foresight. He spoke in the first days of war as only a leader to whom the future was revealed could" (September 15, 1944).

Official Patriotism and Official Honor

The press produced a narrative of "peoples" as symbols of the "unity of the great family" throughout the war.[166] At the outset Stalin had cited regions acquired through the pact with Hitler as Soviet territories. "The enemy has seized a large part of Ukraine, Belorussia, Moldavia, Lithuania, Latvia, Estonia, and a series of other regions," he explained in his second wartime speech, on November 6, 1941.[167] *Pravda*'s commentators followed his lead. "The Uzbek people know their fate will be resolved in Ukraine, on the fields of Belorussia, on the outskirts of Leningrad," wrote a commentator in mid-1942.[168] The literary correspondents, however, usually wrote of soldiers and civilians, not Uzbeks or Ukrainians.[169]

The story of peoples converged with that of "great ancestors" and Pan-Slavism, which gained sway in 1943. *Red Star* editorialized on the "glory" of the Russian, Ukrainian, and Belorussian lands in January of that year.[170] In May editors hailed the "fighting unity of Slavic peoples," with quotes from "the great Russian writer Gogol" on the nature of Slavs.[171] "On the eve of a bitter battle, we say to ourselves, as Suvorov said at such moments to his marvelous fighters: 'We are Russians!'" wrote a columnist.[172] "Patriotism is a feeling formed in our people over centuries. Now, in wartime, we even more warmly and closely sense our blood tie with the founders and creators of Great Russian culture," wrote L. Timofeev in *Red Star* on the fiftieth anniversary of Mayakovsky's birth in July.[173] Werth later wrote of "Stalin's little nationalist orgy" after the Kursk victory in the summer of 1943.[174] Two months later a patriarch of the Orthodox Church was chosen for the first time since the revolution. On New Year's Day, 1944, the press printed the new Soviet anthem. "Great Russia united forever an unbreakable union of free republics," it began. In June 1944 A. Tolstoy's novel *Peter the Great* was widely excerpted, and articles appeared on Russian cultural figures such as Repin, "the great Russian painter," and Chekhov, "pride of the Russian people."[175]

Anti-Semitism, Stalin's as well as that of others, figured in the new nationalism. In August 1942, with Stalingrad at risk, the Central Committee's Department of Agitation and Propaganda, headed by G. F. Aleksandrov, an official philosopher, warned Central Committee secretaries Malenkov, Shcherbakov, and Andreyev that Jews dominated Russian musical and other cultural institutions, as well as the literature and art sections of *Pravda, Izvestiia,* and other newspapers.[176] Purges followed. The initiators included Shcherbakov, chief of the Information Bureau and now also of the army's political administration, and Aleksandrov.[177]

Ortenberg was dismissed along with others and gives an account in his memoirs. "You have many Jews in the editorial section—cut the number," he relates Shcherbakov as having told him in late spring of 1943.[178] "The number is already cut," he replied. "Reporters Lapin, Khatsrevin, Rozenfeld, Shuer, Vilkomir, Slutsky, Ish, and Bernshtein died at the front. They were Jews, and I can cut one more, myself." Shcherbakov fired him on June 30 and refused to give a reason. Ortenberg became chief political officer to Konev's army, which entered Prague the following year. Later in 1943 Simonov wrote Ortenberg of his sense of loss—"for me an organization or institution does not exist by itself, but only through people whom I either love or do not love—in a word, I've cooled off about the newspaper; I hope you understand me."[179] This feeling did not leave him. After the war, in late 1946, when he was editor of the literary journal *New World,* he wrote to the poet A. A. Surkov, who had submitted a poem with a line honoring Ortenberg. "It is dedicated to a man whom I also love, and I want to keep it," he wrote.[180]

Ehrenburg was aware of the new repression. He complained at *Red Star*'s editorial board and the Frunze Military Academy in early 1945 that Soviet soldiers were raping and looting in East Prussia. V. Abakumov, chief of SMERCH, counterintelligence for the Commissariat of Defense, denounced him to Stalin, and Aleksandrov, who had tried to root out Jews as early as 1942, berated him in *Pravda* and *Red Star.*[181] "Comrade Ehrenburg Oversimplifies," was *Red Star*'s caption. He was accused of not distinguishing between Nazis and Germans. Ehrenburg redeemed himself with a fawning letter to Stalin, which began Dear Iosif Vissarionovich! I am sorry to have to take your time in these great days with a personal matter."[182] He later recalled, "I continued to write for *Red Star, Pravda,* and for front-line newspapers, but work became more difficult, something changed; I felt it in myself."[183] Whether the printed criticism was directed to Ehrenburg personally or simply a signal that Germans should no longer be blamed collectively is unclear. Grossman also came under pressure, but he succeeded in publishing his reports on the Holocaust—"Ukraine without Jews" and "The Hell of Treblinka"—although not in major journals or *Red Star.*[184]

The rise and fall of the multiplicity of narratives and viewpoints coincided with the fortunes of the Party, whose membership dropped by a quarter during

1941, after having nearly quadrupled from January 1938 to January 1941. From 1942, membership again grew rapidly, however, nearly doubling the pre-invasion level by the war's end.[185] *Pravda* hailed the return of Soviet authority and officialdom with a spate of articles. "A big day in Iaroslavl," captioned one in 1944. "Secretary of the Provincial [Party] Committee Comrade Larionov in his speech pointed out the immediate material tasks before agricultural workers of Iaroslavl oblast," it read.[186] The bureaucratic imperative returned in a flood of orders. "It is good, Comrades, but we cannot relax. We have no right. Comrade Stalin demands all our strength," a farm chairman announced on May 3, 1943, under the heading "Siberians Respond to the Leader's Order." The old order was coming back with a message: No concessions to wartime feelings and hopes. *Pravda* quoted a peasant in late 1943: "The free Russia of collective farmers and workers existed and will exist."[187]

The two apparent signs of a relaxed official sensibility at this time—dissolution of the Comintern on May 22, 1943, and an agreement with the Russian Orthodox Church in September—were probably intended to influence Western rather than Soviet opinion.[188] *Pravda* featured the announcement by the Comintern's presidium prominently and, a week later, Stalin's explanation to a Reuters correspondent that the measure would facilitate "freedom-loving nations' common pressure against the common foe."[189] *Pravda* gave the Church less attention, noting Stalin's meeting with Metropolitans Sergius, Alexei, and Nikolai in a tiny front-page article on September 4. The announcement of the formation of a Holy Synod, its choice of Sergius as patriarch of Moscow and all Russia, and the Synod's "gratitude to the government of the USSR for its attention to the needs of the Russian Orthodox Church" appeared in a similar report on page 2 on September 8. Thus the Church joined the economy of the gift, and Orthodox priests throughout the country prayed for Stalin's health.[190] There were no pictures, however, and the co-optation of Russian national sentiment proceeded in tandem with the reassertion of Soviet authority.

As the press showed local authorities enjoying the esteem it had once assigned partly to society, cartoonists pictured routed Germans and a humbled Hitler instead of abused women and children. Official honor also reappeared in commentaries on uniforms, medals, and orders. Pictures of new ornate uniforms filled *Red Star* and other papers on January 7, 1943, on the eve of the victory at Stalingrad. "Shoulder straps are not only decoration, but also order and discipline; tell about this," Stalin told Ortenberg.[191] *Red Star* showed marshals' and generals' uniforms on page 1 and the lower ranks on page 2, and Stalin ordered *Pravda* and *Izvestiia* to do likewise.[192] Werth noted a shift from the "thoroughly plebeian" to gold braid, epaulets, and other decorations.[193]

The press emphasized medals and public honor in ways reminiscent of the 1930s. From Stalingrad to the war's end, newspapers printed whole pages listing recipients. Heroes had been decorated earlier, but in 1943 the trickle became a torrent. Medals named for Suvorov, Nevsky, and Kutuzov appeared in 1942; for Bogdan Khmelnitsky, in 1943; for admirals Ushakov and Nakhimov, in 1944; and, in 1943, there was an Order of Glory for common soldiers and an Order of Victory, encrusted with diamonds, for commanders.[194] There were also medals for the liberation of foreign cities, for partisans, and, as before the war, for "labor valor" and "labor excellence."[195] Many brought monetary benefits. "The best masters of sharpshooting are awarded state medals and valuable gifts," read a decree from 1943.[196] The report in May 1942 of awards to families of Major-General Panfilov and twenty-eight guards who perished in the battle of Moscow included a "one-time payment of two thousand rubles," a pension, and housing in Alma Ata.[197]

Stalin prizes were announced in the spring of 1943 for literature and the arts with cash awards of fifty thousand to one hundred thousand rubles.[198] Tolstoy won first prize in literature, and Korneichuk, author of *The Front,* first in drama. Simonov won fifty thousand rubles for his play *Russian People,* more than a hundred times a skilled worker's monthly wage. Official recognition replaced alternate measures of accomplishment in other fields as well. "For the Soviet people, the government's high evaluation of work is the highest of all rewards," an agricultural worker was quoted as saying in early 1944.[199] "Rank and uniform determined a person's position," Ehrenburg recalled, noting the newspapers' failure to mention the death of his friend, the writer Iu. Tynianov in 1943.[200]

The state had never lost control of the definition of dishonor and honor, although it did for a period yield some of its monopoly. From start to finish, Soviet officialdom shamed traitors, slackers, and soldiers taken prisoner. "Yes, I was a prisoner," recalled a general, wounded and captured at Kiev, "and I was much ashamed of it."[201] To adopt the official "code of honor" and conform to its values was to accept an official identity and to model one's behavior accordingly. To internalize the code but to act against it even unwillingly, as had the general captured at Kiev, brought shame. To act against it and not to feel shame was to reject the code and the identity that went with it. After the war Simonov struggled with this conundrum in his novel *The Living and the Dead.* His hero Sintsov is denied reentry into the Party after he loses his Party card— the emblem of an official identity—when wounded in battle. He asks his commanding officer, "What is more valuable: a human being or a piece of paper?"[202] He then notes bitterly his inability to resume his old life without the card, lost by no fault of his own:

> "I now believe that a piece of paper is more valuable," Sintsov went on. "It is lying somewhere in the forest, rotting away and telling me all the time: You think you exist in your own right? No, you're kidding yourself. You are no human being without me. I know it is not your fault; you did not throw me away, but I won't let you live without me."[203]

Many Stories, One Victory

Though Stalin advanced his cult, and newspapers retained and even enlarged the language of performance, a plurality of narratives and meanings persisted. As the war proceeded toward its victorious conclusion, journalists briefly appropriated the flowers and children that the press had previously identified with Stalin and used them to tell a story with other heroes. "Fighters and commanders of the Red Army and Fleet, workers, collective farmers, and employees donate their personal savings to support orphaned children and attend to their upbringing, replacing their lost parents," *Pravda*'s editors wrote on June 14, 1943. Photographers pictured civilians greeting their deliverers with bouquets in Kharkov, in the Donbas, in Poland, in Czechoslovakia, and elsewhere. "The citizens of Kharkov joyfully welcome their liberators," read the caption of a photo in the fall of 1943.[204] "The inhabitants of liberated Prague delightedly greet Soviet troops," read another beneath a picture of a woman waving flowers and another kissing a soldier in September 1944.[205]

Yet by 1945 Stalin's image and paeans to his glory were everywhere.[206] Ehrenburg recalled, perhaps with some self-justification, "Our soldiers piously believed in him."[207] The patriotic prewar slogans—"For the Homeland, for Stalin" and "Where Stalin Is, There Is Victory"—now became prominent, the first in accounts of battles published soon after the German surrender, the second as a slogan in the ceremonial elections for the Supreme Soviet in January 1946.[208] Stalin renewed the logic of the social order in his speech on June 26, 1945, after the victory parade in Red Square, in which he hailed ordinary people as "*vintiki*"—cogs in the state machine. The setting was the Kremlin reception for notable participants in the parade, but Stalin's toast was addressed to those outside the gala Kremlin reception—the vast majority of the people. He emphasized not only service but honor and the acceptance of one's proper place.

> Do not expect me to say something extraordinary. I have the most ordinary toast.
> I wish to drink to people with few ranks and unenviable titles; to people, who are considered "cogs" in the great state mechanism, but without whom all of us—marshals and commanders of fronts and armies— speaking crudely, would not have a leg to stand on.[209]

After Stalingrad, Stalin loomed ever larger, and narratives in which he did not figure faded. "On this morning of peace we think about one person; all glance to him," wrote Ehrenburg on May 10.[210] "This man defended not only our life and dignity, but the very title of the person, which fascism wished to take from us. And because of that, the first spring flowers, the first dawn light, the first sigh of joy go to him, to our Stalin!" wrote the writer Leonid Leonov on the eleventh (May 11, 1945). The mention of flowers signaled the full revival of the cult in all its magic and mystery, and photographs of Stalin with children soon followed. As the Red Army crossed the borders of the old empire, the patriotic war also became a war of liberation, as Stalin had originally envisaged it.

Even as they promoted the cult, however, Ehrenburg, Leonov, and others alluded to other narratives. During the war journalists had appealed to humanistic values uncharacteristic of the 1930s, and the British and American allies had been a faint but real presence in the press. There were frequent quotes from the allied media about Soviet successes, particularly in the last two years of the war. By giving space to such reports, the editors of *Red Star, Pravda,* and other Soviet newspapers broke with a decade of enmity. "Radio San Francisco stressed the enormous expanse of the Soviet troops' attack," read one such comment (January 22, 1944). "London radio communicated a summary of articles from English newspapers in which they comment on the progress and possibilities of the Soviet forces' attack in Ukraine," read another (March 22, 1944). Editors who printed such comments allowed foreigners a legitimacy and authority that contrasted with the xenophobia of the 1930s. "The babies of the world can sleep peacefully in their cradles," Leonov wrote on May 7, 1945. "Soviet troops, and the troops of our Western friends . . . will not return home until the wind of the liberating hurricane makes Germany unfit for the fascist fiend."

Some have argued that the war solidified Stalin's hold on culture and society.[211] Certainly official representations of the wartime experience reinforced his position during the remainder of his lifetime, but the multiple alternative wartime narratives about patriotism, citizenship, motivation, obligation, honor, and courage had a responsive audience. The opening of public space to the emotions and experience of a wider public was part of the national resurgence that brought victory. The values that correspondents expressed resonated with millions of readers. Grossman wrote in *Life and Fate:* "Freedom engendered the Russian victory. Freedom was the apparent aim of the war. But the sly fingers of History changed this: Freedom became simply a way of waging the war, a means to an end."[212]

As the war ended, Stalin and his officials faced the question of how, if ever, they could put the genie of an imagined civil society back in its box. The war spurred new identities, purposes, and courage. To many, victory depended on their own efforts, and not Stalin's. Ehrenburg wrote on May 10, 1945:

> We reached Berlin because there was always another to replace those who had fallen, because Soviet warriors defended every hillock and hollow of their native land, because of vegetable gardens in Moscow suburbs, because of Leningrad suburbs, stones of Sevastopol, tractors of Stalingrad, Kursk meadows, partisans, girls of the "Young Guard," and factories, which sprang up in wasteland, and because for four years the people lived like ascetics.[213]

The plurality of narratives and actors, however, was a casualty of success. While the end was in doubt, participants could promote victory partly in their own way, but as the war was won, Stalin and his government reasserted the primacy of a narrative in which they alone held pride of place. Stalin was acclaimed at home and abroad, and with his pronouncement, made on the October anniversary in 1943 and reiterated afterward, that "the Soviet order has turned out to be not only the best organizational form for the country's economic and cultural growth in years of peaceful building but also the best means of mobilizing all the people's strength to repel the enemy in wartime," he also announced the reimposition of the old order.[214] Yet the mix of narratives reflected participants' own pride in conducting the war and therefore a symbolic transfer of value from state, Party, and leader to "society" in their persons. This, too, was a wartime legacy. Stalin and his supporters worked fiercely to suppress it after the war ended, with only partial success.

Eight

The Theft of the War

STALIN and his supporters entered the cold war with a ruined economy, a traumatized population, and a cluster of potentially hostile client states, but victory empowered them to claim that they had fulfilled their promise to make Russia a great power. The story the press told from May 9, 1945, until Stalin's death on March 5, 1953, was that Stalin had foreseen the war, created the economy necessary to defeat Germany, and saved the Soviet Union and the world from tyranny. Allotting Russians a primary role in these events, Stalin and his government continued the effort to fuse Russian and Soviet nationalism which had begun in the 1930s. By stressing the world's obligation, they appealed to Soviet pride and enlarged the economy of the gift. Although they hesitated at first to demonize their Western antagonists in the cold war, they soon revived the Manicheanism of the 1930s, portraying themselves as humanity's benefactor and their opponents as vicious pretenders to the role and ungrateful beneficiaries of Soviet sacrifices. They likewise revived the public paranoia about domestic enemies.

Narrating postwar events according to this script, Stalin and his supporters increased the population's presumed indebtedness and their own obligation to lie about Soviet life. In conformance with official rituals, the players in Soviet public life were a little like a theatrical company of great reputation, compelled to enact a flawed drama repeatedly before a half-empty house. The undercurrent of dissatisfaction with the official culture was so powerful that within a year of Stalin's death, some of the performers joined hands with the audience to initiate remarkable, if flawed, efforts to revise it fundamentally and even to do away with it entirely.

The project of deifying the aging leader as his mind and body shriveled was inherently implausible. So was the renewed Manicheanism, which answered the needs of the cold war but not those of the new global environment. Most improbable of all was the feat of sustaining the performance after alternate sources of information had become more readily available through the experience of the war itself, postwar travel within the communist bloc, contact with visiting foreigners, and Western propaganda. The very grandiosity of the postwar restaging of Stalinist public culture foreshadowed the reappearance of rival narratives, the collapse of Manicheanism, the dethroning of Stalin under Khrushchev, and the disintegration of the monopoly of information during glasnost under Gorbachev.

In May 1945 Soviet citizens expected benefits, not sacrifices, and the government knew it. One source of concern was the army's exposure to life abroad.[1] "The contrast between living standards in Europe and among us, which millions of fighting people encountered, was a moral and psychological blow that was not so easy for our people to bear despite the fact that they were the victors in this war," Simonov later observed.[2] Lend-Lease was also telling. "In 1945, the streets were full of 'Studebekker' trucks and jeeps with a white star on their doors and hoods—the American hardware we had got on lend-lease," Joseph Brodsky recalled.[3] "The war had hardly finished, and newspapers were already flooded with articles about subservience to the West. And they were aimed largely at us, frontline soldiers, who had crossed Europe from battle to battle," recalled Marshal V. Kulikov.[4]

Some officials feared a repeat of the Decembrist rebellion, when disaffected officers nearly seized power after Napoleon's defeat.[5] The police warned in 1946 of unruly soldiers, workers eager to quit evacuated factories, peasants unwilling to subscribe to the postwar reconstruction loan, and general refusals to work.[6] Agents and informers noted demands for religious and intellectual freedom, reduced work loads and rules, increased bread rations, the breakup of collective farms, and legalization of private trade.[7] In 1945 the government received reports on Shaginian and other writers who complained of "the lack of freedom of speech," workers' living conditions, failures to abide by provisions of the Stalin Constitution, and other shortcomings.[8] Contemporaries later voiced disappointment. "It was painful and humiliating to veterans and everyone that the victory which cost so much blood did not give the country what we dreamed of at the front," recalled a veteran.[9] "Everyone expected something bright and good," noted D. A. Tolstoy, the composer and son of the writer, Alexei Tolstoy.[10] "Although victory had not brought the relief and freedom that were expected at the end of the war, nonetheless the portents of freedom filled the air throughout the postwar period, and they alone defined its historical significance," Pasternak wrote in his epilogue to *Doctor Zhivago*.[11] Advocates, too, had hopes. "Drunk with victory, full of ourselves, we decided that our system was ideal," recalled the writer F. Abramov.[12] The rulers, however, felt the reverse side of the gift equation. Dmitrii Shepilov, editor of *Pravda* from 1953 to 1956, later recalled the millions who had seen superior food, clothing, and housing in Europe with apparent bitterness: "And we were obligated to give people all this."[13]

Peace brought scarcity and repression. Two million people, many of them children, died of hunger and hunger-related diseases in the famine of 1946–48. The Russian historian V. F. Zima blames the government, which requisitioned and exported grain despite drought-related crop failures in European Russia, Ukraine, and Moldavia, as well as a scanty Siberian harvest.[14] People suffered in Moscow and other cities, and starving peasants fled failed farms. The state allotted supplementary food, access to special stores, and other perks to officials down to collective farm chairmen, including favored cultural figures. Khrushchev recalled cannibalism in Ukraine and farmers too weak to work: "I myself had to make a special request from the state for grain to feed our own people," presumably Party people.[15] Interviewing Molotov, the former Soviet poet F. Chuev recalled his own childhood: "I went hungry and was sent to a special play center for children suffering from dystrophia [i.e., malnutrition]. I was six."[16] Molotov replied, "I was not in that situation, . . . but in exile [as a revolutionary in the tsarist period] I sometimes went hungry." The press ignored the famine, although its ravages were painfully evident.

The government celebrated the thirtieth anniversary of Soviet Ukraine with pomp on January 25, 1948. "Soviet Ukraine is on the true and reliable path," Molotov avowed. "We are deeply thankful for the great attention and care for Ukraine shown under Soviet power by the Central Committee of the Bolshevik Party, personally by Vladimir Ilich Lenin, and by the continuer of Lenin's cause, the great Stalin," announced Khrushchev, who later recalled pleading with Stalin to aid the hungry. *Pravda* the next day conveyed the Ukrainian Supreme Soviet's thanks to Stalin. "Ukrainian people will glorify your name eternally from generation to generation as creator of the free Ukrainian state." Playwright A. Korneichuk, who had published *The Front* in *Pravda* during the war, wrote, "We are a happy Ukrainian generation, for we participate in the struggle for the most advanced society, for communism."[17]

The press also ignored repression. Of 5.2 million repatriated citizens, 338,000 were seized by the NKVD, according to official figures.[18] Many émigrés and others, lured back with promises of a good life, were also incarcerated. Arrests were common in liberated areas, and the authorities suspected anyone who had lived beyond the reach of Soviet power. An art specialist recalled questions about whether individuals or their relatives had resided in occupied lands during the war on forms "the Soviet citizen was compelled repeatedly to fill out when getting a passport, taking a job, entering an educational institution, or joining the Komsomol or the Party."[19] According to police data, the gulag's population grew from 1.7 million to 2.5 million from 1945 to 1952.[20] Nationalities deported to camps or punitive exile—Chechens and Ingushi, Kalmyks and Crimean Tatars, Islamicized Georgians, Ukrainians, Balts, Moldavians, Armenians, Volga Germans, and others, perhaps millions in all—added to the toll.[21]

The government addressed the crisis of expectations by expanding the Party and rewarding loyal achievers. The number of members and candidate members reached 5.5 million in 1946, up from 3.9 million in 1941.[22] Two-thirds were younger than thirty-five in 1946, and more than half had attended secondary school, compared to 40 percent before the war.[23] By 1952, membership reached 6.7 million.[24] Russian sociologist Tatyana Zaslavskaia suggested that after the war "the 'social elite' increased substantially, and the contrast between its situation and that of other groups became even more striking."[25] Rewarding good works and loyalty with high-quality goods and services, the state nurtured a privileged minority as it had from the outset.[26] By 1948, *Pravda* had largely abandoned the wartime public for a dialogue with officials and enthusiasts.[27]

Thanking Stalin Again

Pravda's chief postwar domestic story was socialist construction, but from June through December 1945 journalists applauded rather than exhorted.[28] The press played down the wartime theme of sacrifice, despite the deprivations of the era. Typical editorials in May were "A Holiday of Soviet Science" (on scientists "honorably doing their patriotic duty") and "Let Our Great Homeland Prosper and Flourish" (on industry).[29] Exhortations quickly followed, however. In 1946 editorialists urged: "Sow Quickly and Sow Well," "The Country Expects Higher Quality from Workers in the Food Industry," and "The Honorable Task of Workers in Light Industry."[30] Journalists used various metaphors from the 1930s, but the task predominated, as evidenced by this comment from 1946 about the new plan: "Now the greatest tasks of the new Stalinist five-year plan stand before Soviet people."[31]

Journalists identified Soviet life with huge projects embodying the gift, Soviet exceptionalism, and social honor. The press announced the fourth plan (1946–50) on September 12, 1945, a month after Japan surrendered.[32] Stalin discussed it at the Bolshoi Theater on February 9, 1946, promising to restore devastated regions, surpass prewar industrial and agricultural production, and raise living standards.[33] But the figures he gave were for greatly increased output of pig iron and steel, coal, and oil.[34] The plan achieved rapid industrial recovery, but urban living standards stagnated and rural people and agriculture suffered.[35] The industrial recovery drew on prewar capacity, the material and machines appropriated from satellite countries, and the labor of Soviet citizens and two million prisoners of war. By 1950 the value of industrial production was 113 percent of prewar norms in liberated regions, but rural incomes and the availability of consumer goods remained low.[36] As economist Naum Jasny wrote in 1961, "The most important factor contributing to the rapid recovery of the USSR from war devastation was, of course, deprivation of the Soviet population."[37]

The press made it Stalin's plan. "Our people call these plans Stalinist because the great leader of the party and the people, Comrade Stalin, was the soul of the five-year plans, their inspirer, organizer, and real creator," *Pravda* editorialized.[38] Journalists celebrated previous plans as a means of self-improvement. On May Day, 1946, a columnist in *Labor* recounted the success of an orphan who endured the NEP, worked on the first plan, transformed himself in the second, and won a Stalin Prize in the war. "Sergei Davydov began the Second Five-Year Plan as a different person," the author noted.[39] The plan revived the promise of mobility. "You read the law about the new five-year plan, and your heart rejoices. The decision means each of us will participate in a great building, each will contribute part of his labor to the further flourishing of our beloved country," wrote a "tractor driver" in March 1946.[40]

The press showed people flourishing. "Soviet Women's Heartfelt Thanks to the Great Stalin," was *Pravda*'s caption for an article on February 9, 1946, about women who received wartime assistance. "'Beloved Stalin is my father,'" declared a war orphan who had received an education. For most, however, the plan spelled sacrifice, since the government devoted scant resources to raising living standards. In this atmosphere, journalists fervently reasserted the rhetoric of the gift—first for veterans, then for others. On July 19, 1945, the army paper showed the recipient of a red star beside his attractive wife and children and a two-storied house. "Having honorably paid his debt to the homeland, the sergeant returns to his native region," read the report. Another reporter in *Red Star* described a soldier for whom a paltry assistance sufficed:

> Lance Corporal Brysin speaks movingly of the Party's and Soviet government's concern for demobilized troops. Shoes, uniforms, money allowances, provisions for the journey—demobilized soldiers are guaranteed everything. They are also met solicitously and honored as defenders of the fatherland at home. Thanks to the Party, the Soviet government, and Comrade Stalin for their concern for us. We will reciprocate with selfless labor further to strengthen our state's power.[41]

To reimpose the yoke of obligation on a population burning with conflicting expectations, Stalin and his supporters crowned themselves with glory and denied others credit for victory. He shunted aside wartime generals, sent Zhukov to Odessa, and discouraged leading participants from writing and publishing wartime memoirs. In 1947 he made Victory Day an ordinary working day, which it remained until 1965.[42] "Thank you, Comrade Stalin" reverberated in every sphere. Zhukov himself had credited the dictator at the parade in Red Square on June 25, 1945: "We won because we were led by the captain of genius and marshal of the Soviet Union, Stalin," he declared.[43] On June 27 *Pravda* reported Stalin's receipt of a second Order of Victory and the title "Hero of the Soviet Union." His picture filled the front page (Figure 8.1). Above the next day's editorial, "Creator of the People's Victory" was a decree making him generalissimo. "Comrade Stalin foresaw the course of events long before the contemporary war and the German imperialists' attack on the USSR," the editors wrote.[44]

Stalin was again maestro of his cult. In a speech in February 1946 he evaded responsibility for the invasion and attributed victory to his policies.[45] His slogan, "Quickly Heal the Wounds Inflicted by War," served to downplay every aspect of the struggle except his own role.[46] In his report to the Twentieth Party Congress in February 1956, Khrushchev declared: "Not Stalin, but the Party as a whole, the Soviet government, our heroic army, its talented leaders and brave

Figure 8.1. *Pravda,* June 27, 1945 "The Decree of the Supreme Soviet of the USSR Awarding the Title 'Hero of the Soviet Union' to Stalin, Iosif Vissarionovich." The passage above the picture reads: "The heroic Soviet people joyously congratulate the commander and inspired leader of the Soviet people, Comrade Stalin, on the award of a Second Order of Victory and the title 'Hero of the Soviet Union.'"

soldiers, the whole Soviet nation—these are the ones who assured the victory in the Great Patriotic War."[47]

On the first anniversary of victory, editors undercut claims to social honor based on wartime service. An editorial in *Izvestiia* on May 9, 1946, read: "This holiday is not commemorative; it is about our readiness for new feats for the homeland and the happiness of peoples!"[48] Despite poems and recollections, rewards were to be earned in the present, and there was no question of who was in debt to whom. Simonov wrote in *Labor*, "People will always remember the victory of May 9 as the most glorious of the glorious," but his editors told another story. "The victory allowed us to return to socialist building," they wrote.[49] *Pravda*'s chiefs were more blunt: "Celebrating the first year of the great victory over fascist Germany, Soviet people are ready again to struggle selflessly and enthusiastically to fulfill and overfulfill the five-year plan." *Red Star* published the Supreme Soviet's decree awarding the rank of Hero of the Soviet Union to the five soldiers and officers who had raised the Soviet flag over the Reichstag, but only Stalin's picture appeared on the front page (Figure 8.2).[50] All victories had become his.

The press gushed with gratitude. "'Great thanks to our Stalin! Great thanks to him, for preventing the enemy from defiling our holy capital, homes, and factories—great thanks to him for all he did for the people and our victory!'" exclaimed a worker in a report in *Pravda* on June 1, 1945. Stalin was even thanked by those who observed the ritual in film. In 1946 *Pravda* quoted a woman's observation on a scene from *The Oath* in which a female worker thanked Stalin: "I so wished to shout to Comrade Stalin: "Thank you, our beloved leader! Truly we beat the Fascists only because of your leadership. You saved the homeland. Great thanks to you from all the people."[51] Thus Stalin and his cronies, who had tragically misjudged the Nazi threat, were shown to owe citizens nothing, while the populace owed them everything. Indeed, the sphere of obligation soon extended far beyond the victory. "We are endlessly grateful to the Soviet government, to the great Bolshevik Party, and personally to you, Comrade Stalin, for exceptional attention to higher education and science," announced Moscow professors and instructors in *Pravda* in October 1946.[52] When the leader appeared, there were flowers and admiring children, as in *Red Star*'s photo of Stalin and Molotov at the parade of gymnasts in Moscow in July 1946 (Figure 8.3). One of the two photographers credited for the photo was S. Loskutov, who had written so movingly in *Red Star* of his partisan sojourn.

The giving of actual gifts after the war expressed symbolically the reimposition of the culture of the gift. In mid-1946 *Pravda* and *Red Star* reported "A Gift to Comrade I. V. Stalin from the Collective of the Leningrad China Factory" of an urn, two and a half meters high, with his portrait and scenes of victory celebrations (Figure 8.4).[53] Others followed. On August 24, 1948, *Pravda* featured a picture of a crystal vase with a picture of the Kremlin and Stalin's face. The dedication, cited in TASS's report, read in part: "Dear Iosif

Figure 8.2. *Red Star,* May 9, 1946. "The Order of the Minister of the Armed Forces of the USSR" (congratulating citizens on the first anniversary of victory). The editorial is titled "The Holiday of Victory."

ВСЕСОЮЗНЫЙ ПАРАД ФИЗКУЛЬТУРНИКОВ В МОСКВЕ 21 ИЮЛЯ 1946 ГОДА. На снимке: И. В. Сталин и В. М. Молотов принимают цветы от детей.
Фото С. Лоскутова и Ф. Левшина.

Figure 8.3. *Red Star*, July 23, 1946. Photograph by S. Loskutov and F. Levshin. "The All-Union Parade of Gymnasts in Moscow, July 21, 1946. In the picture, I. V. Stalin and V. M. Molotov accept flowers from children."

Figure 8.4. *Red Star,* May 12, 1946 "A Gift to Comrade I. V. Stalin from the Collective of the Leningrad China Factory."

Vissarionovich! We ask you to accept our humble gift, the result of the collective labor of the artists and employees—a crystal vase, which we dedicate to the triumph of Soviet power and personally to you as a mark of our deep thankfulness for your wise and fatherly leadership of our people, for the organization of all its great victories."

By the end of the war Stalin had aged. He appeared infrequently in public, skipped parades, and left keynote addresses to Molotov, G. M. Malenkov, or N. A. Bulganin. He and the cult's promoters redoubled efforts, however. Model citizens had performed the symbolic gesture of nominating him to electoral posts in the late 1930s, and after the war his boosters expanded the practice. On January 2, 1946, *Pravda* announced his nomination as first deputy for the Supreme Soviet in every district. Beside the editorial was a description of a meeting at the Electrozavod Factory: "To the tribune came Master of Electric Light Production, A. A. Slavnova; with all her heart she wants Comrade Stalin to be chosen deputy." On the day before the election Stalin addressed voters, and the press recorded promises to work harder with captions such as "The Collective Farms of the Don Reply to the Leader's Speech."[54] Similar nominations in other elections became obligatory.

The effacement of individuals from the public narrative of Soviet life, which began in the 1930s, continued as the press portrayed Stalin as manager of almost every facet of economic life. Although the press had attributed completed tasks to him in the 1930s, the steady publication of letters and reports addressed to him personally began only late in the war. In 1939 no one overfulfilled the plan to honor his birthday, but after the war, reports to him on fulfillment of the plan flooded the press. In 1947 *Pravda* allotted 21 percent of its front page to such items; in 1948, 12 percent; in 1949, the year of his seventieth birthday, 27 percent; and thereafter more than 10 percent.[55] The authors of these declarations credited Stalin with their own and others' achievements. "Thanks to your fatherly care, Iosif Vissarionovich, and to great help from the glorious Bolshevik Party and our own Soviet government, we raised a big harvest in almost all districts of our oblast," Don farmers affirmed in 1947.[56] In the same famine year, *Pravda* reported "Fulfillment of Obligations," including one from Oblast Party Secretary Leonid Brezhnev (October 16, 1947). "Comrade Stalin, Iosif Vissarionovich," he wrote. "I am glad to inform you, dear Iosif Vissarionovich, that Zaporozhskaia Oblast fulfilled its state grain procurement plan for the 1947 harvest."

Participants understood this as ritual. The writer Vera Panova explained in *Pravda* in late 1951, "The competitions before May Day and the October anniversary, the Stakhanovite efforts, and the labor reports to the great leader, beloved Stalin, have become traditions the people preserve and develop" (October 29, 1951). Officials used this device to affirm that they were honor-bound to work in Stalin's name. "The suggestion by advanced collective farms to send a letter to Stalin was met with great joy throughout the Altai region," wrote the chief of a collective farm in *Pravda* in on March 21, 1947. "All collective farmers unanimously signed and promised Comrade Stalin to gather 120 poods of grain per hectare," he added. To refuse was to risk punishment, but honor was also at stake. "They gave you everything. And there exists the law of reciprocity," recalled the Russian writer Elena Serebrovskaia.[57] She credited "the Russian people," but in the parlance of the time, her debt was to Stalin. "The policy of the knout and the honey cake, of fear and personal devotion, was the basis of his interrelation with all of us, 'cogs' as we were then," recalled Soviet comedian Arkady Raikin.[58]

Journalists reinforced domestic indebtedness with foreign obligation at a time when Stalin's prestige was still high in the West. "We have saved not only our homeland, we have saved universal culture," wrote Ehrenburg the day after Germany's surrender. The following day Boris Polevoi asked citizens of Prague "what they wished to tell Soviet people through *Pravda*" and quoted a professor's reply: "Write that all humanity bows down to Marshal Stalin and that the world has not yet known such a genius of a commander." Acknowledging foreigners' thankfulness did not diminish Soviet citizens' own obligation. "The Soviet people won well-deserved glory as tireless workers, bold transformers and heroes, saviors of its homeland and of the peoples of the whole world from fascist enslavement," editorialized *Pravda* on November 3, 1947. Beside the editorial was a letter to Stalin signed by more than twenty-six million members of the Komsomol youth organization. "We owe you our lives, our education, our happy youth, our todays and our tomorrows," the signatories avowed.

In the international arena, Stalin and Molotov initially used wartime losses to support claims for reparations and territory even though they minimized casualties out of secretiveness or perhaps chagrin, claiming a bare seven million rather than the twenty-six million now accepted. Molotov told Anthony Eden at the London Conference on May 22–27, 1942, that Stalin demanded the restoration of the country's 1941 borders, that is, including the gains from the Nazi-Soviet Pact, and added: "We cannot repudiate this position, especially after the sacrifices made by our country."[59] Some Western leaders were swayed. Churchill recalled that at Yalta he had supported the Soviet claim to the Curzon Line, including the town of Lvov, despite opposition from his own party, because he felt they were entitled to it. "But I had always thought that, after the agonies Russia had suffered in defending herself against the Germans, and her great deeds in driving them back and liberating Poland, the claim was founded not on force but on right."[60] Even President Harry S. Truman inclined to this logic after the war, as did Dean Acheson and Gen. Lucius D. Clay, commander of the U.S. zone in Germany.[61]

Stalin also cited Soviet losses to counter criticism of the Red Army's behavior in Eastern Europe. Yugoslav partisan leader Milovan Djilas recorded Stalin's response in the winter of 1944–45 to his complaint about Soviet soldiers raping and pillaging: "He wept, crying out: 'And such an army was insulted by no one else but Djilas! Djilas, of whom I could least have expected such a thing, a man whom I received so well! And an army which did not spare its blood for you!'"[62]

In accord with Stalin's sentiments, the press depicted foreigners, many of whom were also victims of the conflict, as indebted to the Soviet Union for victory, and in the case of the "peoples' democracies" for a new way of life as well. Journalists often extended foreigners' gratitude in these accounts from Stalin to the Soviet people, inviting citizens to take pride in their international stature, so long as they humbled themselves at home.

The Soviet Union provided food and other goods to war-torn Eastern Europe but extracted considerable reparations and organized very favorable terms of trade. Even in Czechoslovakia, they dismantled former German factories. An economic historian recently concluded that despite the postwar aid, "the guiding Soviet policy in Eastern Europe was to exact the maximum amount of tribute."[63] Whether or not this was true, the press implicitly justified such policies without dwelling on aid or reparations. "The Polish people will be eternally grateful to you," *Pravda* quoted a Polish marshal as saying in a report on the distribution of Polish medals to Soviet officers on May 9, 1946.[64] "The Soviet army brought us not only freedom, but without her valiant liberation struggle we could not carry out land reform in the country, and now this people has given us its dearest treasure—the Soviet peasantry's rich thirty-year experience," stated visiting Hungarians in *Pravda* in the same year.[65] Journalists portrayed Eastern Europe as grateful and dependent, not revolutionary. They noted the demise of the Yugoslav, Bulgarian, and Romanian monarchies, but quietly.

Neither Churchill's Fulton speech in March 1946, which *Pravda* summarized on March 11, nor Soviet Ambassador Nikolai Novikov's telegram from Washington on September 27, 1946, warning that America sought hegemony, sparked an open anti-American campaign.[66] *Pravda*'s editors dismissed Churchill, recalling his ineffectual early opposition to Bolshevism: "Churchill even then marched out of time with history." Three days later Stalin mocked Churchill's "Don Quixote–like antics." Simultaneously, he demanded friendly governments in countries Germany had invaded (Poland, Romania, Bulgaria, and Hungary), as well as Finland, on the grounds that "the Soviet Union lost several times [*sic*!] more people than did England and the United States combined."[67]

The press did not rule out continued allied cooperation. During 1946 and 1947 *Pravda* gave half its space on foreign affairs to stories about peaceful relations and antifascism.[68] During 1946 the paper closely followed Nuremberg and other postwar trials, as well as the United Nations General Assembly. Even in covering Greece, where civil war raged, journalists appealed to an imagined wartime order. Greece belonged to the Western sphere according to the percentages agreement of October 1944, and Stalin had not impeded British installation of a noncommunist government later that year. Greek Communists in May 1946 took the offensive with Tito's backing more than Stalin's.[69] *Pravda* reported "Greek-Fascist Terror," without mentioning Britain's role. The bulk of the article concerned attacks by police on workers in Athens and a description of victims. "None of the bandits has been arrested," the author concluded, as if such arrests might be expected. Readers were invited to speculate about why nothing was being done, but not to blame Britain. Later in the decade, lawlessness and brutality were a given in coverage of the capitalist world. Although the press sometimes labeled individuals and governments as fascist, antifascism virtually vanished during 1947, as did reports of peaceful and productive interactions with the West.[70]

During 1946 and 1947 stories about the bad life abroad, conflicts with the West, and revolutionary situations comprised the remainder of *Pravda*'s foreign coverage.[71] Short reports on life under capitalism in 1946 and 1947 usually concerned natural disasters or social unrest. A mining accident in Germany, unemployment in England and Italy, Egyptian criticism of Great Britain, striking workers in California, and repression in Japan all served.[72] Such stories filled roughly a quarter of *Pravda*'s space on foreign affairs in 1948 but were later supplanted by reports of actual conflicts.[73]

Despite these varied portrayals, the government moved to reinvigorate ideology. Zhdanov had criticized *Pravda*'s "passivity" at the Central Committee on May 15, 1945, and Pospelov, the editor, had acknowledged the need "to unmask the other states' expansionist inclinations."[74] In his memoirs Shepilov blamed the press's inaction on Aleksandrov, head of Agitprop from 1940 through 1947, and recalled that Stalin and the Politburo demanded a sharp response to the West.[75] In that respect, Stalin's interview in *Pravda,* in which he publicly belittled Churchill's speech, was misleading. A commission he authorized to evaluate Soviet propaganda abroad met in June and July of 1946 and also stressed the need for action.[76]

As previously, the authorities chose a few representative targets. On August 9, 1946, the Central Committee's Organizational Bureau discussed the magazines *Star* and *Leningrad,* then considered unruly. At the meeting Stalin damned editors for kowtowing to the West. "We did not build the Soviet order to teach people nonsense," he fumed.[77] He also objected to the printing of translated Western works: "You inculcate extreme respect for foreigners. You inculcate the feeling that we are second class, and they are first. You are pupils; they are teachers. In essence, this is false."[78] How powerfully this view resonated among Stalin's henchmen is evident from Shepilov's subsequent denunciation of the intelligentsia's Westernism after the war. "What shame, what degradation of national dignity!" he wrote.[79]

On August 21 the Central Committee cited editors' "flagrant mistakes" in printing Zoshchenko and Akhmatova. Zhdanov, who in 1944 again had become the Central Committee's secretary for ideology, berated the Leningrad Party organization the next day and chastised a meeting of writers the day after that.[80] On August 22 literary notables pledged in *Pravda* to "eliminate hidden shortcomings."[81] During the following weeks, the press extended the demand for national pride to other fields. On August 29 *Pravda* faulted children's magazines for showing fantasy instead of "the wondrous beauty of our real life."[82] On September 2 the paper condemned theaters. On September 8 the Writers'

Union chided those who "do not know how to portray the best lines and qualities of the Soviet person." On September 21 Zhdanov told "managers of literature" and writers to "be guided by what Soviet literature cannot live without,
that is, politics." *Pravda* warned the next day of "attempts by literary riffraff to
poison our youth's consciousness." In the same issue, critic G. Nikitov reminded musicians that "Soviet music's leading position in international musical culture is indisputable."

In early 1947 the authorities put science both on stage and on trial. In January two investigators claimed to have found a cure for cancer and revealed that
they had shared their findings with Americans. They were interrogated and
"tried" for giving away state secrets by a "court of honor" of their colleagues
before an audience of officials at a Moscow theater.[83] The Council of Ministers
and the Central Committee instituted "courts of honor" at state agencies, as well
as at cultural and scientific organizations.[84] The erring investigators were not
otherwise punished, but on June 14, a week after the trial, the Supreme Soviet
decreed sentences of eight to twenty years for disclosure of "state secrets." A
month later the Central Committee sent a letter to local Party leaders condemning "slavishness and servility to the West" and warning that credit due
Russian science had been "stolen."[85] The cold war had begun.

Cold War Confrontations

The presentation of foreign affairs in the press changed in 1947 and 1948.
Pravda's editors cut space on friendly and neutral relations with noncommunist countries and peaceful international activity from half in 1946 and 1947 to
just over a quarter in 1948, under a fifth in 1949, and less than a tenth in 1952.[86]
Reports on conflicts increased correspondingly. Coverage of the bad life abroad
declined and, after 1948, was integrated into more general coverage of the cold
war. The new "peoples' democracies" never became a prime subject of reportage, however. Reports on foreign communist regimes exceeded 10 percent
of *Pravda*'s space on foreign affairs only in 1949 and 1950, after Mao Zedong's
victory.

The cold war was a struggle of initiatives and counterinitiatives. On the
American side, 1947 was a critical year. In March President Truman won con-
gressional approval for $400 million in aid to Greece and Turkey and an-
nounced support for "free peoples who are resisting attempted subjugation by
armed minorities or by outside pressure," later known as the Truman Doctrine.[87] "This was America's answer to the surge of expansion of communist
tyranny," Truman later recalled.[88] The Marshall Plan followed in June 1947,
the Brussels Treaty in March 1948, and NATO in April 1949. During 1948 and
1949 the Western allies established a West German state. The Voice of America (VOA) and the British Broadcasting Corporation supplemented these ini-

tiatives. VOA began Russian language broadcasts on February 17, 1947, and operated unimpeded until jamming began in the winter of 1948, but even jamming proved ineffective.[89] VOA used commercial programming to present American life in a way that had proved effective elsewhere.[90] There were an estimated five million Soviet shortwave sets, and VOA claimed eight million listeners.[91] A Soviet anti-VOA campaign over the course of several years produced a thousand denunciations of the station.[92]

Soviet démarches included escalation of the Greek civil war in late 1946 and advances in Bulgaria, Romania, and Poland in 1947. In September 1947 Soviet leaders founded the Communist Information Bureau (Cominform) to control foreign Communists, and in 1948 they consolidated power in Czechoslovakia and elsewhere in Eastern Europe. On June 28, 1948, they expelled Yugoslavia from the Cominform and began purging "Titoites" and nationalists elsewhere in Eastern Europe. In July 1948 Soviet authorities imposed a land and water blockade on West Berlin in response to Western currency reforms. In August they launched the World Peace Movement to rally anti-American sentiment and perhaps screen their own aggressive plans. In 1949, after a successful nuclear test, Stalin considered invading Yugoslavia or helping Kim Il Sung conquer the South.[93] In this context, America's might was galling. "America was conducting its foreign policy from a position of strength. . . . I would even say that America was invincible," Khrushchev recalled.[94]

The cold war was a clash of social systems as well as great powers, but Soviet leaders portrayed themselves as benefactors rather than proponents of national interest or revolution abroad. Journalists stressed events that confirmed this story and neglected those that did not. Thus editors largely ignored the Chinese civil war and the Berlin blockade. Stalin may have underestimated the Chinese Communists, and, in any case, the press had no story of Soviet aid to tell. Thus from January 1, 1946, until September 30, 1949, *Pravda* gave China less than 2 percent of the space on foreign affairs, half as much as Greece, which also had a civil war.[95] Coverage of the Berlin crisis of 1948 was likewise scanty. In June 1948 *Pravda* condemned the new West German currency and published the complaints that Marshal Sokolovskii, commander of Soviet forces in Germany, sent to General Clay, but the paper ignored the blockade. On July 11 *Pravda* announced limitations on Western access in a tiny article on page 3 captioned "Transport links between Berlin and the Western zones," but the paper did not discuss the Western airlift that followed.[96] Stalin cited Berlin in his "Answers to *Pravda*'s Correspondent" on October 28, 1948, but also ignored the airlift.[97]

The press downplayed the Cominform's expulsion of Yugoslavia in late June 1948. On September 8, after giving American and British radio six weeks to shape the story unopposed, *Pravda* published "Where Nationalism Leads Tito's Group in Yugoslavia." It was signed "Tseka" instead of TsK, the proper abbreviation for Central Committee. Stalin, with his imperfect command of Russian, is thought to have used this abbreviation, thus leaving a signature no one dared to remove. The author, whether Stalin or not, spoke as teacher and father, chiding ungrateful comrades for "not valuing the friendship" of the Communist Party of the Soviet Union. "Has Tito's group learned the required lesson from these facts?" he asked after listing their sins. "No, Tito's group has not learned the necessary lessons," he concluded. He also interjected a personal note: "Tito's accomplices even urged Stalin to busy himself in this dishonorable campaign to defend Tito's nationalist group from criticism by the Communist Parties of the USSR and other democratic countries." Beside the article was a eulogy of Arco Jovanovic, a Yugoslav general killed while fleeing to Romania after a failed coup attempt.[98] Journalists ignored Tito in 1948, but in 1949, when battle lines hardened, he became an archenemy.

The press fit the Truman Doctrine and Marshall Plan into its narrative by portraying the United States as a false benefactor. *Pravda,* in April 1947, blamed Truman for supporting "antidemocratic elements."[99] The next day the editors compared his stress on America's "noble" aims to Hitler's. "Beneath the 'charitable' mask shows a policy of imperialistic expansion," they wrote. Coverage turned even harsher after the USSR rejected the Marshall Plan in June 1947. Soviet leaders initially softened their hostile response when it appeared they might win assistance without strings, as under Lend-Lease.[100] Molotov visited Paris to evaluate the proposal but left on receiving intelligence reports of American plans to isolate the USSR and rebuild Germany.[101] He denounced the plan on July 2, and the press followed suit. "We claim our due, and not only from Germans," wrote the indefatigable Zaslavskii. "We do not ask for aid, and the world will never see a Soviet person stretch out a hand at the international church door." He demanded that "other peoples, particularly those whose governing classes enriched and fattened on wartime profits, pay their share of the reconstruction of the suffering European countries who fought fascism."[102] On New Year's Day, 1949, *Pravda* featured a cartoon of Uncle Sam as Santa, giving Europeans a pie marked "credit," beside a tree decorated with "crisis," "unemployment," and "atom." The caption was "The Marshallization of the Christmas Tree." The performance could not accommodate two Santas.[103]

The press presented the cold war as a Manichean struggle of "two camps." The metaphor dated from the civil war but now signaled a favorable "correlation of forces," not a Soviet "fortress" and its besiegers. On October 5, 1947, *Pravda* printed the new Communist Information Bureau's description of "two camps"—"the imperialistic and antidemocratic camp, whose basic aim is to destroy democracy and establish the hegemony of American imperialism in the world, and the democratic camp, whose basic aim is to undermine imperialism, strengthen democracy, and liquidate remnants of fascism."[104] On February 9, 1946, Stalin described the October Revolution as a result of imperialism's first crisis and the Soviet victory in World War II a consequence of its second, implying a third would yield a still more favorable outcome.[105] Molotov avowed on the anniversary of the October Revolution in 1947 that "in our time the unified democratic and socialist forces are infinitely stronger than those of the antidemocratic imperialist camp opposing them."[106] This view of the "two camps" doomed the career of the talented economist E. Varga, who had predicted that capitalism might avoid a postwar crisis through fiscal management.[107]

The press employed the metaphors of camps and of the gift to describe the Soviet sponsored "peace movement," launched in early August 1948 at the World Congress of Cultural Activists in Defense of Peace in Brotslav, Western Poland.[108] A. Fadeev, chief of the Soviet delegation and secretary of the Writers' Union, in a speech reprinted in *Pravda,* cited a TASS report identifying Brotslav as the Red Army's gift to Poland: "I was bold enough to recall this because it is not simply words, but the blood of millions of Soviet soldiers."[109] He warned of American efforts "to convert the whole planet into an enormous police station and its population into mute slaves of capital."

In January 1949 Stalin proposed a Soviet-American "peace pact, and the peace campaign moved to the center of the performance.[110] A World Congress of Peace Advocates convened in Paris in April, and *Pravda* reported on the Stockholm Petition to ban nuclear weapons, which had allegedly been signed by five hundred million people. "Who are you with—the five hundred million . . . or the handful of imperialists and their hired agents?" asked Iurii Zhukov, *Pravda*'s Paris correspondent.[111] At issue was the moral merit of the rival superpowers. Fadeev, again chief Soviet delegate, rebuffed the claim that "people of the so-called Atlantic community possess a 'monopoly' on culture and humanism, and we, Soviet people, heirs of Pushkin and Tolstoy, Mendeleev and Pavlov, who have created the first country of socialism in the world with our hands, are somehow the enemies of 'Western,' 'Atlantic' culture."[112] Ehrenburg cited the war to the same purpose:

> When there was a terrible war for culture, for humanity, for life, we led others. We did not count our casualties. There are no scales to weigh lives against dollars, no peoples who want to equate "Stalingrad" and "Lend-Lease." Now a struggle for peace is under way, and we are proud to lead again. We again fight not only for ourselves but for all peoples.[113]

At this juncture science once again appeared on stage, and Stalin promoted activists who would do his bidding, including Trofim Lysenko. In 1947 Lysenko had billed himself as Darwin's heir, promoting his own theory that plants in a species cooperate and the weaker in a cluster "sacrifice" so the stronger may thrive.[114] In 1948 Stalin supported his intervention at the convocation of the All-Union Lenin Academy of Agricultural Sciences, which met from July 31 to August 7, 1948. Lysenko, the academy's much-favored president, portrayed the struggle between his followers and Soviet defenders of biology as a conflict between rival sciences, one Soviet and Michurinist, the other Western ("Mendelist-Morganist").[115] The paper printed some of his colleagues' criticism but cast no doubt on his victory. "The Party Central Committee scrutinized my report and approved it," Lysenko proclaimed in his concluding speech, which Stalin had personally edited.[116] This matched Stalin's interjection of 1935— "Bravo Comrade Lysenko, bravo."[117] *Pravda* hailed his victory in a three-column editorial, "Raise the Banner of Advanced Michurinist Biological Science!"

The authorities hounded Lysenko's opponents and defenders of genetics and expanded his agricultural operations.[118] Biology, agronomy, and genetics went to the chopping block, and Soviet agricultural science fell into a decline from which it never recovered. The impact was similar to that of the Writers' Congress of 1934 on literature and the arts. Scientific activity came on stage, and scientists tried to adapt the obligatory script to their own ends. The performance enveloped pedagogy, medicine, and other sciences, and scientists in these fields found their own Michurins to praise. Physics was spared, not so much because of the bomb as because physicists were not divided among themselves.[119]

On October 20, 1948, two months after Lysenko's triumph, the press announced the approval of "The Great Stalinist Plan to Transform Nature."[120] This super plan called for the planting of thousands of kilometers of shelter-belts of forest along rivers, ravines, and gullies. Collective farms and state farms were to plant trees on nearly six million hectares from 1949 to 1965. More than 44,000 ponds and reservoirs were to be established in Ukraine, Lower Volga, Northern Caucasus, in the black soil regions, and in central Russia. The area under grasses, including clover, was also to be greatly expanded. The planners put Lysenko's theory of cooperation and self-sacrifice of plants into practice, planting 350,000 hectares of land in 1948 with close clusters of acorns rather than well-spaced plantings. Only half the clusters produced saplings and of these most failed, causing Lysenko to lose official support and attract criticism after Stalin's death.[121] The Great Plan was largely abandoned in the mid-1950s, and its overall results are disputed.[122] Nevertheless Lysenko eluded his critics and regained favor under Khrushchev.

Pravda promoted the Great Plan as proof of Soviet superiority. "Capitalism is not only incapable of organizing the planned transformation of nature but of preventing the predatory use of its riches," *Pravda* editorialized on October 24, 1948.[123] The plan was also a gift to Soviet peoples. "No other country in the world could formulate a plan like this," stated an agronomist from Poltava.[124] The press also stressed the plan's Russianness, its inspiration in research of pre-revolutionary Russian agricultural scientists, including V. V. Dokuchaev and P. A. Kostychev. "Millions of agricultural workers should master the teachings of Michurin, Dokuchaev, Kostychev, and Williams, and learn their advanced methods of struggling for the harvest," editorialized *Labor* on October 24, 1948. The press had long cast Stalin as chief actor; now it gave Russians this role vis-à-vis other Soviet peoples. Stalin had pointed the way when the war ended. On May 9 he had portrayed the war as "the age-old struggle of Slavic peoples for their existence and independence," and two weeks later, at the Kremlin victory celebration, he avowed, "I drink most of all to the health of Russian people because they are the most prominent of the nations comprising the Soviet Union."[125]

The promotion of nationalism in science culminated in a session of the Academy of Sciences devoted to history on January 5–10, 1949, which was soon followed by an explosion of official anti-Semitism. The period was perhaps one of the tensest of the cold war. The country was months away from breaking America's nuclear monopoly, the Marshall Plan was succeeding, Western European economies were growing, and their governments were cooperating with one another. The Brussels Treaty for common defense had been signed a year earlier, and NATO was in the works. Tito threatened the integrity of the bloc, and purge trials were planned to stem dissidence elsewhere. The Berlin blockade had failed and would be lifted on May 12. The Chinese civil war continued, but American intervention was possible. Finally, in late 1949, after the successful Soviet A-bomb test and Mao's victory, Stalin ordered a buildup in North Korea for invasion of the South.[126]

Celebrating Russia, participants in the session of the academy enumerated Russia's gifts to the world. S. Vavilov, the academy's president and brother of the great Russian biologist N. Vavilov, who died a victim of Lysenko in an NKVD prison in 1943, set the tone by condemning the hitherto "shameful admiration for foreign authorities cultivated in Russia."[127] *Pravda*'s columnist elaborated: "Throughout its history, the Great Russian people have enriched national and world technology with outstanding discoveries and inventions."[128] Russia was humanity's benefactor in science. "The Airplane Is a Russian Invention" read *Komsomol Pravda*'s header.[129] The author cited "famous Russian scientists and engineers, who many decades ago gave their discoveries and inventions to the world as gifts." He listed prodigious achievements:

> It is impossible to find one area in which Russian people have not blazed new paths. A. S. Popov invented radio. A. N. Lodygin created the incandescent bulb. I. I. Pozunov built the world's first steam engine. The first locomotive, invented by the Cherepanovs, moved on Russian land. The serf Fedor Blinov flew over Russian land in a plane heavier than air, created by the genius Aleksandr Fedorovich Mozhaiskii twenty-one years before the Wright Brothers.

To glorify and enlarge Popov's genuine achievement in advancing radio communication, the government proclaimed May 7 "Radio Day."[130] "Russians were advertised as the first to have discovered or invented anything and everything. Russia is the homeland of the elephant, ran the stock joke," recalled Andrei Sakharov.[131] The full anecdote, which Sakharov abbreviated, has a Soviet delegation to a conference on elephants give a four-part report: (1) classics of Marxism-Leninism-Stalinism on elephants; (2) Russia, the elephant's homeland; (3) the Soviet elephant, the world's best elephant; (4)the Belorussian elephant, the Russian elephant's little brother.

Pravda's editors sandwiched the academy's proceedings between celebrations of the twentieth anniversary of collectivization and the Plan for the Transformation of Nature. Yet what may seem ludicrous in retrospect had a lethal contemporary logic. Imperfection was the twin of perfection in the morality play, and society had to be cleansed of those unsuited for the future. Thus the antithesis of Russian-Soviet became "cosmopolitan" and ultimately Jewish.[132] On January 11, 1949, L. Klimovich published "Against Cosmopolitanism in Literary Criticism" in *Pravda,* chiding authors of a book on Uzbek poetry for linking Uzbek traditions with the Near East, and forgetting Uzbek poets' "burning love for their elder brother, the Russian people." A critic in *Komsomol Pravda* blamed a dearth of science fiction on the "cosmopolitanism" of authors who failed to understand "that Soviet science fiction and adventure literature differs *in principle* from foreign."[133]

Jews were aliens par excellence, particularly after the founding of Israel on May 14, 1948. The Soviet government had been the first to recognize and aid the new state, albeit in order to counter British support of Arabs. On September 3 Golda Meir, Israel's ambassador to the Soviet Union, met Soviet Jews in Moscow, and on September 21 *Pravda* published Ehrenburg's "Response to a Letter," praising the Soviet Union as a homeland for free Jews and promising resolution of the Jews' dilemma through world revolution.[134] Persecution followed. On November 20 the government dissolved the Jewish Antifascist Committee, depicting it as "a center of anti-Soviet information."[135] Shortly afterward, they closed Jewish cultural institutions and began an anti-Semitic campaign. In January 1948 Stalin ordered the murder of the Jewish leader and theater director Solomon Mikhoels, and in February 1949 he had Molotov's Jewish wife, Polina Zhemchuzhina, incarcerated.[136] Jews were expunged from the arts, the professions, and the press.[137] *Pravda* purged its Jewish employees in early March 1949, and *Komsomol Pravda* followed suit in October.[138] *Labor* fired forty Jewish employees from April 1950 to August 1951.[139]

On January 28, 1949, *Pravda* published, in the style of the anonymous editorials of the 1930s, "About One Anti-patriotic Group of Theater Critics," denouncing "a nest of bourgeois aesthetes, who are concealing an anti-patriotic, cosmopolitan, and putrid attitude toward Soviet art." All but two had Jewish names. "The feeling of Soviet national pride is alien to them," the anonymous author wrote. The international situation added urgency. On January 29 the Ministry of Foreign Affairs reported on the North Atlantic Pact and "Anglo-American plans for world hegemony."[140] *Komsomol Pravda* displayed on facing pages the accusation against theater critics and the ministry's statement.[141] Public figures had to join in such campaigns or court danger. "If you keep quiet and don't shout, that means you're not a supporter and you're taking the side of the opposition," a Polish Communist recalled of a similar situation in postwar communist Poland.[142] Simonov resisted, then condemned "the propaganda of bourgeois cosmopolitanism" in a speech published in *Pravda* on February 28. The origins of the anti-Semitic campaign that began can be traced back to Stalin.[143]

The epithet "nest of bourgeois aesthetes" set a hygienic tone. "The anti-patriots eat away at the healthy organism of our literature and art like larvae," noted one of *Pravda*'s commentators on February 26. "Our urgent task is to smoke out these cosmopolites without nation or tribe, who slow the development of Soviet culture, from their burrows," announced another on March 5. Activists also cleansed the past. "These emasculated decadents, who slight Soviet literature, have their own genealogy, their mark, their own primogenitor," noted *Pravda*'s B. Romashov.[144] "His name is Meyerhold, and cosmopolites pray to this evil figure of a typical cosmopolite and anti-Soviet agent," he continued. A. Gerasimov, dean of socialist realist artists and president of the Academy of Artists, censured slanderers of the great Russian painters Surikov and Repin.[145]

The Soviet government had persecuted whole peoples since the civil war. The postwar victimization of Tatars, Volga Germans, Kalmyks, and others was a piece of the same cloth. Yet aside from silence, the press had added little to the stigmatization of these peoples. The persecution of Jews, in contrast, was public. The press made cosmopolitanism the inverse of patriotism, and Jews exemplary heretics. "Fighting cosmopolitanism, the conscious Ukrainian literary public also fights bourgeois nationalism, for these are two sides of the same coin," wrote L. Dmiterko, vice chairman of the Ukrainian Union of Soviet Writers in early 1949.[146] Critics in *Komsomol Pravda* unearthed cosmopolites in popular science, film, sport, pedagogy, and other fields.[147] "The unmasked cosmopolites Volkenshtein, Iutkevich, and Lebedev have now been driven from the GIK [State Institute of Cinematography]," wrote one persecutor of Jews.[148] Another condemned "Gureviches and Sneiders" with Russian pseudonyms: "They preach individualism, careerism, servility to bourgeois sports; they poisoned our best trainers and introduced formalism into physical education."[149]

In April 1949 performers melded the anticosmopolitan campaign with attacks on West European unity, America, and the belittling of Soviet influence, and the focus turned away from Soviet Jews. On April 7 *Pravda*'s commentator defined cosmopolitanism as the antithesis of patriotism: "Cosmopolitanism is advocacy of so-called world citizenship, denial of belonging to a nation, liquidation of peoples' national traditions and cultures in the guise of creating a 'world' culture of all humanity." This was a strange line for Marxists since it clashed with "internationalism." One author, writing in *Labor,* even accused America of using cosmopolitanism "to exterminate workers' patriotic feelings" so as to gain "hegemony over colonized peoples and the Marshallized countries of Western Europe."[150]

From Contiguous Empire to Global Imperium

The strategic balance between the USSR and the West changed after the Soviet A-bomb test of August 29, 1949, and the founding of the Chinese People's Republic on October 1. Participants in the public culture adopted a triumphant tone on almost all topics except the bomb. Soviet strategists had taken America's bomb seriously, and journalists could have billed Soviet possession as a national achievement or as a victory for the international proletariat.[151] Yet neither fit the story of Soviet benevolence and leadership of the peace camp, and journalists largely ignored the bomb. Truman, not Stalin, revealed it on September 23, and on September 25 Soviet newspapers printed a statement from TASS on page 2. *Izvestiia* split its front page between an editorial on Hungarian "enemies of the people" and reports to Stalin on the five-year plan. *Pravda*'s front page was identical, but its editorial longer and reports to Stalin shorter. *Komsomol Pravda* also denounced Hungarian "enemies," while *Labor* editorialized on older workers in production.

TASS revealed that, given Truman's remarks, it was "authorized" to issue a statement, which read in part:

> This announcement signifies that the Soviet Union has already discovered the secret of atomic weapons and this weapon is at its disposal. Scientific circles in America considered V. M. Molotov's announcement a bluff, assuming Russians could not master atomic weapons before 1952. They were mistaken, however, since the Soviet Union mastered the secret of atomic weapons by 1947.
>
> There is no basis for the alarm spread on this account in some foreign circles. The Soviet government, despite its current possession of atomic weapons, maintains its former position on the unconditional prohibition of the use of atomic weapons and will continue to do so in the future.[152]

There was no mention of the test, and the authors implied that the country had succeeded two years earlier.[153] Editors produced a semblance of commentary with excerpts from the foreign press. Foreign comments ranged from remarks on the benefits of peace to considerations of the balance of power. The foreign verbosity contrasted with Soviet silence. *Pravda*'s editorial on October 1, "A Powerful Ideological Weapon of Bolshevism," concerned the eleventh anniversary of Stalin's *Short Course,* not the bomb. Its editorial the next day, "The Just Cause of Peace Will Triumph!" was about the Soviet-led peace movement and foreign spies. In the first instance editors ignored the bomb; in a second they noted only the demise of "atomic diplomacy." *Labor*'s editorial about Soviet science on September 27 concerned the hundredth anniversary of Pavlov's birth, not the bomb. Although journalists and editors did not discuss the bomb, they adopted a triumphant tone. On November 13 Zaslavskii argued in *Pravda* that the bomb, the Chinese Revolution, and the "peace movement" "finally undermined the spiritual equilibrium of some English and American political figures."

TASS reported Mao's announcement of a consultative political assembly on September 23 and the Declaration of the People's Republic on October 2. *Pravda* printed pictures of Mao, Chou En-lai, Liao Shao-chi, and Chu Teh (commander-in-chief of the People's Liberation Army) on October 5 beside a three-column editorial.[154] "This victory multiplies the forces of the front of peace, democracy, and socialism, led by the great Soviet Union," the editors noted. Welcoming China to "the family of democratic peace-loving states," they cited Mao's acknowledgment of the Soviet role in defeating Germany and Japan. *Labor* and *Komsomol Pravda* did likewise, but editors of the youth paper went further. "The birth of the great Chinese democratic power shows once again that the age of capitalism is ending," they wrote.[155] On October 9 and 10 *Pravda* printed the founding declaration of the German Democratic Republic and a week later ran an editorial, "A Turning Point in European History."[156]

The portrayal of enemies in the bloc also changed. Since 1945 *Pravda* had reported repressions of East European fascists and noncommunist politicians without fanfare. The Romanian National-Peasant leader Iuliu Maniu received barely more than a page in 1947, and, despite the prelate's abject confession, Cardinal Mindszenty merited only three short reports in January and February 1949.[157] After Tito's excommunication in June 1948, purging "Tito's agents and spies" became a Soviet objective in East Europe; but the press sounded the tocsin only in late 1949 during the trials of the Hungarian Laszlo Rajk in September and the Bulgarian Traicho Kostov in December.[158] *Pravda* allotted Rajk more than thirteen pages from September 12 through October 4 and Kostov more than nine and a half from December 1 through December 16. Other papers duplicated this coverage.

Reporting the trials, the press showed enemies who appeared as perfidious as those of the 1930s. "There stands accused a band of rotten spies, provocateurs, and murderers," editorialized *Komsomol Pravda* in the Rajk trial.[159] "Judas Tito spread his spies among the peoples' democracies and gave them the task of infiltrating Communist and workers' parties," editorialized *Pravda* (September 21, 1949). The accused, as in the late 1930s, were given criminal pasts that accorded with their roles: Rajk that of a police spy and enemy of communism since 1931 and Kostov that of a wartime fascist. "There is but one defense against rabid dogs, destroy them," announced Rajk's prosecutor (September 22, 1949). Tito figured in these charges, but, unlike Trotsky, he was not the chief target. A week before Rajk's trial, *Pravda* published a cartoon, "The Fascist Hound and His Owner," showing Churchill and Truman cranking a canine Tito who spit slander, and the day after the trial opened another appeared, titled "Thirty Pieces of Silver," showing Tito as Judas and Truman and the U.S. Export-Import Bank a Pontius Pilate (September 1 and 13, 1949).

In the 1920s Bolsheviks had refuted the émigré press, although few readers had access to it. In the 1930s, secure in their monopoly and for the most part denied access by their own censors, they rarely bothered.[160] During the cold war, however, they could not ignore foreign broadcasts. The press used the trials in part to counter foreign news reports of the break with Tito. "Inspired by historic Soviet victories . . . the working people of the peoples' democracies confidently face the future and successfully lay the foundations of socialism," *Pravda* editorialized on the Rajk trial.[161] Positive news of the peoples' democracies now moved to page 1. On September 7, 1949, *Pravda* gave front-page coverage to the opening of "Offices for the Study of Marxism-Leninism" in Czechoslovakia, Bulgarian workers' commemoration of liberation by exceeding production quotas, the growth of agricultural cooperatives in Hungary, the success of Soviet production methods in Romania, and Polish agricultural specialists' enthusiasm for Michurin. In 1949 *Pravda* presented the October anniversary as an affair of the whole socialist camp. "All these historic transformations were accomplished under the powerful Soviet influence," *Pravda* editorialized, referring to central and southeast Europe, China, Germany, and Korea (November 6, 1949).

Stalin's seventieth birthday was a festival of both national and international communism. It was perhaps the most outlandish act of the performance. On December 21, his official birthday, the Central Committee and Council of Ministers lauded him for making the country "a great and invincible power" (December 12, 1949). Molotov, Bulganin, Kaganovich, Beria, Khrushchev, and others praised him as the friend of the world's peoples. A front-page photo the next day, on December 22, showed world communist leaders behind a table heaped with flowers (Figure 8.5). Stalin stood between Mao Zedong and Walter Ulbricht. "From all corners of our Russian Republic, from the far North to the southern banks of the Crimea, from the Baltic to Sakhalin and Korea, the many millions of working people in cities and villages send you a great people's thanks for all the good you have done, for your fatherly concern for people, for the happiness and joy of our life," read a greeting in *Izvestiia*.[162]

Manicheanism reigned. Party and government leaders credited Stalin with purifying Soviet society as well as inventing it. "You pitilessly unmasked the most evil and criminal attempts by enemies of the people to disarm the party ideologically, to shatter its unity, and to destroy Soviet power and the socialist revolution," read the proclamation from the Central Committee and Council of Ministers on December 21, 1949. On the same day individual leaders praised him for crushing internal and external enemies. Molotov stressed his "unwavering vigilance toward class enemies and any sortie by their surviving agents." Beria hailed him for "intransigence toward enemies of communism." Yet Khrushchev, the future dismantler of the cult, outdid the others. "The greatest service of Comrade Stalin," he wrote, "was that he preserved the purity of Leninist teachings and harmony and iron unity in our Party's ranks in the bitter struggle with enemies of the people, Mensheviks, SRs, Trotskyites, Zinovi-

Figure 8.5. *Pravda,* December 22, 1949. "The Festive Meeting at the Bolshoi Theater on the Seventieth Birthday of Iosif Vissarionovich Stalin." The banner reads: "Long Live the Great Leader and Teacher of the Communist Party and the Soviet People, Comrade I. V. Stalin!"

etes, Bukharinites, and bourgeois nationalists." Khrushchev alone among the lieutenants praised Stalin for attacking "rootless cosmopolitanism."

> Comrade Stalin, like a solicitous gardener, grows and educates these cadres in the spirit of passionate Soviet patriotism; he taught and teaches them the Bolshevik style of work and a sharp intransigence toward the slightest appearance of alien bourgeois ideology, the ideology of bourgeois nationalism, rootless cosmopolitanism, or subservience before foreign bourgeois culture.[163]

Never had Stalin appeared more powerful or divine. In 1939 *Pravda* first reported Stalin's sixtieth birthday on December 17 and continued to do so for less than a month. The public ceremony was a Kremlin concert, ignored by the press, and tributes by the army and several other institutions.[164] Party and government leaders, chiefs of republics, and a few notables offered testimonials. In 1949 the press cited events in every major city and the flow of greetings from institutions, organizations, and collectives continued almost until his death in

1953. "Thank you for leading us from the pit of darkness to light and happiness," wrote wartime poet A. Tvardovskii on December 22.[165] The next day *Pravda* printed "words of unlimited love and gratitude," "unanimously approved" by 38,232,867 Komsomol members and young people at meetings around the country. Two thousand young pioneers attended a Moscow gala called "Thank you, Comrade Stalin, for our happy childhood."[166] The Academy of Sciences thanked "the greatest genius of humanity" and adopted Lysenko's suggestion to appoint him to an honorary presidium.[167]

As the day approached, the press printed so many promises to exceed norms and enter "socialist competition" in his honor that by December 6 there was little room for other news. "Together with all Soviet people, komsomols and boys and girls of our country prepare to commemorate the seventieth birthday of the beloved leader and teacher Comrade I. V. Stalin with new labor successes," read *Komsomol Pravda*'s headline on December 8. Moscow city leader N. A. Rossiiskii announced at the Kremlin reception, "Among the innumerable gifts of love and devotion Soviet people have given their leader we give a gift of labor: Industrial Moscow has completed the postwar five year plan for gross production in less than four years."[168] The press also reported that a Caucasian climber had placed Stalin's bust on a peak and that Central Asian climbers had lodged busts on thirty peaks.[169]

Giving Stalin gifts was an authorized way of joining the performance. On December 12 *Pravda* printed a picture of peasant women embroidering "A Gift to Comrade Stalin" (Figure 8.6). "The People Compose Beautiful Songs about Our Wise and Beloved Stalin" read the header. *Izvestiia* displayed his portrait embroidered by a young pioneer and ringed with adoring letters.[170] "Again and Again I thank Comrade Stalin for the Soviet people's happy and joyful life," wrote a house painter from Kuibyshev. Turkmen in Ashkhabad sent a huge carpet showing him talking with champion cotton growers, honored citizens who had fulfilled their obligations.[171] Gifts and letters were exhibited in Moscow and elsewhere.[172] Boris Polevoi described them on December 8, 1949, in a column in *Pravda* captioned "The People's Love." He noted a pipe begun by a soldier at Stalingrad but finished by others after his death. Such gifts were personal, but the press portrayed Stalin as too elevated to use them. Their display nevertheless indicated their symbolic importance.

Foreigners played an important role in the public representation of the Soviet order, and the press underscored their acknowledgment of their debt to Stalin. The writer Leonid Leonov imagined an international holiday "of thanksgiving" when "the working people of all nations greet the great leader."[173] A. Poskrebyshev, the secretive chief of Stalin's secretariat, wrote in *Pravda* on December 21, 1949: "Hundreds of millions of people from the banks of the Pacific Ocean to the Elbe, more than a third of the earth's population are already building a new life according to the great teachings of Marx, Engels, Lenin, and Stalin." In 1939 two foreigners had praised him in *Pravda*—Georgy Dimitrov,

Figure 8.6. *Pravda,* December 12, 1949. "A Gift to Comrade Stalin."

famous for rebutting Nazi charges of having set the Reichstag on fire in 1933, and the legendary orator of the Spanish Civil War, Dolores Ibarrui (La Passionaria).[174] A decade later foreigners were almost as prominent as Soviet well-wishers.

Visitors from abroad matched Soviet citizens in their praise. "We will advance like one man under the banner of Lenin and Stalin," promised Hungarian Communist leader, Matias Rakoshi. The Bulgarian Vylko Chervenkov expressed "profound gratitude to Comrade Stalin for all that he has done and does for our people." Palmiro Tolgiatti, the Italian, claimed, "Without you, Comrade

Stalin, the Italian people would be living in incomparably more difficult conditions." The French Communist, Andre Marty, thanked Stalin, not the Soviet people: "The men and woman of France, in contrast to their government, have not forgotten they owe you their freedom and lives." Mao, more restrained and independent, praised Stalin simply as "leader of the working class of the whole world and of the international communist movement."

There were also foreign gifts. Boris Polevoi described cases of letters at the Museum of the Revolution, some with thousands, even millions of signatures, such as one from North Korea.[175] The press also reported displays in foreign capitals. "Love and Gratitude" was *Izvestiia*'s caption for an article on a display in Prague.[176] "Gifts come from schoolchildren, soldiers, artists, wood carvers, sculptors, furniture makers, machine builders, glass makers, and scientific workers," the author explained. Romanians dispatched more than two thousand items to Moscow, and the Bulgarians organized a special train for their gifts.[177] According to *Pravda,* all France joined the "mass and truly popular sending of individual gifts to Stalin."[178]

The Chinese response was unique. They knew the language of tribute too well to play their assigned part. Mao, who had come to negotiate about territories China had lost to Russia in tsarist times as well as other matters, did not wish to appear as a feudal underling. He brought no retinue of princes and generals, as would have been appropriate for such a mission in Chinese custom, and he rejected General Yang Shangkun's advice to offer tea, porcelain, embroidery, and a big portrait of Stalin.[179] Instead, he produced several wagon loads of Chinese fruits and vegetables, which *Pravda* avoided mentioning. The paper noted only a photograph of Mao with the dedication, "To our leader, Comrade Stalin, from Mao Zedong."[180] Yet little could detract from the chorus of adulation. The whole world seemed to congratulate Stalin in *Pravda*'s daily lists of greetings. One on December 30, 1949, filling half a page, began with the Central Committee of the Communist Party of Paraguay and included the United Free German Trade Unions of the GDR, workers and employees at the Lukoianov Station of the Kazan Railroad, and employees of the publishing house Artistic Literature in Ukraine. Foreign greetings ceased after a year or so, but Soviet ones continued much longer.

The successful A-bomb test, the Chinese Revolution, and the birthday gala all preceded the North Korean invasion of South Korea. In 1949 Kim Il Sung had pressed Stalin for support. After the celebration, he agreed. On January 30, 1950, he instructed the Soviet ambassador in Pyongyang:

> The matter must be organized so that there would not be too great a risk. If he wants to discuss this matter with me, then I will always be ready to receive him and discuss with him. Transmit all this to Kim Il Sung and tell him that I am ready to help him in this matter.[181]

Stalin reinforced the North Korean Peoples Army (NKPA) in February and instructed Soviet advisers to assist in planning the operation.[182] On June 25,

1950, the NKPA crossed the 38th parallel with Soviet-made T34 tanks, and Seoul, less than fifty miles from the border, fell on June 28. On June 27 the Security Council, which the Soviet Union had boycotted since January over China's status, urged members to aid the South. Truman ordered General MacArthur to provide air support, and on June 30 full-scale American intervention began.

The Korean War was the most dangerous moment in the first decade of the cold war, and in no other instance did domestic news dovetail so effectively with a foreign story. As the NKPA advanced in late June and July, the Soviet press focused on several prearranged domestic events that served to highlight the peacefulness of the country and its leader. The first was the "free discussion" of the ideas of deceased linguist Nikolai Marr, which began in *Pravda* on May 9, 1950, with an announcement of shortcomings in Soviet linguistics, and filled two of *Pravda*'s six pages every Tuesday until July 4. A second comprised the meetings of the Supreme Soviet of the USSR, beginning on June 12, and of the Supreme Soviet of the Russian Republic, which met on July 5 to consider "a budget of peace." These were followed by the opening of a Soviet campaign to sign the Stockholm peace petition on June 30, and meetings of peace advocates in Moscow in October and in Warsaw in November. Finally, from June 28 through July 9 a Joint Session of the Academy of Sciences and Academy of Medical Science of the USSR considered Pavlov's legacy.

On June 26 *Pravda* printed the North Korean declaration that the NKPA had crossed the 38th parallel after repulsing a South Korean attack. On June 27 *Pravda* carried Kim Il Sung's speech promising victory, and Western reports of the NKPA's approach to Seoul. The next day the paper denounced Truman's promise to support the South, and on June 29 *Pravda* printed UN General Secretary Trygve Lie's note that the Security Council had urged members to aid the South, the Soviet reply, and a report from Beijing on the fall of Seoul. The anti-American peace-petition campaign commenced on June 30, five days after the invasion.[183] N. S. Tikhonov, war correspondent and writer, headed the Soviet Committee for Defense of Peace. Members included the presidents or chairmen of the Academy of Sciences, the writers' union, the Komsomol, and many other organizations. Sholokhov, Lysenko, Korneichuk, Ehrenburg, Simonov, Shostakovich, and Zaslavskii were among the notables involved.[184] "The Soviet People Vote for Peace!" *Pravda* editorialized on June 30, and the paper later reported that 115,275,940 people had signed from June 30 to August 4.[185] American diplomat Charles E. Bohlen recalled, "I attended a number of meetings at which the CIA discussed ways to counter the 'Hate America' campaign, but we did not come up with anything effective."[186]

TASS reported NKPA victories from Pyongyang without mentioning Soviet involvement. *Pravda*'s correspondent, V. Kornilov, wrote of the bombing of Pyongyang, "Losing battle after battle at the front, the American murderers have decided to kill peaceful people in revenge."[187] In late August he charged MacArthur with using Japanese soldiers and officers, and with "bacteriological sabotage," an accusation which figured in later propaganda campaigns.[188] By mid-July the NKPA had cornered UN forces on the coast, and, with victory at hand, the press touched on North Korea's debt. On July 29 *Labor*'s editorialist reminded readers of previous Soviet aid and observed, "Now [again] Soviet people show solidarity with Korean patriots." On August 15 *Pravda* printed a North Korean declaration on the fifth anniversary of the country's wartime liberation: "Korean people again turn their eyes to their liberator and friend, the Soviet Union, and offer deep thanks to great Stalin and the whole Soviet people." As George F. Kennan has observed, "In Stalin's day, foreign news stories did not appear in the Soviet press unless there was a specific purpose to be served thereby."[189]

MacArthur interrupted this rhetorical shift by landing on September 15 at Inchon, far behind North Korean lines, and inflicting sharp reverses on the NKPA. *Pravda* printed the report of the Central Committee of the Unified Democratic Patriotic Front of Korea on alleged American atrocities seven days later.[190] The press covered the American victories through the lens of the Second All-Union Conference of Peace Advocates, which met in Moscow on October 7. "The powerful peace movement will rip the weapons from the warmongers' dirty hands," declared the president of the Ukrainian Academy of Sciences, A. Palladin.[191] "We are creators of the happiness of peoples," *Pravda*'s columnist avowed on October 10. On the same day, *Pravda*'s columnist depicted rape and murder in captured Seoul. UN forces entered Pyongyang on October 20, and the Second World Congress of Peace Advocates opened in Warsaw soon afterward. *Pravda* and other papers gave the event a third of their space for nearly two weeks. Fadeev, chief Soviet delegate, declared of America, "The country spilled children's blood" (November 19, 1950).

The war turned around again in November after Chinese intervention and the near rout of UN forces in early winter. *Pravda, Labor,* and other papers, who featured tiny reports while UN forces advanced, conveyed the news obliquely in an unsigned article on December 2 about the American response. "In the opinion of the American press, American troops have suffered 'the greatest defeat of the Korean War,'" the author noted. The tone soon became triumphant. "From the peak of the half century we Soviet people see our communist future," *Pravda* editorialized on New Year's Day. Seoul fell again to the Northern forces on January 4, and Kornilov, *Pravda*'s Pyongyang correspondent, exalted: "Looking today into the faces of people going to the front, one firmly believes complete victory is near" (December 13, 1950). A few days later, amid fears of communist invasions elsewhere, *Pravda*'s Paris correspondent, Iurii Zhukov, called Eisenhower "the European MacArthur," and another correspondent warned that "the popular masses of Taiwan know they are not alone in the struggle against imperialism" (January 9, 1951; January 13, 1951). Such thoughts were premature. The allies retook Seoul in March, freed South Korea of communist troops by late May, and a stalemate ensued.

The Manicheanism in coverage of Korea and the "peace movement" was also evident in the commentaries on Marr and Pavlov, which served to contrast the country with warlike America and affirm a Russian-Soviet identity. Stalin intervened three times in the "discussion" about Marr, beginning on June 20, six days before the North Korean attack.[192] Ehrenburg recalled how incongruous this seemed at a time when many feared war: "Stalin busied himself with issues of linguistics, but ordinary citizens bought salt and soap."[193] In fact, the prominence the press gave Marr can hardly be explained without reference to the international context. Marr, who died in 1934, traced Indo-European languages to a core close to Georgian and identified language with superstructure in Marx's schema and hence with a ruling class. This view of language as class-based suited class war and socialist building, but it did not support the combative nationalism of the cold war. Stalin approved the article that opened the anti-Marr campaign on April 10.[194] The planned invasion was but two and a half months away.

Stalin dethroned Marr following the anticosmopolitan campaign in which Soviet was equated with Russian. The day chosen to begin the "discussion" was May 9, the fifth anniversary of Germany's defeat. As events unfolded, Marrists and anti-Marrists disputed word origins, but the crux was the status of Russian. Its glory suited official patriotism, and the Marrists' plea that they treasured Soviet but not tsarist literary language fell on deaf ears.[195] Stalin resolved the issue by proclaiming language to be the people's heritage, independent of class, and therefore part of neither superstructure nor base.[196] He pointed to Pushkin, declaring, "The modern Russian language differs very little in structure from the language of Pushkin," adding that in clashes in which one language died out, "the Russian language . . . always emerged the victor."[197] He relegated the world language some Marxists anticipated to an indefinite future. Asserting the dignity of Russian, Stalin hailed a lingua franca being taught to school children from Berlin to Beijing. Although he may not have fully shared the sentiments Edward Gibbon attributed to the ancient Romans, he would probably have sympathized. "So sensible were the Romans of the influence of language over national manners," Gibbon wrote, "that it was their most serious care to extend, with the progress of their arms, the use of the Latin tongue."[198]

Nationalism also figured in the joint session of the academies held ostensibly to honor Pavlov. Reporting on the opening on June 29, four days after the Korean invasion, *Pravda* denounced Academician L. A. Orbeli, head of Pavlov's Institute of Physiology, for "not combating the influence of the Western American and bourgeois theories against which Academician Pavlov ceaselessly struggled." Yet the meeting differed from the 1948 session of the Academy of Agricultural Sciences at which Lysenko triumphed. First, there was no Lysenko, and second, some participants utilized Stalin's remark in *Pravda* a few days earlier criticizing advocates of Marr for stifling criticism to defend their right to speak.[199] Whether Stalin encouraged openness in science to compete with the West or merely pretended to do so, his words were widely quoted, and *Pravda* even disdainfully noted Orbeli's refusal to denounce himself.[200] Nevertheless, as in linguistics, the press promoted the image of a peaceable government concerned with edifying matters. It also hailed Pavlov's doctrine about the central nervous system as the basis of a new Russian-Soviet medicine and psychology.

Pride in Russian ethnicity had advanced considerably since June 26, 1945, when Stalin had toasted the Russian people. It now became the corollary of empire. In pre-Soviet public culture, the empire figured as a source of enrichment, though the economic aspects of tribute were rarely explicit.[201] The early Bolsheviks stressed the tsarist exploitation of non-Russians and explained their own policies in non-Russian regions as mutually advantageous to the center and the periphery. The press continued this practice during the First Five-Year Plan, printing maps showing investment and enterprise in outlying regions. Stalin and his colleagues gradually changed the emphasis by stressing the Russians' one-sided contribution to other regions and non-Russians' indebtedness. The elevation of Russian ethnicity and implicit denigration of other peoples carried a danger of disunity and disaffection, but cultivation of the threat from abroad in the cold war provided a common foreign enemy and cohesion against it. Anti-Semitism served a similar purpose and may also have diffused resentment over ethnic Russians' preeminence. Yet it was no substitute for the sense of mutual advantage that had hitherto sustained the pre-Soviet imperial project.

The performance intensified as Stalin's life drew to a close, and editorialists adopted a triumphant tone, congratulating readers rather than urging them to work harder.[202] In August and September 1950 the press added "the Great Projects of Communism" to the Great Plan for the Transformation of Nature. These included the Volga Don Canal, the Grand Turkmen Canal, and huge hydroelectric stations on the Volga and elsewhere. In the performance, the grander the accomplishment, the more indebted the citizen, and journalists used these projects to enlarge the cult. "The great projects of communism are new evidence of your tireless concern for further increasing the productive forces of the country, for creating the material and technical base of communism, and for the welfare of the Soviet people," *Pravda*'s editors assured Stalin on November 7, 1950.[203] The Fifth Five-Year Plan was scheduled to run from 1951 to 1955 but the Central Committee announced targets only on August 20, 1952, and gave detailed directives only at the Nineteenth Party Congress in October 1952.[204] Industry again took priority.

Although Stalin withdrew from public life in 1951 and 1952, the cult flourished and he reaffirmed his preeminence on the eve of the Nineteenth Congress by publishing "The Economic Problems of Socialism in the USSR" in *Pravda* on October 3 and 4, 1952.[205] His subject was the Soviet economy, but most striking were his remarks on capitalism's deepening crisis and on the likelihood of war. "To abolish the inevitability of war," he wrote, "it is necessary to abolish imperialism."[206]

The press glorified Stalin, but the issue of succession must have seemed inescapable to participants. Not only had there not been a congress for thirteen years, but the Party had ceased to function as part of the government.[207] Covering the opening of the congress, *Pravda, Labor,* and *Komsomol Pravda* printed a picture of Stalin in the pose of Rodin's thinker, seated alone to the right of Malenkov, who delivered the Central Committee report.[208] The rest of the leadership sat apart. On the final day, *Pravda* and *Labor* again published a photo that emphasized Stalin's distance from other leaders. In what became his last public speech, Stalin discussed the support the country might expect from other nations.[209] He thanked foreign workers for their help during the civil war and their continued help. "Certainly our Party cannot remain indebted to fraternal parties but ought in return support them and their peoples' struggle for liberation and peace." He concluded by recalling early Bolsheviks' hopes. "I think our Party has justified these hopes, especially during the Second World War when the Soviet Union crushed German and Japanese military tyranny and freed peoples of Europe and Asia from the threat of fascist slavery."[210] The foreign obligation was plain.

During the congress, each speaker credited Stalin with the victory, but there were also intimations that government could continue without him. Citing the military victory, Molotov observed, "All this explains why the Party's leading ideological influence has grown so much on all facets of the country's life and why the people's love for the Party is so great."[211] The press also reported socialist competition "in honor of the Party congress," not Stalin (October 7, 1952). Foreign guests, however, clung to old formulas. Maurice Thorez's tribute was typical: "Glory to the teacher and leader of Communists' of all countries, friend and brother of the working people of the whole world, our dear and Great Stalin!" (October 11, 1952). *Pravda*'s editors added, "(stormy, prolonged applause, turning into an ovation. All stand)."

Warnings of the foreign threat capped the congress's agenda. Molotov vowed, "We obviously cannot forget that the Soviet Union lives 'in a system of states,' that there exists an imperialist camp with aggressive adventurist aims, which is arming, fanning war hysteria, and preparing to unleash a new world war" (October 6, 1952). Malenkov, giving the Central Committee's report, stressed the militarization of capitalist economies. Khrushchev recalled, perhaps misleadingly, "In the days leading up to Stalin's death, we believed that America would invade the Soviet Union and we would go to war."[212] Soviet intelligence reports confirmed these worries, and John Foster Dulles had advocated a "policy of boldness" to deter further aggression during the presidential campaign of 1952.[213] Tensions were heightened by the race for the thermonuclear bomb. On the eve of the last burst of official scapegoating, the so-called Doctors' Plot, the Soviet Union was overtaking the United States in the race to produce a deliverable super bomb.[214]

The Party congress coincided with charges against the United States of mass murder, germ warfare, and executions of prisoners in Korea. The press covered

Soviet efforts to press charges in the United Nations and the peace movement. A World Congress of Peoples in Defense of Peace convened in Vienna on December 12, and the press carried more speeches against American militarism. *Pravda* printed photos of dead women and children, "atrocities of American interventionists."[215]Despite heightened tensions, however, the press was slow to invoke the fear of internal enemies, which had been so critical during similar moments in the past. Speakers at the Party congress skirted this topic, although they urged vigilance. Nor did the press promote Czechoslovak leader R. Slansky's trial in November 1952, which Soviet operatives helped organize.[216] *Pravda* commented only once, blaming Washington, American corporations, and George F. Kennan.[217] The press depicted the affair as an extension of earlier trials, but the stress on Jews, Zionism, and economic damage was novel. TASS blamed "Trotskyite-Titoist, Zionist, bourgeois-nationalist traitors and enemies of the Czechoslovak people" who sought to sever the Czechoslovak Republic's "close ties and friendship with the Soviet Union, liquidate its popular democratic order, restore capitalism, return the country to the imperialist camp, and end its independence."[218]

The press pushed internal enemies to the fore in the promotion of the Doctors' Plot in early 1953. The affair resembled the Slansky trial as a communist auto-da-fé but was, in contrast, a full-scale public performance.[219] When *Pravda* opened the affair on January 13, 1953, with a commentary captioned, "Rotten Spies and Murders Masked as Professor-Doctors," the police had already been torturing their victims for months.[220] The anonymous author, citing TASS, accused "doctor-poisoners" working for American intelligence of murdering Zhdanov, Shcherbakov, Gorky, Kuibyshev, and V. R. Menzhinskii (head of the OGPU [Joint State Political Administration], 1926–34) and of trying to poison military leaders. The allegation read in part:

> The majority of participants in the terrorist group, Vovsi, B. Kogan, Feldman, Grinshtein, Etinger, and others, were bought by American secret service. They were enlisted by a branch of the American secret service—the international Jewish bourgeois nationalist organization "Joint." The dirty face of this Zionist organization, which masks its rotten activities with philanthropy, is completely revealed.

The "Joint," the American Jewish Joint Distribution Committee, a philanthropic organization organized in 1914 to help needy Jews, was active in the USSR during the 1920s.[221] Much of the article concerned subversion, and the author cited Stalin's argument that "the more successful our forward movement, the sharper the struggle of the people's doomed enemies, who are driven to despair." The author chided state security, "which did not reveal the wreckers, the doctors' terrorist organization, in time," and the Ministry of Health, which "overlooked the wrecking terrorist activities of the rotten monsters, who sold out to enemies of the Soviet Union." Most striking was the author's concluding words on muddleheadedness: "Besides these enemies, there is still an enemy among us—our people's muddleheadedness. So to liquidate wrecking, we must eliminate muddleheadedness in our ranks."

Foreign observers and subsequent scholars have seen the plot as a product of Stalin's final paranoia, a campaign to unify the country for an anticipated war or as the backdrop to a purge of the leadership. Stalin's behavior may have had a medical cause. His physician, Dr. V. N. Vinogradov, diagnosed arteriosclerosis of the brain in early 1952 and recommended rest, but Stalin, wary of plotters, had him arrested.[222] Whatever Stalin's purpose, it is unlikely that the ill and aging leader actively planned the publicity. Party leaders, including M. A. Suslov (a Central Committee member who had edited *Pravda* and led Cominform) and D. T. Shepilov, who had become *Pravda*'s chief editor, took charge of presenting the plot to the public.[223]

The key words of the initial report were "muddleheadedness," "vigilance," and "Zionism" or "Jewish."[224] The four central newspapers (*Pravda, Izvestiia, Komsomol Pravda,* and *Labor*) published forty-nine articles, including twelve editorials, on vigilance, muddleheadedness, and terrorism from January 13 until *Pravda*'s bulletin on Stalin's declining health on March 5.[225] Of the total, twenty-five concerned the danger of war and twenty-three involved crooks, charlatans, or "dubious people," many of whom were identified as Jews.[226]

The authors of the initial report on the Doctors' Plot accused the United States of organizing the assassination of Soviet leaders and promised retribution. The charges were blunt, and so were the warnings. "Let the warmongers know that the third world war, if they start it, will inevitably destroy the whole capitalist world system," *Komsomol Pravda* threatened on January 28. "The danger of new imperialist aggression, of wrecking, sabotage, and spying from the capitalist world has not been removed," *Pravda* cautioned.[227] Purveyors of these warnings and threats pointed up domestic dangers.

Of the forty-nine articles, thirty-two concerned foreign agents, either separately or together with Soviet internal enemies. *Pravda*'s summary and commentary on TASS's report included the following passage, which contained the only emphasized words in the article:

> The exploiting classes in the USSR were smashed and liquidated long ago, but remnants of bourgeois ideology and of the psychology and morality of private property still exist; and the bearers of bourgeois morality, *living people,* hidden enemies of our people, also exist. These hidden enemies, supported by the imperialist world, are the ones who will carry out sabotage in the future.[228]

The authors of this and other articles implied that such "living people" were likely to be Jews, and Jews appeared in twenty-six of the forty-nine articles. Six of the articles concerned Jews alone. These appeared late in the campaign, and all but one was printed in *Pravda*. A feuilleton reprinted from *Soviet Latvia* recounted the career of Abram Natanovich Khaitin, "a person without a definite occupation," who worked at the poster shop of the Latvian Theatrical Society

(LTO).[229] The authors related how he turned the unit into a private shop, embezzled, and was protected by others with Jewish names. "Only muddleheadedness can explain how Khaitin and company carried out their criminal business for so long in the workshops of the LTO," they concluded. Who could miss the call to persecute and fire Jews. *Labor* urged action: "We should pitilessly battle cosmopolitanism not only ideologically but organizationally and practically, so as to expunge cosmopolitanism and bourgeois nationalism from Soviet reality."[230]

Journalists sounded the alarm. "The muddlehead is dangerous in any area and can greatly harm the cause," editorialized the youth paper.[231] "One must realize that the enemy can use the slightest lapse or muddleheadedness to harm and spoil," wrote two columnists in *Pravda,* who cited carelessness with secret documents as well as treason.[232] The effect was to lump misfits and spies, crooks, traitors, and suspicious people together with Jews. The youth paper's editors reminded readers, "Living human beings, bearers of bourgeois views and morals, are the hidden enemies of our people."[233] Meanwhile, as if to confirm the threat from abroad, although not from America, a bomb exploded at the Soviet mission in Tel Aviv on February 9, wounding several employees and family members. Whether this was a Soviet provocation or a terrorist act is unclear, but more threats and warnings followed.[234]

The campaign was intended, according to some accounts, to justify the planned deportation of Soviet Jews. *Pravda* was to publish a letter from prominent Jews condemning the doctors allegedly involved in the "plot" and requesting transportation to Siberia as protection against the citizens' wrath.[235] The letter has not been found, but Ehrenburg's note to Stalin explaining his refusal to sign and warning that the letter would damage the peace campaign has been discovered. Whatever the truth, reports of deportation were widespread. "After Stalin's death," Sakharov later recalled, "we heard that trains had been assembled in the beginning of March to transport Jews to Siberia and that propaganda justifying their deportation had been set in type, including a lead article for *Pravda* entitled: 'The Russian People Are Rescuing the Jewish People.'"[236]

The denunciations of the doctors halted with Stalin's death in early March, and on April 4 central newspapers published a short announcement from the Ministry of Internal Affairs exonerating the doctors and promising that their accusers would be punished. "Wonderful April events!" wrote Chukovskii in his diary. "The order of amnesty, the reexamination of the affair of the doctor-poisoners, has colored all my days with joy."[237] Sakharov later remembered, "Besides the official communiqué on the doctors' release, we were thrilled by *Pravda*'s editorials on 'The Invincible Friendship of Nations' and 'Socialist Legality Is Inviolable' (April 6). But they were the first and last of their kind."[238] Stalin's death stopped events that appeared to be leading to a horrifying episode of paranoiac homicide, but even his death did not stop the performance.

Stalin survived the war by less than eight years, but the strictures he and his supporters reimposed on communication endured to frustrate the efforts of several generations of would-be reformers. By once again embracing the performance after the war, Stalin and his supporters aggravated the long-standing myopia of the public culture. The global economy was changing; information was becoming the critical factor in economic life; and the very strengths in heavy industry, machine building, and centralized product design that had allowed the country to overcome Nazi Germany were gradually becoming a liability. Yet although Stalin's legacy was burdensome under these circumstances, the leaders who succeeded him ultimately proved unwilling or unable to discard practices and institutions that he and his supporters had made so central to the legitimacy and politics of the Soviet system.

Renewal, Stagnation, and Collapse

STALIN'S final triumph was the enactment of his own funeral. Public figures joined reigning political leaders in a memorial performance rivaling his greatest celebrations. Stalinism itself would soon become a shameful and often suppressed memory, but for another forty years his successors struggled to maintain key elements of the system that he and Lenin had created, including, among others, the state's monopoly on public information, the illusion that state and society were one, and the presumption of a single official narrative of national life. At the same time, Stalin's successors cautiously opened the media to new voices, allowed limited scope for reforms and commentary, and tried to instill sufficient vitality into the unitary narrative to keep it alive. The dual effort was internally inconsistent and doomed to failure, but participants in Soviet public life doggedly sustained it until the collapse of communism in 1991.

Stalin suffered a stroke or was poisoned on the night of February 28 or in the early morning hours of March 1, 1953. He was found at midday on March 1 by a chambermaid who entered unbidden when he failed to emerge as usual.[1] His colleagues initially denied him treatment, but he eventually received some medical care and clung to life without regaining consciousness until 9:30 on the evening of March 5. On March 4 *Pravda* reported "a serious illness," and on March 5 newspapers carried a medical bulletin on his declining health and an appeal for unity. The press announced his death on March 6 in a statement by the Central Committee, the Council of Ministers, and the Presidium of the Supreme Soviet. A medical bulletin gave the time of death as 11:30 P.M., not 9:30 P.M., when it is presumed to have occurred. Moscow radio reported the event early on the morning of March 6 to the accompaniment of the allegretto from Beethoven's Seventh Symphony.[2] The announcement in the newspapers, in which the Party and government warned of internal and external enemies and of a readiness to repel invaders, bespoke an effort to maintain continuity in an atmosphere of uncertainty and vulnerability.

Stalin's colleagues reorganized the government when they discovered his condition, and on March 7 the press reported G. M. Malenkov as head of the Council of Ministers, with Beria, Molotov, Bulganin, and Kaganovich as deputy heads of the Council of Ministers. Voroshilov, Stalin's aged comrade from the civil war, chaired the Presidium of the Supreme Soviet, replacing, without explanation, N. M. Shvernik, who had held the position since 1946. The press did not report or discuss rivalries among Stalin's heirs. Nor were the deaths of the 109 people later crushed at his funeral publicly acknowledged.[3]

On March 7 *Pravda, Izvestiia, Labor,* and *Komsomol Pravda* printed the same photomontage of Stalin's successors observing his body in the Hall of Columns at the House of Trade Unions, an eighteenth-century building with an ornate interior. On one side stood government and Party leaders. On the other lay the dead Stalin, five times larger than the living, a composite of all the larger-than-life heroes the press had projected since the 1930s (Figure Epi.1). His bier was awash with flowers, as befitted the mystery of his departure. "Everything is drowned in a sea of living flowers," reported *Komsomol Pravda.*[4] Two days later, on March 9, Aleksei Surkov, the poet and war correspondent, Stalin prizewinner, and literary bureaucrat, rhapsodized in *Pravda:* "Flowers and bouquets brought from everywhere into the Hall of Columns—this is but one revelation of the people's love, but how significant is the mute language of flowers!"[5] *Izvestiia,* on March 11, showed a long stretch of the Kremlin wall banked with blossoms. "Moscow, Red Square. Wreaths laid by the working people of the Soviet Union at the burial place of Iosif Vissarionovich Stalin," read the caption. Yet Stalin was not buried but entombed and displayed, his name engraved under Lenin's on the mausoleum. Nor did flowers spring spontaneously from the people's love, however grief-stricken the populace may have been. They were flown in from the south at great expense, and it was so difficult for unofficial people to buy them in Moscow that the family and friends of Sergei Prokofiev, whose death on March 5 was ignored by the press, used cuttings from house plants to honor the composer.[6] Those who raved about "the language of flowers" knew this language for what it was and performed accordingly.

The press also incorporated children in the final drama. On March 9 *Pravda*'s feature, "Children Bid the Leader Good-bye," included a picture of a girl beside his coffin (Figure Epi.2). The author explained that she had given Stalin flowers on the past May Day and now again presented a bouquet.

> "From children," she whispers barely audibly, and looks into the familiar face.
>
> Stalin is immobile. He does not lift his hands to embrace the girl as he had earlier. His eyes are forever closed, his face calm.
>
> And the girl steps quietly from the pedestal. Grief grips her young heart: Stalin is not there.
>
> Stalin lives! He lives in all the great national deeds.

Flowers and children had long signified his fatherhood of Soviet society. Now the press employed these symbols of divine authority to immortalize his presence despite his corporeal passing.

The public presentation of Stalin's death was a managed event, albeit not designed in advance. Konstantin Simonov recalled a meeting of the Central Committee, the Council of Ministers, and the Supreme Soviet on the evening of

Figure Epi.1. *Pravda*, March 7, 1953. "In the Hall of Columns in the Kremlin Palace of Congresses. The leaders of the Party and the government at the bier of Comrade I. V. Stalin."

Дети прощаются с вождем

Figure Epi.2. *Pravda,* March 9, 1953. "Children bid the leader good-bye" in the Hall of Columns in the Kremlin Palace of Congresses.

March 5 to discuss Stalin's illness, after which D. T. Shepilov, the editor of *Pravda,* invited him and other prominent literati, including Fadeev, Korneichuk, Surkov, and Tvardovskii, to his office.[7] At *Pravda,* after Shepilov received a phone call announcing Stalin's death, they set to work allocating tasks. Simonov recalled, "I do not remember who agreed to do what, or what we agreed to do and write. I said that I would write verses, but I did not know whether I could write these verses. I did know that I was incapable of anything else at the moment." He went on to describe how he and others wept, and how the words *loss* and *grief* were everywhere. "There are no words to convey / all the unbearable pain and sadness / no words with which to say how we mourn over you / Comrade Stalin," he wrote in his poem "As You Taught" in *Pravda* on March 7.

The journalists may have expressed genuine grief for the loss of the architect of the society that had given them material rewards, Stalin prizes, appreciation, and, for some, a sense of accomplishment for the greater good. From March 7 through March 11 newspapers printed testimonials and commentaries on reactions to Stalin's death. During these six days *Pravda* and *Izvestiia* gave less than the sum of two single columns to other news, and *Labor* and *Komsomol Pravda* gave none at all.[8] The press had long shown Stalin as a supreme moral being, and on his death it allowed for no other concerns. Participants in this last Stalinist performance utilized the metaphors of past decades, including the path, family, school, and construction, to bind the nation to him once more.

The beneficiaries of his long rule outdid one another in crediting him with accomplishments and in expunging all but his script from history. Shepilov, editor of *Pravda,* recalled "a flood of telegrams, letters, and articles" from people who wished to publish testimonials to Stalin.[9] The press showed Stalin's legatees overseeing a future in which he still ruled, or, more precisely, they ruled as his proxies. "The Party's plans for the future, the precise outlook and path of our forward movement, depends on the knowledge of economic laws and on the science of building a communist society worked out by Comrade Stalin," *Pravda* editorialized on March 7.[10] As earlier, praise for Stalin sustained the economy of the gift. No one voiced the survivors' obligation better than Boris Polevoi, war correspondent, novelist, and winner of a Stalin Prize in 1949, when he cited two anonymous mourners:

"Well, I would give up my life without a thought if it would extend his life a year."

"Really—only you? Millions of people would give their lives."[11]

Tikhonov, head of the Soviet Peace Committee, war correspondent, and winner of three Stalin Prizes, set the tone: "This man, who showed humanity the path to happiness and defended peaceful peoples from oppression, was known and loved in all small and large countries."[12]

Those who eulogized the dead leader borrowed from the rhetoric of Christianity by emphasizing Stalin's testament, his immortal teachings, and his disciples' sacred duties, but their claims were limited. No one intimated that Stalin had died for his or her sins or transgressions against the communist order. The call was to action, to produce and build, rather than to faith or repentance. The representation of Stalin's death was an apotheosis of the economy of the gift. The spontaneous emergence (spontaneous, at least, on the part of the directors of the performance) of this treatment at a time of stress shows the resilience of the Stalinist cultural system in the mid-1950s. The slogan "Stalin Is with Us," caption to Polevoi's front-page summary of the funeral in *Pravda* on March 7, was apt. The press displayed a shared identity.[13] Malenkov invoked an extended political community in his funeral speech on March 9 when he said, "Stalin's cause will live for ages, and grateful descendants such as you and I will glorify his name."

For all its similarity to past ceremonies, Stalin's funeral differed from its antecedents. Stalin's charisma, following Max Weber's usage, did not long survive his death. Stalin had inherited Lenin's charismatic authority through his followers' recognition of his revolutionary power to transform the world.[14] Like Lenin, he occupied a place in the Soviet system analogous to that of prophets of new religions and leaders of great political movements. Through his personal charisma he helped produce the "social big bang," the explosion of new meanings and understandings that usually accompanies the invention of a new society.[15] The performative culture lacked many qualities of great religions and long-lasting civilizations, but it had some, and Stalin's charisma was its prime unifying force.

Stalin, in Max Weber's terms, was the prophet of a community that extended far beyond Lenin's limited following. As his charisma was routinized, he became its teacher and lawgiver. Hence the ceaseless invocation of his speeches and writings. The result was akin to what the sociologist Talcott Parsons has described in his commentary on Weber's *Sociology of Religion* as a "sacralized polity"; namely, a "politically organized society in which the religious and the secular aspects of organization are not differentiated at the higher collectivity levels—in Western terms, a community which is both 'church' and 'state' at the same time."[16]

Through his charisma, Stalin established the "otherness" of the Soviet experience, its exceptionalism and independence from strictures that governed other societies. By accepting him as leader and prophet, participants in the performative culture were able to enhance their own power, justify the rightness of their cause, and deny the applicability of all other standards of behavior and morality. By proclaiming their distinctness from nonbelievers, including schismatics, they facilitated the vast persecutions of the Soviet era. The gratitude they expressed in what I have described as the moral economy of the gift can be understood as a personal expression of gratefulness to Stalin and of the bond between them. The officials, activists, and enthusiasts who enjoyed this bond with Stalin were the government's link to the general populace, and the leaders of the Party used the word link (*zveno*) to identify such people, including the intelligentsia. This is why the pedagogical function of the performance was so important. Participants who comprised the "link" rehearsed the routines of the social order and so communicated their understanding of "the facts of life" to others.[17]

Stalin's funeral, although long on pomp and ceremony, was insufficient to extend his charisma beyond his life. Weber noted the possibility of a transfer of charisma from a dead prophet to a disciple and the "routinization of charismatic authority" in a shift from personal charisma to the charisma of office or even, in a reduced form, to an institution.[18] That neither occurred in 1953 is evident from the new leaders' unwillingness to compete for the succession by citing Stalin, as Stalin himself had once cited Lenin against Trotsky. Malenkov attempted something of the sort at the funeral by imitating Stalin's famous oath to Lenin and having *Pravda* print a doctored photograph of him with Stalin and Mao, but he quickly abandoned the attempt and the others hardly tried.[19]

Within days, the successors attempted to legitimize themselves rationally on the basis of the efficacy of their policies. Dispensing with Stalin's prophetic authority, they also began to jettison Soviet society's essential otherness. Weber denied charisma to revolutionary and communist movements precisely because he thought their efforts to organize the masses were "dependent on 'value rational' appeals to their disciples, and on arguments from expediency (*zweckrational*) in their [external] propaganda."[20] Stalin's successors behaved as Weber might have expected, and the Stalinist cultural system eroded under this treatment until its ultimate collapse.

Two days after Stalin's death, on March 7, the Central Committee and the Council of Ministers proclaimed in bold type the "Erection of a Pantheon as a memorial to the eternal glory of the great people of the Soviet Union." Stalin's name was not in the caption, and it followed Lenin's in the small type of the text. The Pantheon was never built, but the two mummified leaders continued to symbolize the state until Khrushchev cast Stalin out in 1961. In significant departures from the norm of the performance, Stalin's fallibility was implicitly admitted as some of his policies were reversed: The terror was relaxed, the doctors were freed, and limited amnesties were declared (first for common criminals and then for select political prisoners). Malenkov's stress on peace and prosperity in his funeral speech was another deviation.[21] So was the failure to rename anything after the dead leader, for whom everything had once been named. A subtle shift was in train. Rather than dwelling on gifts already delivered, as Stalin had, his heirs shifted to promises of change in the near future. Malenkov pledged an "abundance of consumer goods in two to three years" and Beria came up with a rash of far-reaching projects, including the end of Stalin's cult and the promotion of non-Russian nationalities to high positions, but it was left to Khrushchev to try to realize a program of reforms.[22]

There were also changes in society. For many, the opening shot in the intelligentsia's campaign against official culture was V. Pomerantsev's essay "On Sincerity in Literature," which appeared in the December 1953 issue of *New World*. His appeal for truthfulness constituted a clear rejection of the pedagogic ethic of the performance. Other writers went further in probing the falseness of the public culture and questioning its polarity of good and evil. Ehrenburg, in his novella of mid-1954, *The Thaw*, contrasted two artists. One lived well but wasted his talent on official commissions. The other lived miserably but painted from the heart. In Vladimir Dudintsev's novel of 1956, *Not by Bread Alone*, the opposing heroes are an inventor, who lives outside "the invisible empire of bureaucracy" and is true to himself and "honorable" and an insincere industrial manager, given to making speeches and playing by the official rules.[23] Demanding honesty as well as personal honor, Dudintsev questioned the norms of nearly three decades of Soviet public life.

Writers advocated a return to professionalism, including true criticism, as some had during 1945 and 1946. Fadeev, who had joined the anticosmopolitanism campaign, wrote to the Presidium of the Central Committee on August 25, 1953, to urge an end to the "bureaucratic distortion," which he considered "the main obstacle to the development of art and literature in our time."[24] Under the guise of professionalism, writers reasserted their right to a personal and a metahistorical voice. "An author writes a book because he must tell people something of himself," Ehrenburg proclaimed in October 1953.[25] Grossman appealed to Khrushchev on February 22, 1962, a year after the seizure of his manuscript of *Life and Fate,* to save his book "in which there are no lies or slanders but in which there is the truth."[26] Rejecting his request, Suslov, one of the Party's reigning ideologues and a chief organizer of Stalin's seventieth birthday celebration, suggested that such a book could not be published for 100 or even 250 years.[27] Writers who made such requests seem to have felt that the government could agree to what they asked without jeopardizing the Soviet system. They were wrong.

Stalin had screened the performance from unfriendly scrutiny with the repressive power of the state. By repudiating Stalin, his cult, and the wholesale terror, if not the threat of it, at the Twentieth Party Congress (February 14–25, 1956), Khrushchev introduced a more secular and rational style of public life. He began to weaken the monopoly on public expression and allowed others to do so, opening the press to limited discussions on a variety of topics. Yet his initiative failed or was aborted mid-way. Once the contest of ideas had been "replaced by the administrative mechanism," to use Trotsky's phrase from the 1920s, political leaders who had risen in the Stalinist system were unable to tolerate criticism. [28] Khrushchev had chased a will-o'-the-wisp in seeking a moderate "Leninist" style of political life that in many respects had never existed and wartime feelings that were in practice unrecoverable. In the end, faced with challenges in East Europe and failures at home, he reverted to a contemporary version of the performative culture.

Khrushchev oversaw the relatively stable Soviet-American rivalry that followed Stalin's death and emphasized the quality of Soviet life as the key to defeating capitalism. In his speech greeting Vice President Richard Nixon at the American National Exhibition in Moscow in July 1959, the site of the famous "kitchen debate," he vowed, "We are sure our country will soon catch up with our American partner in peaceful economic competition, and then, at some way station, draw equal with him, give a greeting, and move on."[29] The metaphor remained that of the path. *Pravda* did not cover the kitchen debate.

Khrushchev's stress on living standards culminated in the pledge at the Twenty-second Party Congress (October 17–31, 1961) to establish communism. The authors of the program, which was first printed in *Pravda* on July 30, 1961, promised that in the decade from 1961 to 1970 the Soviet Union would not only "surpass the strongest and richest capitalist country, the United States, in per capita production," but "everyone will live in easy circumstances" and "hard physical labor will disappear."[30] To describe this transformation as immediately pending was to employ the Stalinist understanding of time in which the present bridged the richly embellished past and future. "Not only our descendants, but you and I, Comrades, our generation of Soviet people, will live under communism!" Khrushchev avowed.[31] A "collective farm clerk" wrote in *Pravda,* "All Soviet people greet the projected program of the CPSU as a document of the epoch of communism" (October 11, 1961). Welcoming the congress, *Pravda* featured a ghostly Lenin and a few battered-looking early Bolshevik fighters floating above a multitude of prosperous and happy contemporary citizens (October 17, 1961).

The press even presented Stalin's disinterment in the style of the performance. *Pravda,* on October 31, 1961, printed the congress's resolution, "On the Mausoleum of Vladimir Ilich Lenin," announcing that given "the serious violation of the Leninist testament, abuse of power, mass repression against honorable Soviet people, and other actions in the period of the cult of personality" it was impossible "to leave the coffin with his [Stalin's] body in the mausoleum of V. I. Lenin." *Pravda* showed delegates voting unanimously for disinterment and printed selected speeches. Most remarkable was that of a woman, an old Bolshevik from Leningrad, D. A. Lazurkina, who announced, "Yesterday I sought Ilich's advice, and it was as if he stood before me alive and said: It is unpleasant for me to be beside Stalin, who brought so much harm to the Party" (October 31, 1961). Without describing Stalin's removal, *Pravda* printed a large picture on November 2: "Moscow. Red Square, November 1, 1961. At the Mausoleum of Vladimir Ilich Lenin." The anniversary of Lenin's death, commemorated on January 22, the day after his death in Stalin's time, now became a major media event celebrated on January 21, and Lenin's birthday, which had hitherto been largely ignored, was commemorated as well.[32]

Soviet authorities tried to modify the performative culture, but they could not abandon it. Brezhnev in 1964 inherited from Khrushchev an economy that was spending prodigiously to catch up and overtake its capitalist antagonists but nevertheless falling more and more behind. When the attempted reforms and controlled liberalization of the early 1960s did not yield the desired results, he and his government reasserted the old-style performance with an almost comic banality, decrepitude, and cynicism. Most participants in Soviet society largely followed the script and were therefore limited in their efforts to identify and describe developments that undermined the social order they supported. Even as difficulties and problems mounted, the press employed the rhetoric of the Stalinist era enshrined in slogans such as "The Party and the People Are One" and "The Path to Communism."

During the thaw under Khrushchev, however, the rules of the performance had changed. Although the old Stalinist rhetoric persisted, writers and other public figures began speaking out on hitherto forbidden issues, ranging from the environment to love and marriage.[33] These discussions and commentaries were an extension of the easing of censorship following Stalin's death and were affirmed during the thaw. Open resistance to the official regimen also surfaced. The rise of the dissident movement in the 1970s, the struggle for Jewish emigration, and the reassertion of national identity among non-Russian peoples signified the emergence of a more active public sphere and the expression of increasingly independent opinions. As a result, the official press found itself increasingly entangled in a heterogeneous discourse originating within society. Yet the past weighed heavily on the present.

In no area was the official discourse as rigid as in portrayals of Russian and non-Russian identities. In the evolution of Stalin's treatment of the nationalities, the state's gift to non-Russian republics on the periphery became increasingly Russia's gift. To make other nationalities passive beneficiaries of Russian achievement was to reverse the pre-1917 image of the empire as a treasure trove from which Russians drew riches.[34] This reversal intensified in the late 1920s, when maps associated with the five-year plan showed the periphery as the recipient of fruitful Soviet investment. Promoters of the central government's generosity toward the national republics may have unwittingly devalued the empire in the eyes of ethnic Russians, who were told they gave much but received little. A remarkable ceremonial expression of Russian beneficence was Khrushchev's transfer of the Crimea, which after the exile of the Crimean Tatars was inhabited largely by Russians, from the Russian Republic to Ukraine on the three hundredth anniversary of Russia's annexation of Ukraine. D. S. Korotchenko, chairman of the Presidium of the Ukrainian Supreme Soviet, lauded this expression of "the Russian people's boundless confidence and love for the Ukrainian people" and promised that "this decision will be met with gratitude and approval by the whole Ukrainian people." [35] Representing this decision as an act of friendship, both national and Ukrainian leaders invoked the image of Russian beneficence within the Soviet family of peoples.

The scale of Russian benevolence expanded as the Soviet bloc grew and aid flowed to potential allies. Stalin had used the presumption of Soviet benevolence as a thin veil over Soviet interests, although many could see through it. Khrushchev and his successors operated with greater constraints and were more involved in dispensing favors to clients. This orientation was apparent even at the time of Stalin's death. Surkov wrote in *Pravda* on May Day, 1953: "Soviet peoples help those whose countries are embarking on the socialist path . . . not from self-interest or to enslave them politically or economically, but out of a brotherly dependence based on mutual advantage."[36]

This notion of beneficence may have encouraged a sense of superiority that proved hard to suppress. "So why must we come across as so arrogant all the time?" asked a bewildered Khrushchev in his memoir, reflecting on how the Soviet Union invariably offended its friends.[37] Another negative feature of the international economy of the gift from the Soviet standpoint was the role of benefactor itself. In retrospect we may ask why the Soviet Union impoverished itself subsidizing an empire that its citizens did not value. In fact, to bargain with their allies effectively and to defend their own economic interests, Soviet leaders would have had to give up the image of themselves as benefactors and take on another one for which they had not yet written a script. With the escalation in world oil prices after 1973 and the Soviet reluctance to respond appropriately, subsidies to Eastern European satellites and other allies became very large. In stressing the Soviet Union's role as benefactor, journalists unwittingly communicated the one-sidedness of this relationship. Convincing Russians that the foreign and domestic empire was a drain on their resources, the press prepared the way for their lack of protest at its collapse, as well as psychological regret for lost glory.

Brezhnev innovated within the performance by evoking the memory of wartime suffering, which Stalin had largely suppressed. Attention to loss first crept into commemorations toward the end of Khrushchev's rule, but the press's observance of the twentieth anniversary in 1965 differed from the fifteenth.[38] As the country failed to match rising living standards in Western Europe and North America, Brezhnev made Victory Day a holiday, stressing the war's cost and the country's losses. In that respect, it was, as he said: "The more the war years retreat from us into history, the fuller and clearer is the great heroic feat of the Soviet people, who courageously defended our country in the uniquely bitter struggle with fascism for socialism."[39]

After the twentieth anniversary in 1965, Victory Day became ever grimmer, and in 1975, 1980, and 1985 pictures of joyful victors gave way to images of melancholy veterans contemplating tombs and memorials. Brezhnev captured this tone in his speech on the thirtieth anniversary in 1975: "The path to victory was difficult. Many were lost on this path, and today we think most of all of those who did not return from the front, who perished defending the land of their fathers, the homeland of socialism" (May 9, 1975). The trope of the gift and foreign indebtedness remained, but in 1975 the domestic equation changed as the press cited the younger generation's obligation to the older, while promoting Brezhnev as an exemplary heroic elder (May 7, 1975). "Thank You, Veterans," *Pravda* editorialized on May 11, 1980. Five years later, in 1985, Mikhail Gorbachev, the new Party chief, practically repeated Brezhnev's words when he exclaimed, "The country is obligated to you, Comrades, for the victory, and she will never forget what you accomplished" (May 9, 1985). Since he was speaking as a nonveteran who was fourteen when the war ended, however, he articulated the state's obligation to society in the person of the veterans as much as society's obligation to the state. The curtain was descending on the performance; seasoned actors were leaving the stage.

People experienced the official public culture individually and with a range of reactions and implications. The difficulty, however, of maintaining separate personal and public understandings of "the facts of life," with distinct vocabularies and repertoires of social practices, was undoubtedly very great. The norms of the performance, including its magical power and representations of agency, were embedded in the Russian language and ultimately shared by or imposed on virtually all who used it. Anatoly Dobrynin, longtime Soviet ambassador to the United States, unwittingly pointed this out when he recalled in his memoir, *In Confidence,* how in 1944, at the age of twenty-five, he was summoned to the Central Committee headquarters and told, "There is an opinion to send you to study at the Higher Diplomatic School." He writes, "I should note that the Russian expression *yest mnieniye,* or there is an opinion—without ever clarifying whose opinion it was—used to be quite popular in the vocabulary of the Communist Party and the Soviet government. It had a touch of secrecy and power: you did not know to whom you could appeal, and the only way out was to consent."[40] What Dobrynin urbanely refers to as "a touch of secrecy and power" had become the sine qua non of Soviet public life under Stalin.

Soviet sociologists who studied the press in the late 1960s discovered that journalists viewed their work much more negatively than their readers.[41] In the case of *Labor,* for example, only 8 percent of the journalists in one survey felt they did a good job of covering trade unions compared to 26 percent of the readers. The journalists revealed their uneasy sense of their calling and, one might say, their weariness with the performance, but their readers, who knew less of what went into newspaper stories, were less dissatisfied. Yet change affected even those who seemed to disregard the symbolic world of communism. Vaclav Havel, in his essay "The Power of the Powerless," depicts the impact of the Soviet type of press commentary on the wider society. He presents the example of a green grocer who puts the slogan, "Workers of the World, Unite," in his window. The grocer does not think about the slogan but nevertheless upholds the system by displaying it. "The primary excusatory function of ideology, therefore," Havel writes, "is to provide people, both as victims and pillars of the posttotalitarian system, with the illusion that the system is in harmony with the human order and the order of the universe."[42]

The ideology, enshrined in the official press, had the same function in the Stalinist system, with the difference that disobedience was more severely punished. Havel acknowledged the diminution of punishment when he called on people to begin "living in truth" by ceasing to display the slogan, that is, to deny the ideology in the face of punitive but not lethal consequences. Removing the placard on which the slogan was written left an empty space, even among those adept at seeing the beets and onions through it or beyond it.

The divergence between the demands of the performance and of daily life were painfully evident in the official moral economy. Advocates of the public "gift" masked private payoffs, undermined the legitimacy of market exchange, and attributed even individual achievement to the "bounty" of Stalin and the state. In effect, the metaphor of the public gift created a rhetorical economy in which individual effort was valued only as a partial repayment of the gift. Since the gift was too great to repay completely, the value of individual effort was always inferior to that of the state and its leader. The proponents of this idea reinforced a central tenet of Soviet economic theory: that, under communism, exchange value (as determined through the market) disappears because private demand is eliminated. All demand emanates from the state in the name of the collective good. But at the same time they stood the labor theory of value on its head, since, in Stalin's moral economy, labor was not the source of value, as Marx would have said, but, rather, value was determined by the state. Stalin and his supporters made this change in the 1930s, when they moved from the collective valorization of workers and peasants to lionizing individuals for exceptional service to the state.

After Stalin's death, the official public culture became an increasingly significant obstacle to economic growth. Although Khrushchev's government and later that of Brezhnev made huge and often productive investments in science, technology, and industry, they imposed on themselves and their confederates in the socialist camp, cultural constraints that would eventually lead to technological stagnation, scientific backwardness, and economic decline. The global economy after World War II diverged increasingly from that of the 1930s, and tremendous opportunities opened up for those who were flexible and innovative about products and processes.[43] Multinational operations and international capital flows became more important. Science was progressively internationalized and information became the critical factor in economic life, sparking the creation of new industries and the restructuring of older ones. Technological innovation surged, and changes in communication and transportation shrank time and space. The cosmopolitanism and diversity of public expression in democratic market-oriented societies sustained these dramatic transformations. The rigidity, centralization, and insularity of the performative culture did not. Unable to match the postwar dynamism of North America, Japan, and Western Europe, Soviet society decayed from within until it was unable to withstand the challenges before it.

Brezhnev died on November 10, 1982, and was replaced as general secretary by the aging and ill Yuri Andropov, formerly head of the KGB, who was followed in February 1984 by the feeble Konstantin Chernenko, who died on March 10, 1985. The day after Chernenko's death, Gorbachev met with members of the Central Committee, was elected general secretary, and, according to his own account, stressed "the need for transparency (*glasnost'*) in the work of Party, Soviet, state, and public organizations."[44] Well over a year later he opened the media to a variety of opinions in the hope of gaining support for his policies, particularly from the intelligentsia. *Glasnost'* was a word borrowed from the early years of Alexander II's rule, when "the tsar liberator" permitted the press and society to speak more freely on the eve of the 1861 emancipation of the serfs; "restructuring" (*perestroika*), the other half of Gorbachev's initial program, harkened back to the late 1920s and early 1930s, when Stalin and his government reorganized the economy and society under the First Five-Year Plan and collectivization. Neither word captured the magnitude of the changes that followed. Despite Gorbachev's depiction of his policies as a return to Leninism, he broke the monopoly on information so dear to communism's founders. In doing so he ensured the demise of the style of commentary and observation that Stalin and his supporters had set in place half a century earlier. By the time Boris Yeltsin forced Gorbachev from power in 1991, the public culture of Soviet Communism no longer existed.

With the privilege of hindsight, we can say that Soviet public culture, like the Soviet economy, failed. It failed not because it lacked complexity or richness, but because, in the end, it left little room for a critical commentary adequate to recognize its own defects and to provide a nuanced understanding of its accomplishments. Despite changes following Stalin's death, the official culture retained its power, and the Soviet polity could not modify its self-image sufficiently to prolong its existence. As the revolution in information, the third industrial revolution, took hold in America, Europe, and Japan, the Soviet government clung to a system of public expression and a self-referential view of the world that effectively precluded participation in the global integration of information. The government monopoly of information had little room for the informal and international exchanges of knowledge that might have sustained the country's economic competitiveness in the second half of the century. Nor was there foresight to see the approaching end. In communism's twilight, Brezhnev and his colleagues did not publicly discuss the destruction of the physical environment in which they lived, the tremendous waste and loss throughout the economy, or the growing corruption of their society. Yet within the public culture their government appeared to be the only possible one. At the end of communist rule there was no recognized opposition. There were no alternative programs, nor even publicly expressed and commonly shared judgments about what had gone wrong.

In 1998 the stories that filled *Pravda* and *Izvestiia* as recently as seven years ago are largely forgotten. Nothing of the old order disappeared so completely as the official public rhetoric. Its long hegemony did not win it even a momentary reprieve. Certainly, for those who at the end genuinely believed the literal message, the dismantling of the structures of Soviet Communist expression and effacement of its ornate emblems were a devastating shock.

With the Soviet system's demise came the hardships and challenges of the post–Soviet era. We face a vexing question in our own time: How could citizens so well educated and so accomplished in other dimensions have been so oblivious to the impending collapse and so ill-prepared to rebuild? Many observers would answer that the leaders knew but lied and enforced the lies through censorship. On some issues this answer is correct; individual leaders certainly knew facts that were covered up. But the suppression of information and censorship is not a sufficient explanation. Simple lies cannot fully deceive an educated public, and the Soviet public ultimately became one of the most discerning in human history in its mastery of sophisticated literature and its education in math and science. The full answer lies in the function of the press in creating a stylized, ritualistic, and internally consistent public culture that became its own reality and supplanted other forms of public reflection and expression.

Freed of slogans and constraints of the cultural performance, Russia is now recovering its past, finding new public voices, and preparing to participate on new terms in the international public culture of the twenty-first century. The process has been and remains arduous, and the outcome has yet to be seen.

Notes

Prologue

1. Jeffrey Brooks, "The Zemstvos and the Education of the People," in *The Russian Zemstvo*, ed. Terence Emmons and Wayne S. Vucinich (Cambridge, 1982), 266–78.

2. *Russkii istoriko-etnograficheskii atlas "Russkie"* (Moscow, 1963).

3. Jeffrey Brooks, *When Russia Learned to Read: Literacy and Popular Literature, 1861–1917* (Princeton, N.J., 1985); and idem, "Two Tandem Revolutions in Russian Culture: The Modern and the Pop," *Common Knowledge* (Winter, 1998–99). See also Louise McReynolds, *The News under Russia's Old Regime* (Princeton, N.J., 1992); A. Reitblat, *Ot Bovy k Bal'montu* (Moscow, 1991); A. V. Blium, "Russkaia lubochnaia kniga vtoroi poloviny xix veka," *Kniga. Issledovaniia i materialy* (Moscow, 1981), 94–114; Richard Stites, *Soviet Popular Culture: Entertainment and Society in Russia since 1900* (Cambridge, 1992).

4. Brooks, *When Russia Learned to Read,* 360, 366; Paolo Cherchi Usai, Lorenzo Codelli, Carlo Montanaro, and David Robinson, eds., *Silent Witnesses, Russian Films, 1908–1919* (London, 1989), 16–18.

5. Abram Tertz (Andrei Sinyavsky), *The Trial Begins,* trans. Max Heyward; and *On Socialist Realism,* trans. George Dennis (New York, 1960), 147.

6. Czeslaw Milosz, *The Captive Mind,* trans. Jane Zielonko (New York, 1955), 4–24.

7. *Pravda,* September 1, 1943.

8. My argument is informed by observations about human agency in Charles Taylor, *Human Agency and Language. Philosophical Papers* 1 (Cambridge, 1985), 15–44, 97–114); idem, *Sources of the Self: The Making of the Modern Identity* (Cambridge, Mass., 1989); and Harry G. Frankfurt, "The Freedom of the Will and the Concept of the Person," *Journal of Philosophy* 63, no. 1 (January 1971): 5–20. Carlos J. Moya summarizes this literature in *The Philosophy of Action: An Introduction* (Cambridge, 1990). I also draw on Paul Ricoeur's distinction between act and event in *Oneself as Another,* trans. Kathleen Blamey (Chicago, 1992), 67–87.

9. E. P. Thompson utilized "moral economy" to describe a "consistent traditional view of social norms and obligations of the proper economic functions of several parties within the community in "The Moral Economy of the English Crowd in the 18th Century," *Past and Present* 50 (1971): 79.

10. Quoted in Evgenii Ermolin, *Materializatsiia prizraka. Totalitarnyi teatr sovetskikh massovykh aktsii 1920–1930-x godov* (Iaroslav', 1996), 48.

11. The Russian is *daesh'.* See Boris Efimovich Galanov, *Zapiski na kraiu stola* (Moscow, 1996), 25; *"Daesh' iasli"* (1930), in *Affiches constructivistes Russes* (Moscow, 1992), 89; *"Daesh' BAM!"* (1980), in *Plakat v rabochem stroiu* (Moscow, 1980), 15; and the journal *Daesh'* (1929).

12. Andre Siniavksii notes Stalin's theatricality in "Stalin—Kak geroi i khudozhnik stalinskoi epokhi," *Sintaksis* 19 (1987): 106–25, as does A. Antonov-Ovseenko in *Teatr*

Iosifa Stalina (Moscow, 1995). See also Steven Kotkin, *Magnetic Mountain: Stalinism as a Civilization* (Berkeley, 1995).

13. *Khrushchev Remembers: The Glasnost Tapes,* trans. and ed. Jerrold L. Schecter and Vyacheslav V. Luchkov (Boston, 1990), 104.

14. Varlam Shalamov, *Kolyma Tales,* trans. John Glad (New York, 1994), 284.

15. The editor of *Krasnaia zvezda,* D. Ortenberg, notes that the Soviet Information Bureau reported the loss of Smolensk in mid-August, a month late (*Iiun'–Dekabr' sorok pervogo* [Moscow, 1986], 98). I did not find a report in *Pravda.*

16. L. Kosheleva, V. Lel'chuk, V. Naumov, O. Naumov, L. Rogovaia, and O. Khlevniuk, eds., *Pis'ma I. V. Stalina V. M. Molotovu, 1925–1936 gg. Sbornik dokumentov* (Moscow, 1995), 207.

Chapter One
The Monopoly of the Printed Word:
From Persuasion to Compulsion

1. *O partiinoi i sovetskoi pechati. Sbornik dokumentov* (Moscow, 1954), 173.

2. John Reed, *Ten Days That Shook the World* (New York, 1960), 354, 356.

3. *O partiinoi i sovetskoi pechati,* 179.

4. *V. I. Lenin o pechati* (Moscow, 1974), 359–64; Neil Hardin, *Lenin's Political Thought* (Atlantic Highlands, N.J., 1983), 1:162–762, 2:210; Peter Kenez, "Lenin and Freedom of the Press," in *Bolshevik Culture: Experiment and Order in the Russian Revolution,* ed. Abbott Gleason, Peter Kenez, and Richard Stites (Bloomington, Ind., 1985); Robert Service, *Lenin: A Political Life. Worlds in Collision* (Bloomington, Ind., 1991), 2:224–26.

5. V. I. Lenin, *Polnoe sobranie sochineniia,* 5th ed. (Moscow, 1960–70), 35:51–52.

6. A. Z. Okorokov, *Oktiabr' i krakh russkoi burzhuaznoi pressy* (Moscow, 1970), 155–56.

7. Quoted in E. A. Dinershtein, *I. D. Sytin* (Moscow, 1983), 215.

8. Okorokov, *Oktiabr',* 56–57; the quote is from I. Skvortsov-Stepanov, a Bolshevik publicist.

9. *Dekrety oktiabr'skoi revoliutsii* (Moscow, 1933), 1:17.

10. Ibid.

11. Okorokov, *Oktiabr',* 394; *Dekrety,* 49–55.

12. *Izdatel'skoe delo v pervye gody sovetskoi vlasti (1917–1922)* (Moscow, 1972), 17–18; A. V. Blium, *Za kulisami "Ministerstva Pravdy": Tainaia istoriia sovetskoi tsenzury, 1917–1929* (Saint Petersburg, 1994), 40.

13. *Izdatel'skoe delo v pervye gody,* 55.

14. *O partiinoi sovetskoi pechati. Sbornik dokumentov* (Moscow, 1954), 180–81, 347–50.

15. The decree is reprinted in *Izdatel'skoe delo v pervye gody,* 17–18; see also 169; and see Blium, *Za kulisami.*

16. *O partiinoi sovetskoi pechati,* 175–76.

17. Kenez, "Lenin and Freedom of the Press," 142; Blium, *Za kulisami,* 36–44.

18. Blium, *Za kulisami,* 49–80.

19. Quoted in ibid., 36.

20. Ibid., 82–93.

21. Comments by Anthony Adamovich in *The Soviet Censorship,* ed. Martin Dewhist and Robert Farrell (Metuchen, N.J., 1973), 71–72.

22. Cited in D. Soldatenkov, *Politicheskie i nravstevennye posledstviia usileniia vlasti VKP(b) 1928–1941 (iiun')* (St. Petersburg, 1994), 16.

23. Blium, *Za kulisami,* 88.

24. M. V. Zelenov, "Glavlit i istoricheskaia nauka v 20–30-e gody," *Voprosy istorii,* no. 3 (1997): 25.

25. Blium, *Za kulisami,* 125–33; T. M. Goriaeva, ed., *Istoriia sovetskoi politicheskoi tsenzury. Dokumenty i komentarii* (Moscow, 1997), 257–84.

26. Blium, *Za kulisami,* 124.

27. Ibid., 128.

28. Ivan Gronskii, *Iz proshlogo . . . Vospominaniia* (Moscow, 1991), 119–20.

29. Ibid., 128.

30. TsSU SSSR, *Narodnoe obrazovanie, nauka i kul'tura v SSSR. Statisticheskii sbornik* (Moscow, 1971), 20.

31. Ibid., 20; Alex Inkeles, *Public Opinion in Soviet Russia* (Cambridge, Mass., 1950), 234–53.

32. Angus Roxburgh, *Pravda: Inside the Soviet News Machine* (New York, 1987), 9; Ellen Propper, *Media and the Russian Public* (New York, 1981), 51; Kenez, "Lenin and Freedom of the Press," 131–50; Peter Kenez, *The Birth of the Propaganda State* (Cambridge, 1985), 1–14; Richard Taylor, *The Politics of the Soviet Cinema, 1917–29* (Cambridge, 1979), 26–29; and Inkeles, *Public Opinion,* 143–74.

33. Ia. Shafir, *Rabochaia gazeta i ee chitatel'* (Moscow, 1926), 27, 228.

34. Ibid.

35. *Pravda,* July 1, 1923.

36. *Rabochaia Moskva,* June 7, 1923.

37. *Bednota,* February 6, 13, 17, 1923.

38. Jeffrey Brooks, "Russian Cinema and Public Discourse, 1900–1930," *Historical Journal of Film, Radio, and Television* 11, no. 2 (1991): 144.

39. The columns are from *Pravda.* See also Jeffrey Brooks, "Studies of the Reader in the 1920s," *Russian History,* nos. 2–3 (1982): 187–202; Sheila Fitzpatrick, "Supplicants and Citizens: Public Letter-Writing in Soviet Russia in the 1930s," *Slavic Review* 55 (1996): 78–105; and idem, "Readers' Letters to *Krest'ianskaia gazeta,* 1938," *Russian History* 24, nos. 1–2 (spring–summer 1997), 149–70.

40. The *aktiv* included non-Party activists as well as Party members. See Sosnovskii, in *Pravda,* July 5, 1925.

41. *Rabochaia Moskva,* February 7, 1923.

42. *Rabochaia gazeta,* March 1, 1922.

43. *Krest'ianskaia gazeta,* May 24, 1926.

44. Brooks, "Studies of the Reader"; Mathew E. Lenoe, "Reader Response to the Soviet Press Campaign Against the Trotskii-Zinov'ev Opposition," *Russian History* 24, nos. 1–2 (spring–summer 1997), 89–116.

45. Iu. M. Steklov, ed., *Sovetskaia demokratiia. Sbornik* (Moscow, 1929), 203; V. A. Kozlov, *Kul'turnaia revolutsiia i krest'ianstvo, 1921–1927* (Moscow, 1983), 160–76; G. V. Zhirkov, *Sovetskaia krest'ianskaia pechat'—odin iz tipov sotsialisticheskoi pressy* (Leningrad, 1984).

46. *Rabochaia gazeta,* February 12, 1924.

47. Ibid., February 20, 1924.

48. Ibid., February 12, 1924. The Russian is *obshchestvennoe mnenie.* On the government's use of letters to study public opinion, see A. K. Sokolov, ed., *Golos naroda. Pis'ma i otkliki riadovykh sovetskikh grazhdan o sobytiiakh, 1918–1932 gg.* (Moscow, 1998), 14.

49. A. Meromskii and P. Putnik, *Derevnia za knigoi* (Moscow, 1931), 37.

50. *Krest'ianskaia gazeta,* April 27, 1926, February 27, 1926.

51. *Rabochaia gazeta,* May 5, 1925.

52. Ibid., November 15, 1923, November 6, 1924.

53. A. Glebov, *Pamiatka sel'kora* (Moscow, 1926), 13.

54. Michael Schudson, *Discovering the News: A Social History of American Newspapers* (New York, 1978), 152–53; Robert W. Desmond, *Windows on the World: The Information Process in a Changing Society, 1900–1920* (Iowa City, 1980).

55. Thomas C. Leonard, *The Power of the Press: The Birth of American Political Reporting* (Oxford, 1986); Daniel J. Czitrom, *Media and the American Mind, from Morse to McLuhan* (Chapel Hill, 1982); Ronald Steel, *Walter Lippmann and the American Century* (Boston, 1980).

56. Thomas C. Leonard, *News for All: America's Coming-of-Age with the Press* (New York, 1995), 65–89; there were American films in which journalists fell short of the ideal, as Bernard Weinraub points out in the *New York Times,* October 13, 1997. Journalists appear in a few Soviet films but as representatives of the state rather than society, as in Sergei Gerasimov's 1967 film *Zhurnalist.*

57. Jurgen Habermas, *The Structural Transformation of the Public Sphere: An Inquiry into a Category of Bourgeois Society* (Boston, 1989); John Keane, ed., *Civil Society and the State* (London, 1988).

58. Dominique Colas, *Le Glaive et le fléau. Genéalogie du fanatisme et de la sociéte civile* (Paris, 1992). In German the same term is used for both civil and bourgeois society; whether Marx imagined a civil society distinct from civil administration under communism remains unclear.

59. George Orwell, *1984* (New York, 1983), 62.

60. Hannah Arendt, *Totalitarianism.* Part 3 of *The Origins of Totalitarianism* (San Diego, 1968), 39.

61. Jacques Ellul, *Propaganda: The Formation of Men's Attitudes* (New York, 1965), x.

62. Russel Lemmons, *Goebbels and Der Angriff* (Lexington, Ky., 1994), 42. On the official Nazi Party newspaper, *Volkischer Beobachter* (The racial observer), see Oron J. Hale, *The Captive Press in the Third Reich* (Princeton, N.J., 1964), 29–31.

63. Cited in Ralf Georg Reuth, *Goebbels* (New York, 1994), 91.

64. Ibid., 94.

65. Lemmons, *Goebbels and Der Angriff,* 62.

66. Adolf Hitler, *Mein Kampf,* ed. Alvin Saunders Johnson and John Chamberlain (New York, 1940), 137.

67. *Pravda*'s circulation on the eve of World War I ranged from 40,000 to 130,000 (Angus Roxburgh, *Pravda: Inside the Soviet New Machine* [New York, 1984], 17).

68. Robert Gellately, "Denunciations in Twentieth-Century Germany: Aspects of Self-Policing in the Third Reich and the German Democratic Republic," in *Accusatory*

Practices: Denunciation in Modern European History, 1789–1989, ed. Sheila Fitzpatrick and Robert Gellately (Chicago, 1996), 187.

69. Sheila Fitzpatrick and Robert Gellately, "Introduction to the Practices of Denunciation in Modern European History," in idem, *Accusatory Practices,* 9.

70. Reuth, *Goebbels* 172.

71. Ibid., 212–13.

72. Ibid., 316; on Goebbels use of euphemisms, see John Wesley Young, *Totalitarian Language: Orwell's Newspeak and Totalitarian Language and Its Nazi and Communist Antecedents* (Charlottesville, Va., 1991), 224.

73. Reuth, *Goebbels,* 313.

74. TsSU SSSR, *Narodnoe obrazovanie,* 21.

75. *Vsesoiuznaia perepis' naseleniia 1926 goda,* vol. 17 (Moscow, 1929), 2–3, 48–49.

76. *Bednota,* March 27, 1918.

77. Ibid., January 10, 1922–January 17, 1922.

78. M. Kalinin, in *Bednota,* March 4, 1924. He claimed sixty thousand subscriptions mostly from individual subscribers by March 1, 1924.

79. Ibid., March 12, 1925.

80. *Krest'ianskaia gazeta,* September 4, 1928, December 25, 1929.

81. *Rabochaia gazeta,* December 12, 1926.

82. Ibid.

83. Ibid., March 29, 1927.

84. I. Vareikis, *Zadachi partii v oblasti pechati* (Moscow, 1926), 11.

85. Kotkin, in *Magnetic Mountain,* describes the process of learning to speak "Bolshevik."

86. *Bednota,* January 24, 1923.

87. M. I. Slukhovskii, *Kniga i derevnia* (Moscow, 1928), 118. The Russian term was *innostranshchina.*

88. Shafir, *Rabochaia gazeta,* 221; see also Patrick Seriot, "On Officialese: A Critical Analysis," *Sociocriticism* 2, no. 1 (1986): 195–215.

89. *Derevenskaia politprosvetrabota* (Leningrad, 1926), 220–21.

90. Meromskii and Putnik, *Derevnia,* 169.

91. Slukhovskii, *Kniga,* 120.

92. Ia. Shafir, *Gazeta i derevnia,* 2nd ed. (Moscow, 1924), 28.

93. M. A. Smushkova, *Pervye itogi izucheniia chitatelia* (Moscow, 1926), 37–39; Shafir, *Gazeta i derevnia,* 71–72, 75–82; Slukhovskii, *Kniga,* 119–21; Meromskii i Putnik, *Derevnia,* 170–71. See also M. Selishchev, *Iazyk revoliutsionnoi epokhi* (Moscow, 1928).

94. Neologisms, acronyms, and foreignisms in this period are discussed in Selishchev, *Iazyk.*

95. Brooks, "Studies of the Reader"; Mark von Hagen, *Soldiers in the Proletarian Dictatorship: The Red Army and the Soviet Socialist State, 1917–1930* (Ithaca, N.Y., 1990), 272–73; Orlando Figes, "The Russian Revolution and Its Language in the Village," *Russian Review* 56, no. 3 (July 1997): 323–45.

96. *Izdatel'skoe delo v pervye gody,* 39.

97. McReynolds, *The News,* Table 6. Combined circulation of *Pravda, Izvestiia, Bed-*

nota, Rabochaia gazeta, Krest'ianskaia gazeta, and *Gudok* for 1924 was 1,319,000 (Jeffrey Brooks, "The Breakdown in the Production and Distribution of Printed Material, 1917–1927," in *Bolshevik Culture,* ed. Abbott Gleason, Peter Kenez, and Richard Stites [Bloomington, Ind., 1985], 151–74).

98. Louise McReynolds, "News and Society: Russkoe Slovo and the Development of a Mass Circulation Press in Late Imperial Russia," Ph.D. diss., University of Chicago, 1984, p. 219.

99. *Izdatel'skoe delo v pervye gody,* 106–10.

100. *Istoriia knigi v SSSR* (Moscow, 1985), 2:214; *Rabochaia Moskva,* May 5, 1923. *Izvestiia* (May 4, 1923) gives the figures 2.7 million for January 1922 and 1.4 million for December 1922.

101. Brooks, "The Breakdown," 151–74.

102. Ibid., 167. Smaller, more primitive machines for which no figures are available were functioning before 1917, but these also diminished between 1921 and 1926.

103. *Piatiletnii plan khoziaistva pechati SSSR* (Moscow, 1929), 198.

104. *Rabochaia Moskva,* February 7, 1923, February 2, 1923.

105. A. I. Nazarov, *Oktiabr' i kniga* (Moscow, 1968), 227; E. Dinershtein, *I. D. Sytin,* 174; *Istoriia knigi v SSSR,* 2:197; *Pravda,* July 6, 1923.

106. *Istoriia knigi,* 2:205.

107. *Krest'ianskaia gazeta,* April 13, 1924.

108. *Bednota,* October 12, 1922.

109. *Pravda,* July 26, 1923.

110. Shafir, *Gazeta i derevnia,* 99–128.

111. Ibid., 113.

112. Ibid., 112, 99–118.

113. Vareikis, *Zadachi,* 8.

114. Ibid.

115. *Piatiletnii plan,* 229.

116. Ibid., 283–84.

117. *Sovetskaia pechat' v dokumentakh* (Moscow, 1961), 62; A. G. Egorov and K. M. Bogoliubov, eds., *KPSS v rezoliutsiiakh i resheniiakh s'ezdov, konferentsii i plenumov TsK* (Moscow, 1984), 109.

118. *Krest'ianskaia gazeta,* March 9, 1924.

119. Brooks, "Studies of the Reader"; Evgeny Dobrenko, *The Making of the State Reader: Social and Aesthetic Contexts of the Reception of Soviet Literature,* trans. Jesse M. Savage (Stanford, 1997).

120. N. D. Rybnikov, ed., *Massovyi chitatel' i kniga* (Moscow, 1925), 48. I discuss the material in "Studies of the Reader," 187–202.

121. Rybnikov, *Massovyi chitatel',* 76.

122. Shafir, *Rabochaia gazeta.*

123. There were 7,483 replies of a circulation of 200,000 copies in May 1924 (Brooks, "Studies of the Reader").

124. A. Bek and L. Toon, *Litso rabochego chitatelia* (Moscow, 1927).

125. S. Romanov, "Kniga s otzyvami chitatelei," *Krasnyi bibliotekar'* 6 (1927): 29.

126. Meromskii and Putnik, *Derevnia,* 143.

127. This is the view of Karl Mannheim, *Ideology and Utopia* (1936; reprint, New York: Mentor, n.d., 6–7).

128. Sheila Fitzpatrick makes this argument in *Education and Social Mobility in the Soviet Union, 1921–1934* (Cambridge, 1979).

129. E. M. Kovalev, ed., *Golosa krest'ian: Sel'skaia Rossiia xx veka v krest'ianskikh memuarakh* (Moscow, 1996), 249.

Chapter Two
The First Decade: From Class War
to Socialist Building

1. Sheila Fitzpatrick stresses the civil war's impact on state formation in "The Civil War as a Formative Experience," in *Bolshevik Culture*, ed. Gleason, Kenez, and Stites (Bloomington, Ind., 1985), 74; Orlando Figes discusses rural repression in *Peasant Russia, Civil War: The Volga Countryside in Revolution (1917–1921)* (Oxford, 1989).

2. Yuri Buranov, *Lenin's Will: Falsified and Forbidden* (Amherst, N.Y., 1994), 33–34, reprints original and edited versions of Lenin's article.

3. The document appears in Valentina Vilkova, *The Struggle for Power: Russia in 1923* (Amherst, N.Y.: 1996), 307–9; see also 236–41, 252, 273–76, 299.

4. Pierre Broue, *Trotsky* (Paris, 1988), 411.

5. Buranov, *Lenin's Will*, 63–103. On Lenin's view of Trotsky, see Richard Pipes, *The Unknown Lenin: From the Secret Archive*, ed. Richard Pipes, trans. Catherine A. Fitzpatrick (New Haven, Conn., 1996), 9–10.

6. Kosheleva et al., *Pis'ma I. V. Stalina V. M. Molotovu*, 11–30, 40–42.

7. Edward Hallett Carr, *Socialism in One Country, 1924–1926* (New York, 1960), 115–30.

8. Broue, *Trotsky*, 522–23.

9. Moshe Lewin, *Political Undercurrents in Soviet Economic Debates: From Bukharin to the Modern Reformers* (Princeton, N.J., 1974), 21–22; Stephen F. Cohen, *Bukharin and the Bolshevik Revolution: A Political Biography, 1888–1938* (New York, 1973), 291–336.

10. Quoted in Broue, *Trotsky*, 492.

11. On agenda setting, see Shearon A. Lowery and Melvin L. DeFleur, *Milestones in Mass Communication Research* (New York, 1988), 327–52; For a discussion on schemata, see Doris A. Graber, *Processing the News: How People Tame the Information Tide* (New York, 1988), 131–33, 184–266.

12. Graber, *Processing the News*, 28, 119–78.

13. On "media frames," see Todd Gitlin, *The Whole World Is Watching* (Berkeley, 1980), 7; see also William A. Gamson and Andre Modigliani, "Media Discourse and Public Opinion on Nuclear Power: A Constructionist Approach," *American Journal of Sociology* 95 (July 1989): 1–37; and Gamson and Kathryn E. Lasch, "The Political Culture of Social Welfare Policy," in *Evaluating the Welfare State: Social and Political Perspectives*, ed. S. E. Spiro and E. Yuchtman-Yaar (New York, 1983) 397–415.

14. *Pravda*, December 3, 1919.

15. V. I. Lenin, *Sochineniia*, 4th ed. (Moscow, 1941–62), 26:209; idem, *Collected Works* (Moscow, 1960–70), 26:240 (hereafter, *CW*) (I have slightly simplified the official translation).

16. *Pravda*, November 19, 1917; Lenin, *CW*, 26:297.

17. *Pravda*, March 30, 1922.

18. These and other similar generalizations given below are derived from a sample of every tenth editorial on domestic topics in *Pravda* from 1921 through February 1952 (hereafter, cited as the *Pravda* editorial sample). When the subject was foreign affairs, I chose the next domestic editorial. My print run for 1918–20 was incomplete, however, and that sample included only seventeen editorials for 1918, sixteen for 1919, and fourteen for 1920. The word *we* appeared in 82 percent of these editorials in 1918, 75 percent in 1919, 64 percent in 1920, and 53 percent in 1921.

19. *Pravda,* December 3, 1918.

20. Based on the *Pravda* editorial sample, institutional actors appear in 55 percent in 1918–20 (199 articles in 6 issues), 55 percent in 1921–22 (335 articles in 18 issues), 48 percent in 1923–26 (460 articles in 12 issues), and 52 percent in 1927 and early 1928 (141 articles in 3 issues). On passive constructions, see M. Gus, Iu. Zagorianskii, and N. Kaganovich, *Iazyk gazety* (Moscow, 1926), 221–22.

21. Baruch Knei-Paz, *The Social and Political Thought of Leon Trotsky* (Oxford, 1978), 372–80.

22. On Soviet usage, see M. Lewin, *Russian Peasants and Soviet Power: A Study of Collectivization* (New York, 1968), 71–78.

23. *Pravda,* October 30, 1919.

24. Ibid., April 2, 1921.

25. On the cognitive importance of metaphors, see George Lakoff, *Women, Fire, and Other Dangerous Things* (Chicago, 1987); Eva Feder Kittay, *Metaphor: Its Cognitive Force and Linguistic Structure* (New York, 1987); George Lakoff and Mark Johnson, *Metaphors We Live By* (Chicago, 1980), 14–24; and James W. Fernandez, ed., *Beyond Metaphor: The Theory of Tropes in Anthropology,* (Stanford, 1991). Roger Pethybridge notes the militarization of Russian life in *The Social Prelude to Stalinism* (New York, 1974), 73–131. The words *front* and *bor'ba* appeared frequently. Military metaphors had an orientational function in 7 of 48 articles in the *Pravda* editorial sample (1918–19) and 67 of 119 articles in a random sample of several issues over the same period.

26. *Pravda,* December 21, 1919.

27. Lynn Mally, *Culture of the Future: The Proletkult Movement in Revolutionary Russia* (Berkeley, 1990).

28. *Pravda,* February 27, 1924.

29. Enemies figured in every one of 48 editorials in the *Pravda* editorial sample (1918–20) and in more than 60 percent of the 119 articles in my random sample.

30. *Pravda,* January 3, 1918.

31. Ibid., November 23, 1919.

32. Aleksandr Solzhenitsyn, *The Gulag Archipelago, 1918–1956: An Experiment in Literary Investigation,* vol. 1, parts 1–2, trans. Thomas P. Whitney (New York, 1991 [1973]), 352–67.

33. *Pravda,* June 8, 1922.

34. Self-denial was stressed in more than a third of 494 sampled cases of obituaries, human-interest stories, and reports of contests published in *Pravda* from 1921 through mid-1927 (hereafter, cited as my individual sample). These include living people or obituaries in which an individual's origins or past are cited except for Lenin whom I excluded from the tally. The sample includes 494 lives in *Pravda* in 1921, 1923, 1925, and the first half of 1927. The genres include biographies for contests (29 percent of the

total); human-interest stories (17 percent); anniversaries of national figures (5.5 percent); and obituaries (45 percent).

35. *Pravda,* January 1, 1921.

36. Ibid., March 15, 1925.

37. Ibid., November 3, 1925.

38. Lenoe, "Reader Response to the Soviet Press Campaign," 89–116; Von Hagen, *Soldiers,* 43–44.

39. Women rarely wrote for *Pravda.* There were 24 articles written or coauthored by women of a random sample of 961 articles in 1918–27, and 7 of 338 in 1928–32. On images of self-denial, see Anna Krylova, "In Their Own Words? Soviet Women Writers and the Search for Self," in *Russian Women Writers,* ed. Adele Barker and Jehanne Gheith (Cambridge, 1998).

40. *Pravda,* January 17, 1923.

41. Only 7 percent of my individual sample featured a comment on home or family, and these were almost exclusively negative.

42. *Pravda,* April 3, 1921; September 2, 1921.

43. The Russian word is *predannost'.*

44. *Pravda,* July 17, 1921.

45. Of the articles in my individual sample, 43 percent contain references to life under the old regime. Other life-shaping experiences include the civil war (25 percent) and education (20 percent). See Jeffrey Brooks, "Revolutionary Lives: Public Identities in *Pravda* during the 1920s," *New Directions in Soviet History,* ed. Stephen White (Cambridge, 1991), 27–40.

46. *Pravda,* March 8, 1923.

47. For a summary of arguments about the NEP, see R. W. Davies, "Changing Economic Systems an Overview," in *The Economic Transformation of the Soviet Union, 1913–1945,* ed. R. W. Davies, Mark Harrison, and S. G. Wheatcroft (Cambridge, 1994), 8–13. The NEP's success is emphasized in Holland Hunter and Janusz M. Szyrmer, *Faulty Foundations: Soviet Economic Politics, 1928–1940* (Princeton, N.J., 1992); and Paul R. Gregory, *Before Command: An Economic History of Russia from Emancipation to the First Five-Year Plan* (Princeton, N.J., 1994). I agree.

48. Quoted in Edward Hallett Carr, *The Bolshevik Revolution, 1917–1923 (A History of Soviet Russia)* (Harmondsworth, Eng., 1971), 2:276.

49. Lenin, *CW,* 32:495; Lenin, *Sochineniia,* 4th ed., 32:472. The French is given in the English version but not in the earlier Russian version. The source of the text is not given in either.

50. The Russian words are *vopros* and *problema.*

51. *Pravda,* March 31, 1923; May 12, 1923; June 17, 1923; August 14, 1923.

52. Ibid., February 14, 1923.

53. More than half my random sample in *Pravda* in 1923 and 1924 were pragmatic discussions. This is an evaluation of 256 articles in nine sampled issues of *Pravda* in 1923 and 84 articles in two sampled issues in 1924.

54. *Pravda,* September 7, 1922.

55. Ibid., August 6, 1925.

56. Steven R. Coe, "Peasants, the State, and the Languages of NEP: The Rural Correspondents' Movement in the Soviet Union, 1924–1928," Ph.D. diss., University of

Michigan, 1993; and Jennifer Clibbon, "The Soviet Press and Grassroots Organization: The Worker Correspondent Movement, NEP to the First Five-Year Plan," Ph.D. diss., University of Toronto, 1993. See also Julie Kay Mueller, "A New Kind of Newspaper: The Origins and Development of a Soviet Institution, 1921–1928," Ph.D. diss., University of California, Berkeley, 1992.

57. Enemies figure in roughly half my random sample of *Pravda* from 1921 through 1927 and in somewhat more than a third of the *Pravda* editorial sample.

58. *Pravda,* June 28, 1924.

59. Solzhenitsyn, *The Gulag Archipelago,* vol. 1, parts 1–2, 367–70.

60. *Pravda,* January 8, 1924. On Kol'tsov, see David Joravsky, *The Lysenko Affair* (Cambridge, Mass., 1970), 224; and Alexander Vucinich, *Empire of Knowledge: The Soviet Academy of Sciences* (Berkeley, 1984), 76, 174–75.

61. *Pravda,* February 17, 1924.

62. Ibid., February 26, 1927; January 1, 1927; February 10, 1924.

63. V. N. Ipatieff, *The Life of a Chemist: The Memoirs of V. N. Ipatieff,* ed. Khenia Joukoff Eudin, Helen Dwight Fisher, and Harold H. Fisher, trans. Vladimir Haensel and Mrs. Ralph H. Lusher (Stanford, 1946), 367.

64. *Pravda,* February 6, 1927.

65. Ibid., April 1, 1923.

66. Ibid., January 19, 1926.

67. *O partiinoi i sovetskoi pechati. Sbornik dokumentov* (Moscow, 1954), 343–47; the document is excluded from *Kommunisticheskaia Partiia Sovetskogo Soiuza v resoliutsiiakh i resheniiakh, konferentsii i plenumov TsK* (Moscow, 1984), 3:108.

68. This is based on all articles on the arts published in the first four months of 1924 and 1925.

69. *Pravda,* January 4, 1924.

70. *Bednota,* September 3, 1922.

71. *Krest'ianskaia gazeta,* May 24, 1926.

72. *Bednota,* October 8, 1922.

73. *Krest'ianskaia gazeta,* May 1, 1924.

74. Ibid., January 11, 1927; January 18, 1927.

75. *Bednota,* August 11, 1922.

76. *Krest'ianskaia gazeta,* January 11, 1927. The Russian word is *vrediteli.*

77. Jeffrey Brooks, "Official Xenophobia and Popular Cosmopolitanism in Early Soviet Russia," *American Historical Review* (December 1992): 1431–48.

78. This is based on a random sample of nine issues per year from January 1, 1921 to July 1, 1928 (hereafter, my foreign random sample). The sample was designed to permit no more than a month between sample issues. The sample included 2,653 articles: 1,656 in *Pravda;* 699 in *Trud;* and 298 in *Krest'ianskaia gazeta. Trud* was unavailable for 1924–25. England, Germany, France, and the United States account for more than half the space given to foreign affairs from 1921 through 1928 in *Pravda* and *Krest'ianskaia gazeta,* and more than 60 percent in *Trud,* where concern for unions swelled coverage. East Central Europe accounted for 10 percent in each, and the Baltic and Scandinavian states less than 5 percent. The residue mostly concerned issues linked to the West. China comprised 6 percent in *Pravda* and *Krest'ianskaia gazeta* but only 3 percent in *Trud.*

79. These and the following comments are based on my foreign random sample.

80. I. V. Stalin, *Sochineniia* (Moscow, 1946–52), 7:197–98; he repeated the argument at the Fourteenth Party Congress in December 1925 (Stalin, *Sochineniia,* 7: 354–56).

81. V. I. Lenin, *Speeches at Party Congresses (1918–1922)* (Moscow, 1971), 143.

82. F. Chuev, *Sto sorok besed s Molotovym* (Moscow, 1991), 92.

83. Knei-Paz, *The Social and Political Thought of Leon Trotsky,* 333, 302–33; see also Richard B. Day, *Leon Trotsky and the Politics of Economic Isolation* (Cambridge, 1973).

84. This was included in a speech to the Fourteenth Party Congress printed in *Krest'ianskaia gazeta,* December 22, 1925, but I could not find it in Stalin's collected works.

85. "Report at the Eighth Congress of Soviets, December 21, 20," in Alvin Z. Rubinstein, *The Foreign Policy of the Soviet Union* (New York, 1960), 70–72; Jerry Hough, *Russia and the West* (New York, 1988), 53–54.

86. *Pravda,* November 17, 1927; see the "Platform of the Bolshevik-Leninist (Opposition) to the Fifteenth Party Congress," in *Kommunisticheskaia oppozitsiia v SSSR, 1923–1927,* ed. Iu. Fel'shinskii (Benson, Vt., 1988), 4:135.

87. *Pravda,* October 26, 1927.

88. Nikolai Shmelev and Vladimir Popov, *The Turning Point: Revitalizing the Soviet Economy* (New York, 1989), 221–22; Franklyn Holzman, "Foreign Trade," in *Economic Trends in the Soviet Union,* ed. Adam Bergson and Simon Kuznets (Cambridge, Mass., 1963); Michael R. Dohan, "The Economic Origins of Soviet Autarchy, 1927–28— 1934," *Slavic Review* 35 (December 1976): 603–35.

89. See M. S. Agurskii, *Ideologiia natsional-bol'shevizma* (Paris, 1980); and Mikhail Agursky, *The Third Rome: National Bolshevism in the USSR* (Boulder, Colo., 1987). See also Dmitry Shlapentokh, "Bolshevism, Nationalism, and Statism: Soviet Ideology in Formation," in *The Bolsheviks in Russian Society: The Revolution and the Civil Wars,* ed. Vladimir N. Brovkin (New Haven, Conn., 1997), 271–97; idem, *The French Revolution and the Russian Anti-Democratic Tradition* (New Brunswick, N.J., 1997), 213–19.

90. *Pravda,* October 22, 1922.

91. *Krest'ianskaia gazeta,* September 21, 1924.

92. Positive reports accounted for 18 percent of the cumulative space given to foreign affairs in *Pravda,* 13 percent in *Labor,* and 23 percent in *The Peasant Newspaper,* partly owing to the promotion of foreign agricultural practices. Neutral reports of events abroad, briefs from foreign newspapers, and other commentaries bring the total to a quarter of the cumulative space on foreign affairs in each newspaper.

93. *Pravda,* March 21, 1922.

94. *Krest'ianskaia gazeta,* January 17, 1928.

95. *Pravda,* June 17, 1922.

96. Ibid., January 11, 1921.

97. *Trud,* May 6, 1921.

98. Foreign opinion is cited in 6 percent of the articles about foreign affairs in *Pravda,* 8 percent in *Labor,* and 13 percent in *The Peasant Newspaper,* where reporters extolled foreign workers for their support of the Soviet Union. The references in the three papers were primarily to foreign workers or to foreigners generally and not to foreign Communists.

99. *Pravda,* May 17, 1922.

100. *Krest'ianskaia gazeta,* February 18, 1924.

101. *Pravda,* September 7, 1922.

102. Ibid.

103. Ibid., July 22, 1927.

104. *Trud,* January 17, 1928.

105. I discuss this in more detail in "The Press and Its Message: Images of America in the 1920s and 1930s," in *Russia in the Era of NEP,* ed. A. Rabinovich and Richard Stites (Bloomington, Ind., 1991), 231–53.

106. The following is based on a sample of articles on America in *Pravda* in 1921–28, 1931, 1933, 1935. The sample included every fifth article of more than 132 lines and every tenth article of fewer than 132 lines. All articles on America in *Krest'ianskaia gazeta* from 1923 to 1928 were counted.

107. Kendall E. Bailes, "The American Connection: Ideology and the Transfer of American Technology to the Soviet Union, 1917–41," *Comparative Studies in Society and History* 23, no. 3 (July 1981): 421–48; Richard Stites, *Revolutionary Dreams: Utopian Vision and Experimental Life in the Russian Revolution* (New York, 1989), 145–64. Hoover's American Relief Administration at its peak fed eleven million Soviet citizens a day (H. H. Fisher, *The Famine in Soviet Russia, 1919–23* [New York, 1927], 553, 556–57).

108. *Rabochaia Moskva,* April 4, 1923; *Krest'ianskaia gazeta,* June 21, 1927.

109. *Bednota,* February 23, 1922.

110. *Rabochaia gazeta,* January 24, 1923; see also *Pravda,* August 30, 1923.

111. *Pravda,* February 24, 1924; see also Kuibyshchev's remarks in ibid., March 9, 1924.

112. Ibid., September 30, 1923.

113. In *The Foundations of Leninism,* in I. V. Stalin, *Works,* (Moscow, 1952–55), 6:196.

114. *Pravda,* February 15, 1921; *Rabochaia gazeta,* July 8, 1924.

115. *Rabochaia gazeta,* May 3, 1926.

116. Antonio Gramsci, *Selections from the Prison Notebooks,* ed. and trans. Quintin Hoare and Geoffrey Nowell Smith (New York, 1971), 302–3. See also Charles S. Maier, "Between Taylorism and Technocracy," *Journal of Contemporary History* 5, no. 2 (1970): 29.

117. See "Ford at Shipka," an article about "Soviet Fords" (*Sovetskie fordy*), *Rabochaia gazeta,* January 1, 1928.

118. Stites stresses this with respect to the cult of Ford and Taylor in *Revolutionary Dreams,* 148; David Joravsky links Taylorism with scientific rationality in *Russian Psychology: A Critical History* (Oxford, 1989), 344.

119. T. P. Korzhikhina, "Osnovnye cherty administrativno-komandnoi sistemy upravleniia," in *O formirovanie administrativno-komandnoi sistemy,* ed. V. P. Dmitrenko (Moscow, 1992), 146–64.

120. The Russian is *sotsialisticheskoe stroitel'stvo.*

121. *Pravda,* October 21, 1926.

122. Ibid., April 19, 1927.

123. Brooks, *When Russia Learned to Read,* 235–37.

124. *Pravda,* April 8, 1926.

125. Ibid., June 16, 1925.

126. *Krest'ianskaia gazeta,* June 23, 1925.

127. The Soviet Union had good relations with Italy during the 1920s. See Larry Ceplair, *Under the Shadow of War: Fascism, Anti-Fascism, and Marxists, 1918–39* (New York, 1987), 106–9. The word *fascism* appeared in articles filling 6–7 percent of the foreign sample; articles about fascism occupied less than a third of that.

128. *Trud,* May 17, 1922.

129. *Krest'ianskaia gazeta,* August 11, 1925.

130. Ibid., March 2, 1926.

131. *Trud,* September 14, 1923. "Palestine" here refers to a native place and has nothing to do with the actual Palestine.

132. *Pravda,* September 9, 1927.

133. The problem for American foreign policy in the 1950s is conceptualized in David J. Finlay, Ole R. Holsti, and Richard R. Fagen, *Enemies in Politics* (Chicago, 1967), 1–24.

134. *Pravda,* May 12, 1923.

135. On Moor and Deni, see Stephen White, *The Bolshevik Poster* (New Haven, 1988), 41–60.

136. *Rabochaia Moskva,* May 15, 1923.

137. Ibid., May 12, 1923.

138. *Pravda,* May 27, 1927; May 28, 1927.

139. Ibid., May 28, 1927.

140. Ibid., June 2, 1927.

141. *Bednota,* August 13, 1927.

142. *Pravda,* June 9, 1927.

143. Ibid., June 9, 1927.

144. Alfred G. Meyer, "The War Scare of 1927," *Soviet Union* 5, no. 1 (1978): 1–25; Stalin, *Sochineniia,* 10:41–59.

145. *Pravda,* September 27, 1927.

146. Ibid., May 13, 1923.

147. Ibid., July 6, 1927.

148. Average space on world revolution in the peasant paper dropped by half in 1923 and 1927, and by two-thirds in 1928 to a mere 7.5 percent of all space given to foreign affairs in my foreign sample. Between 1926 and 1927 coverage of world revolution dropped in *Labor* from 44 percent to 27 percent, and in *Pravda* from 36 percent to 22 percent.

149. Elisabeth Noelle-Neumann, *The Spiral of Silence: Public Opinion—Our Social Skin* (Chicago, 1984), 78.

150. Kendall E. Bailes, *Technology and Society under Lenin and Stalin* (Princeton, N.J., 1978), 64.

151. T. H. Rigby, *Communist Party Membership in the USSR* (Princeton, N.J., 1968), 59–62.

152. Institut Marksizma-Leninizma pri TsK KPSS, *Istoriia Kommunisticheskoi Partii Sovetskogo Soiuza* 4, book 1 (Moscow, 1970), 16.

153. Ibid., 480–81.

154. Don K. Rowney, *Transition to Technocracy: The Structural Origins of the Soviet Administrative State* (Ithaca, N.Y., 1989), 152; Fitzpatrick, *Education and Social Mobility,* 62, 181–87; Akademiia obshchestvennykh nauk pri TsK KPSS Kafedra istorii

sovetskogo obshchestva, *Sovetskaia intelligentsiia (Istoriia formirovaniia i rosta, 1917–65)* (Moscow, 1968), 141.

155. *Bednota,* December 19, 1922.
156. Ibid., February 8, 1921.
157. *Krest'ianskaia gazeta,* April 13, 1926.
158. Knei-Paz, *The Social and Political Thought of Leon Trotsky,* 367–78.
159. *Rabochaia Moskva,* August 15, 1922.
160. *Krest'ianskaia gazeta,* January 25, 1927.
161. Ibid., May 17, 1926.
162. Ibid., January 6, 1925; May 17, 1926; December 21, 1924; December 21, 1924.
163. Ibid., January 20, 1924; April 19, 1927.
164. *Bednota,* June 14, 1922.
165. *Rabochaia Moskva,* March 14, 1922.
166. *Bednota,* February 24, 1923.
167. *Krest'ianskaia gazeta,* March 2, 1926.
168. *Bednota,* October 17, 1922.
169. *Rabochaia Moskva,* May 12, 1922.
170. Ibid., September 17, 1922.
171. Ibid., September 14, 1922.
172. Von Hagen, *Soldiers,* 127, 308–25.
173. *Rabochaia Moskva,* May 23, 1922.
174. *Bednota,* February 20, 1923.
175. *Krest'ianskaia gazeta,* May 25, 1924.
176. *Bednota,* March 31, 1923.
177. Ibid., December 30, 1922.
178. Ibid., September 6, 1922.
179. *Krest'ianskaia gazeta,* July 7, 1925.
180. Ibid., August 30, 1927.
181. *Bednota,* September 14, 1922.
182. Ibid., May 24, 1923.
183. *Krest'ianskaia gazeta,* November 29, 1927.
184. *Rabochaia Moskva,* March 17, 1922.
185. *Bednota,* March 4, 1923; December 21, 1922.
186. Ibid., August 17, 1926.
187. Shlapentokh, "Bolshevism, Nationalism, and Statism," 277–95.
188. The Russian word is *zadacha.* Lexicographer Vladimir Dal defined it as "a question for resolution, a riddle, or a lesson" (V. Dal', *Tolkovyi slovar' zhivogo velikorusskogo iazyka* [Moscow, 1978] [based on the 1880–82 edition]). The task appears as a key or governing metaphor in 6 of 48 sampled editorials and 7 of the 119 articles in the general sample.
189. *Pravda,* December 29, 1918.
190. Ibid., September 3, 1925.
191. On orientational metaphors, see Lakoff and Johnson, *Metaphors We Live By,* 14–24. The Russian word is *put'.*
192. Lenin, *CW,* 32:419; Lenin, *Sochineniia,* 4th ed. (Moscow, 1950), 32:397. I have translated *put'* as "path" rather than "road" as in the official English version.
193. White, *The Bolshevik Poster,* 99, 102, 118.

194. Mikhail German and Aleksandr Kokovkin, eds., *Serdtsem slushaia revoliutsiiu—iskusstvo pervykh let oktiabria* (Leningrad, 1985), 78.

195. White, *Bolshevik Poster,* 11.

196. *Serdtsem slushaia revoliutsiiu,* 81.

197. The Russian word is *poputchik.*

198. *Pravda* printed a speech he gave on January 28 in its February 12, 1924, issue.

199. *Pravda,* February 12, 1924.

200. Ibid., 2/12/25, 7/22/27.

201. *Ogonek,* December 18, 1927.

202. The Russian word is *liniia.*

203. *Pravda,* August 1, 1926.

204. Ibid., November 11, 1926. The Russian words are *magistral'* and *etapy.*

205. Such stories comprise more than a quarter of all articles in the general sample and slightly more than a fifth of the editorial sample. The Russian word is *stroitel'stvo.*

206. *Pravda,* 1/28/1919.

207. Ricoeur discusses act and event in *Oneself as Another,* 67–87.

208. Articles framed by the idea of class war declined during the 1920s in my general sample from a high of 25 percent in 1918–20 to 16 percent of the total in 1921–22, 12 percent in 1923–26, and only 8 percent in 1927 to early 1928.

209. Andrey Platonov, *The Foundation Pit,* trans. Mirra Ginsburg (Evanston, Ill., 1994).

210. *Pravda,* November 6, 1927.

211. A. K. Sokolov, ed., *Golos naroda. Pis'ma i otkliki riadovykh sovetskikh grazhdan o sobytiiakh, 1918–1932 gg.* (Moscow, 1998), 56.

212. Ibid., 97.

213. From a selection of peasant letters in V. Kabanov, T. Mironova, and E. Khandurinaia, "'Sotsializm—Eto rai na zemle.' Krest'ianskie predstavleniia o sotsializme v pis'makh 20-x gg," *Neizvestnaia Rossiia xx vek,* ed. I. D. Koval'chenko (Moscow, 1993), 3:211.

214. Sokolov, *Golos naroda,* 137–38.

215. Ibid., 107.

216. Kabanov, Mironova, and Khandurinaia, "Sotsializm," 204.

217. Sokolov, *Golos naroda,* 209.

218. Ibid.

Chapter Three
The Performance Begins

1. *Pravda,* May 1, 1939.

2. Hannah Arendt describes a break with rationality in *The Origins of Totalitarianism* (New York, 1958). Raymond Aron disagrees in "The Essence of Totalitarianism According to Hannah Arendt," in *In Defense of Political Reason: Essays by Raymond Aron,* ed. Daniel J. Mahoney (Lanham, Md., 1994), 97–112.

3. Brooks, "Studies of the Reader"; Dobrenko, *The Making of the State Reader.*

4. J. D. Barber and R. W. Davies, "Employment and Industrial Labour," in *The Economic Transformation of the Soviet Union, 1913–45,* ed. R. W. Davies, Mark Harrison, and S. G. Wheatcroft (New York, 1994), 102; R. W. Davies, *The Soviet Economy in Tur-*

moil, 1929–1930 (Cambridge, Mass., 1989), 86–88; Holland Hunter and Janusz M. Szyrmer, *Faulty Foundations: Soviet Economic Policies, 1928–1940* (Princeton, N.J., 1992) 26–41, 232–33. E. A. Osokina, *Ierarkhiia potrebleniia. O zhizni liudei v usloviiakh stalinskogo snabzheniia, 1928–1935 gg.* (Moscow, 1993).

5. Barber and Davies, "Employment and Industrial Labor," 103–4.

6. Ibid., 102–4.

7. Moshe Lewin, *The Making of the Soviet System: Essays in the Social History of Interwar Russia* (New York, 1985), 121–41. Robert Conquest, in *Harvest of Sorrow: Soviet Collectivization and the Terror-Famine* (Oxford, 1986), 301, calculates almost 14.5 million deaths. Michael Ellman, in "A Note on the Number of 1933 Famine Victims," *Soviet Studies* 43, no. 2 (1991): 375–79, estimates 7–8 million. S. G. Wheatcroft and R. W. Davies, in "Population," in *The Economic Transformation of the Soviet Union,* 68, estimate "several million" famine deaths and somewhat more than 5 million persecuted as kulaks.

8. Wheatcroft and Davies, "Population," 74.

9. R. W. Davies, "Industry," in *The Economic Transformation of the Soviet Union,* 137–38.

10. Mark Harrison, "National Income," in *The Economic Transformation of the Soviet Union,* 45.

11. Alfred D. Chandler Jr., *Scale and Scope: The Dynamics of Industrial Capitalism* (Cambridge, Mass., 1990).

12. K. M. Simonov, *Glazami cheloveka moego pokoleniia: Razmyshleniia o I. V. Staline* (Moscow, 1990), 63.

13. *Sovetskaia intelligentsiia (Istoriia formirovaniia i rosta, 1917–65)* (Moscow, 1968), 141; Institut Marksizma-Leninizma pri TsK KPSS, *Istoriia Kommunisticheskoi Partii Sovetskogo Soiuza* 4, book 1 (Moscow, 1970), 480–81; Sheila Fitzpatrick, *Education and Social Mobility in the Soviet Union, 1921–34* (New York, 1979), 87–110, 171–73, 241; Lewin, *The Making of the Soviet System,* 241–57.

14. *Krest'ianskaia gazeta,* March 21, 1931; *Encyclopedia of Russia and the Soviet Union,* ed. Michael T. Florinsky (New York, 1961), 110; Stephen Merl, "Social Mobility in the Countryside," in *Social Dimensions of Soviet Industrialization,* ed. William G. Rosenberg and Lewis H. Siegelbaum (Bloomington, Ind., 1993), 45.

15. *Istoriia Kommunisticheskoi Partii Sovetskogo Soiuza* (Moscow, 1970), 5:27.

16. Merl, "Social Mobility," 45.

17. Ibid.

18. *Pravda,* October 16, 1927.

19. Hunter and Szyrmer, *Faulty Foundations,* 137–39.

20. *Pravda,* November 7, 1928.

21. Ibid., October 10, 1932.

22. Robert Conquest shows, in *The Harvest of Sorrow,* 322–28, that Soviet leaders concealed the famine.

23. George Orwell, *Shooting an Elephant and Other Essays* (San Diego, 1945), 110.

24. O. V. Kalintseva, *Nashi: Semeinaia khonika, (1886–1986)* (Sverdlovsk, 1992), 183.

25. Max Weber, *Economy and Society: An Outline of Interpretive Sociology,* ed. Guenther Roth and Claus Wittich, trans. Ephraim Fischoff, Hans Gerth, A. M. Anderson et al. (Berkeley, 1978), 215–16, 241; Edward Shils, *The Constitution of Society*

(Chicago, 1982), 93–117. I disagree with Carl J. Friedrich and Zbigniew K. Brzezinski, who deny Stalin's charisma for lack of religiosity. See their *Totalitarian Dictatorship and Autocracy* (Cambridge, Mass., 1956), 24–25.

26. Clifford Geertz, *Nagara: The Theatre State in Nineteenth-Century Bali* (Princeton, N.J., 1980), 11–25, 104; and idem, *Local Knowledge: Further Essays in Interpretative Anthropology* (New York, 1983), 121–48.

27. Richard S. Wortman, *Scenarios of Power: Myth and Ceremony in Russian Monarchy from Peter the Great to the Death of Nicholas I*, vol. 1 (Princeton, N.J., 1995), 81.

28. Boris Souvarine, *Stalin: A Critical Survey of Bolshevism* (New York, 1939), 397.

29. He did not print Stalin's speech "The International Situation and the Defense of the USSR" (August 1, 1927). It appears in Stalin, *Sochineniia,* 10:1–91.

30. Kosheleva, Lel'chuk, and Naumov, *Pis'ma I. V. Stalina V. M. Molotovu,* 161, 165; Boris Bazhanov, *Bazhanov and the Damnation of Stalin,* trans. David W. Doyle (Athens, Ohio, 1990), 95.

31. O. V. Khlevniuk, A. V. Kvashonkin, L. N. Kosheleva, and L. A. Rogovaia, eds., *Stalinskoe politbiuro v 30-e gody,* (Moscow, 1995), 95.

32. The chief editors are listed in Angus Roxburgh, *Pravda: Inside the Soviet News Machine* (New York, 1987), Appendix 2.

33. Nikita Khrushchev, *Khrushchev Remembers,* trans. and ed. Strobe Talbot (New York, 1970), 274.

34. Gronskii, *Iz proshlogo . . . vospominaniia,* 124, 135, 145.

35. Kornei Chukovskii, *Dnevnik, 1930–1969* (Moscow, 1994), 141.

36. On Mussolini's image, see Lawrence Rainey's review of Enrico Sturani's *Otto Millioni Di Cartoline Per Il Duce* (Centro Scientifico, 1997), "Making History," *London Review of Books,* January 1, 1988, 18–20.

37. Nina Tumarkin, *Lenin Lives! The Lenin Cult in Soviet Russia* (Cambridge, Mass., 1983), 152–74. Stalin's oath stood out for its religiosity.

38. Blium, *Za kulasami,* 127.

39. Edvard Radzinsky, *Stalin,* trans. H. T. Willetts (New York, 1996), 12–14.

40. *Pravda,* December 22, 1929.

41. Ibid.

42. Quoted in *Dnevnik "Velikogo Pereloma" (mart 1928–avgust 1931)* (Paris, 1991), 175.

43. *Izvestiia,* December 22, 1929.

44. *Komsomol'skaia pravda,* December 21, 1929.

45. *Krest'ianskaia gazeta,* December 25, 1929.

46. Khrushchev, *Khrushchev Remembers,* 46–47.

47. *Pravda,* January 1, 1931.

48. Ibid. The term *shock work* (*udarnaia rabota*) refers to work exceeding the norm.

49. *Krest'ianskaia gazeta,* November 6, 1933.

50. *Pravda,* July 28, 1927; Stalin, *Works,* 9:337–38.

51. *Pravda,* July 15, 1928; see also ibid., June 26, 1928, and July 3, 1928.

52. *Beseda* can have a religious connotation, as in "conversations about the immortality of the soul." See V. I. Dal', *Tolkovyi slovar' zhivogo velikorusskogo iazyka* 1 (Moscow, 1978), 85. Stalin published other *besedy,* as in *Pravda,* September 9, 27.

53. *Pravda,* February 10, 1930.

54. Stalin, *Works,* 12:190, 192; I use the title from the text in *Pravda.*

55. Many commentators trace the cult to Stalin. See Andre Sinyavksy, *Soviet Civilization: A Cultural History,* trans. Joanne Turnbull with the assistance of Nikolae Formozov (New York, 1990) 94; and "Stalin—Kak geroi i khudozhnik stalinskoi epokhi," *Sintaksis* 19 (1987): 106–25. A. Antonov-Ovseenko, in *Teatr Iosifa Stalina,* attributes Stalin's roles to acting. Leonid Gozman and Alexander Etkind suggest Soviet citizens were treated as infants, in *The Psychology of Post-Totalitarianism in Russia,* trans. Roger Clarke (London, 1992), 16.

56. Jeffrey Brooks, "Russian Nationalism and Russian Literature," in *Nation and Ideology,* ed. Ivo Banac, John G. Ackerman, and Roman Szporluk (Boulder, Colo., 1981), 315–34.

57. *Ukhod velikogo startsa,* dir. Iakov Protazanov and Y. Thiemann (Moscow, 1912), Thiemann and Reinhardt.

58. Robert C. Tucker, *Stalin in Power: The Revolution from Above, 1928–1941* (New York, 1990), 554–55; and Roy Medvedev, *Let History Judge the Origins and Consequences of Stalinism,* trans. George Shriver (New York, 1989), 831. Also see his poem published at age sixteen in 1895, in Richard Kosolapov, *Slovo tovarishchu Stalinu* (Moscow, 1995), 3–4. Stalin may have identified with Peter and Ivan, as Tucker has argued, but the press does not attest to this. The comparison was more evident in films.

59. Il'ia Erenburg, *Liudi, gody, zhizn': Vospominaniia v trekh tomakh* (Moscow, 1990), 2:224.

60. *Pravda,* November 30, 1928; Stalin, *Works,* 11:305.

61. *Pravda,* January 11, 1935.

62. Ibid., January 10, 1933; Stalin, *Works,* 13:219.

63. Lenin was cited in 33 of 201 editorials in 1921–27; Stalin in 32 of 169 in 1928–32; and Stalin in 135 of 247 in 1933–39. After 1936 there was a similar trend on certain holidays—May Day, Press Day (May 5), the anniversary of the revolution, International Women's Day (March 8), and Constitution Day (December 8).

64. *Pravda,* March 17, 1939.

65. *Trud,* September 27, 1935.

66. *Komsomol'skaia pravda,* November 7, 1936.

67. *Pravda,* December 6, 1936.

68. Radzinsky, *Stalin,* 357.

69. Excerpts appear in Veronique Garros, Natalia Korenevskaya, and Thomas Lahusen, eds., *Intimacy and Terror: Soviet Diaries of the 1930s* (New York, 1995), 181.

70. Quoted in Sarah Davies, *Popular Opinion in Stalin's Russia: Terror, Propaganda and Dissent, 1934–1941* (Cambridge, 1997), 46.

71. *Pravda,* December 21, 1939; *Komsomol'skaia pravda,* December 21, 1939; *Izvestiia,* December 22–23, 1939;

72. *Pravda,* August 21, 1936.

73. Katerina Clark notes religious and ritualistic elements in Soviet novels in *The Soviet Novel: History as Ritual* (Chicago, 1985), and modifies and develops these ideas in *Petersburg, Crucible of Cultural Revolution* (Cambridge, Mass., 1995), particularly 242–60; Gleb Prokhorov, in *Art under Socialist Realism: Soviet Painting 1930–1950* (Roseville East, Australia, 1995), describes this in painting.

74. Moshe Lewin stresses a "peasant outlook" in *The Gorbachev Phenomenon: A Historical Interpretation* (Berkeley, 1991), 34; and in *Russia/USSR/Russia* (New York, 1995), 140–44. See also Boris Mironov, "Peasant Popular Culture and the Origins of

Soviet Authoritarianism," in *Cultures in Flux: Lower-Class Values, Practices, and Resistance in Late Imperial Russia,* ed. Stephen P. Frank and Mark D. Steinberg (Princeton, N.J., 1994), 54–73.

75. Richard Pipes, *Russia under the Bolshevik Regime* (New York, 1995), 503–5.

76. Leszek Kolakowski, *Main Currents of Marxism: Its Origin, Growth, and Dissolution,* trans. P. S. Falla (Oxford, 1978), 3:1–5; Andrzej Walicki, *Marxism and the Leap to the Kingdom of Freedom: The Rise and Fall of the Communist Utopia* (Stanford, 1995), 2–3, 398–410.

77. Boris Groys, *The Total Art of Stalinism: Avant-Garde, Aesthetic Dictatorship, and Beyond,* trans. Charles Rougle (Princeton, N.J., 1992), 64; Clark, *Petersburg,* 52.

78. Some peasants called Lenin "Father" in letters to *Krest'ianskaia gazeta.* See Sokolov, *Golos naroda,* 119.

79. See Don K. Rowney, *Transition to Technocracy: The Structural Origins of the Soviet Administrative State* (Ithaca, N.Y., 1989); and Fitzpatrick, *Education and Social Mobility,* 238. See also Sheila Fitzpatrick, "The Great Departure: Rural-Urban Migration in the Soviet Union, 1929–33," in *Social Dimensions of Soviet Industrialization,* ed. Rosenberg and Siegelbaum, 15–40. Family life is described in Wendy Z. Goldman, *Women, the State, and Revolution: Soviet Family Policy and Social Life, 1917–1936* (Cambridge, 1993). The geographic and social disruption are stressed in Lewin, *The Gorbachev Phenomenon,* chaps. 1–3.

80. Lewin, *Russia,* 88.

81. Lion Feukhtvanger, *Moskva, 1937 god* (Moscow, 1937); the cited passages are reprinted in M. P. Lobanov, ed., *Stalin v vospominaniiakh sovremennikov i dokumentakh epokhi* (Moscow, 1994), 302–3.

82. Tumarkin, *Lenin Lives!,* 134–206.

83. Ibid., 174, cites Nikolae Valentinov (N. V. Vol'skii), *Novaia ekonomicheskaia politika i krizis partii posle smerti Lenina,* ed. J. Bunyan and V. Butenko (Stanford, 1971), 90–92.

84. *Pravda,* March 30, 1929.

85. Davies, *Popular Opinion,* 150.

86. Clifford Geertz attributes power of this sort to dramatic ritual in *Nagara* and elsewhere. Victor Turner, in *From Ritual to Theatre: The Human Seriousness of Play* (New York, 1982), claims that ritual and drama resolve social conflict.

87. James L. Watson, "The Structure of Chinese Funerary Rites: Elementary Forms, Ritual Sequence, and the Primacy of Performance," in *Death Ritual in Late Imperial and Modern China,* ed. James L. Watson and Evelyn S. Rawski (Berkeley, 1988), 3–19.

88. Mikhail Baitalsky, *Notebooks for the Grandchildren: Recollections of a Trotskyist Who Survived the Stalin Terror,* ed. and trans. Marilyn Vogt-Downey (Atlantic Highlands, N.J., 1995), 309.

89. Herbert Marcuse, *Soviet Marxism: A Critical Analysis* (New York, 1961), 72–73.

90. Brooks, *When Russia Learned to Read,* 166–213.

91. Khrushchev, *Khrushchev Remembers,* 72–73.

92. Robert C. Tucker makes this point in *Stalin in Power,* 215.

93. Erving Goffman, in *Frame Analysis* (New York, 1974), 202–5, uses the term *disattention* to describe performers' oblivion to what is outside the frame of their activities.

94. This theory is developed by the sociologist Harold Garfinkel in *Studies in Ethnomethodology* (Cambridge, 1994 [1967]), 76.

95. Ibid., 41–42.

96. Ibid., 175.

97. Of seventy-six editorials in my *Pravda* sample (1933–39) in which Stalin was cited, metaphors of friendship and family figured in twenty-three, military metaphors in fifteen, school metaphors in twelve, and tasks and other models of leadership such as "the path" and the "line" in nineteen. Of thirty-one cases in my random sample in which Stalin was cited as an authority, his name was coupled with metaphors of family and friendship in eighteen, the military in five, the school in five, and taskmaster in three. Prokhorov notes paintings of Stalin with women in *Art under Socialist Realism,* 96.

98. *Pravda,* June 29, 1936. I have translated *rodina* as homeland and the more emphatic *rodina-mat'* as motherland. *Pravda* also published a picture of this girl embracing Stalin on January 30, 1936 following the reception.

99. Heller and Nekrich, *Utopia in Power,* 282.

100. V. V. Glebkin, *Ritual v sovetskoi kul'ture* (Moscow, 1998), 114–17.

101. Sarah Davies, "The 'Cult of the Vozhd': Representations in Letters, 1934–1941," *Russian History* 24, nos. 1–2 (spring–summer 1997): 131–47.

102. *Pravda,* October 29, 1933; smiles appear in a montage by Klutsis on the October anniversary. The flowers are noted in Heller and Nekrich, *Utopia in Power,* 281.

103. Markoosha Fischer, *My Lives in Russia* (New York, 1944), 110.

104. Jack Goody, *The Culture of Flowers* (Cambridge, 1993).

105. M. Chapkina, *Khudozhestvennaia otkrytka: K stoletiiu otkrytki v Rossii* (Moscow, 1993); Gosudarstvennyi Istoricheskii muzei, *Torgovaia reklama i upakovka v Rossii, XIX–XXvv.* (Moscow, 1993); Mikhail Anikst and Elena Chernevich, *Russian Graphic Design, 1880–1917* (New York, 1990).

106. M. Anikst, *Soviet Commercial Design of the Twenties* (New York, 1987); T. I. Bolodina, ed., *Agitatsionno-massovoe iskusstvo. Oformlenie prazdnestv* (Moscow, 1984), tablitsy (plates).

107. Turner, *From Ritual to Theatre,* 24–28; idem, *The Anthropology of Performance,* 22–24.

108. Arnold van Gennep, *The Rites of Passage,* trans. Monika B. Vizedom (Chicago, 1970), 21; Turner discusses the phases in *From Ritual to Theatre,* 24–25.

109. Turner, *From Ritual to Theatre,* 54.

110. Turner, *Anthropology of Performance,* 21. The phrase is Milton Singer's in *When a Great Tradition Modernizes* (New York, 1972); Turner, in *From Ritual to Theatre,* 33–41, uses "liminoid" to distinguish performances of modern industrial societies from those that are sacred ritual. I use it because the Soviet performance was somewhere between the two. On time, see also Clark, *The Soviet Novel,* 145–46; and Evgeny Dobrenko, "The Petrified Utopia: Time, Space, and Paroxysms of Style in Socialist Realism," in *Socialist Realism Revisited,* ed. Nina Kolesnikoff and Walter Smyrniw (Ontario, 1994), 13–27.

111. Conquest, *Harvest of Sorrow,* 184. On the confusion as to whose property was being protected, see Sheila Fitzpatrick, *Stalin's Peasants: Resistance and Survival in the Russian Village after Collectivization* (New York, 1994), 73, 178.

112. *Pravda,* August 9, 1932.

113. Valentine M. Berezhkov, *At Stalin's Side: His Interpreter's Memoirs from the October Revolution to the Fall of the Dictator's Empire,* trans. Sergei V. Mikheyev (New York, 1994), 170.

114. Svetlana Alliluyeva, *Only One Year,* trans. Paul Chavchavadze (New York,

1969), 25. Sheila Fitzpatrick called this fakery "Potemkinism," in *Stalin's Peasants*, 16–18, 262–85.

115. *Pravda*, August 17, 1939.

116. Ibid., August 1, 1939; August 2, 1939.

117. Ibid., August 2, 1939; Boris I. Nicolaevsky, *Power and the Soviet Elite: "The Letter of an Old Bolshevik" and Other Essays by Boris I. Nicolaevsky*, ed. Janet D. Zagoria (New York, 1965), 58.

118. *Pravda*, August 1, 1939.

119. Ibid.

120. Ibid.

121. The number of editorials that mentioned non-Russian people were 12 of 201 for 1921–27, 19 of 169 for 1928–32, and 78 of 172 for 1933–39.

122. See the unsigned photomontage in *Pravda*, November 7, 1930. The nationalities first appeared in Soviet stamps on the tenth anniversary of the October Revolution in 1927, and from April through July 1933 the government issued a series of twenty-one stamps representing the peoples of the USSR. See *Katalog pochtovykh marok Rossii, 1857–1995* (Moscow, 1995), 32, 36–37.

123. These figures are based on the first three days of *Pravda*'s coverage of the two congresses. I counted government leaders as Russians even though their nationalities varied. "Russians" in 1933 account for more than half the space in these days. The dates were February 16–18, 1933, and February, 11–13, 1935.

124. *Pravda*, November 26, 1936.

125. Ibid., August 20, 1938. The Russian is *rodina-mat'*.

126. Gerhard Simon, *Nationalism and Policy Toward the Nationalities in the Soviet Union: From Totalitarian Dictatorship to Post-Stalinist Society*, trans. Karen Forster and Oswald Forster (Boulder, Colo., 1991), 73; George O. Liber, *Soviet Nationality Policy, Urban Growth, and Identity Change in the Ukrainian SSSR, 1923–1934* (Cambridge, 1992), 2–3, 34–37, 45, 107–8.

127. Liber, *Soviet Nationality*, 148–59.

128. *Pravda*, February 5, 1931.

129. Stalin, *Works*, 13:41.

130. The Russian words are *otechestvo, rodina,* and *rodina-mat'*.

131. Stalin, *Works*, 13:41.

132. Nationalism figured in 17 of 250 sampled editorials from 1933 through 1939; science, technology, and progress figured in 125. Popular writers in late Imperial Russia often identified with the land rather than its rulers, as I note in *When Russia Learned to Read*, 214–45. Robert Tucker describes Stalin's "popular traditionalism" in *Stalin in Power*, 325.

133. *Pravda*, October 14, 1939; April 10, 1937.

134. *Krest'ianskaia gazeta*, February 10, 1937.

135. James von Geldern and Richard Stites, eds., *Mass Culture in Soviet Russia: Tales, Poems, Songs, Movies, Plays, and Folklore, 1917–1953* (Bloomington, Ind., 1995), 329.

136. *Trud*, September 24, 1935.

137. *Pravda*, February 11, 1937.

138. Anthony Giddens, *Modernity and Self-Identity: Self and Society in the Late Modern Age* (Stanford, 1991), 21–23.

139. Mikhail Bakhtin wrote "Forms of Time and the Chronotope in the Novel" and began his doctoral dissertation on Rabelais, which appeared as *Tvorchestvo Fransua Rable i narodnaia kul'tura srednevekov'ia i Renessansa* (Moscow, 1965), between 1936 and 1941, perhaps partly in response to Soviet official time. See Katerina Clark and Michael Holquist, *Mikhail Bakhtin* (Cambridge, Mass., 1984), 263.

140. Wolfgang Leonhard, *Child of the Revolution,* trans. G. M. Woodhouse (Chicago, 1958), 13–14.

141. *Pravda,* February 11, 1937.

142. *Krest'ianskaia gazeta,* February 10, 1937.

143. Tucker analyzes the text in *Stalin in Power,* 530–50.

144. *Pravda,* September 14, 1938.

145. Ibid., September 13, 1938.

146. Ibid., September 19, 1938. Sheila Fitzpatrick notes a worker using this analogy of leaders alienated from the masses in a letter, in "Supplicants and Citizens: Public Letter-Writing in Soviet Russia in the 1930s," *Slavic Review* 55, no. 1 (spring 1996), 92.

147. *Pravda,* September 19, 1938. According to the text in *Pravda* and in *The Short Course,* the source of this quotation is Stalin's speech "On the Shortcomings in Party Work." The passage does not appear in this speech published in *Pravda* on March 29, 1937. On Stalin's sense of history as the present, see Simonov, *Glazami cheloveka moego pokoleniia,* 160–64.

148. *Pravda,* September 14, 1936; December 4, 1936; June 17, 1938; and September 19, 1939.

149. Matthew Cullerne Bown, *Art under Stalin* (New York, 1991), 104.

150. Ibid., 37–38.

151. *Pravda,* June 29, 1930.

152. Ibid., July 14, 1930; July 15, 1930. See also Tucker, *Stalin in Power,* 96.

153. The phrase first appears in my *Pravda* editorial sample on November 16, 1931; it appears as a headline on January 1, 1932.

154. Richard Stites, *Revolutionary Dreams,* 145–64.

155. Valentine Kataev, *Time, Forward,* trans. Charles Malamuth (Bloomington, Ind., 1976), 6.

156. These calculations are based on all articles on science and technology in a random sample of 9 issues per year. The sample included a total of 378 articles from 1921 through 1939. With the exception of 1921 and 1922, the paper was largely the same size in both periods.

157. *Pravda,* January 11, 1929.

158. Andre Gide, *Return from the USSR,* trans. Dorothy Bussy (New York, 1937), 33.

159. *Pravda,* October 1, 1931.

160. David Joravsky, *Russian Psychology: A Critical History* (London, 1989), 323–26; and *The Lysenko Affair* (Cambridge, Mass., 1970), 208–17.

161. *Pravda,* February 1, 1935.

162. Ibid., May 18, 1935.

163. Ibid., January 1, 1933.

164. The *Oxford English Dictionary* defines the subjunctive mood of a verb as contingent or hypothetical. I did not code for time in my random sample for the period up to 1928, but I did for the editorials and these results seem sufficient. Roughly half the

editorials and other articles in 1928–32 were about what should be done rather than, or in addition to, what was actually happening, compared to only 12 percent of editorials in 1924–27.

165. *Pravda,* October 5, 1930.

166. Ibid., January 1, 1939.

167. Ibid., January 2, 1936.

168. Michael Ignatieff, "Whispers from the Abyss," *New York Review of Books* 63, no. 15 (October 3, 1996): 4.

169. *Izvestiia,* August 5, 1939.

170. Ibid.

171. Shils, *The Constitution of Society,* 113.

172. Arkadii Raikin, *Vospominaniia* (St. Petersburg, 1993), 150.

173. D. A. Tolstoi, *Dlia chego vse eto bylo: Vospominaniia* (St. Petersburg, 1995), 40, 85.

174. Solomon Volkov describes the intelligentsia's use of "bureaucratese" in *St. Petersburg: A Cultural History* (New York, 1995), 379. Sheila Fitzpatrick notes learning "the language of *Pravda,*" in "Supplicants and Citizens," 94.

175. Vasily Grossman, *Forever Flowering,* trans. Thomas P. Whitney (New York, 1972), 229.

Chapter Four
The Economy of the Gift: "Thank You, Comrade Stalin, for a Happy Childhood"

1. This limits the Nietzschean aspect of Soviet heroes, which some scholars have stressed. See Mikhail Agursky, "Nietzschean Roots of Stalinist Culture," in *Nietzsche and Soviet Culture: Ally and Adversary,* ed. Bernice Glatzer Rosenthal (Cambridge, 1994), 256–86; and Margarita Tupitsyn, "Superman Imagery in Soviet Photography and Photomontage," in idem, *Nietzsche and Soviet Culture,* 287–310.

2. E. E. Evans Prichard, "Introduction," to Marcel Mauss, *The Gift: Forms and Functions of Exchange in Archaic Societies,* trans. Ian Cunnison (New York, 1967), ix. Jacques Derrida suggests that a gift considered a gift by both giver and receiver does not create obligation; see his *Given Time: Counterfeit Money,* trans. Peggy Kamuf (Chicago, 1992), 14, 64. The state's control over the outlay of goods and services is stressed in Ferenc Feher, Agnes Heller, and Gyorgy Markus, *Dictatorship over Needs: An Analysis of Soviet Societies* (New York, 1983).

3. Leonid Maksimenkov, *Sumbur vmesto muzyki: Stalinskaia kul'turnaia revoliutsiia, 1936–1938* (Moscow, 1997), 264–69.

4. *Pravda,* March 8, 1936.

5. On this notion of the gift, see William Ian Miller, *Humiliation and Other Essays on Honor, Social Discomfort, and Violence* (Ithaca, N.Y., 1993), 15–52.

6. Karen Petrone, "Life Has Become More Joyous Comrades": Politics and Culture in Soviet Celebrations, 1934–1939," Ph.D. diss., University of Michigan, 1994, 75–77.

7. N. Vatolina's, "Spacibo rodnomu Stalinu," which was published in 1939 as a postcard and taken from a poster, is reproduced in M. Chapkina, *Khudozhestvennaia otkrytka: K stoletiiu otkrytki v Rossii* (Moscow, 1993), 229 n. 377. On unofficial representations of Stalin as benefactor, see Davies, *Popular Opinion,* 155–67.

8. Avishai Margalit, *The Decent Society,* trans. Naomi Goldblum (Cambridge, Mass., 1996), 44–45.

9. Cited by Vladimir Dal', *Tolkovyi slovar' zhivago velikorusskogo iazyka* (Moscow, 1882), in his definition of *unizhat'.*

10. The citation is from G.W.F. Hegel's *Phenomenology of Mind* and is cited in Margalit, *The Decent Society,* 109–10.

11. Quoted in Davies, *Popular Opinion,* 171.

12. From 1921 through mid-1927, workers comprised 7 percent and peasants 2 percent of my individual sample of 494 lives described in *Pravda* in 1921, 1923, 1925, and the first half of 1927. From 1928 through 1932, workers comprised 25 percent and peasants 2 percent of the cases of 59 lives in a sample of every tenth issue of *Pravda;* from 1933 through 1939, workers comprised 19 percent and peasants 2 percent of 65 lives described in a sample of every tenth issue of *Pravda.* The decline in workers from 1928–32 to 1933–39 reflects increasing coverage of the military, flyers, and explorers.

13. *Pravda,* September 5, 1935. Ordzhonikidze's discovery of Stakhanov and the origins of the movement are described in Oleg V. Khlevniuk, *In Stalin's Shadow,* trans. David J. Nordlander (Armonk, N.Y., 1995), 78–84. The context and campaign in *Pravda* is discussed in Louis H. Siegelbaum, *Stakhanovism and the Politics of Productivity in the USSR, 1935–1941* (New York, 1988), 72–75.

14. Siegelbaum, *Stakhanovism,* 179–86; Donald Filtzer, *Soviet Workers and Stalinist Industrialization: The Formation of Modern Soviet Production Relations, 1928–1941* (Armonk, N.Y., 1986), 179–207.

15. Gennady Andreev-Khomiakov, *Bitter Waters: Life and Work in Stalin's Russia,* trans. Ann E. Healy (Boulder, Colo., 1977), 54–55.

16. *Trud,* September 8, 1935.

17. *Pravda,* November 15, 1935.

18. Ibid.

19. In my individual sample from 1928 through 1932 I coded the two most significant cohort experiences. Revolutionary activity was cited in 49 percent of the cases, the civil war in 25 percent, joining the Party in 15 percent, education in 14 percent, and work in 12 percent. Of twenty-nine lives described in *Pravda* from 1933 through 1937, pre-revolutionary experience was cited as the most important in 48 percent, life under new Soviet order in 55 percent, education in 21 percent, the civil war in 10 percent, and personal achievements in 10 percent. In *Pravda,* in 1921–27, life under the old regime (43 percent), participation in the civil war (25 percent), and education (20 percent) were most important.

20. *Pravda,* February 14, 1933.

21. Ibid., November 22, 1935.

22. Ibid., August 3, 1933.

23. Louis H. Siegelbaum describes rural competitions in "Dear Comrade, You Ask What We Need": Socialist Paternalism and Rural 'Notables' in the Mid-1930s," *Slavic Review* (spring 1998): 107–32.

24. Quoted in Davies, *Popular Opinion,* 38–39.

25. Davies, *Popular Opinion,* 33.

26. Of my individual sample of 494 lives (1921–27), 16 percent were women. Of 59 lives in the sample of every tenth editorial from 1928 through 1932, 10 percent were women. Of 65 lives in the sample of every tenth issue from 1933 through 1939, 23 per-

cent were women. My findings tally with those of Victoria E. Bonnell in *Iconography of Power: Soviet Political Posters under Lenin and Stalin* (Berkeley, 1977), 66–67, 78, 101–23.

27. *Pravda,* March 8, 1923.

28. Ibid., March 8, 1928.

29. Ibid., March 8, 1934.

30. This is based on every tenth issue of *Trud* in 1936–38 and of *Pravda* in 1938. More women wrote for *Pravda* in this period, but they remained a tiny percentage of all contributors. In *Pravda,* from 1918 through 1927, 24 of a random sample of 961 articles were written or coauthored by women; in 1928–32, 7 of 338; and in 1933–39, 25 of 479.

31. Tucker, *Stalin in Power,* 356–58.

32. *Pravda,* June 28, 1936.

33. On physical culture day, see *Pravda,* July 25, 1934; on parades, see *Pravda,* June 14, 1935 and July 1, 1935, when 120,000 athletes paraded in Moscow. Artists such as A. Deineka and A. Rodchenko helped to formulate new eroticized images of the body. See Deineka's poster "Moscow, 1933," in *Rossiia—XX vek (Istoriia strany v Plakaty)* (Moscow, 1993), 116; and Rodchenko's photographs of parades held in 1936 in Museum of Modern Art, *Aleksandr Rodchenko: Painting, Drawing, Collage, Design, Photography* (New York, 1998), 296–97; see also Maksimenkov, *Sumbur vmesto muzyki,* 197–211.

34. *Pravda,* July 7, 1936.

35. In the *Pravda* editorial sample, non-Russians make up 2 percent of the cases in 1928–32 and 10 percent in 1933–39.

36. Liber, *Soviet Nationality Policy,* 148.

37. Simon, *Nationalism,* 138–45; Liber, *Soviet Nationality Policy,* 2–3, 34–37, 45, 107–8, 148–59.

38. Tucker, *Stalin in Power,* 57.

39. Ibid., 151–53.

40. *Pravda,* January 1, 1936.

41. Ibid., December 4, 1936.

42. In *Pravda's* editorials on domestic themes, consideration of the nationalities jumped from 6 percent in 1921–27 to 11 percent in 1928–32 and to 31 percent in 1933–39.

43. *Pravda,* August 20, 1936.

44. Frank J. Miller, *Folklore for Stalin: Russian Folklore and Pseudo-folklore of the Stalin Era* (Armonk, N.Y., 1990), 11, 21–22. He dates the new Stalinist folklore from 1935. See also Stites, *Russian Popular Culture,* 165–66.

45. Earlier the phrase was used literally, as in the phrase "*Stakhanovskaia dekada,*" *Pravda,* January 29, 1936. The chronicle *Kul'turnaia zhizn' v SSSR, 1928–1941. Khronika* (Moscow, 1976) lists two festivals before 1936: "a week of Soviet Belorussia," which *Izvestiia* relegated to page 5 (January 3, 1931) and a "festival of the Belorussian Academy of Sciences in 1933, also covered in the back pages (*Pravda,* February 3, 1931; February 11, 1931).

46. Maksimenkov, *Sumbur vmesto muzyki,* 164–65.

47. *Pravda,* May 25, 1937.

48. Festivals are indexed under *dekada* in *Kul'turnaia zhizn' v SSSR, 1928–1941.*

49. *Pravda,* October 19, 1939.

50. Quoted in Greg Castillo, "Peoples at an Exhibition," in *Socialist Realism without Shores,* a special issue of *The South Atlantic Quarterly,* ed. Thomas Lahusen and Evgeny Dobrenko, 94:3 (summer 1995), 733; Castillo discusses the autarchic quality of the display.

51. *Pravda,* December 3, 1936.

52. Ibid., December 4, 1936.

53. Ibid., August 20, 1938.

54. *Pravda* published sixteen editorials on science and technology from 1921 through 1927, fifty-four from 1928 through 1932, and eighty-four from 1933 through August 1937. On one source of Soviet scientism, see Dmitry Shlapentokh, "The Fedorovian Roots of Stalinism," *Philosophy Today* 40, no. 3/4 (fall 1996): 388–404; and idem, "Bolshevism as a Fedorovian Regime," *Cahiers du Monde russe* 37, no. 4: 429–66.

55. From 1921 to mid-1927, half the lives in the *Pravda* individual sample were of managers, party leaders, administrators, and educators. In 1928–32, managers, leaders, and administrators dropped to a quarter of fifty-nine sampled lives. In a sample of sixty-five lives in 1933–37, delegates to gatherings numbered ten; workers, seven; peasants, two; pilots and other heroes, ten; and soldiers, nine—comprising nearly 60 percent of the total—in contrast to managers, two; political figures, three; and activists, five.

56. My remarks about favored scientists are based on a sample of the first ten scientists described each year and the first ten scientists who wrote in *Pravda* in the years 1932–37, as well as all editorials on science and technology from 1921 to 1937.

57. *Pravda,* November 26, 1936. Stalin, *Sochineniia* 1 (14), ed. Robert H. McNeal (Stanford, 1967), 182. This is a continuation of the thirteen-volume Soviet edition, the publication of which was halted after Stalin's death.

58. David Joravsky, *The Lysenko Affair* (Cambridge, Mass., 1970), notes that Michurin was a precursor of Lysenko but credits him with producing valuable new plant stock if not new varieties (40–53).

59. *Pravda,* June 9, 1931; September 18, 1934.

60. On this and also on the inferior quality of his work, see A. A. Nikonov, *Spiral' mnogovekovoi dramy: Agrarnaia nauka i politika Rossii (XVIII–XX vv.)* (Moscow, 1995), 202–5, 215.

61. Zhores A. Medvedev, *The Rise and Fall of T. D. Lysenko,* trans. I. Michael Lerner (Garden City, N.Y., 1971), 90–91.

62. *Pravda,* April 3, 1935.

63. Ibid., August 7, 1927. Medvedev, in *The Rise and Fall of T. D. Lysenko,* rates these experiments generally successful (11–12); Joravsky, in *The Lysenko Affair,* discusses the *Pravda* article and the failure of winter peas, 58–59; Nikolai Krementsov, in *Stalinist Science* (Princeton, N.J., 1997), 63, notes Lysenko's use of the press.

64. *Pravda,* October 15, 1934.

65. These tales of "orphans" resemble the formula of the prerevolutionary success story, which I describe in *When Russia Learned to Read,* 269–94, but prerevolutionary orphans did not owe their success to the community or the state.

66. *Pravda,* March 16, 1937.

67. Ibid., July 29, 1938.

68. Ibid., July 16, 1936; July 18, 1936.

69. Ibid., September 27, 1929; September 27, 1934; February 28, 1936. *Izvestiia* featured Pavlov more prominently.

70. *Pravda,* September 10, 1934.

71. Ibid., February 2, 1937.

72. Vera Tolz, *Russian Academicians and the Revolution: Combining Professionalism and Politics* (Houndmills, Eng., 1997), 83.

73. *Pravda,* September 10, 1934.

74. Ibid., February 28, 1936.

75. Bailes, *Technology and Society under Lenin and Stalin,* 386–89.

76. John McCannon describes Chkalov's career in *Red Arctic: Polar Exploration and the Myth of the North in the Soviet Union, 1932–1939* (New York, 1998), 68–72, 107–8. Chkalov was also shown kissing Stalin.

77. Stakhanov notes five hundred to six hundred rubles a month as his salary before his feat (*Pravda,* November 15, 1935).

78. *Pravda,* July 25, 1936.

79. Simonov, *Glazami cheloveka moego pokoleniia,* 64.

80. Faked photos were common. See David King, *The Commissar Vanishes: The Falsification of Photographs and Art in Stalin's Russia* (Edinburgh, 1997).

81. McCannon describes Shmidt's career in *Red Arctic,* 33–35, 61–70. See also Loren Graham, who is more positive about Schmidt's standing, in *Science in Russia and the Soviet Union: A Short History* (Cambridge, 1993), 117–18.

82. *Trud,* April 21, 1934.

83. *Pravda,* February 1, 1935.

84. McCannon, *Red Arctic,* 142.

85. *Pravda,* June 30, 1938.

86. John R. Searle discusses this linguistic operation in *The Construction of Social Reality* (New York, 1995), 23–26, 37–39.

87. *Pravda,* August 20, 1936.

88. Ibid., May 24, 37.

89. Ibid., September 27, 1934.

90. Milan Kundera, *The Unbearable Lightness of Being,* trans. Michael Henry Heim (New York, 1984), 253; on overcoming death, see Shlapentokh, "The Fedorovian Roots of Stalinism," 388–404.

91. In my *Pravda* individual sample there were twenty-five obituaries from 1928 through 1930, two in 1931 and 1932, and only eight from 1933 through 1939.

92. *Pravda,* October 12, 1928.

Chapter Five
Literature and the Arts: "An Ode to Stalin"

1. Maksimenkov, *Sumbur vmesto muzyki,* 52.

2. See Boris Starkov, "Trotsky and Ryutin," in *The Trotsky Reappraisal,* ed. Terry Brotherstone and Paul Dukes (Edinburgh, 1992), 78–82; Boris Starkov, "Narkom Ezhov," in *The Stalinist Terror: New Perspectives,* ed. J. Arch Getty and Roberta T. Manning (New York, 1993), 23; Robert Conquest, *Stalin: Breaker of Nations* (New York, 1991), 176–78; and Vadim Rogovin, *Vlast i oppozitsiia* (Moscow, 1993).

3. His note appears in D. L. Babichenko, ed., *Literaturnyi front: Istoriia politicheskoi tsenzury, 1932–1946 gg.* (Moscow, 1994), 13.

4. Quoted in D. L. Babichenko, *Pisateli i tsenzory* (Moscow, 1994), 10–11.

5. Erenburg, *Liudi,* 2:30.

6. Nadezhda Mandelstam, *Hope Abandoned,* trans. Max Hayward (New York, 1974), 419–20.

7. *Pravda,* August 17, 1934; Stalin and Gorky had fallen out at the time. See Viacheslav V. Ivanov, "Why Did Stalin Kill Gorky?" *Russian Studies in Literature* 30, no. 4 (fall 1994): 33.

8. This chapter is based on 1,816 articles about literature and the arts published in *Pravda* during the first four months of 1921, 1924, 1927, 1929, 1930, 1933, 1936, and 1939. Also included were the first two months of 1925 and 1938, the first eight months of 1934, and the days of the writers' conference. The sample was chosen to include periods of continuous coverage. Additional months and years were added to answer specific questions.

9. *Krest'ianskaia gazeta,* usually four pages, gave the congress a full front page on August 15 (with the same photo of Stalin and Gorky that Deni used as the basis for his sketch in *Pravda*) and an undated special edition with the same front page.

10. Quoted in Evgenii Gromov, *Stalin: Vlast' i iskusstvo* (Moscow, 1998), 155. See also A. Kemp-Welch, *Stalin and the Literary Intelligentsia, 1928–39* (New York, 1991), 120–32.

11. *Pravda,* May 6, 1934.

12. The story is "How Robinson Was Created," I. Il'f and E. Petrov, *Sobranie sochinenii* (Moscow, 1961), 3:193–97.

13. The Russian words are *pravil'no* and *pravdivost'.*

14. Blium, *Za kulisami "Ministerstva Pravdy",* 11.

15. *Pravda,* February 10, 1934.

16. Ibid. Notes on participants in the 1934 writers' congress appear in *Pervyi vsesoiuznyi s'ezd sovetskikh pisatelei: Stenograficheskii otchet 1934. Prilozheniia* (Moscow, 1990), 81.

17. Ivanov, "Why Did Stalin Kill Gorky?" 33.

18. *Pravda,* April 22, 1934.

19. Louis Fischer in *The God That Failed,* ed. Richard Crossman (New York, 1949), 205.

20. There is a large literature on socialist realism. I discuss some of it in "Socialist Realism in *Pravda:* Read All About It," *Slavic Review* (winter 1994): 973–91. I disagree with Regine Robin and others who tie socialist realism to the Russian literary tradition. See her *Socialist Realism: An Impossible Aesthetic* (Stanford, 1992).

21. E. Dobrenko notes a conjunction of official and fictional heroes in *Metafora vlasti: Literatura stalinskoi epokhi v istoricheskom osveshchenii* (Munich, 1993), 39–43; as does Stites, *Russian Popular Culture,* 66–72.

22. *Krest'ianskaia gazeta,* August 17, 1934.

23. On this aspect, see Dobrenko, *The Making of the State Reader,* 289–90.

24. *Pravda,* August 18, 1934.

25. During 1936 *Pravda* devoted roughly ten pages per month to the arts, four times the pre-congress coverage.

26. *Pravda*, August 17, 1934. The cartoonists were M. V. Kuprianov, P. N. Krylov, and N. A. Sokolov.

27. The Russian word is *predannost'*.

28. *Pravda*, August 18, 1934.

29. Ibid.

30. Quoted without a citation in Arkady Vaksberg, *Stalin's Prosecutor: The Life of Andrei Vyshinsky*, trans. Jan Butler (New York, 1991), 201.

31. *Pravda*, September 4, 1934.

32. Joravsky, *Russian Psychology*, 329–30. Graham in *Science in Russia and the Soviet Union*, 162, makes a similar point about Stalin's view of engineers.

33. Cited in Bailes, *Technology and Society*, 117–18.

34. Hiroaki Kuromiya, "Stalinist Terror in the Donbas: A Note," in *Stalinist Terror: New Perspectives*, ed. J. Arch Getty and Roberta T. Manning(Cambridge, 1993), 217.

35. *Pravda*, February 2, 1931; November 22, 1932. In mid-1935 these were replaced by "Cadres decide all" (*Pravda*, May 6, 1935).

36. The Russian words are *master* and *podmaster'e*.

37. Erenburg, *Liudi*, 2:32–38.

38. I disagree with Boris Groys and others who see a confluence. See his *The Total Art of Stalinism: Avant-Garde, Aesthetic Dictatorship, and Beyond*, trans. Charles Rougle (Princeton, N.J., 1992).

39. Abram Tertz (Andrei Sinyavsky) notes the importance of the final objective or purpose (*tsel'*) and the path (*put'*) in "Chto takoe sotsialisticheskii realizm," in his *Fantasticheskii mir Abrama Tertsa* (New York, 1967), 409–14.

40. The Russian words are *zadacha* and *zadanie*.

41. Metaphors of art as construction occur in articles that filled more than half the space given to the arts in the first four months of 1930 and 1933.

42. *Pravda*, January 29, 1929.

43. Ibid., April 13, 1933.

44. Gromov chronicles his interventions in *Stalin: Vlast' i iskusstvo*.

45. *Pravda*, April 15, 1930.

46. Ibid., February 6, 1927.

47. Roxburgh, *Pravda*, 29; he cites A. Gayev, "Kak delaetsyia 'Pravda,'" *Ost-Probleme*, no. 37 (1953): 1567f.

48. *Pravda*, August 17, 1934.

49. Participants writing in languages other than Russian constituted 48 percent of the delegates, but Russians made longer speeches. See *Pervyi vsesoiuznyi s'ezd*, appendix.

50. This was much less than their proportion at the congress by nationality (65 percent) but probably equivalent to their importance as calculated by length of speeches. See *Pervyi vsesoiuznyi s'ezd*, appendix. *Izvestiia* gave the congress less front-page space than *Pravda*, but its coverage was also extensive.

51. *Pravda*, August 20, 1934.

52. Simon, *Nationalism*, 138–45; Liber, *Soviet Nationality Policy*, 2–3, 34–37, 45, 107–8.

53. *Pravda*, August 21, 1934.

54. *Krest'ianskaia gazeta*, August 17, 1934.

55. *Trud*, August 17, 1934.

56. *Pravda,* August 25, 1934.

57. Ibid., August 18, 1934.

58. Ehrenburg, *Liudi,* 2:32.

59. *Pravda,* August 27, 1934.

60. On Stalin's literary image, see Agursky, "Nietzschean Roots of Stalinist Culture," 280.

61. *Pravda,* August 24, 1934.

62. Babichenko, *Literaturnyi front,* 11.

63. The painting is reproduced in A. I. Morozov, *Konets utopii: Iz Istorii iskusstva v SSSR 1930-x godov* (Moscow, 1995), 24–25.

64. *Pravda* August 16, 1934.

65. Ibid., August 17, 1934.

66. Ibid., August 26, 1934.

67. Nadezhda Mandelstam, *Hope against Hope: A Memoir,* trans. Max Haywood (New York, 1970), 203. The ode has been read variously. See the review by James L. Rice, *Slavic Review* 57, no. 2 (summer 1998): 481–82.

68. *Pravda,* March 19, 1930.

69. Tucker, *Stalin in Power,* 278–79.

70. *Pravda,* March 14, 1936.

71. Ibid., March 23, 1936.

72. Ibid., January 8, 1938.

73. See Marcus C. Levitt, *Russian Literary Politics and the Pushkin Celebration of 1880* (Ithaca, N.Y., 1989).

74. *Pravda,* February 11, 1938.

75. Ibid., February 16, 1939.

76. Ibid., March 28, 1939.

77. Jeffrey Brooks, "Popular Philistinism and the Course of Russian Modernism," in *Literature and History,* ed. Gary Saul Morson (Stanford, 1986), 90–110, 308–10.

78. *Pravda,* February 27, 1938.

79. Ibid., January 26, 1929.

80. See ibid., January 4, 1936.

81. Brooks, "Russian Nationalism and Russian Literature," 315–334.

82. *Pravda,* March 24, 1936; April 8, 1936. Peter Kenez, *Cinema and Soviet Society: 1917–1953* (Cambridge, 1992), 145.

83. *Pravda,* February 10, 1939.

84. Kenez, *Cinema and Soviet Society,* 147–48.

85. *Pravda,* January 12, 1939.

86. Ibid., January 8, 1938.

87. Sheila Fitzpatrick, in *The Cultural Front: Power and Culture in Revolutionary Russia* (Ithaca, N.Y., 1992), 207, suggests that modern Western music was not publicly performed after the articles appeared.

88. *Pravda,* January 28, 1936; February 6, 1936.

89. D. D. Shostakovich, *Testimony: The Memoirs of Dmitrii Shostakovich as Related to and Edited by Solomon Volkov,* ed. Solomon Volkov, trans. Antonina W. Bouis (New York, 1979), 113. The book's authenticity, once questioned, is now largely accepted.

90. On antiformalism in art, see Matthew Cullerne Bown, *Socialist Realist Painting* (New Haven, 1998), 189.

91. *Pravda,* January 28, 1938.

92. Maksimenkov, *Sumbur vmesto muzyki,* 211.

93. Shostakovich, *Testimony,* 271.

94. There were critical attacks in *Pravda* and reports on meetings of architects (February 22, 1936; February 26, 1936), film workers (February 27, 1936; March 6, 1936), and artists and children's illustrators (March 1, 1936).

95. *Pravda,* March 6, 1936.

96. Ibid., February 27, 1936.

97. Ibid., March 11, 1936; Maksimenkov, *Sumbur vmesto muzyki,* 158–96.

98. *Pravda,* March 15, 1936.

99. Ibid., March 16, 1936.

100. Elliott Mossman, ed., *The Correspondence of Boris Pasternak and Olga Freidenberg, 1910–1954,* trans. Elliott Mossman and Margaret Wettlin (London, 1982), 158–59.

101. Ibid., 158.

102. Ibid., 162.

103. In a conversation with Platonov, quoted in M. Heller, "Les Annees Trente," in *Histoire de la Littérature russe. Le xxe siècle: Gels et dégels,* ed. E. Etkind, G. Nivat, I. Serman, and V. Strada (Paris, 1990), 143.

104. T. J. Clark, *The Painting of Modern Life: Paris in the Art of Manet and His Followers* (Princeton, N.J., 1984), 184–85.

105. Quoted in Dmitry and Vladimir Shlapentokh, *Soviet Cinematography: Ideological Conflict and Social Reality* (New York, 1993), 29; the citation is from *Sovetskaia kul'tura,* June 4, 1988.

106. Babichenko, *Pisateli i tsenzory,* 11.

107. Ibid., 12.

108. The phrase is Pierre Bourdieu's in *Language and Symbolic Power* (Cambridge, Mass., 1991), 239.

109. Quoted in E. Pasternak, *Boris Pasternak. Materialy dlia biografii* (Moscow, 1989), 511.

110. Frank Kermode, *The Art of Telling: Essays on Fiction* (Cambridge, Mass., 1983), 169.

111. The phrase is Pasternak's from an April 29, 1939, letter to his parents about *Hamlet;* quoted in Pasternak, *Boris Pasternak,* 540.

112. *Pravda,* June 10, 1934; January 18, 1936; March 5, 1939.

113. See Seveltana Boym, *Death in Quotation Marks: The Cultural Myth of the Modern Poet* (Cambridge, Mass., 1991); on Voloshin, see Barbara Walker, "Maximilian Voloshin's 'House of the Poet': Intelligentsia Social Organization and Culture in Early 20th-Century Russia," Ph.D. diss., University of Michigan, 1994; on Mandelstam, see Gregory Freidin, *A Coat of Many Colors: Osip Mandelstam and his Mythologies of Self-Presentation* (Berkeley, 1987); on Pushkin, see Catherine Theimer Nepomnyashchy's introduction to Avram Tertz's (Andrei Sinyavsky), *Strolls with Pushkin* (New Haven, 1993), trans. Catherine Theimer Nepomnyashchy and Slava I. Yastremski; see also her introduction to *Russian Studies in Literature* (winter 1991–92).

114. Marietta Chudakova, in "Pasternak i Bulgakov: rubezh dvukh literaturnykh tsiklov," in *Literaturnaia obozrenie* 5 (1991): 11–17, notes Bulgakov's and Pasternak's preoccupation with Stalin. The article appears in English in *Russian Studies in Literature* (winter 1995–96): 83–102.

115. Vitaly Shentalinsky, *The KGB's Literary Archive,* trans. John Crowfoot (London, 1993), 184. He attributes this version to Nadezhda Mandelstam without a citation. The word also appears in a police report on Andrei Platonov from the 1930s, given by Shitalinsky: "He is popular among writers and considered a master" (210).

116. Translated by Bernard Meares, in *Twentieth-Century Russian Poetry,* selected and introduced by Evgeny Yevtushenko, ed. Albert C. Todd and Max Heyward (with Daniel Weissbort) (New York, 1993), 107.

117. Anna Akhmatova, "Requiem," trans. Daniel Weissbort, in *Twentieth-Century Russian Poetry,* ed. John Glad and Daniel Weissbort (Iowa City, 1992), 90.

118. Akhmatova, "Requiem," 92–94.

119. Boris Pasternak, *Doctor Zhivago,* trans. Max Hayward and Manya Harari (New York, 1991 [1958]), 559.

Chapter Six
Honor and Dishonor

1. There is a large literature on honor. I have drawn on Margalit, *The Decent Society,* who uses the concept of "social honor"; Frank Henderson Stewart, *Honor* (Chicago, 1994); and William Ian Miller, *Humiliation and Other Essays on Honor, Social Discomfort, and Violence* (Ithaca, N.Y., 1993).

2. Honor's importance in Russia before 1917 is evident from the place-system (*mestnichestvo*), the table of ranks, civic punishment (*grazhdanskaia kazn'*), and use of the word itself (*chest'*). Such group honor can be lost and there are rules for maintaining it, but it can rarely be won. See Steward, *Honor,* 145–46; Bruno Lefebvre, "L'argent et le secret: Dégredations et recompositions," in *L'Honneur: Image de soi ou don de soi un idéal équivoque,* ed. Marie Gautheron (Paris, 1991), 142–67.

3. Vladimir Dal', *Tolkovyi slovar' zhivogo velikorusskogo iazyka* (Moscow, 1978–80 [1880–82]); Akademiia Nauk SSR, Institut Russkogo Iazyka, *Slovar' russkogo iazyka* (Moscow, 1961); and *Bol'shoi anglo-russkii slovar' v dvukh tomakh* (Moscow, 1977).

4. The Russian is *orden.* See, for example, *Pravda,* August 6, 1938.

5. The term for the last is *znak pocheta.*

6. A designation of rank in the arts was "*Pochetnoe zvanie zasluzhennogo deiatelia iskusstva,*" *Pravda,* August 26, 1928. In mid-1939 officials of the writers' union sent a list to A. A. Andreev, a member of the Politburo, who consulted with Beria, minister of internal affairs, and sent it on to Stalin himself (Babichenko, *Literaturnyi front,* 38–40).

7. *Pravda,* May 14, 1935. The word for holders of orders, *ordenonosets,* does not appear in Vladimir Dal', *Tolkovyi slovar' zhivogo velikorusskogo iazyka* (Moscow, 1881).

8. See, for example, awardees from the Red Army (*Pravda,* August 17, 1936), awards to theater personnel (ibid., June 3, 1937), and awards to Ukrainian farmers (ibid., February 10, 1939).

9. Roy A. Medvedev, *Nikolai Bukharin: The Last Years,* trans. A.D.P. Briggs (New York, 1980), 102.

10. Tucker, *Stalin in Power,* 323.

11. *Stalin's Letters to Molotov, 1925–1936,* 219. The letter is from September, 28, 1930. I use this translation except for *chestno,* which I translate as honorably, as I believe it is closer to the original. The original is in Kosheleva, Lel'chuck, and Naumov et al., *Pis'ma I. V. Stalina V. M. Molotovu,* 225.

12. *Pravda,* September 6, 1934; February 24, 1933. Stewart describes the tendency to associate honor with moral qualities in nineteenth-century Europe in *Honor,* 46–48. The Russian words are *chest'* and *pochet.*

13. Stewart, in *Honor,* 55, notes that *fama* is not personal honor because the rules for losing it are unclear.

14. *Pravda,* January 25, 1935. The Russian is *pochet.*

15. Mandelstam, *Hope against Hope,* 311.

16. *Pravda,* October 24, 39. The Russian phrases are *znatnye liudi* and *doverennye litsa.* See also ibid., April 15, 1934; July 7, 1938. Tucker, *Stalin in Power,* 321–22.

17. The painting is reproduced in Hubertus Gassner and Evgeniia Petrova, eds., *Agitatsiia za schast'e: Sovetskoe iskusstvo stalinskoi epokhi* (Dusseldorf-Bremen, 1994), 111.

18. The poster is reproduced in A. Fedotova, *Zhivopis' pervoi piatiletki. Khudozhnik i vremia* (Leningrad, 1981), unnumbered page.

19. "Iz dnevnikov Ol'gi Berggol'ts," *Neva,* no. 5 (1990): 174. The Russian word is *chest'.*

20. Richard Pipes, *The Russian Revolution* (New York, 1990), 790–91.

21. On anti-Semitism in popular culture, see Brooks, *When Russia Learned to Read,* 231–33; in antireligious campaigns in 1921, see Orlando Figes, *A People's Tragedy: The Russian Revolution, 1917–1924* (London, 1996), 749–50; on Stalin's and Soviet anti-Semitism in general, see Arcady Vaksberg, *Stalin against the Jews,* trans. Antonina W. Bouis (New York, 1994); and G. Kostyrchenko, *V plenu u krasnogo faraona* (Moscow, 1994). Kamenev was half-Jewish but was considered a Jew, according to Agursky, *The Third Rome,* 320.

22. Pierre Pascal, *Mon état d'âme. Mon journal de Russie,* Vol. 3: 1922–26 (Lausanne, 1982), 187.

23. Agursky, *The Third Rome,* 305–9, 320–21.

24. Vadim Rogovin, *1937* (Moscow, 1996), 154–59.

25. The 1931 poster of unknown authorship is reproduced T. V. Izmailova, ed., *Stalin s nami?* (Moscow, 1991), portfolio of unnumbered pages.

26. Mary Douglas, *Purity and Danger: An Analysis of the Concepts of Pollution and Taboo* (London, 1994 [1966]), 105.

27. *Pravda,* August 1, 1928.

28. Quoted in Stephen Kotkin, "Peopling Magnitostroi: The Politics of Demography," in *The Social Dimensions of Soviet Industrialization,* William G. Rosenberg and Lewis H. Siegelbaum, eds. (Bloomington, Ind., 1933), 86. He cites *Magnitogorskii rabochii,* February 17, 1933.

29. Medvedev, *Let History Judge,* 245–48.

30. Stalin, *Works,* 10:306.

31. Ibid., 11:180; *Pravda,* July 14, 1928.

32. Stalin, *Works,* 12:173; *Pravda,* December 29, 1929; L. Kosheleva, Lel'chuk, and Naumov et al., *Pis'ma I. V. Stalina V. M. Molotovu,* 141–43.

33. In 1921–26, enemies were named in 71 of 171 (42 percent) of *Pravda'*s editorials; in 1927, 18 of 30 (60 percent); in 1928–32, 89 of 169 (53 percent); and in 1933–39, 143 of 250 (57 percent). In 1921–26, enemies were identified with hostile projects in 43 of 141 of *Pravda'*s editorials (30 percent); in 1927, 14 of 30 (47 percent); in 1928–32, 59 of 169 (35 percent); and in 1933–39, 108 of 250 (43 percent).

34. The holidays are January 1, International Women's Day, Press Day, May Day, and the anniversary of the October Revolution.

35. T. M. Goriava, ed., *Istoriia sovetskoi politicheskoi tsenzury. Dokumenty i komentarii* (Moscow, 1997), 285.

36. Goriava, *Istoriia sovetskoi politicheskoi tsenzury,* 285.

37. Joravsky, in *Soviet Marxism and Natural Science,* 233, suggests that the great break in science lasted from mid-1929 to early 1932; Bailes, in *Technology and Society,* 69–85, notes *Pravda*'s prominence in promoting the Shakhty trial; the importance of the press in this affair is detailed in Aleksey E. Levin, "Expedient Catastrophe: A Reconsideration of the 1929 Crisis at the Soviet Academy of Science," *Slavic Review* 2 (1988): 261–79.

38. *Pravda,* May 9, 1928.

39. Shitts, *Dnevnik,* 40. On this, see also Bailes, *Technology and Society,* 79–80.

40. On Stalin's views, see Kosheleva, Lel'chuk, and Naumovet al., *Pis'ma I. V. Stalina V. M. Molotovu,* 181–232.

41. Ibid., 216–18.

42. *Pravda,* November 26, 1930.

43. On this, see also Shitts, *Dnevnik,* 29.

44. Cited in Dmitry Shlapentokh, "Popular Support for the Soviet Political Trials of the late 1920s and the Origins of the Great Purges," in *State-Organized Terror: The Case of Violent Internal Repression,* ed. P. Timothy Bushnell, Vladimir Shlapentokh, Christopher K. Vanderpool, and Jeyaratnam Sundram (Boulder, Colo., 1991), 270.

45. *Pravda,* July 6, 1928.

46. Ibid. The Russian term is *obshchestvennaia rabota.*

47. Conquest, *Harvest of Sorrow,* 184; on the confusion as to whose property was being protected, that of the state or the collective farm, see Fitzpatrick, *Stalin's Peasants,* 73, 178.

48. *Pravda,* August 9, 1932.

49. Lynne Viola describes gleaning and pilfering immediately after collectivization in *Peasant Rebels: Collectivization and the Culture of Peasant Resistance* (New York, 1996), 221–26.

50. The merging of images of kulaks and clergy is noted in Glennys Young, *Power and the Sacred in Revolutionary Russia: Religious Activists in the Village* (University Park, Pa., 1997), 263–71.

51. Mary Douglas identifies fear of contagion of the social order as "the final paradox of the search for purity" in her *Purity and Danger,* 163.

52. These are the translations in *The Oxford Russian-English Dictionary* (Oxford, 1984). The term was used in editorials in *Pravda* on January 25, 1935; June 16, 1935; October 4, 1937; December 16, 1937; and many other occasions.

53. *Pravda,* May 8, 1928.

54. Ibid.

55. See editorial in *Pravda,* December 17, 1930; see also articles in *Krest'ianskaia gazeta,* May 11, 1931.

56. *Pravda,* August 7, 1930.

57. The writer is Anatolii Sysoev, who is quoted in Zakhar Dicharov, ed., *Raspiatye pisateli—zhertvy politicheskikh repressii,* vol. 1 (St. Petersburg, 1993), 8–9.

58. *Komsomol'skaia pravda,* June 26, 1930.

59. *Pravda,* March 8, 1930.

60. *Trud,* November 7, 1930.

61. Ibid., January 16, 1935.

62. On the relationship between the persecutions and purges, see Robert T. Manning, "The Soviet Economic Crisis of 1936–1940 and the Great Purges," in *Stalinist Terror: New Perspectives,* ed. J. Arch. Getty and Roberta T. Manning, 116–41; Vadim Rogovin, *Vlast' i oppozitsii* (Moscow, 1993); and *Stalinskii neonep* (Moscow, 1994).

63. Ivanov, "Why Did Stalin Kill Gorky?" 35; and L. Spiridonova, *M. Gor'kii: Dialog s istoriei* (Moscow, 1994), 284–96. On Kirov, see Dmitri Volkogonov, *Stalin: Triumph and Tragedy* (Rocklin, Calif., 1992), 207–9.

64. On scapegoats, see René Girard, *The Scapegoat,* trans. Yvonne Freccero (Baltimore, 1986).

65. On the stabilizing feature of rituals of sacrifice, see René Girard, *Violence and the Sacred,* trans. Patrick Gregory (Baltimore, 1970), 284.

66. *Pravda,* December 2, 1934.

67. Ibid., December 4, 1934.

68. Ibid., December 7, 34. *Trud, Komsomol'skaia pravda,* and even Bukharin's *Izvestiia* did not immediately emphasize vengeance as did *Pravda,* but they printed the same speeches and announcements. Initially they stressed grief. "Good-bye, our Kirov; you will be with us in the struggle," read the legend on the cover of *Komsomol'skaia pravda* on December 6. Medvedev, in *Nikolai Bukharin,* 96–98, notes that Bukharin followed Stalin's views in his editorial, but he did not print diatribes from "the masses" that appeared in other newspapers.

69. *Pravda,* January 16, 1935.

70. Ibid., December 22–23, 1934; January 17, 1935; and *Trud,* December 22, 1934.

71. *Pravda,* December 24, 1934.

72. For earlier medical charges, see *Pravda,* June 8, 1938.

73. Robert Conquest, *The Great Terror: A Reassessment* (New York, 1990), 375–90; Kostyrchenko, *V plenu u krasnogo faraona,* 324–26.

74. Peter Holland, in "Maid, Man, and Jew," in *The New York Review of Books,* June 12, 1997, 51, notes that Jewish men were accused of breast-feeding in early modern Europe.

75. *Pravda,* June 15, 1937.

76. Saul Friedlander, *Nazi Germany and the Jews,* Vol. 1: *The Years of Persecution, 1933–1939* (New York, 1997).

77. *Pravda,* September 14, 1938.

78. Ibid., January 24, 1937.

79. *Trud,* January 18, 1935; the remark literally is "get the bad weed out of the field" (*Khuduiu travu s polia von!*).

80. *Pravda,* August 24, 1936.

81. Ibid., January 30, 1937.

82. *Pravda* devoted five of its six pages on December 12, 1934 to this topic; ibid., January 3, 1935.

83. Ibid., January 30, 1937.

84. Ibid., January 31, 1937.

85. Davies, *Popular Opinion,* 87.

86. *Pravda,* January 31, 1937.

87. Ibid., August 17, 1936.

88. Ibid., August 21, 1936.

89. The available data are summarized in Vadim Rogovin, *Partiia rasstreliannykh* (Moscow, 1997), 479–89.

90. Aleksandr I. Solzhenitsyn, Roy Medvedev, and Robert Conquest brought the scale of atrocities to light. Conquest, in "Excess Deaths and Camp Numbers: Some Comments," *Soviet Studies* 43, no. 5 (1991): 949–52, posits a high figure; see also his *The Great Terror,* 484–69. The authors of *Le Livre noir du communisme. Crimes, terreur, et répression,* ed. Stéphane Courtois and Remi Kauffer (Paris, 1997), support a higher figure. Alec Nove, in "Terror Victims: Is the Evidence Complete?" *Europe-Asia Studies* 46, no. 3 (1994): 535–37, suggests a low one, citing documents that 4,060,306 were condemned by the Cheka and its successors in 1921–53 and, of these, 799,455 were shot (681,692 in 1937–38).

91. See the previous note.

92. Rogovin, *Partiia rasstreliannykh,* 481.

93. Veronique Garros, Natalia Korenevskaya, and Thomas Lahusen, eds., *Intimacy and Terror: Soviet Diaries of the 1930s* (New York, 1995), 139.

94. Stalin, *Works,* 12:277.

95. Ibid., 13:67.

96. *Pravda,* March 7, 1930; May 17, 1932.

97. Ibid., November 16, 1930.

98. Ibid., December 17, 1929.

99. The Russian is *Sovetskaia obshchestvennost'*. There is no easy translation. The 1958 Academy of Science dictionary defined *obshchestvennost'* as "the advanced part, the advanced portion of society," *Slovar' russkogo iazyka,* 2nd ed. (Moscow, 1958), 2:576. A. V. Golubev, in "Zapad glazami sovetskogo obshchestva (osnovnye tendentsii formirovaniia vneshne politicheskikh stereotipov v 30-x godax)," *Otechestvennaia istoriia,* no. 1 (January–February 1996): 116, defines it as the intelligentsia, lower party functionaries, and the *aktiv.* On earlier uses of *obshchestvo,* see Edith W. Clowes, Samuel D. Kassow, and James L. West, "Introduction: The Problem of the Middle in Late Imperial Russian Society," in *Between Tsar and People: Educated Society and the Quest for Public Identity in Late Imperial Russia,* ed. Clowes, Kassow, and West (Princeton, N.J., 1991), 3–9.

100. *Pravda,* February 18, 1928.

101. Ibid., July 23, 1931.

102. The phrase was sometimes replaced by "Party responsibility" (*partiinoi otvetstvennosti*) (ibid., July 31, 1932).

103. Based on my editorial sample, *Pravda*'s editorialists used *we* in 82 percent of editorials in 1918; 75 percent in 1919; 64 percent in 1920; 53 percent in1921; 61 percent in 1922; 67 percent in 1923; 72 percent in 1924; 59 percent in 1925; 60 percent in 1926; 47 percent in 1927; 70 percent in 1928; 84 percent in 1929; 67 percent in 1930; 50 percent in 1931; 53 percent in 1932; 60 percent in 1933; 58 percent in 1934; 67 percent in 1935; 31 percent in 1936; 54 percent in 1937; 41 percent in 1938; 31 percent in 1939; and 6 percent in 1940.

104. The Russian is *zveno;* see *Pravda*'s editorial, May 9, 1929. The commanding tone can be gauged by headers with imperative verbs or words such as task (*zadacha*). Only 3 percent of articles in a random sample of 252 in 1924–27 had commands in head-

ers compared to 12 percent of 338 articles in 1928–32. The difference in editorials was sharper—4 percent of 116 editorials in 1924–27 compared to 43 percent in 1928–32.

105. The words are roughly the same as Stalin's, "U nas ne dolzhna kruzhit'sia golova" (*Pravda*, September 19, 1929). Stalin's speech was on March 2, 1930.

106. *Pravda*, February 24, 1929.

107. Ibid., February 20, 1930.

108. Ibid., March 9, 1929.

109. Nearly half the 124 interactive articles in my random sample from this period are critical comments on shortcomings.

110. *Pravda*, February 24, 1931.

111. *Izvestiia*, December 3, 1936.

112. Unsigned entry in *Biulleten' oppozitsii*, no. 50 (May 1936): 3.

113. See note 103. The same downward trend is apparent in the newspaper as a whole. In a random sample of domestic articles in two issues per year, *we* was used in 90 of 338 (27 percent) in 1928–32, and in 71 of 479 (15 percent) in 1933–39. Maksimenkov notes a similar usage of *we* in the mid-1930s in *Sumbur vmesto muzyki*, 125.

114. *Pravda*, January 1, 1933.

115. Ibid., November 7, 1934.

116. Ibid., June 21, 1934.

117. *Izvestiia*, December 5, 1936.

118. *Pravda*, March 26, 1937.

119. Chukovskii, *Dnevnik*, 113. The Russian word is *nash*.

120. *Pravda*, January 9, 1936.

121. Ibid.

122. Ibid., February 10, 1937; April 3, 1935.

123. *Izvestiia*, December 21, 1939.

124. O. V. Kalintseva, *Nashi: Semeinaia khronika (1886–1986)* (Sverdlovsk, 1992), 5.

125. Davies, *Popular Opinion*, 128.

126. Sylvia R. Margulies, *The Pilgrimage to Russia: The Soviet Union and the Treatment of Foreigners, 1924–1937* (Madison, Wis., 1968); Stephen Koch, *Double Lives: Spies and Writers in the Secret Soviet War of Ideas against the West* (New York, 1994).

127. *Pravda*, January 29, 1936.

128. Ibid.

129. Ibid., June 30, 1935; July 5, 1935.

130. The letter to Esther Marchard is quoted in Bernard Duchatelet, ed., *Cahiers Romain Rolland. Voyage à Moscou (juin–juillet 1935)* (Paris, 1992), 63. He intervened with Stalin for Victor Serge. Serge later censured Rolland for not condemning the purge trials (Victor Serge, *Memoirs of a Revolutionary, 1901–1941*, trans. Peter Sedgwick (London, 1963), 316–20, 333–34).

131. See Rolland's journal of his 1935 trip and his correspondence following his return in his *Voyage à Moscou*, particularly 140, 173–75 (about Victor Serge), 289–90, 307–24.

132. Stephen Spender, in *The God That Failed*, ed. Richard Crossman (New York, 1949), 272.

133. Gide, *Return from the USSR*, xiv.

134. In 1934–39, only 10 of 214 (5 percent) of *Pravda*'s editorials concerned foreign affairs; in 1940, only 2 of 36 (6 percent).

135. Cited from *Vsesoiuznaia perepis' 1930 goda* by A. V. Golubev, in "Zapad glazami sovetskogo obshchestva (osnovnye tendentsii formirovaniia vneshne politicheskikh stereotipov v 30-x godov," *Otechestvennaia istoriia,* no. 1 (January–February 1996): 120.

136. Golubev, "Zapad glazami sovetskogo obshchestva, 112.

137. Ibid.

138. Khrushchev, *Khrushchev Remembers,* 126.

139. *Pravda,* November 7, 1934.

140. Ibid., March 8, 1933.

141. *Izvestiia,* December 5, 1936.

142. The poster by N. M. Kochergin is reproduced in *Dorogi iunosti* (Moscow, 1968), 137. The picture, a diagram purporting to show "the numbers of fascist military organizations" in different countries, showed the largest concentration in the United States, then Italy, followed by Poland, and finally Nazi Germany.

143. Quoted in Golubev, "Zapad glazami sovetskogo obshchestva," 113.

144. François Furet, *Le Passé d'une illusion: Essai sur l'idée communiste au xxe siècle* (Paris, 1995), 280.

145. *Izvestiia,* December 5, 1936.

146. Boris Efimov, "Vernost' prizvaniiu," in *Bol' i pamiat'* (Moscow, 1993), 29.

147. Vaksberg, *Stalin against the Jews,* 89.

148. *Pravda,* August 3, 1936.

149. Ibid., August 16, 1936.

150. Ibid., August 23, 1936.

151. Furet, in *Le Passé d'une illusion,* presents Soviet Communism and fascism as mutually dependent.

152. *Pravda,* July 9, 1937. The Russian word, *Bogatyr',* is the caption of the lead editorial (ibid., July 15, 1937).

153. Quoted in Anthony Read and David Fisher, *The Deadly Embrace: Hitler, Stalin, and the Nazi-Soviet Pact of 1939–1941* (New York, 1988), 237.

154. *Pravda,* September 3, 1939.

155. Ibid., September 5, 1939.

156. Ibid., August 3, 1940.

157. The document appears in Goriava, *Istoriia sovetskoi politcheskoi tsenzury,* 319–20.

158. *Pravda,* November 18, 1940.

159. Gennadi Kostyrchenko, *Out of the Red Shadows: Anti-Semitism in Stalin's Russia* (Amherst, N.Y., 1995), 289 n. 114.

160. Read and Fisher, *The Deadly Embrace,* 252.

161. N. Khrushchev, *The Glasnost' Tapes,* trans. and ed. Jerrold L. Schecter, with Vyacheslav V. Luchkov (Boston, 1990), 48.

162. Garros, Korenevskaya, and Lahusen, *Intimacy and Terror,* 371–72; police reports indicate that such reactions were typical.

163. Davies, *Popular Opinion,* 98.

164. Sakharov, *Memoirs,* 39.

165. G. Patrick March, *Eastern Destiny: Russia in Asia and the North Pacific* (West-

port, Conn., 1996), 216–17; on Russian losses, see Roger R. Reese, *Stalin's Reluctant Soldiers: A Social History of the Red Army, 1925–1941* (Lawrence, Kans., 1996), 169–70.

166. *Pravda,* August 28, 1938.

167. The first instance I found was in *Trud,* October 26, 1938. See also *Komsomol'skaia pravda,* August 6, 1939; *Pravda,* April 16, 1939; and an article by Alexei Tolstoi in *Pravda,* December 25, 1939.

168. Losses were 1,139 killed and 2,383 wounded. See Reese, *Stalin's Reluctant Soldiers,* 170.

169. *Pravda,* December 2, 1940.

170. Ibid., March 13, 1940.

171. Reese, *Stalin's Reluctant Soldiers,* 171.

172. *Pravda,* July 31, 1940.

173. Michael Parrish, *The Lesser Terror: Soviet State Security, 1939–1953* (Westport, Conn., 1996), 53–109.

174. Figures on deportations are from Bohdan Mahaylo and Victor Swoboda, *Soviet Disunion: A History of the Nationalities Problem in the USSR* (New York, 1990), 88–89; and Read and Fisher, *The Deadly Embrace,* 469. The number of Balts rounded up in June 1941 came to 25,711, according to Courtois and Kauffer, in *Le Livre noir,* 236.

175. Courtois and Kauffer, *Le Livre noir,* 237.

176. The issue was raised in Viktor Suvorov, *Ledokol; Den' "M"* (Moscow, 1994 [1989]). The dispute is summarized in Iu. N. Afanas'ev, ed., *Drugaia voina, 1939–1945* (Moscow, 1996); and in *Russian Studies in History,* 36:2 (fall 1997), and 36:3 (winter 1997–98). See also V. A. Nevezhin, *Sindrom nastupatel'noi voinyi* (Moscow, 1997). Alexander Werth, in *Russia at War, 1941–1945,* 121–27, suggested that Stalin may have intended to attack Germany in 1942.

177. No transcript of the speech has appeared; V. A. Nevezhin, "Rech Stalina 5 maia 1941 goda i apologiia nastupatel'noi voiny," in Afanas'ev, *Drugaia voina,* 106–31; reprinted from *Otechestvennaia istoriia,* no. 2 (1995).

178. Nevezhin, "Rech Stalina," 110; the author is Vs. Vishnevskii.

179. Nevezhin, in *Sindrom,* 186–251, describes directives to the press and cites a note of A. S. Shcherbakov indicating that newspapers, particularly *Izvestiia* and *Pravda,* should not openly promote military alertness.

Chapter Seven
Many Wars, One Victory

1. David Ortenberg, *Iiun'–dekabr' sorok pervogo: Rasskaz-khronika* (Moscow, 1986), 11; Stalin made the appellation official with his order as commander on November 7, 1944. The war was also called the "war of liberation" by Stalin and others (*Pravda,* May 1, 1942; November 8, 1943).

2. Ortenberg, *Iiun'–dekabr',* 10–11; Suvorov, in *Ledokol; Den' "M",* 6, suggests that Stalin ordered Lebedev-Kumach to write the poem in February 1941 as part of preparations for an attack on Germany. He may have adapted a WWI song.

3. Ortenberg, *Iiun'–dekabr',* 10–11.

4. Ibid., 9.

5. *Pravda,* August 11–12, 1941.

6. *Krasnaia zvezda,* April 24, 1943.

7. Alexander Werth, *Moscow War Diary* (New York, 1942), 102. In his *Russia at War, 1941–1945* (New York, 1964), 741–42, he takes a different view and cites a tension between "Holy Russia" and the Soviet Union.

8. On Soviet superiority in wartime production, see Richard Overy, *Why the Allies Won* (New York, 1995), 208–44, and tables on 331–32.

9. See also Dmitrii Volkogonov, *Triumf i tragediia. I. V. Stalin,* book 2, part 1 (Moscow, 1989), 158–62.

10. *Pravda,* July 3, 1941.

11. Georgii Zhukov, "Velikii podvig naroda," in M. I. Stepichev et al., eds., *Zhivaia pamiat'. Velikaia Otechestvennaia pravda o voine. V trekh tomakh* (Moscow, 1995), 3:472 (editors of vol. 3: Igor Grebtsov and Viktor Khokhlov).

12. Erenburg, *Liudi,* 2:233.

13. According to the chronology in *Kto byl kto v Velikoi Otechestvennoi voine, 1941–1945* (Moscow, 1995), Soviet troops left Minsk on June 28.

14. *Pravda,* July 4, 1941.

15. V. D. Danilov, "Stalinskaia Strategiia nachala voiny: Plany i real'nost'," in Afanas'ev, *Drugaia voina, 1939–1945,* 149.

16. Iurii Razliv, *Dnevniki, pis'ma, stikhotvoreniia, 1936–1942,* ed. Evgenii Starshinov (Iaroslavl, 1988), 131.

17. *Pravda,* August 26, 1941.

18. M. A. Gareev, "Faktory, opredelivshie voennye poteri v Velikoi Otechestvennoi voine," in *Liudskie poteri SSSR v period vtoroi mirovoi voiny. Sbornik statei,* ed. N. A. Aralovets, O. M. Verbitskaia, V. B. Zhiromskaia, Iu. A. Poliakov, and A. I. Repinetskii (St. Petersburg, 1995), 14.

19. Volkogonov, *Triumf i tragediia,* 208. Werth argues in *Russia at War,* 207, that Stalin may have been right since the battle for the city delayed the German assault on Moscow; *Krasnaia zvezda,* September 22, 1941; Ortenberg, *Iiun'–dekabr',* 176.

20. David Ortenberg, *Stalin, Shcherbakov, Mekhlis i drugie* (Moscow, 1995), 60–61. Ehrenburg eventually wrote about Kiev, and a month later, on November 14, 1941, wrote in *Krasnaia zvezda* of several captured cities.

21. Mossman, *The Correspondence of Boris Pasternak and Olga Freidenberg,* 203.

22. Vladimir Nikolaev, "Voina nastupaet na iunost'," in Stepichev et al., *Zhivaia pamiat',* 1:63 (editors of vol. 1: Semen Borzunov and Vladimir Smolin).

23. Ibid., 65.

24. Vadunur Baskakov, "Opolchentsy," in Stepichev et al., *Zhivaia pamiat',* 1:138.

25. Aleksandr Rubashkin notes this in *Il'ia Erenburg: Put' pisatelia* (Moscow, 1990), 314–15. On Leningrad, see *Pravda,* September 30, 1941. *Pravda* cited air battles near Moscow on October 6, 1941 and again on the ninth. The first mention of a battle for the city was October 15, 1941.

26. Ortenberg, *Stalin, Shcherbakov, Mekhlis i drugie,* 62.

27. *Pravda,* October 21, 1941; Werth, *Russia at War,* 240; Ortenberg, *Iiun'–dekabr',* 222–24.

28. David Ortenberg, *Sorok tretii rasskaz-khronika* (Moscow, 1991), 208.

29. *Pravda,* October 25, 1941.

30. *Pravda,* November 7, 1941.

31. John Barber and Mark Harrison, *The Soviet Home Front, 1941–1945: A Social*

and Economic History of the USSR in World War II (London, 1991), 28–30; G. F. Krivosheev, "Poteri vooruzhennykh sil SSSR," in *Liudskie poteri SSSR,* gives a figure of four million Soviet losses for this period (77–78); Danilov, in "Stalinskaia strategiia," gives a figure of one hundred thousand German losses.

32. E. M. Andreev, L. E. Darskii, and T. L. Khar'kova, "Liudskie poteri SSSR vo vtoroi mirovoi voine: Metodika otsenki i rezul'taty," in *Liudskie poteri SSSR,* 42; Barber and Harrison, *The Soviet Home Front,* 41–42.

33. On casualties, see A. K. Sokolov, "Metodolicheskie osnovy ischisleniia poter' naseleniia SSSR v gody Velikoi Otechestvennoi voiny," in *Liudskie poteri SSSR,* 22–23.

34. A. A. Sherviakov, "Gitlerovskii genotsid i repatriatsiia sovetskogo naseleniia," in *Liudskie poteri SSSR,* 179.

35. *Pravda,* March 14, 1946.

36. *Krasnaia zvezda,* January 15, 1942.

37. Stalin, *Sochineniia,* 2 [15]: 75.

38. Itskhak Arad, "Katastrofa sovetskogo evreistva," in *Unizhtozhenie Evreev SSSR v gody nemetskoi okkupatsii (1941–1944),* ed. Itskhak Arad (Jerusalem, 1992), 1–30. In addition, a quarter million fell in battle, eighty thousand were shot as prisoners, and tens of thousands died in Leningrad and in surrounding regions.

39. Ortenberg, *Iiun'–dekabr',* 6.

40. Mordekhai Al'tushuler, Itskhak Arad, and Shmuel' Krakovskii, eds., *Sovetskie evrei pishut Il'e Erenburgu* (Jerusalem, 1993), 125–26.

41. *Krasnaia zvezda,* August 1, 1942.

42. Ibid., August 6, 1942.

43. Ibid., November 1, 1942.

44. A. S. Shcherbakov, secretary of the central committee and the bureau's chief, relayed the order to Ortenberg, and he assumed it was Stalin's. Ortenberg, *God 1942* (Moscow, 1988), 201–3.

45. Stalin was cited in 42 percent of *Pravda*'s editorials from 1933 through June 23, 1941, but in only 25 percent from January 1, 1940, to June 22, 1941. He was cited in 52 percent of editorials from June 23, 1941, to December 31, 1941; 44 percent in 1942; 40 percent in 1943; 61 percent in 1944; and 66 percent in 1945. Of 498 general articles in a random sample of domestic reportage, he was cited in 18 percent from June 23, 1941, to December 31, 1941; 22 percent in 1942; 28 percent in 1943; 21 percent in 1944; and 15 percent in 1945—slightly higher than prewar totals.

46. Based on all front pages, *Pravda* allotted the equivalent of nine and a half pages to pictures in which he appeared from January 1, 1940, to June 23, 1941, but barely six in the following two and a half years.

47. Erenburg, *Liudi,* 2:237.

48. Stalin was chief agent in 16 of 303 sampled editorials from 1933 to June 22, 1941; 1 of 55 from June 23, 1941, to December 31, 1942; 6 of 32 in 1943; 14 of 32 in 1944; and 7 of 13 from January 1 to May 9, 1945.

49. "For Stalin, for the Homeland" appeared after the victory at Khasan Lake in 1938. "The slogan of heroes of Khasan—'for Homeland, for Party, for Stalin'—is the slogan of the whole Soviet people," editorialized *Labor* on the October anniversary in 1938. "For Stalin! For the Homeland!" appeared on the anniversary of the battle and sporadically thereafter. See *Komsomol'skaia pravda,* August 6, 1939; *Pravda,* April 16, 1939;

and Alexei Tolstoi in *Pravda,* December 25, 1939. "Where Stalin Is, There Is Victory" arose on Stalin's sixtieth birthday in 1939 (*Komsomol'skaia pravda,* December 21, 1939). E. S. Seniavskaia, in *1941–1945: Frontovoe pokolenie. Istoriko-psikhologich-eskoe issledovanie* (Moscow, 1945), 132–33, notes that troops were ordered to shout "For the Homeland, for Stalin" but often ignored the second phrase. Iaroslavskii promoted the slogans in *Pravda,* June 23, 1941; see also *Pravda*'s editorial, September 1, 1941; and *Krasnaia zvezda,* March 31, 1942.

50. *Krasnaia zvezda,* December 13, 1941.

51. Werth, *Russia at War,* 418, cites a speech by Stalin, but there is no such order in Stalin, *Sochineniia,* 2 [15].

52. *Krasnaia zvezda,* July 30, 1942, did not print the order beside its masthead.

53. Ortenberg stressed the abruptness of the communication in *Stalin, Shcherbakov, Mekhlis i drugie,* 145.

54. David Ortenberg, *God 1942: Rasskaz-khronika* (Moscow, 1988), 17; and Ortenberg, *Stalin, Shcherbakov, Mekhlis i drugie,* 148–49. *Pravda* printed the list of commanders on January 3, 1942.

55. Ortenberg, *Stalin, Shcherbakov, Mekhlis i drugie,* 149.

56. Erenburg, *Liudi* 2:235–36; the word is *shtampy.*

57. *Krasnaia zvezda,* August 15, 1941; August 12, 1942.

58. Ortenberg, *Iiun'–dekabr',* 39.

59. Ibid., 31.

60. Ortenberg, *Stalin, Shcherbakov, Mekhlis i drugie,* 7.

61. Ibid., 8–9, 18.

62. Ibid., 19–20.

63. The account of the Commissariat of Defense's Press Bureau is taken from A. Gaev, "Sovetskaia pechat' na voine," *Vestnik journal mitteilungen* (Institut po izucheniyu . . . kultury SSSR), 47–61.

64. Ortenberg, *God 1942,* 164–65.

65. Ortenberg, *Stalin, Shcherbakov, Mekhlis i drugie,* 133.

66. Ibid., 131–32.

67. Ibid., 31–40; D. L. Babichenko, *Pisateli i tsenzory: Sovetskaia literatura 1940-kh godov pod politicheskim kontrolem TsK* (Moscow, 1994), 28.

68. Ortenberg, *Stalin, Shcherbakov, Mekhlis i drugie,* 36–37.

69. On wages, see Barber and Harrison, *The Soviet Home Front,* 80.

70. Ortenberg, *Stalin, Shcherbakov, Mekhlis i drugie,* 26.

71. *Krasnaia zvezda,* October 21, 1941.

72. Ibid., November 14, 1941.

73. Ibid., January 6, 1942.

74. Ilya Ehrenburg and Konstantin Simonov, *In One Newspaper: A Chronicle of Unforgettable Years* (New York, 1985), 5.

75. *Krasnaia zvezda,* December 17, 1941.

76. David Ortenberg, "Voinskii podvig grafa Tolstogo. Zameki redaktora i pisatelia," in Stepichev et al., *Zhivaia pamiat',* 3:264–65.

77. *Pravda,* August 31, 1941.

78. Ibid., May 1, 1942.

79. *Krasnaia zvezda,* January 24, 1942.

80. Rubashkin, *Il'ia Erenburg,* 336.

81. *Pravda,* August 31, 1941.

82. *Krasnaia zvezda,* August 18, 1943; see also August 26, 1943, and September 9, 1943.

83. *Krasnaia zvezda,* November 30, 1943.

84. Konstantin Simonov, *Pis'ma o voine, 1943–1979* (Moscow, 1990), 17.

85. Ortenberg, *Stalin, Shcherbakov, Mekhlis i drugie,* 20–22.

86. John and Carol Garrard, *The Bones of Berdichev: The Life and Fate of Vasily Grossman* (New York, 1996), 53.

87. Garrard and Garrard, *The Bones of Berdichev,* 81, 91–99.

88. Ibid., 113

89. Ibid., 122–25.

90. Joshua Rubenstein, *Tangled Loyalties: The Life and Times of Ilya Ehrenburg* (New York, 1996), 16–22.

91. Quoted in Shimon Redlich, *War, Holocaust, and Stalinism: A Documented Study of the Jewish Anti-Fascist Committee in the USSR* (Australia, 1995), 23.

92. Redlich, *War, Holocaust, and Stalinism,* 23–24, 445–50.

93. Redlich prints the relevant documents in *War, Holocaust, and Stalinism,* 347–70.

94. *Krasnaia zvezda,* December 17, 1943; he continued his comments on December 18 and 19, 1943.

95. Garrard and Garrard, *The Bones of Berdichev,* 137–38.

96. *Krasnaia zvezda,* October 12, 1943. "Ukraine without Jews" appeared in the *Einikeit,* the paper of the Jewish Anti-Fascist Committee, in late 1943. "The Hell of Treblinka" appeared in *Znamia* in November 1944.

97. *Krasnaia zvezda,* August 6, 1944.

98. Ibid., November 13, 1942.

99. Ibid., November 25, 1942.

100. Vasily Grossman, *Life and Fate. A Novel,* trans. Robert Chandler (New York, 1980), 29; on *Life and Fate,* see also Nina Tumarkin, *The Living and the Dead* (New York, 1994), 113–17.

101. Boris Pasternak, *Doctor Zhivago,* trans. Max Hayward and Manya Harari (New York, 1958), 507.

102. Semyon Lipkin, *Zhizn' i sud'ba Vasiliia Grossmana* (Moscow, 1990), 9; quoted in Garrard and Garrard, *The Bones of Berdichev,* 135.

103. Grossman, *Life and Fate,* 809.

104. *Pravda,* March 12, 1942; *Krasnaia zvezda,* May 26, 1942.

105. *Pravda,* March 9, 1942.

106. Percentages of articles in *Pravda* with a bureaucratic agent dropped from 64 percent in sampled issues in June 1940 to May 1941 to 16 percent in June 1941 to December 1942. But in 1943 the percentage was 54 percent, and in 1944–45, 53 percent. In terms of space, articles of this type declined from 72 percent to 8 percent over the same period but rose to 43 percent in 1943 and to 50 percent in 1944–45.

107. *Krasnaia zvezda,* November 18, 1941.

108. Erenburg, *Liudi,* 2:256–57.

109. *Pravda,* June 23, 1941.

110. Ibid., July 3, 1941.

111. Ibid., August 24–27, 1942. On the importance of the play, see Alexander Werth,

The Year of Stalingrad (New York, 1947), 289–90; and Stites, *Russian Popular Culture,* 107.

112. Simonov, *Glazami cheloveka moego pokoleniia,* 356.

113. *Krasnaia zvezda,* October 26, 1941.

114. Simonov reports on his conversation with Konev in *Glazami cheloveka moego pokoleniia,* 251.

115. Ibid., 264.

116. Both posters appear in *Istoriia strany v plakate,* 124, 133; V. Koretskii's poster appeared in *Pravda,* August 5, 1942. The Russian word for "motherland" was *rodina-mat'*.

117. *Pravda,* July 19, 1942.

118. Ibid., August 15, 1942.

119. Ortenberg, *Stalin, Shcherbakov, Mekhlis i drugie,* 130–31.

120. *Krasnaia zvezda,* August 27, 1942.

121. Ibid., August 8, 1943.

122. Quoted in Ortenberg, *Iiun'–dekabr',* 15.

123. *Krasnaia zvezda,* July 16, 1942.

124. Ibid., December 25, 1941.

125. Ibid., November 30, 1941.

126. *Pravda*'s use of *we* (exclusive of the narrow editorial *we*) dropped off sharply on the eve of the war and did not recover fully during the war. From 1933 through June 21, 1940, *we* appeared in 59 percent of all sample editorials. *We* appeared 31 percent in 1939 but only 2 percent in 1940 and the first half of 1941. In 1942 *we* was used in 45 percent of the editorials in *Red Star,* compared to 31 percent in *Pravda.* In the first months of 1943 *we* appeared in 43 percent of the *Red Star* editorials, compared to 6 percent in *Pravda.* From June 22, 1941, through 1945 *we* appeared in 23 percent of the *Pravda* editorials.

127. Kalintseva, *Nashi,* 276.

128. James Tobin, *Ernie Pyle's War: America's Eyewitness to World War II* (New York, 1997), 202–23.

129. Rubashkin, *Il'ia Erenburg,* 340–41; the letters are in Ehrenburg's archive in TsGALI.

130. Ibid., 339.

131. Erenburg, *Liudi,* 2:323.

132. It appeared only in a French edition. Ilya Ehrenburg, *Cent Lettres,* trans. A. Roudnikov (Paris, 1945).

133. *Krasnaia zvezda,* October 18, 1941.

134. A. Sutzkever, *Selected Poetry and Prose,* trans. Barbara and Benjamin Harshav (Berkeley, 1991), 151.

135. *Krasnaia zvezda,* November 16, 1941.

136. Ibid., April 2, 1943.

137. Ibid., May 9, 1943.

138. Translated by Lubov Yakovleva in *Twentieth-Century Russian Poetry,* ed. Todd and Heyward, 624. Ortenberg says Simonov offered it to him for *Red Star,* but he felt it too sad to publish (*Sorok tretii,* 113). Valerii Agranovskii suggests in *Poslednii dolg* (Moscow, 1994), 66–75, that the poem was composed earlier about the camps and that Simonov adopted it.

139. Nicolas Berdyaev, *The Origin of Russian Communism* (Ann Arbor, 1960), 9.

140. A. F. Losev, *"Mne bylo 19 let . . . " Dnevniki. Pis'ma. Proza.,* ed. A. A. Takhogodi (Moscow, 1997), 273.

141. *Pravda,* March 20, 1942.

142. Konstantin Simonov, *The Living and the Dead,* trans. R. Ainsztein (New York, 1962), 243.

143. *Krasnaia zvezda,* September 22, 1944.

144. Ibid., December 28, 1941; November 21, 1944.

145. Ibid., March 15, 1945.

146. Editorial in *Pravda,* September 7, 1941.

147. "Posetiteli Kremlevskogo Kabineta I. V. Stalin," *Istoricheskii arkhiv,* nos. 2–5/6 (1996).

148. Ortenberg, *God 1942,* 262–64, 373, 375.

149. Ibid., 375.

150. Ibid., 301.

151. E. S. Seniavskaia notes the hostility of the villagers in *1941–1945 Frontovoe pokolenie,* 140–42; the reports are in *Pravda,* January 27, 1942, and February 18, 1942.

152. Ortenberg, *Stalin, Shcherbakov, Mekhlis i drugie,* 89.

153. Babichenko, *Pisateli i tsenzory,* 82–84.

154. Simonov, *Glazami cheloveka moego pokoleniia,* 357–58.

155. Khrushchev, *Khrushchev Remembers,* 170.

156. *Pravda,* November 6, 1942; November 7, 1942.

157. The Russian word is *prikazy.* According to my sample in *Pravda,* the frequency of these orders rose from four out of thirteen from August to December 1943 (31 percent) to thirteen out of thirty-two in 1944 (41 percent) to seven out of twelve from January to June 1945 (58 percent).

158. *Pravda,* September 1, 1943.

159. Werth, *Russia at War,* 684–85. Werth was mistaken about this being the first; the first of the "orders" of this type appeared in *Pravda,* July 25, 1943.

160. *Pravda,* December 19, 1942.

161. Ortenberg, *Stalin, Shcherbakov, Mekhlis i drugie,* 150.

162. See *Pravda,* January 1, 1943.

163. Ibid., January 30, 1943.

164. Ibid., February 22, 1943.

165. *Krasnaia zvezda,* November 6, 1942.

166. *Pravda,* July 20, 1942.

167. Ibid., November 7, 1941.

168. Ibid., July 20, 1942.

169. Werth describes the nationalities' increased role beginning in late 1942 in *The Year of Stalingrad,* 295–97.

170. *Krasnaia zvezda,* January 22, 1943.

171. Ibid., May 11, 1943.

172. Ibid., May 22, 1943.

173. Ibid., July 19, 1943.

174. Werth, *Russia at War,* 684.

175. *Krasnaia zvezda,* June 3, 1944; June 8, 1944; August 5, 1944; July 11, 1944; and August 15, 1944.

176. The document was discovered by Kostyrchenko, who reprints much of it in *Out of the Red Shadows*, 15–18.

177. Ibid., 24–25.

178. Ortenberg, *Sorok tretii*, 339.

179. Simonov, *Pis'ma o voine*, 22–23.

180. Konstantin Simonov, *Sobranie sochinenii. Pis'ma, 1943–1979* (Moscow, 1987), 12:41.

181. L. Lazarev discusses this issue in "True Tales and Fables," *Russian Studies in Literature* (fall 1996): 53, reprinted from *Znamia*, no. 10 (1994): 183–99. The author of the article was G. Aleksandrov, but Ehrenburg, according to his American biographer, took the article as a general rebuke, which it probably was, and wrote to Stalin, who never answered (Rubenstein, *Tangled Loyalties*, 222–25).

182. The letter, dated April 15, 1945, is reprinted in D. L. Babichenko, *Literaturnyi front*, 156–57.

183. Erenburg, *Liudi*, 2:322.

184. A. V. Blium, *Evreiskii vopros pod sovetskoi tsenzuroi, 1917–1991* (Saint Petersburg, 1996), 91–92.

185. The figures cited include members and candidate members (Institute Marksizma-Leninizma pri TsK KPSS, *Istoriia Kommunisticheskoi Partii Sovetskogo Soiuza*, vol. 5 [Moscow, 1970], 27, 372).

186. *Pravda*, January 22, 1944.

187. Ibid., November 1, 1943.

188. Volkogonov, *Stalin: Triumph and Tragedy*, 486–87.

189. *Pravda*, May 22, 1943; May 30, 1943.

190. Heller and Nekrich, *Utopia in Power*, 410.

191. Ortenberg, *Sorok tretii*, 15–17.

192. *Pravda*, January 7, 1943.

193. Werth, *The Year of Stalingrad*, 289.

194. V. A. Durov, *Russkie i sovetskie boevye nagrady* (Moscow, 1990), 76–99.

195. *Pravda* July 17, 1943.

196. Ibid., May 3, 1943.

197. Ibid., May 3, 1942.

198. *Krasnaia zvezda*, May 20, 1943.

199. *Pravda*, March 22, 1944.

200. Erenburg, *Liudi*, 2:228.

201. Aleksandr Vasil'ev, in "Neuzheli ia eshche zhiv?" Stepichev et al., *Zhivaia pamiat'*, ed. Grebtsov and Khokhlov, 3:495, quotes a remark of General Petr Sysoevich Il'in at a gathering of veterans.

202. Simonov, *The Living and the Dead*, 458.

203. Ibid., 459.

204. *Krasnaia zvezda*, August 24, 1943.

205. Ibid., September 16, 1944.

206. But I did not find the famous slogans promoted in *Pravda* or *Krasnaia zvezda*. There was, however, a postcard, "For the Homeland! For Stalin!" See Chapkina, *Khudozhestvennaia otkrytka*, 257.

207. Erenburg, *Liudi*, 2:263.

208. *Krasnaia zvezda*, June 21, 1945; *Pravda*, January 11, 1946; February 11, 1947.

Neither was widely proclaimed. "Where Stalin is, there is victory" was used as a password (see Seniavskaia, *1941–1945 Frontovoe pokolenie,* 132–34).

209. *Krasnaia zvezda,* June 26, 1945.

210. *Pravda,* May 10, 1945.

211. Volkogonov, *Triumf i tragediia,* 174–75; Barber and Harrison, *The Soviet Home Front,* 208.

212. Grossman, *Life and Fate,* 48; Vasily Grossman, *Zhizn' i sud'ba. Roman* (Moscow, 1990), 369.

213. *Pravda,* May 10, 1945.

214. *Krasnaia zvezda,* November 7, 1943.

Chapter Eight
The Theft of the War

1. Seniavskaia, *1941–1945,* 202.

2. Simonov, *Glazami cheloveka moego pokoleniia,* 91.

3. Joseph Brodsky, *Less Than One: Selected Essays* (New York, 1986), 24.

4. Seniavskaia, *1941–1945,* 164.

5. Ibid., 198–203.

6. Vladislav Zubok and Constantine Pleshakov, *Inside the Kremlin's Cold War from Stalin to Khrushchev* (Cambridge, Mass., 1996), 36–37; Iurii Aksiutin summarizes these complaints in his "Pochemu Stalin dal'neishemu sotrudnichestvu s soiuznikami posle pobedy predpochel konfrontatsiiu s nimi?" in *Kholodnaia voina: Novye podkhody, novye dokumenty,* ed. I. V. Gaiduk, M. L. Korobochkin, M. M. Narinskii, and A. O. Chubar'ian (Moscow, 1995), 48–63.

7. Aksiutin, "Pochemu Stalin," 48–63; E. Iu Zubova, "Stalin i obshchestvennoe mnenie v SSSR," in *Stalin i kholodnaia voina,* ed. I. V. Gaiduk, N. I. Egorova, and A. O. Chubar'ian (Moscow, 1997), 274–80.

8. Babichenko, *Literaturnyi front,* 161–74.

9. Quoted in Seniavskaia, *1941–1945,* 165–66, from V. Kondrat'ev and V. Kozhemiako in *Pravda,* June 20, 1991.

10. D. A. Tolstoi, *Dlia chego vse eto bylo* (St. Petersburg, 1995), 259.

11. Pasternak, *Doctor Zhivago,* 519.

12. Quoted in E. Iu. Zubkova, *Obshchestvo i reformy 1945–1964* (Moscow, 1993), 33, from *Izvestiia* February 3, 1990.

13. D. T. Shepilov, "Vospominaniia," *Voprosy istorii* 5 (1998): 11.

14. V. F. Zima, *Golod v SSSR, 1946–1947 godov: proiskhozhdenie i posledstviia* (Moscow, 1996), 178–79. I rely on this book for my remarks on the famine.

15. Khrushchev, *Khrushchev Remembers,* 232.

16. Chuev, *Sto sorok besed s Molotovym,* 368.

17. *Pravda,* January 26, 1948.

18. A. A. Sherviakov, "Gitlerovskii genotsid i repatriatsiia sovetskogo naseleniia," in *Liudskie poteri SSSR,* 181.

19. M. F. Kosinskii, *Pervaia polovina veka* (Paris, 1995), 342; such forms remained in use in some successor states until 1994.

20. John L. H. Keep, *The Last of the Empires: A History of the Soviet Union, 1945–1991* (New York, 1995), 12–13; see also Nicholas Werth and Gaël Moullec, eds., *Rap-*

ports Secrets Soviétiques, 1921–1991: La Société russe dans les documents confidentiels (Paris, 1994), 395.

21. Aleksandr M. Nekrich, *Punished Peoples* (New York, 1978); Bohdan Nahaylo and Victor Swoboda, *Soviet Disunion: A History of the Nationalities Problem in the USSR* (New York, 1989), 95–108.

22. T. H. Rigby, *Communist Party Membership in the USSR* (Princeton, N.J., 1968), 52.

23. Cynthia S. Kaplan, "The Impact of World War II on the Party," in *The Impact of World War II on the Soviet Union,* ed. Susan J. Linz (Totowa, N.J., 1985), 160–61.

24. Rigby, *Communist Party Membership,* 52.

25. Tatyana Zaslavskaia, *The Second Socialist Revolution: An Alternative Soviet Strategy,* trans. Susan M. Davies with Jenny Warren (Bloomington, Ind., 1990), 25.

26. Zaslavskaia notes the rise of an elite sharply differentiated from the rest of society particularly in the postwar period in *The Second Socialist Revolution,* 25. See also Vera S. Dunham, *In Stalin's Time: Middle-Class Values in Soviet Fiction* (Cambridge, 1976), 13.

27. The percentages of *Pravda*'s editorials addressed to the *apparat* from May 19, 1945, through March 3, 1953, based on my sample of 275, are 1945 (25 percent), 1946 (26 percent), 1947 (31 percent), 1948 (50 percent), 1950 (32 percent), 1951 (49 percent), and 1952 (57 percent).

28. The subject of domestic editorials from May 19, 1945 through March 3, 1953, based on my sample of 275 was socialist construction in roughly three-quarters of the cases. The differences from year to year did not appear significant

29. *Pravda,* June 11, 1945; October 29, 1945.

30. Ibid., May 6, 1946; May 19, 1946; May 31, 1946.

31. Ibid., September 25, 1946. When two or more metaphors were employed, I chose one as the shaping metaphor. By this rough measure, shaping metaphors from May 19, 1945, through March 3, 1953, include task (*zadacha* and *zadanie*) (33 percent), the path (8 percent), construction (7 percent), the military (4 percent), the gift (2 percent), others (5 percent), and none (42 percent). Secondary metaphors, often used to define authority, include the task (*zadacha* and *zadanie*) (24 percent), school (9 percent), duty (7 percent), the military (5), the family (3 percent), others (8 percent), and none (45 percent). The metaphor of the gift was often implicit. The word *struggle* (*bor'ba*) was often associated with the tasks, as in struggle for (*za*) rather than struggle against.

32. *Pravda,* August 30, 1945; *Trud,* September 12, 1945. It was formally introduced half a year later; see *Pravda,* February 22, 1946.

33. *Pravda,* February 10, 1946.

34. Naum Jasny, *Soviet Industrialization, 1928–1952* (Chicago, 1961), 253.

35. Jasny, *Soviet Industrialization,* 245.

36. Iu. A. Prikhod'ko, *Vosstanovlenie industrii, 1942–1950* (Moscow, 1973), 233.

37. Jasny, *Soviet Industrialization,* 245.

38. *Pravda,* February 22, 1946.

39. *Trud,* May 1, 1946.

40. *Pravda,* March 23, 1946.

41. *Krasnaia zvezda,* July 10, 1945.

42. Tumarkin, *The Living and the Dead,* 101–5.

43. *Krasnaia zvezda,* June 26, 1945.

44. *Pravda,* June 28, 1945.

45. Ibid., February 10, 1946.

46. Ibid., May 18, 1945; September 21, 1946.

47. Nikita S. Khrushchev, *The Crimes of the Stalin Era. Special Report to the 20th Congress of the Communist Party of the Soviet Union,* annotated by Boris I. Nicolaevsky (New York, 1956), 43.

48. *Izvestiia,* May 9, 1946.

49. *Trud,* May 9, 1946.

50. *Krasnaia zvezda,* May 9, 1946.

51. *Pravda,* August 8, 1946.

52. Ibid., October 24, 1946.

53. *Pravda* and *Krasnaia zvezda,* May 12, 1946.

54. *Pravda,* February 13, 1946.

55. This was based on a random sample of eighteen issues a year. The figures are 21 percent in 1947, 12 percent in 1948, 27 percent in 1949, 11 percent in 1950, 14 percent in 1951, and 13 percent in 1952.

56. *Pravda,* August 23, 1947.

57. Elena Serebrovskaia, *Mezhdu proshlym i budushchim* (St. Petersburg, 1994), 7. The Russian word is *vzaimnost'.*

58. Raikin, *Vospominaniia,* 198.

59. The Soviet summary of this conversation is reprinted in Oleg A. Rzhesevsky, ed., *War and Diplomacy: The Making of the Grand Alliance. Documents from Stalin's Archives,* trans. T. Sorokina (Amsterdam, 1996), 75–76.

60. Winston S. Churchill, *The Second World War: Triumph and Tragedy* (Boston, 1953), 367.

61. John Lewis Gaddis, *We Now Know: Rethinking Cold War History* (Oxford, 1997), 32.

62. Milovan Djilas, *Conversations with Stalin,* trans. Michael B. Petrovich (New York, 1962), 95. Djilas tells other stories of the giving and receiving of gifts on pages 14, 55, 63, 83, and 92.

63. Randall W. Stone, *Satellites and Commissars: Strategy and Conflict in the Politics of Soviet-Bloc Trade* (Princeton, N.J., 1996), 27.

64. This kind of obligation was expressed in 45 of 222 articles on Eastern Europe and the Balkans (excepting Greece and Yugoslavia) in a random sample of articles on foreign affairs in nine issues per year in *Pravda* from 1946 through 1952 (the *Pravda* random sample on foreign affairs).

65. *Pravda,* July 27, 1949.

66. The Novikov telegram is translated in Kenneth M. Jensen, ed., *Origins of the Cold War: The Novikov, Kennan, and Roberts 'Long Telegrams' of 1946* (Washington, D.C., 1993); Zubok and Pleshakov, in *Inside the Kremlin's Cold War from Stalin to Khrushchev,* 124, cite Zhdanov's secret note identifying Churchill's Fulton speech as a failure.

67. *Pravda,* March 14, 1946.

68. According to my random sample, *Pravda* allotted 50 percent of the space given to foreign affairs in 1946 and 1947 to peaceful relations with other countries. Of this, 8 percent concerned Eastern Europe and 10 percent antifascism.

69.. On the lack of Soviet support, see Zubok and Pleshakov, *Inside the Kremlin's Cold War,* 126–27.

70. According to my random *Pravda* sample, articles on peaceful and productive re-

lations with the capitalist world filled the following percentages of total space allotted to foreign affairs: 1948 (12 percent), 1949 (6 percent), 1950 (4 percent), 1951 (4 percent), and 1952 (3 percent). Antifascism comprised 4 percent in 1948 and less than 1 percent thereafter.

71. According to my *Pravda* random sample, in 1946 and 1947 articles about the bad life filled 23 percent of the space allocated to foreign affairs; conflicts with the West, 7 percent; and situations of conflict not involving the West, 12 percent.

72. *Pravda,* February 29, 1946; June 21, 1946; October 26, 1946; December 8, 1946; July 25, 1947; February 11, 1947; and February 27, 1946.

73. In 1949 such reports comprise 17 percent of the total space *Pravda* allotted to foreign affairs in my sample; in 1950, 14 percent; in 1951, 3 percent; and in 1952, 8 percent.

74. Quoted in V. O. Pechatnov, "'Strel'ba kholostymi': Sovetskaia propaganda na zapad v nachale kholodnoi voiny (1945–1947)," in *Stalin i kholodnaia voina,* 175.

75. Shepilov, "Vospominaniia," *Voprosy istorii* 5 (1998): 11–13.

76. Pechatnov, "'Strel'ba kholostymi,'" 180–81.

77. Babichenko, *Literaturnyi front,* 203.

78. Ibid., 200. For inculcate, he used *privivat',* meaning to inoculate or graft, suggesting contagion.

79. Shepilov, "Vospominaniia," 11.

80. The account is from Babichenko, *Pisateli i tsenzory,* 136–37.

81. *Pravda,* August 22, 1946.

82. Ibid., August 29, 1946; specifically, Kornei Chukovskii's story "Murzilka."

83. Krementsov describes the campaign and honor courts in *Stalinist Science,* 131–43.

84. G. V. Kostyrchenko, "Ideologicheskie chistki vtoroi poloviny 40-x godov: Psevdopatrioty protiv psevdokosmopolitov," in *Sovetskoe obshchestvo: Voznikonovenie, razvitie, istoricheskii final,* ed. Iu. N. Afanas'ev (Moscow, 1997), 2:106–9.

85. Krementsov cites it as authored by Zhdanov and edited by Stalin in *Stalinist Science,* 138–39. The decree was not reported in *Pravda* or *Izvestiia.*

86. According to my random sample, peaceful, friendly, or neutral coverage of foreign affairs, including antifascist articles, comprise the following percentages of the space allotted to foreign affairs: 1946 (55 percent), 1947 (45 percent), 1948 (28 percent), 1949 (17 percent), 1950 (15 percent), 1951 (12 percent), and 1952 (8 percent).

87. Quoted in Martin Walker, *The Cold War: A History* (New York, 1993), 49.

88. Harry S. Truman, *Memoirs by Harry S. Truman: Years of Trial and Hope* (Garden City, N.Y., 1956), 2:105.

89. Walter L. Hixson, *Parting the Curtain: Propaganda, Culture, and the Cold War, 1945–1961* (New York, 1997), 32–33.

90. Reinhold Wagonleitner, *Coco-Colonization: The Cultural Mission of the United States in Austria after the Second World War* (Chapel Hill, N.C., 1994); on Soviet worries about VOA, see V. S. Lel'chuk and E. I. Pivovar, "Konfrontatsiia dvukh sistem i mentalitet sovetskogo obshchestva," in *SSSR i kholodnaia voina,* ed. V. S. Lel'chuk and E. I. Pivovar (Moscow, 1995), 18.

91. Alex Inkeles, *Social Change in Soviet Russia* (Cambridge, Mass., 1968), 345–79; Hixson, *Parting the Curtain,* 33. Inkeles estimates 1–1.5 million sets able to receive broadcasts. I assume Hixson's recent figure of 5 million is more reliable.

92. Up to March 31, 1951. Inkeles, *Social Change,* 345–79.

93. Ivo Banac, *With Stalin, Against Tito: Cominformist Splits in Yugoslav Communism* (Ithaca, N.Y., 1988), 129–42; Gaddis, *We Now Know,* 74–75.

94. Khrushchev, *Khrushchev Remembers,* 361–52.

95. This according to my random sample. This figure on China correlates with that given for 1947–1948 by Alex Inkeles in *Public Opinion in Soviet Russia* (Cambridge, Mass., 1950), 163.

96. For comments on the German currency, see *Pravda,* June 26, 1948.

97. *Pravda* published M. Marinin's commentaries on the "so called Berlin crisis" (November 2–March 1948). He rebutted foreign journalists, cited documents published by the Ministry of Foreign Affairs, and blamed the West, without mentioning the airlift.

98. Banac, *With Stalin, Against Tito,* 129–30.

99. *Pravda,* March 14, 1947.

100. On June 16 *Pravda*'s columnist B. Leontev denounced American aid to Europe as an extension of the Truman Doctrine. See also *Pravda,* June 21, 1947; Chuev, *Sto sorok besed s Molotovym,* 88; and Zubok and Pleshakov, *Inside the Kremlin's Cold War,* 104–5. At first, American press did not consider the proposal important either. See Martin Walker, *The Cold War: A History* (New York, 1993), 51.

101. Zubok and Pleshakov, *Inside the Kremlin's Cold War,* 105.

102. *Pravda,* October 16, 1947.

103. See the article by B. Gribor'ev, "Novogodnie 'dary' g-na garrimana," in *Trud,* January 8, 49.

104. *Pravda,* October 5, 1947. According to one account, Stalin approved the phrase at the last minute. See Vojtech Mastny, *The Cold War and Soviet Insecurity* (New York, 1996), 31; on the "two camps," see William Curti Wohlforth, *The Elusive Balance: Power and Perceptions during the Cold War* (Ithaca, N.Y., 1993), 71.

105. Stalin, *Sochineniia,* 3 [16]: 1–22.

106. *Pravda,* November 7, 1947.

107. *Pravda,* January 26, 1948; see also Nezhinskii and Chelyshev, "Problemy venshnei politiki," 48.

108. *Pravda,* August 26, 1948.

109. Ibid., August 29, 1948.

110. Ibid. and *Izvestiia,* February 2–5, 1949, also gave foreign comments on Stalin's remarks.

111. *Pravda,* April 7, 1949.

112. Ibid., April 27, 1949.

113. Ibid., April 25, 1949.

114. Lysenko survived an attack by Zhdanov's son Iurii, who retracted his view in a letter in *Pravda* (August 7, 1948). Valery N. Soyfer, *Lysenko and the Tragedy of Soviet Science,* trans. Leo Gruliow and Rebecca Gruliow (New Brunswick, N.J., 1994), 164, 179–82.

115. *Pravda,* August 4, 5, 10, 1948; other newspapers did not cover the event. Joravsky, in *The Lysenko Affair,* shows the conflict's complexity, 306–13.

116. *Pravda,* August 10, 1948; Krementsov, *Stalinist Science,* 180.

117. *Pravda,* February 15, 1935.

118. Medvedev, *The Rise and Fall of T. D. Lysenko,* 122–30.

119. David Holloway *Stalin and the Bomb: The Soviet Union and Atomic Energy, 1939–1956* (New Haven, 1994), 186–88, 210.

120. Lazar Volin, *A Century of Russian Agriculture: From Alexander II to*

Khrushchev (Cambridge, Mass., 1970), 312–21; Nikonov in *Spiral' mnogovekovoi dramy,* 275–77; Joravsky, *The Lysenko Affair,* 300–303.

121. On inspected areas in 1949, see Soyfer, *Lysenko and the Tragedy of Soviet Science,* 205–11; on critical evaluations of Lysenko's theories by agricultural officials in 1952, see Joravsky, *The Lysenko Affair,* 154–55.

122. Some studies favor shelter-belts. See Nikonov, *Spiral',* 274–75; and James H. Bater, *The Soviet Scene: A Geographical Perspective* (London, 1989), 134–36.

123. *Pravda,* October 24, 1948.

124. Ibid., October 26, 1948.

125. Stalin, *Sochineniia,* 2 [15]: 203–4; his radio address on May 9 was printed in *Pravda* on May 10, 1945. Echoes in *Pravda* include June 11, 1945; September 16, 1945; and March 7, 1946.

126. Gaddis, *We Now Know,* 74–75.

127. *Pravda,* January 6, 1949.

128. Ibid., January 9, 1949.

129. *Komsomol'skaia pravda,* January 9, 1949.

130. *Trud,* May 7, 1950.

131. Sakharov, *Memoirs,* 123.

132. Critics damned pro-Western "cosmopolites" in philosophy journals in mid-1948. See Werner G. Hahn, *Postwar Soviet Politics: The Fall of Zhdanov and the Defeat of Moderation, 1946–53* (Ithaca, N.Y., 1982), 78, 82–83.

133. *Komsomol'skaia pravda,* January 8, 1949.

134. *Pravda,* September 21, 1948. Vaksberg, in *Stalin against the Jews,* 186, suggests that Ehrenburg may not have written this.

135. Vaksberg, *Stalin against the Jews,* 198–99.

136. Ibid., 189–90, 203–5.

137. Kostyrchenko, *Out of the Red Shadows,* 179–247.

138. Ibid., 181–93.

139. Ibid., 189.

140. *Pravda,* January 29, 1949.

141. Ibid.

142. Stefan Staszewski, interviewed in Teresa Torganska, *"Them": Stalin's Polish Puppets,* trans. Agnieszka Kolakowska (New York, 1987).

143. Nadzharov, "Stalinskii Agitprop," 219–22.

144. *Pravda,* February 26, 1949.

145. Ibid., February 10, 1949.

146. *Trud,* March 17, 1949.

147. *Komsomol'skaia pravda,* March 2, 1949; March 23, 1949.

148. Ibid., March 22, 1949.

149. Ibid., March 6, 1949.

150. *Trud,* March 12, 1949.

151. Holloway, *Stalin and the Bomb,* 237–50. He cites a pamphlet by Major General G. I Pokrovskii published in 1946.

152. *Izvestiia,* September 25, 1949.

153. Holloway points this out in *Stalin and the Bomb,* 266.

154. *Pravda,* October 5, 1949.

155. *Komsomol'skaia pravda,* October 6, 1949.

156. *Pravda,* October 9–11, 1949; October 19, 1949.

157. *Pravda* published only three reports on the trial (January 5, 1949; February 5, 1949; February 7, 1949). On other trials briefly covered, see *Pravda,* June 21, 1948; October 29, 1948; November 2, 1948; and November 4, 1948.

158. This is Czech historian G. P. Murashko's evaluation of Soviet objectives based on Russian archival material in "Politicheskii arkhiv xx veka: Delo Slanskogo," *Voprosy istorii,* no. 4 (1997): 5.

159. *Pravda,* September 18, 1949.

160. In 1927 the government denied even high Party officials access to émigré publications. See Glolubev, "Zapad glazami sovetskogo obshchestva, 113.

161. *Pravda,* September 25, 1949.

162. *Izvestiia,* December 22, 1949.

163. *Pravda,* December 21, 1949.

164. Comedian Arkadii Raikin was called at 5:00 A.M. to perform for Stalin himself at the festivities which had continued since the previous night (Raikin, *Vospominaniia,* 195–96).

165. *Pravda,* December 22, 1949.

166. *Komsomol'skaia pravda,* December 20, 1949.

167. *Pravda,* December 23, 1949.

168. Ibid.

169. *Trud,* December 27, 1949; *Pravda,* December 20, 1949.

170. *Izvestiia,* December 13, 1949.

171. *Pravda,* December 14, 1949.

172. *Pravda,* December 6, 1949. One exhibit was at the Museum of the Revolution of the USSR.

173. *Pravda,* December 18, 1949.

174. Ibid., December 21, 22, 1939.

175. Ibid., December 8, 1949.

176. *Izvestiia,* December 14, 1949.

177. Ibid., December 15, 1949.

178. *Pravda,* December 5, 1949.

179. I rely on Harrison E. Salisbury, *The New Emperors: China in the Era of Mao and Deng* (Boston, 1992), 93–95. His account is based in part on personal interviews.

180. *Pravda,* December 8, 1949.

181. The document appears in Kathryn Weathersby, "Korea, 1949–1950: To Attack, or Not to Attack? Stalin, Kim Il Sung, and the Prelude to War," in *Cold War International History Project Bulletin* 5 (Spring, 1995): 9.

182. Kathryn Weathersby, "New Russian Documents on the Korean War," in *Cold War International History Project Bulletin* 6–7 (winter 1995–96): 31.

183. Zubok and Pleshakov, *Inside the Kremlin's Cold War,* 64; Charles E. Bohlen, *Witness to History, 1929–1969* (New York, 1973), 295.

184. *Pravda,* June 30, 1950.

185. Ibid., August 4, 1950.

186. Bohlen, *Witness to History,* 295.

187. *Pravda,* August 1, 1950.

188. Ibid., July 30, 1950; August 11, 1950.

189. George F. Kennan, *Memoirs, 1950–1963* (Boston, 1972), 2:42–43.

190. *Trud,* September 24, 1950.

191. *Pravda,* October 8, 1950.

192. He commented in *Pravda* on June 20, 1950; July 4, 1950; and August 2, 1950. His comments on August 2, 1950, consisted of three replies to letters, which, together with his earlier remarks, were reprinted as a separate booklet.

193. Erenburg, *Liudi,* 3:154.

194. Yuri Slezkine, "N. Ia. Marr and Soviet Ethnogenetics," *Slavic Review* 55, no. 4 (winter 1996): 857.

195. *Pravda,* June 6, 1950; July 13, 1950; July 13, 1950.

196. Stalin, *Sochineniia,* 3 [16]: 114–71. *Pravda, Komsomol'skaia Pravda,* and *Trud* featured his remarks prominently.

197. The translation is that given in Bruce Franklin, ed., *The Essential Stalin: Major Theoretical Writings, 1905–1952* (Garden City, N.Y., 1972), 410, 426–27.

198. Edward Gibbon, *The History of the Decline and Fall of the Roman Empire,* ed. David Womersley (London, 1994), 1:64–65.

199. Franklin, *The Essential Stalin,* 427–28.

200. David Joravsky, in *Russian Psychology,* 404–14, suggests that he may have wished to encourage competition; *Pravda,* August 2, 1950.

201. Brooks, *When Russia Learned to Read,* chap. 6.

202. The percentage of editorials captioned with exhortatory headings declined from over 50 percent in 1946–48 to 43 percent percent in 1949, and to a third or less from 1950 through 1952.

203. *Pravda,* November 7, 1950.

204. Iasny, *Soviet Industrialization,* 252.

205. I follow the explanation in Stalin, *Sochineniia,* 3 [16]: 189. This compendium began to appear under his name in February 1952.

206. I use the translation in Franklyn, *The Essential Stalin,* 473.

207. Khrushchev, *Khrushchev Remembers,* 276–77.

208. *Pravda, Trud,* and *Komsomol'skaia pravda,* October 6, 1952; *Izvestiia* printed a picture of Malenkov at the podium and Stalin seated beside members of the Presidium.

209. *Pravda,* October 15, 1952.

210. *Trud,* October 15, 1952.

211. *Pravda,* October 6, 1952.

212. Nikita Khrushchev, *Khrushchev Remembers: The Glasnost Tapes,* trans. Jerrold L. Scheter with Vyacheslav V. Luchkov (Boston, 1990), 100.

213. Zubok and Pleshakov, *Inside the Kremlin's Cold War,* 154; cited in Gaddis, *We Now Know,* 107.

214. On the superiority of the Soviet bomb, see Holloway, *Stalin and the Bomb,* 307.

215. *Pravda,* December 14, 1952.

216. *Pravda* allotted two pages to Slansky's trial (November 25, 1952). No correspondents published on-site reports, and neither *Komsomol Pravda, Trud,* nor *Izvestiia* editorialized on the topic as they had earlier (N. Tarakanov, "Delo Slanskogo," *Voprosy istorii* 3 [1997]: 3–20).

217. *Pravda,* November 25, 1952.

218. Ibid., November 21, 1952.

219. Official transcripts concerning the secret trial of the Jewish Anti-Fascist Com-

mittee, which was closely related to the Doctors' Plot, appear in *Nepravednyi sud: Polsednii stalinskii rastrel, Stenogramma sudebnogo protessa nad chlenami Evreiskogo antifashistskogo komiteta,* ed. V. P. Naumov (Moscow, 1994).

220. Kostyrchenko, in *Out of the Red Shadows,* 291, attributes it to Stalin.

221. Redlich, *War, Holocaust, and Stalinism,* 57 n. 54.

222. Louis Rapoport, *Stalin's War Against the Jews: The Doctors' Plot and the Soviet Solution* (New York, 1990), 148; Kostyrchenko, *Out of the Red Shadows,* 264.

223. Ibid., 289.

224. The Russian words were *bditel'nost'* and *rotozeistvo.*

225. This includes fifteen articles in *Pravda,* seventeen in *Komsomol'skaia pravda,* eleven in *Trud,* and six in *Izvestiia.* Of these, *Pravda* published three editorials, *Komsomol'skaia pravda* seven, and *Trud* and *Izvestiia* one each.

226. *Bditel'nost'* appears in the captions of 14 articles, *rotozeistvo* in four; but both words figured in most of the articles.

227. *Pravda,* January 31, 1953.

228. Ibid., January 13, 1953.

229. Ibid., February 1, 1953.

230. *Trud,* February 18, 1953.

231. *Komsomol'skaia pravda,* January 20, 1953.

232. *Pravda,* January 31, 1953.

233. *Komsomol'skaia pravda,* February 12, 1953.

234. Vaksberg, in *Stalin against the Jews,* 256–57, suggests it was a provocation; Kostyrchenko, in *Out of the Red Shadows,* 295, does not speculate.

235. Vaksberg, in *Stalin against the Jews,* 258–70, describes the process of creating the letter and prints Ehrenburg's response. Kostyrchenko, in *Out of the Red Shadows,* 294, notes that official documentary evidence is lacking.

236. Sakharov, *Memoirs,* 162.

237. Chukovskii, *Dnevnik,* 197.

238. Sakharov, *Memoirs,* 166.

Epilogue
Renewal, Stagnation, and Collapse

1. The most complete description is in Radzinsky, *Stalin,* 566–82.

2. Ludmila Alexeyeva and Paul Goldberg, *The Thaw Generation: Coming of Age in the Post-Stalin Era* (Pittsburgh, 1990), 66.

3. Khrushchev gave the figure in his "second secret speech" at the Polish United Workers' Party in Warsaw, March 20, 1956, *Cold War International History Project Bulletin,* 10 (March 1998): 47.

4. *Komsomol'skaia pravda,* March 7, 1953.

5. *Pravda,* March 9, 1953.

6. On Prokofiev and flowers, see Radzinsky, *Stalin,* 579.

7. Simonov, *Glazami cheloveka moego pokoleniia,* 228–34.

8. Based on a coding of all articles in *Pravda* from March 7 to March 11, 1953, domestic stories account for 66 percent of the space, bloc countries for 14 percent, foreign Communist Parties 11 percent, and noncommunist countries 8 percent.

9. D. T. Shepilov, "Vospominaniia," *Voprosy istorii* 3 (1998): 16.

10. *Pravda,* March 7, 1953.

11. Ibid., March 8, 1953.

12. Ibid., March 9, 1953.

13. *We* is used in 38 percent of 148 domestic articles in *Pravda* from March 7 to March 11, 1953.

14. Weber, *Economy and Society,* 241–45, 1111–57.

15. The phrase is Serge Moscovic's in *The Invention of Society: Psychological Explanations for Social Phenomena,* trans. W. D. Halls (Cambridge, 1993), 113–35. I draw on his views as well as those of Max Weber, who stressed the importance of charisma in social change.

16. Talcott Parson, "Introduction," in Max Weber, *The Sociology of Religion,* trans. Ephraim Fischoff (Boston, 1963), xxxvii.

17. Garfinkel, in *Studies in Ethnomethodology,* develops this approach to social knowledge.

18. Weber, *Economy and Society,* 1139–41.

19. *Pravda,* March 10, 1953. In the press coverage in *Trud, Izvestiia,* and *Pravda* on March 11, 1953, there was little attention to this. On the photo, see Roxburgh, *Pravda,* 41.

20. Weber, *Economy and Society,* 154.

21. *Pravda,* March 10, 1953.

22. Iasny, *Soviet Industrialization,* 252; Heller and Nekrich, *Utopia in Power,* 518–19.

23. Vladimir Dudintsev, *Not by Bread Alone,* trans. Edith Bone (New York, 1957), 257, 312.

24. *Okrug Fadeeva. Neizvestnye pis'ma, zametki i dokumenty (Iz Rossiiskogo Gosudarstvennogo Arkhiva literatury i iskustva),* ed. S. N. Esin (Moscow, 1996), 81.

25. Quoted in Rubenstein, *Tangled Loyalties,* 279.

26. *Istoriia sovetskoi politicheskoi tsenzury. Dokumenty i komentarii,* ed. T. M. Goriaeva, (Moscow, 1997), 15–17

27. *Istoriia sovetskoi politicheskoi tsenzury,* 15–17; on Suslov, see R. A. Medvedev, *Oni okruzhali Stalina* (Moscow, 1990), 314–16.

28. Quoted in Broue, *Trotsky,* 492.

29. *Pravda,* July 25, 1959.

30. The translation is that used in *The New Soviet Society. The Final Text of the Program of the Communist Party of the Soviet Union,* ed. Herbert Ritvo (New York, 1962), 114–15; the final program appears in *Pravda,* November 2, 1961.

31. *Pravda,* October 19, 1961.

32. See for example *Pravda,* April 22, 1962, which is almost entirely devoted to the dead leader. Lenin's birthday did not become a holiday, but the first Sunday after it became a day of unpaid labor.

33. On discussions of love, see Vladimir Shlapentokh, *Love, Marriage, and Friendship in the Soviet Union* (New York, 1984).

34. Brooks, *When Russia Learned to Read,* 241–45.

35. *Pravda,* February 27, 1954.

36. Ibid., May 1, 1953.

37. Khrushchev, *Khrushchev Remembers,* 137–38.

38. See *Pravda's* editorial, May 9, 1960.

39. *Pravda,* May 9, 1965.

40. Anatoly Dobrynin, *In Confidence* (New York, 1995), 13.

41. Vladimir Shlapentokh, *Soviet Public Opinion and Ideology: Mythology and Pragmatism in Interaction* (New York, 1986), 69.

42. Vaclav Havel, *Living in Truth,* ed. Jan Vladislav (London, 1987), 43.

43. See Michael J. Piore and Charles F. Sable, *The Second Industrial Divide: Possibilities for Prosperity* (New York, 1984); Richard R. Nelson, ed., *National Innovation Systems: A Comparative Analysis* (New York, 1993); and Louis Galambos, "The U.S. Corporate Economy in the Twentieth Century," in *The Cambridge Economic History of the United States,* vol. 3 (Cambridge, 2000).

44. Mikhail Gorbachev, *Memoirs* (New York, 1996), 167.

Index